Susanne Langer
in Focus

Susanne Langer in Focus

The Symbolic Mind

Robert E. Innis

Indiana University Press

BLOOMINGTON AND INDIANAPOLIS

This book is a publication of

Indiana University Press
601 North Morton Street
Bloomington, IN 47404-3797 USA

http://iupress.indiana.edu

Telephone orders   800-842-6796
Fax orders   812-855-7931
Orders by e-mail   iuporder@indiana.edu

The paper used in this publication meets the
minimum requirements of American National
Standard for Information Sciences—Permanence
of Paper for Printed Library Materials,
ANSI Z39.48-1984.

Manufactured in the United States of America

Library of Congress Cataloging-in-Publication Data

Innis, Robert E.
    Susanne Langer in focus : the symbolic mind /
Robert E. Innis.
        p. cm. — (American philosophy)
    Includes bibliographical references and index.
      ISBN 978-0-253-35278-1 (cloth : alk. paper) —
ISBN 978-0-253-22053-0 (pbk. : alk. paper) 1. Langer,
Susanne Katherina Knauth, 1895–1985. I. Title.
    B945.L274I56 2009
    191—dc22
                                            2008029698

1 2 3 4 5   14 13 12 11 10 09

For Marianne, once again

In the fundamental notion of symbolization . . . we have the keynote of all humanistic problems.

Susanne K. Langer, *Philosophy in a New Key*

Contents

Preface and Acknowledgments

The goal of this book is to bring as clearly as possible the total range of Susanne Langer's work "into focus." Its unifying theme is "the symbolic" or "the symbolific" mind. I have set as my task to "free the line" of Langer's work or, with a gesture to Michelangelo's conception of the role of the sculptor, to free the form of her work from the massive block of text in which it lies. Not that Langer is not herself clear about the points she wants to make, but there are numerous side-glances in her work, references to current debates, massive amounts of empirical details, and polemical engagements that are quite unnecessary to reproduce in the present context. I have for the most part, in order to avoid undue complexity and unnecessary scholarly quarrels and nit-picking, restricted engagement with the secondary literature and with parallel positions to controlled allusions within the text itself. Rolf Lachmann's *Susanne K. Langer: Die lebendige Form menschlichen Fühlens und Verstehens* (2000) and William Schultz's *Cassirer and Langer on Myth* (2000) have given rather differently focused discussions of Langer and contain extensive bibliographies. I have accordingly indicated in each chapter a limited set of pertinent articles and books, including book chapters, that deal with the matters at hand, both positively and negatively. Readers can take off from there, but I have seen no reason to qualify each assertion about Langer in this book with a reference to a dissenting opinion or evaluation. At the same time I have been concerned to indicate points of confluence between Langer's work and some of the great figures of the American philosophical tradition.

I would like to thank especially Donald Dryden for his selfless and open-spirited support of this project. His willingness to share his vast knowledge of

Langer's work, his superb and fundamental articles about Langer, and his keen reading of this manuscript are deeply appreciated. He was responsible also for a fine meeting with Leonard Langer, Susanne Langer's son, during the summer of 2006, where important biographical issues were discussed. John Stuhr has been from the beginning an interested and engaged advocate for the book. Dee Mortensen, at Indiana University Press, has been a model of benign patience, waiting for a long-overdue manuscript. I have benefited from serious discussions about Langer with Beebe Nelson, Vincent Colapietro, Felicia Kruse, Jaan Valsiner, Dines Johansen, SunHee Kim Gertz, and many others who are intrigued by new ways of doing philosophy in light of the "semiotic turn," which is not some arcane, private academic preserve with its various warring tribes and chieftains and specialized, or even specious, terminology. The semiotic turn in philosophy involves simply a recognition that humans are truly the "symbolic species" and is an attempt to find out what philosophizing, in some important respects, and human life, in all respects, would look like if we took that notion with the utmost seriousness.

My aim in the book has been, first, to determine just what positions Langer wanted to propose and why she proposed them and, second, to indicate which of them are worth both defending and extending. My method, then, can be seen as deliberately oscillating between critical presentation and analysis and a firm, yet responsibly nuanced, advocacy.

Biographical Note

Susanne K. Langer was born Susanne Katherina Knauth in New York City on 20 December 1895 and died on 17 July 1985 in Old Lyme, Connecticut. After cremation, her ashes were scattered near her beloved cabin in the Catskills, where she had done much of her creative work.

She graduated from Radcliffe College, which at that time offered the equivalent of a Harvard degree for women, in 1920 with a B.A. in philosophy. The following year she married William Langer, and together they spent some months in Vienna, where her husband did archival research and she participated in courses at the University of Vienna. There she made the acquaintance of Karl Bühler, who was clearly a model for her interdisciplinary interests. Langer received her M.A. in philosophy from Radcliffe in 1924 and in 1926 received her Ph.D. in philosophy from Radcliffe. Her extremely spotty and untraditional academic career was made up of a set of temporary appointments at various institutions throughout the country, and she held only one permanent appointment, at Connecticut College from 1954 to 1962, when she retired. This "external career" was counterbalanced by a remarkable scholarly and intellectual career of the highest order and by a broad and refined aesthetic sensibility. Her personal life played very little role in her thought, which was marked by deep and persistent theoretical concerns. From the philosophical point of view her work was her life.

Her original interests in philosophical methodology and symbolic logic, presented in her first published books, *The Practice of Philosophy* (1930) and *An Introduction to Symbolic Logic* (1936), were followed by *Philosophy in a New Key* (1942), which explored the philosophical implications of taking the notion of "symbolic transformation" as the "new key" in philosophy, opening up a new idea and standard of human rationality and meaning-making. In 1946 appeared Langer's translation, with an illuminating introduction, of Ernst Cassirer's *Language and Myth,* a theme, and topic, that lay at the very center of her philosophical concerns. In 1953, Langer published what many consider her most original work, *Feeling and Form,* which presented a full theory of art focusing on the central category of the "art symbol," which was expanded and applied, with a lighter hand, in the essays published in 1957 in her book *Problems of Art.* She also published a collection of primary source materials, *Reflections on Art: A Source Book of Writings by Artists, Critics, and Philosophers* (1961).

Langer then turned to an even more ambitious project, to construct a naturalist model of mind under the rubric of "feeling." The results of this research project were first presented in *Philosophical Sketches* (1962) and then in a massive trilogy, *Mind: An Essay on Human Feeling,* the installments of which appeared in 1967, 1972, and 1982. An abridged version by Gary van den Heuvel in one volume appeared in 1988. Langer published a small number of articles, both scholarly and popular, in the course of her career, but her essential contributions to philosophy are her books.

Dryden (2003) gives a nuanced and more detailed overview of her life as well as a selected bibliography. Lachmann (2000) also has important biographical information as well as a comprehensive bibliography.

Abbreviations and Langer Bibliography

PP   *The Practice of Philosophy*. New York: Holt, 1930.

ISL   *Introduction to Symbolic Logic*. Boston: Houghton Mifflin, 1937; London: Allen and Unwin, 1937; 3rd rev. ed., New York: Dover, 1967.

PNK   *Philosophy in a New Key: A Study in the Symbolism of Reason, Rite and Art*. Cambridge, Mass.: Harvard University Press, 1942; 3rd ed., with new preface by the author, Cambridge, Mass.: Harvard University Press, 1951; 3rd ed., with new preface by the author, Cambridge, Mass.: Harvard University Press, 1957.

FF   *Feeling and Form: A Theory of Art Developed from* Philosophy in a New Key. New York: Scribner's, 1953; London: Routledge and Kegan Paul, 1957.

PA   *Problems of Art: Ten Philosophical Lectures*. New York: Scribner's, 1953; London: Routledge and Kegan Paul, 1957.

RA   *Reflections on Art: A Source Book of Writings by Artists, Critics, and Philosophers*. Baltimore, Md.: Johns Hopkins University Press, 1958.

PS   *Philosophical Sketches: A Study of the Human Mind in Relation to Feeling, Explored through Art, Language, and Symbol*. Baltimore, Md.: Johns Hopkins University Press, 1962; London: Oxford University Press.

M-I   *Mind: An Essay on Human Feeling*. Vol. 1. Baltimore, Md.: Johns Hopkins University Press, 1967.

M-II   *Mind: An Essay on Human Feeling*. Vol. 2. Baltimore, Md.: Johns Hopkins University Press, 1972.

M-III   *Mind: An Essay on Human Feeling*. Vol. 3. Baltimore, Md.: Johns Hopkins University Press, 1982.

M-A   *Mind*. Abridged ed. Abridged by Gary van den Heuvel. Foreword by Arthur C. Danto. Baltimore, Md.: Johns Hopkins University Press, 1988.

Introduction

Links, Themes, and Intersections

Langer's Philosophical Project

The task that Susanne Langer made the focal point of her philosophical career was to explore how human life must be thought of as a continuous process of meaning-making effected through processes of symbolic transformation of experience. In a set of precise, nuanced, and comprehensive works she proceeded to examine the various forms, "symbolic forms," such processes gave rise to and operated within: language, ritual, myth, art, science. Her ultimate goal was to construct a model of human mentality under the rubric of the "symbolic mind" that would encompass all the major dimensions encompassed by what we call "mind" in the distinctively human sense.

At the very beginning of her intellectual career, and even much later with a nod to William James, Langer asserted that philosophy as a distinctive discipline was fundamentally concerned with the descriptive and critical analysis of *meanings and their orders* and not, like the sciences, with the discovery of facts. Langer wanted to determine "how to make our ideas clear" about meaning, a deeply pragmatist concern. At the same time Langer, like the pragmatists, famously proposed a "new key" in philosophy: the way philosophy, as more an activity than a doctrinal superscience, was to be "practiced," already the theme of her first book, was to recognize once and for all that meanings are *"embodied* in forms" that have a distinctive kind of "logic" and history, both "ideal" and "real."

Under the influences of Henry Sheffer, her logic teacher, Alfred North White-head, her "great teacher and friend," and the polymath German scholar, Ernst Cassirer, Langer thought the analysis of meanings had to be rooted in a precise and comprehensive account of the "logic of signs and symbols" and of the "symbolic forms" this logic both structured and made possible. Such a way of thinking distanced Langer not so much from the concerns and procedures of Anglophone analytic philosophy, which came to dominate the American philosophical scene, as from their use of ordinary and formal language and discursive rationality as the normative measure of human meaning-making. At the same time, while admitting that C. S. Peirce had made great strides in developing such a logic of signs and symbols under the rubric of a philosophical "semeiotic," she did not take over any of the Peircean technical terminology, although she reconstructed, or at least duplicated, his chief distinctions, using different sources. The "logical" and "semiotic" schemata she worked out in her first book, *The Practice of Philosophy* (1930; hereafter *PP*) and then deepened, expanded, and applied in her classic *Philosophy in a New Key* (1942; hereafter *PNK*), were never repudiated. These schemata relied upon the radical distinction between *indexicality* (indication) and *symbolicity* (symbolization) and between *discursive* and *presentational* symbols or symbol systems. They function as a categorial and critical backbone for her whole work, with implications for the theory of art presented in her *Feeling and Form* (1953; hereafter *FF*) and for the naturalist, but non-reductive, "metaphysics" of mind that Langer ultimately tried to construct, culminating in her trilogy, *Mind: An Essay on Human Feeling* (1967, 1972, 1982; hereafter *M-I, M-II, M-III*). This trilogy parallels in important respects John Dewey's *Experience and Nature* and Peirce's mature metaphysical reflections and speculations.

The present book will chart the steps in the development of these schemata, trying to extract the permanently valid philosophical discoveries and conceptual innovations made by Langer.

American Philosophical Themes

One of the focal points in this book will be the thematic concerns and methodological procedures shared by Langer and the classic American philosophical tradition that join them together in mutual reinforcement, supplementation, and vital tension. I find both philosophical frameworks equally engrossing and necessary. This dual commitment will inform much of the following discussion. The thread that stitches together Langer's philosophical project and the American philosophical tradition, broadly conceived, is Langer's crucial and indispensable insight that a focus on the "logic" of signs, symbols, and meanings, her lifelong concern, does not take philosophical reflection away from "experience," the axis point of American philosophy, but throws new light on just how experience itself is structured and accessed through semiotic tools and instruments, topics I have explored at length elsewhere with close attention to American philosophical sources, especially those of Peirce and Dewey (see Innis 1994 and 2002). Moreover, relying on the "founding texts" of American philosophical tradition, John McDermott has in his *The Culture of Experience* (1976) and *Streams of Experience* (1986) taken up the theme of "experience" in American philosophy and given it classic reformulations, interpretations, and extensions to primary existential spaces of our lives. These works exemplify, in rather different register, the relevance of philosophical analysis and reflection to lived experience, something that Langer's work also displays. This is a deep and strong "tie that binds," and I have tried to show that Langer's work is not just abstract analysis but engagement with life's deep structures, expressed in art, ritual, myth, in our encounters with death, and in profound civilizational conflicts.

While, then, American philosophy in any traditional sense was neither a source nor a resource for Langer, her philosophical project can be an additional resource for it and for development of its continuing relevance and analytical and creative power. It supplies independent confirmation of some of American philosophy's central theses and focal concerns and supplies new sets of conceptual tools for broadening its appeal and exemplifying its essentially open character. As a consequence, although in this book I will present, analyze, and evaluate Langer's distinctive contribution to philosophy quite generally, I will also indicate, in ways that do not blur our organizing focus on the "symbolic mind," points of intersection between her substantive theses and the American philosophical tradition.

As was the case for the classic thinkers of the American philosophical tradition, the more abstract "logical" dimension of the practice of philosophy was complemented for Langer by a more concrete "hermeneutical" dimension, an engagement with "formed content." Langer thought of philosophy as fundamentally both an interpretive and a constructive discipline. For Langer it certainly is interpretation, in practically any format, but it is also constructive and analytical: philosophy, on Langer's account, studies the contexts, means, criteria, consequences, and contents of interpretation. These are pivotal features of the mature work of C. S. Peirce and of Josiah Royce. Langer shares with these two American thinkers both a love of logic and a passion to interpret. Royce, for his part, tried especially in chapters 12, 13, and 14 of his *The Problem of Christianity*

(1913) to draw out the implications of Peirce's doctrine of signs for interpreting a paradigm case of "formed content," namely, an articulated historical religion. Langer nevertheless deliberately avoided what she clearly took to be the unnecessary complications of Peirce's typology of signs, while matching the universality of his interests.

Instead, against the background, but without the thematic use, of the tripartite paradigm of "ascending" or increasingly dematerialized sense-functions of *expression, representation,* and *pure signification* that informs the third volume of Ernst Cassirer's *The Philosophy of Symbolic Forms* (1929), Langer, like Cassirer, wanted to show how the world *at every level* is accessed, projected, and interpreted through the construal as well as the construction of signs and symbols. They argued that the world of interpretations, the experienced continuum of embodied meanings, goes far beyond language and its close cousins, logic and mathematics, to encompass the whole realm of cultural forms as well as the perceptual field itself. Interpretation as meaning-making, which is often thought of as a "higher-level" activity, is importantly and insightfully "pushed down" by Langer to the primary stratum of awareness or sentience, just as the great pragmatists Peirce and Dewey, with different emphases, oscillate between the logical and the psychological. What I am calling here "interpretation" and "construction" are dimensions or aspects of what Langer calls quite generally "symbolic transformation" on the human level, the "new key" in philosophy, but what Peirce calls, quite generally, "semiosis" (or "semeiosis") and Dewey "minding." The multiform and multileveled duality of a *sign and meaning* model is to replace the old duality of a *percept and concept* model as the axle around which the philosophical wheel turns. This is the "semiotic turn" in philosophy that Langer, and clearly Peirce and the later Royce, were concerned to effect. It joins their projects together non-competitively—and intersects with Dewey's own "logical" interests in how "qualitative" thought, which marks all aspects of experiencing, goes out into symbolization and in turn is informed by it (see Dewey 1931b and Innis 1999, where Dewey's essential link to Peirce's theory of quality, which will inform parts of our discussion, is explored).

Semiotic Links to Naturalism

Langer's whole project can, or even should, also be seen as a double-sided attempt, firstly, to update and validate Ernst Cassirer's philosophy of symbolic forms especially through the exploitation of its relevance for the theory of art (*Feeling and Form*) and as a model of philosophical reflection—a form of expansive updating—and, secondly, inspired clearly by Whitehead, but paralleled by the deepest thrust of the main currents of American philosophy, to establish and to find the implications of a non-reductive naturalism for, and an anti-substantialist approach to, the rise of mind and its embodiment in objective symbolic structures (*Mind* trilogy). Rolf Lachmann (1997), Donald Dryden (1997), and Vincent Colapietro (1997, 1998, 2007) have explored in scholarly detail this theme, which we will take up in later chapters. Langer's repudiation of a substantialist metaphysics at all levels is ultimately due to the permanent, though ambiguous, influence of Whitehead on her thought, although she is not a "process philosopher." Her attacks on "soul-substance" in *Philosophy in a New Key* clearly show this—the book was dedicated to Whitehead, just as *Feeling and Form* was dedicated to Cassirer—but her reflections on art and her reflections on the rise and nature of mind avail themselves of the contentious *act-concept,* which she admits to having taken from Whitehead and used in her own way. Her world, like Whitehead's, is a processual world, a world of events and relations, not of stable "things" embodying "essences." Organisms, on Langer's conception, which is developed systematically and in empirical detail, are self-organizing and self-unifying matrices of acts. They are dynamic wholes. In this she certainly is close to Dewey's naturalist metaphysical vision of "minding" in *Experience and Nature,* whose Langerian equivalent, as I have noted, is her *Mind* trilogy. At the same time, like Dewey, she will not accept any form of pan-experientialism, which she finds also in Whitehead and which has been developed by others, often with theological intent. This position she firmly opposes in the name of a sober, but by no means pessimistic, naturalism. Langer shares a strong anti-speculative bent that makes her, in this respect, closer to Dewey than to Peirce, although her position on the self, while naturalistic, is intrinsically semiotic, even if with a biological twist. In this she merits close comparison with Peirce's account of the self, a theme pursued with precision and depth by Vincent Colapietro (1989). Langer, for her part, offers, we will see, deep-grounded insights into the "semiotic body," in both its endosomatic (intra-bodily) and exosomatic (extra-bodily) forms. Meaning-systems exist both "inside" and "outside" our "natural" bodies.

Empirical Dimensions

Langer, like many in the American philosophical tradition, wanted to put philosophy into a close relationship to the empirical sciences and to exploit them for concepts that can be utilized and validated by means of progressive generalization and exemplification. What she took from biology and psychology, her (and Dewey's) principal empirical sources, was precisely this *act-concept* and the generalized notion of *sentience* as a *phase* of biological processes, not a new "ontological" level. Langer, as opposed to Peirce, tries to specify, with the help of developmental biology and neurophysiology, the exact mechanism for the emergence of mind and sentience, without the ambiguous recourse to the temptations of objective idealism to which Peirce was susceptible (see Hausman 1993, "objective idealism" in index). Mind for Langer is *an emergent dimension of sentience,* not an aboriginal cause or source of sentience. The rise of symbolically informed sentience, which is also Terrence Deacon's thematic concern (Deacon 1997), is fruitfully connected by Langer, relying on some classic French researches by Th. Ribot (1926), Jean Philippe (1903), and Philippe Fauré-Fremiet (1934, 1940), with the power of imagination and the internalization of symbolic processes *prior to external articulation.* Human mentality is rooted in an organism that undergoes a riot of spontaneously formed images, founded upon certain cerebral shifts and conditions. Peirce himself thought, without contradicting Langer's point, that it was consciousness of signs as such and their explicit use and control that marked human mentality as a process of semiosis. Langer supplies Peirce's systematic insight with grounded genetic and empirical support that merits the closest attention.

The distinctively human ambient, Langer argues, in a way reflecting the semiotic biology and the construction of a "theory of meaning" on a biological base pursued by Jakob von Uexküll (1940), is a symbolic or symbolically transformed ambient, with both endosomatic and exosomatic dimensions. The organism's "natural body" is constituted by the exchange of messages and meanings just as the "semiotic body" of the human organism is constituted by objective symbolic structures in which we are embodied and which we, in Michael Polanyi's terminology, "indwell" (see Polanyi 1958, chapter 4 on "skills," and Innis 1994, chapter 3, and Innis 2002a, chapters 1 and 4). But, as we will see, Langer's important, maybe even revolutionary, thesis is that the human ambient arises and is supported through the internalization and use for symbolization of an *immanent process of generating images.* When images, initially spontaneously produced by reason of cerebral development, whether in dreaming or waking, no longer directly evoke or express various types of reactions, positive or negative, but are *used* to give rise to a conceived or symbolized, internal or external, world, when, that is, images not only function but are *recognized as means of symbolization and conceptualization,* even of self-consciousness, *that* is the movement to the human ambient. Consciousness of images not as things to be dealt with or undergone but *as symbolic tools,* as primary carriers of "significance," allows the human organism to abstract and to fix a world, to stabilize the flow of experience even prior to language. But this stabilizing, on the operative level, is already a qualitatively *new type* of grasp and constitution of meaning or meaningful wholes. Langer, then, goes a different methodological route, the genetic, than Peirce, but she still, like

Peirce and Dewey, pushes semiosis, sign-reading and sign-making, "down" before pushing it "up."

Anti-Foundationalism

It is a paradoxical non-foundational search for a "base" of meaning and knowledge that binds together Langer, Peirce, James, Dewey, and, totally outside the American pragmatist tradition, Cassirer. All four thinkers, in different but complementary ways, undermine any temptation to remain committed to epistemology "as we have known it," with its abstract dialectic of knower and known, or subject and object. Dewey (1908) went so far as to call the theory of knowledge "that confirmed species of intellectual lockjaw." Langer, by exploiting and developing a "new key" in philosophy, wants to put our jaws in motion and give us something substantial to chew on. Langer pinpoints a fusion of symbolic *action*, exemplified in the spontaneous production and systematic elaboration of images, and meaning-making quite generally. This is a deeply pragmatist insight and thesis. James and Dewey especially foreground this actional aspect of knowing perhaps a bit more than Langer does, at least from the more explicitly psychological, as opposed to the biological, side. At the same time, Langer gives empirical support, in fact if not in explicit intention, to Whitehead's distinction between "causal efficacy," the massive unthematized background "withness of the body," and "presentational immediacy" and to Whitehead's notion that "affective tones," not "objects," mark as well as inform our first encounter with the continuum of experience and effect its primary segmentation.

Aesthetic Aspects

At the core of Langer's work is a systematic, well-grounded, and *sui generis* treatment of aesthetic issues, which we will examine in later chapters (see Dryden 2001 and 2004 for important arguments for the deep *philosophical* significance of art for Langer). One of her greatest and most challenging philosophical achievements is to have worked out a comprehensive theory of art that is not a mere corollary to her other interests, a kind of philosophical footnote or "application" of a differently ordered systematic frame. The aesthetic dimension for Langer is absolutely central, indeed, indispensable, to our understanding of what a human mind is and as an exemplification of what it can do. Langer asks in the most fundamental way what type of "thing" an artwork is and what "work" it does. The artwork is, Langer asserts, a "symbol of feeling" and it effects a "work" of meaning wherein an "import" is "expressed." The artwork functions as a "psychological lure to long contemplation" (*FF* 397) and it is *a heuristic key to mind.* On the one hand, our encounter with these pregnant forms gives us experience and insight at the same time. The art symbol, as source of *understanding,* must be *experienced* just as much as the aesthetic experience must be embodied in some meaning-bearing frame or imaginative (and recollected) schema. On the other hand, the art work is itself a symbolic image of the mind, or type of mind, that is its source.

The reason is that the essence of art, for Langer, is symbolic formulation, in the presentational mode, of what she calls the "morphology of feeling" in all its varieties and nuances and its exemplification in the primary illusions created by the various art genres. This, Langer claims, "sets it apart as an autonomous, creative function of a typically human mind" (*FF* 36). Langer asserts that "all levels of feeling are reflected, explicitly or implicitly, in art" (*M-I* 208), revealing and articulating the "logic of sentience": order, pattern, rhythm, growth and diminution of energies, sense of effort and release, dynamism and relaxation, and so forth. Clearly, for Langer the symbolic dimension is inextricably intertwined with the experiential with all its gradients: "Gradients of all sorts—of relative clarity, complexity, tempo, intensity of feeling, interest, not to mention geometric gradations . . . —permeate all artistic structure" (*M-I* 211)—and experiential structures, too. Her work is a treasure house of precise, provocative, and empirical exemplifications of these gradients, especially in "The Import of Art" section of *Mind* (*M-I* 73–253) and in the discussion of the great orders of art in *Feeling and Form,* which Langer studies in light of her key notion of the types of abstraction that give rise to each art genre's primary illusions or distinctive symbolic work. We will pay close attention to these matters.

Plan and Scope of the Book

The present book, then, is an attempt to present and to evaluate Langer's contribution to philosophy. It is not a biography in any sense of that term, although it could be considered a kind of intellectual or philosophical biography that charts the major steps in Langer's philosophical trajectory. Langer pursued such a complicated project for the most part uninfluenced by external events either in the world or in her personal life, about which she was extremely reticent even to the point of saying of herself that she was "a social porcupine" (Wesley Wehr, "Susanne K. Langer: The Evolution of a Friendship," unpublished manuscript). She was also, in a sense, a kind of "philosophical porcupine," since she did not easily fit into any of the major strands and schools of twentieth-century philosophy. She did acknowledge many influences on her path of thinking, but they make up an extremely heterogeneous group, the members of which contributed to her work in diverse, even hidden, ways.

My procedure in this book, however, will not be to follow all the byways and detours of Langer's "way" but to cut as straight a path as possible through her major works by presenting her major theses and their import and by highlighting her pivotal concepts and distinctions. The chapters in the book deal successively with Langer's major book-length publications, following the main threads of her evolving pattern as she weaves her philosophical tapestry.

Chapter 1 will engage Langer's first book, *The Practice of Philosophy,* where she lays down what is in effect the ground plan of her life's philosophical project and where the preliminary delineation of most of the main themes of her later investigations are to be found. Chapters 2 and 3 will be devoted to Langer's most famous, as opposed to perhaps her most important, book, *Philosophy in a New Key,* focusing on her mature formulation of her notions of symbolic transformation, the distinctions between types of signs and symbols and between the two major symbolic modes, discursive and presentational, and their exemplifications in language, ritual, myth, and art. Chapters 4 and 5 discuss Langer's *Feeling and Form,* her major contribution to aesthetics and the philosophical theory of art. Here are taken up, first, against the background of *Philosophy in a New Key,* the general framework that Langer constructs to frame the art symbol as a "form of feeling," relying on the cognate notions of abstraction, expression, form, interpretation, and other subsidiary notions. Then, secondly, the exemplification of Langer's general conceptual framework is examined, with specific attention to Langer's treatment of the visual arts (painting, sculpture, and architecture), dance, and literature. The three following chapters deal with Langer's great *Mind* trilogy. Chapter 6 treats the issue of why Langer uses "feeling" as the general term of "minding," chapter 7 presents Langer's argument that symbolization in the distinctively human sense is the culmination of a process of producing and exploiting the power of images, and chapter 8 examines the cultural and moral aspects of the rise and destiny of a "symbolic animal" that lives out its life within a world of objective symbolic structures. Chapter 9 briefly sums up the major conclusions drawn in the course of the book about the validity and enduring value of Langer's work as a whole.

1

The Roots of Langer's Philosophical Project

On the "Logic" of Meaning

Philosophy as Analysis of Meanings

In *The Practice of Philosophy* (*PP*), her first published book from 1930, Langer puts forth a central claim that she will explore and defend in all her later work. The job of philosophy is to "see *possibilities of interpretation*" rather than to engage in the demolishing of "literal propositions" (x). It is precisely the distinction between and the autonomy of the realms of the "literal" and the "non-literal" that will play a central, though not exclusive, role in her intellectual journey. In her *An Introduction to Symbolic Logic* (*ISL*), from 1937, Langer distinguishes, in a way that will reverberate throughout her whole work, *interpretation* from *abstraction*. "Interpretation is the reverse of abstraction; the process of abstraction begins with the real thing and derives from it the bare form, or concept, whereas the process of interpretation begins with an empty concept and seeks some real thing which embodies it" (*ISL* 38). Its role, consequently, is constructive, indeed hermeneutical, and not destructive or negatively critical. Strangely enough, in light of her later interest in "thick" cultural phenomena, at the center of Langer's core proposal, as it was for Royce, too, is the expressed need for a thorough study of the logic of relations, which she presented in more formal fashion in her *An Introduction to Symbolic Logic.* Such a study not only would supply, as she already said in *The Practice of Philosophy,* "a powerful instrument of metaphysical thought," but is also "the most elementary, restricted and definite philosophical science" (x). Langer clearly thinks, in her first work, and repeats emphatically in *Philosophy in a New Key,* that philosophy is in a kind of crisis situation. Already Langer was anticipating—in spite of her fondness for Bertrand Russell—the "emancipation of modern philosophy from common-sense and *from the method and interests of natural science*" (*PP* 5). Langer admits that what she is doing can be described as "logical" or "analytic" philosophy—but this is not "scientific" philosophy (*PP* 17). It is concerned with "logical foundations" (*PP* 17), to be sure, but Langer will develop in a very different way the philosophical dimensions of logic without contradicting the main thrust of modern developments in logical theory. These she fully accepts, while at the same time being concerned with its conceptual premises and a rather different way of applying its core ideas. She will be concerned, to use a later formulation, with the *logic of sentience,* the *logic of consciousness,* the *logic of cultural forms.* Her goal in *The Practice of Philosophy* is to "attain a *new* orientation" (*PP* 19), to transcend the old positions and analytical methods, not just adjust them—or adjust to them (*PP* 19).

In order to make philosophy "a definite branch of human learning" (*PP* 21) and to avoid the flounderings, methodological broodings, and formulations of much of contemporary philosophy, which she always held herself rather distant from, Langer proposes "a guiding principle that will define our field, dictate our procedure (of which the analytic method is a perfectly assignable, integral part), and give philosophy a working basis as well as an ultimate aim: this principle is the pursuit of meaning" (*PP* 21). This is, as she rightly puts it, and as her whole intellectual project showed, "an arduous and complicated task" (*PP* 22). Admitting the polymorphous nature of the concept of "meaning," Langer at the beginning of her career firmly opposes any sort of monolithic reductionism and asserts that she will use the term "meaning" not in "any one restricted sense, but in all its varieties, shadings and fulnesses" (*PP* 22). Langer never repudiated this position—it became one of the hinges of her thought. This allows the philosopher, in fact, to not shy away from what she calls "the study of trivial examples" (*PP* 25). In her sourcebook, *Reflections on Art,* from 1958, Langer will assert that "the chief virtue of a fertile theory is that it allows philosophical inquiry (i.e., conceptual analysis and construction) to go into detail" (xiii). Note the characterization of philosophical inquiry. Examples, however, are to be studied in terms of fundamental relations, conceptual relations. While necessarily concerned with "facts," philosophy is nevertheless a "rational science," engaged not in the actual pursuit of facts for their own sake but of the *meanings* of facts (*PP* 31).

Philosophy as a rational science, as conceived by the early Langer and ruthlessly practiced by the later Langer, develops by following up the "implications of a few fundamental ideas" (*PP* 33). In light of this notion Langer states her "central thesis," with a conscious gesture toward her master, Whitehead: "All philosophy is a study of what is *implied* in the fundamental notions which are our natural unconscious formulations of experience" (*PP* 35). Here we have a preliminary statement, involving a special kind of hermeneutics, of the importance of "prescientific" knowledge that Langer explores in part 1 of *Mind*. Philosophy, however, is for Langer at this point and even later, as it turns out, a kind of holding company. "*Philosophy, which is the systematic study of meanings, comprises all the rational sciences.* Philosophy is a group of disciplines which are all governed by the principle of seeking *implications,* i.e., *logical connections*" (*PP* 36), in contrast to science, which seeks *causal connections*. The aim of philosophy, as Langer sees it, is "to see all things in the world in proportion to each other, in some order, i.e. to see reality as a system, or at least any part of it as belonging to some system" (*ISL 40*). A parallel case, once again, is the example of Josiah Royce's turn to logic, a turn that Oppenheim (1987: 43–87 and 2005 passim) emphasizes and develops.

In a sense not unlike Karl Popper's, Langer is seeking a demarcation criterion to determine what does or does not belong to philosophy, what its method is to be (not chiefly analytic in any restricted sense), and what its subject matter is. "*Logical analysis* is to philosophy just what *observation* is to science—namely the first step in finding and formulating a problem, and a means of testing the answer" (*PP* 37). For Langer a philosophical problem concerns the *import* of an idea (*PP* 37), including, as will become clear in later work, the import of the very idea of art, namely, its import for discovering the essential nature of human mentality. This is the theme of the core part of *Mind.* Hence, "to establish as fully as possible the meaning of a concept is the guiding principle of philosophy" (*PP* 38).

Langer will focus on the concepts of symbolization and the symbolic transformation of experience as distinguishing marks of humans, symbolic animals *par excellence.* Connections of fact are the province of science, both natural and cultural. Langer, it is clear, wants first and foremost to establish the distinctiveness and autonomy of philosophy and its non-identity with, yet essential relation to, science. Philosophy, on Langer's first position, can "pass over" into or utilize science—but it can never itself become science (*PP* 41). Philosophical propositions can never be "replaced" by scientific ones (*PP* 41), a point that Campbell (1997) seems to have missed but that it is important to always keep in mind, nor, *contra* James Campbell, does Langer offer "simply an exquisite solution *to her self-imposed problem* of granting primacy, at least philosophical primacy, to discursive meaning" (1997: 138). Furthermore, logic, while not all of philosophy, is nevertheless the "common foundation" of the philosophical sciences (*PP* 42). "Logic . . . is the study of forms; and forms are derived from common experience, reality, life, or whatever we choose to call it, by *abstraction*. The science of logic is a steady progression from the concrete to the abstract, from contents with certain form to those forms without their content, from instances to kinds, from examples to concepts" (*ISL* 240). But philosophy for Langer will nevertheless return to the concrete through the abstract. Symbolization will rely upon and exploit our ability to see forms *exemplified* in different contents or mediums. Nevertheless, as Langer puts it, "if we would . . . really gain insight into the great storehouse of forms which may be interpretable physically, or psychically, or for any realm of experience whatever, we must consider abstracted patterns as such—the orders in which any things whatsoever may be arranged, the modes under which anything whatever may present itself to our understanding" (*ISL* 39). Langer's whole philosophy could be thought of as an exploration of such a "great storehouse of forms." Rather than staying on the abstract level she plunges into the content of these forms, too, and not just their formal structures. In this she rather unexpectedly shares an orientation, with rather different concerns, with the later work of Josiah Royce, which, as I have said, attempted to explore the philosophical implications of Peirce's logic of relations for the philosophy of religion and the "problem" of Christianity. (See Royce 1913 for an exemplification of a rigorous interpretation of "formed content" carried out with logical acuity.)

Beween Intuition and Abstraction

Arthur Danto contentiously remarks in his preface to the abridged edition of *Mind* (*M-A*), however, that Langer was not always faithful, at least as regards the rhetoric of presentation, to this idea of philosophy. In his opinion the supporting material adduced in *Mind* "obscures the philosophical architecture, like a dense scaffolding, and renders inaccessible to philosophical scrutiny one of the most audacious philosophical visions of recent times" (vi). The philosophical architecture erected, or rather sketched, in her early work remained, however, fundamentally in place, and Langer's "rejection" of traditional philosophy and its relation to the empirical sciences, anticipated in *The Practice of Philosophy*, and supported and grounded in *An Introduction to Symbolic Logic*, merely became more explicit in *Mind* just as it remained operative in *Philosophy in a New Key* and *Feeling and Form*.

The logical foundation of philosophy, as Langer conceives it in *The Practice of Philosophy*, entails that philosophy cannot rest upon "intuition" as its foundation, though intuition will later function as a central topic, whose own "logic" remains to be explicated. "Intuition," she writes, "is not a method, but a natural phenomenon. It occurs; it cannot be invoked or taught. Moreover, its result is not knowledge, but that fundamental experience which knowledge is *about* . . . intuition never yields a proposition, but presents us with the subjects of propositions. It is our source of direct contact with the world. Contact, however, is not understanding" (*PP* 44–45). For understanding we need perspective and distance, as in standing away from a painting. Understanding, for its part, requires a medium, and understanding is "mediate knowledge, more or less colored by intervening factors in the knowledge-relation" (*PP* 45). These "intervening factors," rooted in our bio-psychological constitution, will become the focal point of *Mind*. Intuition, then, supplies us with the *given* in experience (*PP* 45). The medium that understanding requires is *abstraction* (*PP* 46), which is "always operative in reason, and perhaps never in intuition" (*PP* 46). Then, in a fantastic footnote (*PP* 46), Langer, in a moment of reflective hesitation, sets herself a problem that she will still be wrestling with at the end of her life. "I do not know," she writes, "whether intuition ever involves abstraction. The subject has never, to my knowledge, been conclusively treated." Seven years later, however, she will say explicitly that "the power of recognizing similar forms in widely various exemplifications, i.e. the power of discovering analogies, is logical intuition" (*ISL* 33). It is this idea of exemplification of forms that will be such a powerful generative idea especially for Langer's conception of art. The deep affinity between forms of sentiency and the forms of art is rooted in this type of intuition, in this case, aesthetic intuition, which has its own "logic."

By the time Langer wrote the essays collected in *Problems of Art* (hereafter: *PA*), which form a kind of bridge between *Feeling and Form* and *Mind*, intuition has become the same as Locke's "natural light" (*PA* 66). Intuition, as Langer sees it there, has become "the fundamental intellectual activity, which produces logical or semantical understanding. It comprises all acts of insight or recognition of formal properties, of relations, of significance, and of abstraction and exemplification" (*PA* 66). This is clearly quite a power, with a comprehensive range of application. Still, she problematically holds even at a much later stage to the position that is first articulated in *The Practice of Philosophy*, but that also is operative in *An Introduction to Symbolic Logic*. Intuition, she writes, "is not true or false, but simply present" (*PA* 66). "Abstraction" in *The Practice of Philosophy* is a concern with "the *general* condition which certain particular examples illustrate" (*PP* 47). Speaking of the case of "transience," Langer seemingly holds to a very traditional, indeed realist, view of abstraction. "Transience," she writes, "is that bare common element which is embodied in every instance" (*PP* 48). In her early book Langer thinks of abstraction in the received terms of "taking away," that is, "treating separately, some *integral aspect* of the whole situation" (*PP* 48). This is what she will later call "generalizing abstraction." But generalization, Langer rightly notes, "far from being a hindrance to true thought, is the source of all thought-economy" (PP 47). Moving us beyond the immediacy of the moment, generalization and abstraction are the conditions of language and thought, properly speaking. Without them, Langer remarks, there would be "no knowledge, only sense" (PP 50). The goal of abstraction, however, is not to generate the materials for a set of blanket assertions. The elements that we "single out from the great flux of reality, those abstracted ingredients, are our *concepts*" (PP 50)—a formulation that evokes the mixed company of James, Whitehead, and Cassirer. Concepts can enter into many more relations with one another than there are actual relations in the world. Possibility is even infinitely greater than existence. Langer then concludes, in a comment pregnant with meaning for her later thought and its focus on art and its import, "Thus the art of abstraction, by giving us the pure concept, liberates the human mind from the finitude of actuality and opens to it the endless reaches of *potentiality*" (PP 51). Here is a first—in the present context unexploited and undeveloped—key to the infinity of art and of aesthetic ideas (or concepts) and, indeed, of the infinity of mind and its products. But the type of abstraction functioning in art will change to an abstraction focused on *form*, rather than *generalized concepts*. That is, there will be another "art of abstraction" that will be the condition of the possibility of the "abstraction of art."

The Early Notion of Form

In fact, Langer's early conception of *form*, while focused on "logical" form, already foreshadows the broadening of this notion under the impetus of Gestalt psychology. Langer traces the weakness of classical logic not to its formalism, but to "the paucity of its forms" (PP 83). Logic is the "science of forms as such, the study of patterns" (PP 83), though it is not a branch of mathematics, but rather its trunk. What accounts for the differences of form? Langer answers in a rich and provocative remark: "Differences of *form*, whether of propositions, geometric figures, musical compositions, *or any other matter* [my emphasis], depend upon the presence of different sorts of *relation* within the structure of the thing in question" (PP 87). Already we can see that the idea of "form" goes far beyond the "discursive" dimension. The form of a thing (anything) is "*the way its parts are put together*" (PP 87). It is not dependent upon the material parts themselves but upon the relations between the parts—(an insight common, I might add, to the structuralist model of the sign, derived from Ferdinand de Saussure, and to Karl Bühler's Husserl-inspired "principle of abstractive relevance," issues I have treated at length elsewhere [Innis 1994 and Innis 2002a]). Suits of the same form, to use Langer's example, which reappears, with a host of others, in *An Introduction to*

Symbolic Logic, are not dependent upon the same materials any more than chess sets are dependent upon identical materials in order to be chess sets or melodies are dependent upon the instruments upon which they are played. But not only suits (or chess sets or melodies) but "all other things in the world exemplify some form, which might conceivably be exemplified by some other materials. And this *form,* regardless of the *content,* is the thing that concerns us in logic" (*PP* 88). This will become one of the cardinal theses of Langer's logic book and allows her to make a confident translation from symbolic logic to the logic of aesthetic symbols. The pursuit of meaning becomes the pursuit of form, even forms, that is, patterns of relation, that do not yet exist—or could not exist except in our imaginative construction of them. In this way, thinks Langer, we obtain a kind of "cosmic knowledge" (*PP* 90), linked to the creative imagination, which clearly runs in multiple channels. This will be one of Langer's most lasting insights and themes.

Speaking in a kind of metaphysical mode, Langer holds that the systematic investigation of form entails "the appreciation of general uniformities and general contrast in the world . . . the appreciation of world order" (*PP* 89). World order, as we will see, however, is both discovered and created. Systematic investigation, rooted in appreciation, is the "key to all understanding, the basis of science and philosophy" (*PP* 89). Logic, nevertheless, does not study just forms in their totality. The ultimate aim is "the formal understanding of *systems*" (*PP* 95), a point made by Langer's honored teacher, Henry M. Sheffer, which she duly acknowledged. But the scope of such a knowledge of systems clearly points to its extension to the aesthetic or artistic domain, in particular, such as visual or auditory systems, and to other imaginative constructs, quite generally, an idea that Langer will extensively exploit. Langer notes (*PP* 99) that when we know that two systems exemplify the same pattern, "we know that any essential configuration in one system will find its analogue in the other." In a way "proleptically" reminiscent of Nelson Goodman (1976 and 1978; see also Innis 1977, where Langer and Goodman are brought into dialogue), Langer avails herself once again of the example of the relation of a suit to its paper pattern, namely, that alterations to one can be made in the other. (I would like to note in passing the wide range of "domestic" examples in Langer's work, even in the symbolic logic book.) Both changes are, in Langer's terminology, *expressions* of a change in the general form. Langer makes the comment that "by mutilating a pattern we express to the tailor what changes he shall make in the suit" (*PP* 99), the changes functioning as a Peircean "energetic interpretant" of the pattern, that is, eliciting and controlling an action or reaction. This is another one of Langer's generative insights: "Thus any logical construct in a system can be *expressed* by an analogous logical construct in any other system having the same form" (*PP* 99).

But suits and suit patterns are not, in the traditional sense, "logical constructs." They are both "made things," one of them a "symbolic thing," and the pattern, in the strict sense, "means" the suit, not vice versa. It is a semiotically charged artifact. One of the roots of Langer's mature philosophy and the aesthetics founded on and growing out of it is found here: *possession of a common form by two systems*. The same logical form, Langer notes, can be possessed by two very different systems. Reflecting on the relations between mathematics and natural systems, Langer clearly sees that the level of intricacy on nature's side demands the creation and further extension of "elaborate systems of mathematical concepts" (*PP* 100), such as the calculus. This can, indeed does, involve ascension to higher levels of abstraction, the finding or inventing of "abstracter forms" (*PP* 101). The invention of different types of forms will mark a different type of "ascension." The intricacy of the life of sentience will demand a parallel development of "concreter" forms by means of a different type of abstraction and very differently constructed systems of imaginative forms that give us true "knowledge" of feeling.

The logical and the metaphysical are not separated in Langer's early work any more than in her later work, although she did not return thematically to logical concerns in the traditional sense as her thought matured. In a concluding passage from chapter 4 of *The Practice of Philosophy* we see a signpost pointing both to later developments in her first book and to her later thought as a whole. Such a passage enables us also to see how Langer's first book is actually the informing and contextual frame of the technical sections of *An Introduction to Symbolic Logic*.

> Yet every advance in logic is a gain in metaphysical insight. Even the novice in philosophy can gain understanding only as he gains the logical power of recognizing relations, systematic form, and analogies. The recognition of *orders* in the world is a prerequisite for the discovery of meanings. For meaning is expression, which depends upon order; and the art of expressing very subtle ideas is the art of seeing very subtle forms, very delicate patterns in nature, thought, and feeling. (*PP* 102)

There is a transformation in philosophy, with Kantian echoes, already limned here in the fateful triad: nature, thought, and feeling. But the "art of seeing very subtle forms" will become the mark of the artist, the myth-maker, even the scientist, working "abstractly" with the totality of "concrete" forms that mark, indeed symbolize, the life of sentience *qua tale*.

The Turn to the Aesthetic Dimension

Langer's approach to art and aesthetics, which plays such a central role in her later thought, is already predefined by her commitment to a particular view of philosophy. "The idea that philosophy is the pursuit of meaning is rather disturbing to conscientious thinkers" (*PP* 105). But what is disturbing, she thinks, is the "logical" demand that there be a common *basis* for meaning that does not swallow all the diversity of meanings to be found in the world. What is needed, she reasons, is "some general *structural* similarity, an abstract logical pattern, which is *the general pattern of all meaning-situations*" (*PP* 108). This will become a pivotal issue in her work. Citing, illuminatingly and provocatively, Whitehead and Wittgenstein as reaching "very similar conclusions by their similar researches" (*PP* 108) on the "formal structure of meaning," which is constituted by a "perfectly definite correlation" between two items, that is, a pairing of symbol and thing, Langer asserts one of the fundamental theses of her work, which will also be central to its aesthetic expansion. "Anything that may be distinguished"—names, concepts, thoughts, a distinguishable quality, tables, persons—"that is a member of any class of entities, may be a term in the relation of symbol and object" (*PP* 109). While denotation, which is central to language, may be "the simplest sort of meaning" (*PP* 111), it is not for Langer the prime model. Her real model at this stage is "syntactical," not strictly referential. *Meaning belongs to structure as a principle not so much of reference as of "articulation."* Langer takes from Wittgenstein and Russell the notion that "*the sentence may denote any fact which has a structure similar to that which we call the syntax*" (*PP* 112)—however contentious such a notion, baldly stated, may be. But her point is that integrated concepts can and must be rendered in sentences or sentence-like structures by discursive syntactical forms (*PP* 114), exemplified also clearly in the case of algebra, which is eminently a matter of the eye, led intuitively by the forms of expression (here is a connection with Peirce's theory of iconism, which Langer parallels, but does not mention, in the "discursive" sections of *An Introduction to Symbolic Logic*). Langer's aesthetic theory, as well as her theory of myth, religion, and ritual, will then see the key to understanding art in the expanded notion of a *non-discursive* syntax that not so much "denotes" facts as *exemplifies* or *expresses* the "forms of feeling" and forms of meaning that are not able to be objectified in discursive terms, transcending, as they do, the "sayable."

Langer straightforwardly asserts that "the expressiveness of any thing which functions as a symbol depends upon its logical structure: the more elaborate the structure, the more detail it can express" (*PP* 115). Since, however, *anything* can function as a symbol ("A symbol is any device whereby we are enabled to make an abstraction" [*FF* xi]), it is clear that Langer is already committed to an even more general principle: "expression depends upon structure" (*PP* 117), the structure reproduces a "logical" pattern, but the restriction of "logic" to the discursive is on the verge of being exploded. Langer is equating, in effect, the "logical" with the "structural." Thus she is able to assert "the importance of configuration for any sort of meaning relation, from the simple denotation of names or suggestiveness of natural signs, to the most intricate symbolic expression, in literal notation or poetic metaphor" (*PP* 121). *This,* I think, is the real lesson Langer learned from Wittgenstein. It is not a lesson directly dependent, either in its formulation or in its consequences, on the contention of the picture theory of language that there are "atomic facts" or "atomic objects." A cursory examination of Langer's account of language, primarily as it will be treated in *Philosophy in a New Key,* will show that it is only externally connected with Wittgenstein's *Tractatus* and its "picture theory" of language, which functions rather as a metaphor, apart from technical detail and claims. The real "sources" of Langer's approach to language are Philipp Wegener 1991 and Karl Bühler (see Innis 2002a: 51–98), as we shall see in a later chapter.

Expanding the Notion of Logical Form

Langer thinks that "every entity has some logical form" (*PP* 123), whether the entities be "conventional" or "natural." But "conventional entities" that are restricted to "words and signs" in the literal sense never allow us to "get to that which poetic spirits, less cautious than the scientific and therefore often more enlightened, call the 'deeper meaning' of certain symbolic structures" that are "philosophically interesting": "problems of scientific description, artistic truth, unconscious symbolization . . . the literal understanding of language, the reactions of dogs to dinner-bells or the inference from 'honk-honk' to automobile" (*PP* 127). Readers of *Philosophy in a New Key* will recognize this collection of philosophically interesting topics, to which we will return. Langer here uses, for the first time, the notion of a "symbolic form" (*PP* 128) to circumscribe the scope of her investigations. The mark of the human is the ability "to *find* meanings deliberately, rather than acquire them with passive unconsciousness" (*PP* 128). This finding of meaning is the work of abstraction, which is, it becomes clear, not identical with generalization. "Abstraction," Langer writes, "is the explicit recognition of a *form* which may be variously exemplified" (*PP* 130). While theoretical science begins with "the step from generalization to abstraction, from the classification of entities or events to the appreciation of forms" as the step "from inductive beliefs to logical insight, from a codification of actualities to a survey of possibilities" (130), it is by no means determinative of what can count as a form. Langer, echoing Cassirer, considers a class-concept to be a "form, according to which certain entities may be conceived" (131). Theoretical science "is based not only upon generalized observation, but upon *principles of interpretation,* which are purely formal, and determine our recognition of events and entities" (*PP* 132). Formal principles of interpretation are "logical." This acknowledgment of autonomous principles of interpretation will open the way to "other principles" that are not "theoretical," that is, not discursive, but that nevertheless have their own logic. But at this point in her discussion Langer makes a fateful, and fruitful, comment. Our recognition of a "conceived form where it is expressed in nature" involves "a new primitive notion, which the Germans have called 'Gestalt'" (*PP* 132).

The notion of "Gestalt," which makes its appearance here, will enable Langer to make a fundamental and permanent connection between the "logical" and the "perceptual." It characterizes, at the most basic level, the mind's "ability to *find meanings.* Instead of depending upon chance associations to make a sign out of a sensory stimulus, we are able to apprehend the stimulus as a form, and make of it a *symbol* for experiences which follow the same pattern" (*PP* 132). The formulation of this insight in *Philosophy in a New Key* was that "meaning . . . accrues essentially to forms" (*PNK* 90). In short, *wherever there is form, there is meaning.* Meaning is "pushed down" to the level of perception, understood as primary "articulation." Not only do (perceptual) "forms," as potentially symbolic structures, give us access to objects, objects are themselves forms and, as Langer will conclude, can become or be used as symbolic structures. Just as there is no *the* meaning of a symbol, there is no "only one pattern" (*PP* 134), no one unique form, of an object, and therefore no *one* symbol that can capture it, nor can it function univocally as *one* symbol by reason of its "semantic plenitude" or connotational richness. Logical structures—embedded in symbolic systems—are always expressed, Langer writes, "in terms of certain primitive entities" (*PP* 134). These primitive entities, Langer claims, belong to the system, not to existent things as such, which, indeed, are accessible only under some system. There is "no such thing as *the form* of a real thing, or of an event. There is no such thing as pure experience" (*PP* 135). Langer then makes, in light of and as an extension of the preceding comment, with its pragmatist echoes, an observation that she never repudiated.

> Just as all thought must have some logical constants, though these may be variously chosen, so all experience must have some specific pattern, wherein it may be sensed, though there are many patterns possible within the same reality. All expe-

rience, of sense or thought or of feeling, is selective; it must formulate its material in some way, and in just one way at a time. All concrete reality has a multiplicity of possible forms, and when it is known to us it has one actual form, with an amorphous "content." (*PP* 136)

Hence, the relation between form and content is "an elusive affair" (*PP* 136). There is no such thing as an absolute description of anything, no perspective that fuses and relates all other perspectives. When, therefore, Langer says that "logical perspectives exclude each other; they cannot be ideally put together" (*PP* 137), she is not using "logical" in any narrow sense. A logical perspective is "not partial in the sense that it leaves out certain portions of the object. It is abstract not sectional" (*PP* 137). The whole reality is given to us under, and by means of, the form. A logical perspective, hence, is a form of symbolic projection that subsumes all the features of an object or system of objects *under its constitutive point of view.*

Multiple Realities

What is the upshot here? Reality, Langer writes, can be seen under *"several adequate descriptions"* (*PP* 138). Logically diverse systems can "mean" a concrete experience. This experience "is capable of exemplifying various forms, though it can display only one form at a time. Any system which fits the real experience exactly, and leaves none of its structural properties indeterminate, is an adequate description" (*PP* 138). Because, as Langer says a few pages further on, "a symbol is not a reproduction of its object, but an *expression*—an exhibition of certain relevant moments, whose relevance is determined by the purpose in hand" (*PP* 141), it is clear that, on Langer's early position, there can be many *true* symbolic transformations of the experiential field. "All expression," she writes, "is based upon abstract features wherein symbol and object coincide; but as an object may have various and variously expressible aspects, all symbolization is necessarily selective" (*PP* 142). Because all understanding, as selective, must be "most appropriate to certain purposes" (*PP* 142), it is already valuational. The selectiveness of understanding entails that "facts themselves might be differently formulated, according to the notions through which they are apprehended" (*PP* 143). Reality, Langer says, admits of many truth-forms, and so "there is probably in one experiential matrix a disjunction of individual facts" (*PP* 143). Think of the so-called conflict between the scientific and the religious-mythical symbolizations of "creation" and the "origin" of the world. This "disjunction" is not merely empirical. Speaking for the moment of scientific data, Langer rightly points out that they are "significant only in the light of some logical system of *rendering* the facts" (*PP* 149).

The ways of rendering are interpretations. Indeed, "we cannot formulate reality otherwise than by the pattern it actually has from the points of reference we have chosen. *Any entity* [my emphasis] which expresses such a pattern is a symbol: it is 'true' to experience in so far as the analogy holds" (*PP* 150). A symbol allows us to "grasp" experience, to "understand" it. Philosophy's ideal of understanding is "*systematic* interpretation, the discovery of syntactical meanings in the world," the "appreciation of all connecting orders in the world" (*PP* 151). This will, in fact, become a reflection upon symbolic forms and consequently upon the meaning-systems carried by these forms. Thus, the semiotic or symbolic turn in philosophy is already present in Langer's early work and radically conditions how she initially formulates matters concerning myth and art, a formulation that gets carried into her later work and given a definitive treatment.

Types of Understanding: Myth, Art, and the Non-discursive

In *The Practice of Philosophy* Langer distinguishes a type of understanding that she calls "non-discursive reasoning" (*PP* 152). It is different from verbal expression "only by peculiar characteristics of its symbolism" (*PP* 152). She calls it "insight." Insight, as she puts it, "is a constituent in ordinary intelligence, and, like all knowledge, involves the appreciation of symbolic structures *qua* symbolic" (*PP* 152). The discussion of "insight" is a direct attack upon "the sins of narrowness which logical philosophy is supposed to avert" by making room for such phenomena as "the significance of Art . . . and the existence of incommunicable knowledge" (*PP* 152). Insight, in the original formulation, gives us access to emotional and aesthetic experience, which Langer assimilates to the recognition of intrinsic values. These items cannot be adequately accessed by means of a discursive type of symbolism. The object of insight "is at least sometimes expressible, though not verbally definable" (*PP* 154). Indeed, an object's complexity, we have already seen, can defy our apperception and thus evade any one exclusive symbolic form. This pluralism is derived from another one of Langer's generative and most important insights: "[T]here are ideas which no definition can render . . . ideas that haunt the human mind, yet are never satisfactorily stated in words" (*PP* 156). For Langer, at this stage of her thought, the prime exemplar of such an idea is the type that is incarnated in myths. Myth arises, she thinks, when what we want to articulate has no previous concept. In this way we can apprehend a concept before we can comprehend it. "The kernel of a myth is a remote idea, which is *shown*, not stated in the myth. It is only the myth that is stated in words" (*PP* 158). The move away from thinking of "rationality" as "scientific" and "literal" is already taken in Langer's very first book. Her whole intellectual project will be to explore its implications. Without falling into a Wittgensteinian position on the "inexpressibility," and hence non-rationality or mystical character, of mythical ideas, Langer merely states that the language of myth and the language of propositions are not the same, without measuring the one by the other, although myths are themselves in need not just of engagement but also of interpretation. Discursive symbolism is, says Langer, using a Wittgensteinian mode of expression, a "picture" of a fact; but we are also able, by means of our universal intelligence, "to see in any sort of fact a 'picture' of a general condition" (PP 158)—and this is the function of myth. It constructs a picture of a general condition without describing it in literal terms. Langer explicitly follows Cassirer here in what is surely one of the earliest references to his *Philosophy of Symbolic Forms* in the English-speaking philosophical world, long before the appearance of this monumental trilogy in translation.

But Langer goes even further, in a comment that will be also crucial for her later work and will become a fulcrum of central chapters in *Feeling and Form.* "All representative art," she asserts, "is a myth" (PP 160). In what does its significance reside? Not in the object, she responds, "but in that which its particular formulation of the object is capable of expressing," a formulation that is "inexhaustibly individual" (PP 160). The irrelevance of the object is matched by the all-importance of its conception. But what does Langer, at this stage, specify as belonging to the "conception"? Note the seriation of, albeit predominantly visual, items: balance of values, line and color and light, "and I know not what other elements" (PP 160). They are, she says, so related that "no verbal proposition could hope to embody its pattern. Yet the totality is an indescribably perfected *rhythm* (which is 'pattern' in a more developed sense), for which we find equally indescribable meanings in our world of experience" (PP 160). While it is pretty clear that Langer is thinking of a constructed visual form here, it should be noted that already in *The Practice of Philosophy* she foregrounds music as "the purest of symbolic media" (PP 160)—doing this for both personal and semiotic reasons—and asks, anticipating the aesthetic pivot of *Philosophy in a New Key* and all of her later work, whether "the final object of musical expression" might not be "the endlessly intricate yet universal pattern of emotional life" (PP 161). Langer had not yet adopted *feeling* as a *terminus technicus*, but it is clear what she means.

The central distinction between discursive and presentational forms, which is the axis of *Philosophy in a New Key* and which clearly informs the concerns of *An Introduction to Symbolic Logic*, is, then, already made in *The Practice of Philosophy*, though Langer had not settled on a stable vocabulary. Her first way of formulating the distinction is to divide the functions of symbolism into the *presenta-*

tive and the *representative*. Distinguishing for the sake of contrast "reason" from "intuition," a distinction she will not hold to, she claims that the former, that is, reason, works through discursive language while intuition works through non-verbal symbolism (*PP* 161). Langer at this point in her thought made a most interesting hedge. On the one hand, she asserted that while ideally everything could be said, it is so only ideally, for we cannot master an infinite vocabulary and an infinite syntax. Here the limitation seems to be psychological and, indeed, a limitation of human faculties. On the other hand, she then goes on to say that while words are our most definite and certain means of communication, nevertheless "the paucity of language is astounding" (*PP* 161). Linguistic structures are unable to mediate, by reason of their (syntactic) form, what Langer here calls an *intensive* knowledge. But intensive knowledge is not distinguished as a different faculty. Langer points out that the intensive meanings are apperceived by a process that is the same as that of understanding a sentence (*PP* 162). This leads her to state that "the symbolic quality of empirical things is just the same as what Russell has called the 'transparency' of an asserted proposition. But since the symbolic *possibilities* of a concrete experience are probably infinite, and no abstract meaning is fixed by convention, as in language, insight into rhythms and forms which elude words is apt to be incommunicable" (*PP* 162)—that is, discursively incommunicable. This is the power and achievement of "direct intensive symbolization" (*PP* 164).

Langer is not completely consistent in her terminology here, oscillating between the pairs "representative" and "presentative" and "discursive" and "intensive." But her point, independently of terminology, is the same. And she further contends, as does Peirce, that almost every act of cognition utilizes both forms.

> There is no knowledge without form; and probably no form is unique; therefore all knowledge can find symbolic expression. But it is the types of expression rather than the organ of recognition that determines the difference between insight and inference. In general, each type of expression is appropriate to a certain type of subject-matter which the other cannot adequately render, yet there are some conceptions that fall as easily into the one form as into the other. For instance, one person can understand through a graph what another can only grasp through an algebraic formula, and *vice versa*. (*PP* 165)

The ideal types, which are contrasted here, are the scientist, who, in Langer's conception, aims at "literal" expression and the artist, who "must find symbolisms in nature; but his expression is intensive, and only clarifies the material to the point of making the hunch vaguely contagious" (*PP* 166). The gesture toward vagueness points not to laxness but to richness and to the necessity, as Peirce so clearly saw, of *application* in the interpretation of the symbolic form (see Innis 2002: 47–48). Both the scientist and the artist, it turns out, are dependent upon "insight." "But the scientist must have insight to convey intellectual knowledge, and the artist must have insight to inspire insight" (*PP* 166). Langer will not totally abandon, strangely enough, this contrast. In *Feeling and Form* she will say that the "import" of a work of art can be only exhibited, not stated.

That the nucleus of *Philosophy in a New Key*, and Langer's other later works, is latent in *The Practice of Philosophy* is further indicated when Langer asserts that it is the perception of patterns that is the foundation of insight or intuition. She uses, once again, in a way that foreshadows her later emphases, the notion of Gestalt, which is form "in a really general sense" (*PP* 166). Here she foregrounds "the process of generalizing an apprehended configuration, be it verbal, visual, or even emotional; finding for it possible meanings in our further experience" (*PP* 166). This process is not "alogical," Langer says; "rather it seems to me that the recognition of patterns without the help of conventional associations, the personal discovery of meanings through myth, ritual, art, highly individual, and awe-inspiring by its subtlety, is the very acme of logical procedure, and the refinement of intelligence" (*PP* 166). This is a most helpful remark. Note the pivotal concepts, especially the emphasis on the broadened notion of reason that plays such a rhetorical role in *Philosophy in a New Key*, the notion of an "apprehended configuration," the contrast between novel patterns and conventional associations, and so forth. The point being made here is, for Langer, universal. It informs both her conception of philosophy and her conception of the tasks of the analysis of presentational forms in all their varieties and especially for the development of Langer's mature aesthetics and her account of the rise of cultural forms in volume three of *Mind*. "Every experience," she writes, "illustrates rational order of some sort, although we may lack the conceptual outfit to symbolize that order. There is no known limit to the mind's capacity for constructions. The shifts, the changes of logical *Gestalt*, are unpredictable" (*PP* 218). The task of philosophy, as well as of art, then, is to develop, analogous to the "mechanic's feel" discussed by Robert Pirsig in *Zen and the Art of Motorcycle Maintenance* (1974: 323–324), "true expertness in recognizing universal forms, in finding world-patterns" (*PP* 215). These world-patterns are embodied in symbolic forms. World-patterns are interpretations that themselves need, from the philosophical side, to be interpreted and ordered. The semiotic and the hermeneutical are hence joined from the very beginning in Langer's philosophical project.

In *The Practice of Philosophy* it must be admitted that the analysis of the various presentational forms in general and of the aesthetic dimension in particular is not fully thematized—primarily because Langer did not believe the fundamental categories had been established in an appropriately formal fashion. Just as good and evil may not be fundamental categories in ethics, so beauty and ugliness, she cautiously claimed, are not fundamental in aesthetics. We will discuss this thesis later, when we turn to *Feeling and Form*. Langer, in this first book, believes, without developing the point, that ethical and aesthetic values "must be *products* of ethical and aesthetic systems rather than their terms; they should emerge, where they are not presupposed as indefinable ingredients at all" (*PP* 210). But even here we can see, in outline, the path Langer will take. As she saw matters in 1930, aesthetics, perhaps her greatest philosophical love as a *theoretical* discipline, was still in the "mythical" stage, and philosophy, while "mythical in origin" must be "scientific in destination" (*PP* 178). In her conception "every myth must be redeemed by a scientific inspiration" (*PP* 211). By "scientific" Langer clearly means theoretical and conceptual. It is, however, one must note, not art that passes over into such a scientific stage but our reflections on art—and on myth, ritual, sacrament—that must do so, that is, philosophy. There is a (certainly unintended) Hegelian echo here—a kind of distant hoot of the owl of Minerva.

What types of hints as to a viable non-mythical aesthetics, and a general philosophy of presentational forms, does Langer give? First, Langer thinks that such a "scientific" and philosophical hermeneutics and aesthetics must work with some principle of *proportion*. We face, at the outset, she thinks, the task of defining a "*system of possible proportions*" and then of applying such a system to "select certain patterns, the ones we call 'artistic,' i.e. the members of the *actual* system" (*PP* 211). This is not, however, a psychological, but rather a logical, matter. Secondly, Langer (certainly influenced by Whitehead) thinks we need a clearly defined idea of *harmony*, "a norm, an abstract conception of harmony . . . some abstract form that could be exemplified in all media, physical, conceptual, or what-not" (*PP* 212). Thirdly, we need some completely general formulation of *rhythm*. Or, maybe some category that would reduce harmony and rhythm to some further abstraction—perhaps this "further abstraction" will be the pivotal notion of "living form" that will play such a central role in *Feeling and Form* and in *Mind*, as we will see and as Rolf Lachmann and Donald Dryden have emphasized. This would give us, Langer argues, the beginnings at least of a metaphysics of art, and, I think, of symbolic forms quite generally, which is not reducible to a psychology of appreciation, although, as we will see, Langer's utilization of the resources of psychology will be extensive. These resources will contribute substantially to her development of a nuanced, naturalistic model of mind. The metaphysics of art, which in fact Langer never did really develop under that rubric, would deal with postulated forms and their possible elaborations in the world's art. But Langer's account of symbolic forms ultimately goes far beyond art to encompass all the products of mind. It is a kind of metaphysics of mind that Langer ultimately develops, even if it has an aesthetic core and a semiotic or symbolic frame.

Langer's metaphysics of mind, defined as it was by a distinctive conception of logic, was itself then to be configured semiotically and ultimately, in a nonreductive way, naturalistically, rooted in what became for her the logic of sentience. Rather than a *metaphysics* of mind and art that trod a purely formal and abstract path, she ended up pursuing a *semiotics* of mind and art and of all symbolic forms, but a semiotics distinctively, though not uniquely, her own. It was a semiotics grounded empirically in the psychology of perception and of imagination and in a fruitful exploitation of theoretical and practical sources far removed from "traditional" philosophy. The "practice" of philosophy for Langer already entailed a "transformation" of philosophy.

Toward the Later Philosophy

From the seed sown in *The Practice of Philosophy* and *An Introduction to Symbolic Logic* the flower of Langer's distinctive approach to the "symbolic mind" and its expressions, especially its expression in art, grew. With relation to the domain of aesthetics, still missing is the development of the idea of *semblance* or *Schein*, which Langer attributes first and foremost to Friedrich Schiller, whose primary debt in his *Aesthetic Letters* was to Kant. But Kant actually plays little systematic or direct role in Langer's work, both earlier and later, although there are clearly Kantian elements. Indeed, Langer's thoroughgoing cognitivism with respect to the mythic and aesthetic dimensions stands in what seems to be polar opposition to Kant's way of thinking about these symbol-drenched domains. Further, the deep thematization of the imagination and its connection with abstraction that marks *Mind* is only vaguely hinted at. But it is nevertheless recognized as a problem and a focal concern. Langer will mine a very different set of "sources" here, especially French works from the first third of the twentieth century, which we will examine in a later chapter. One will not be surprised by Langer's later focusing on the imagination. An account of imagination is, indeed, demanded for a coherent expansion of the early formulated frame. For how else could one see possibilities in and beyond actual experience? The notion of *living form*, of the *vital image*, which will play such a role in *Mind*, is likewise not thematically present in *The Practice of Philosophy*. At the same time, the emphasis on proportion, harmony, and rhythm as essential features already includes an "organic" orientation and shows a further, even if rather unacknowledged, influence of Whitehead. And, finally, the notion of a "primary illusion" as distinctive of each great order of art is not present in *The Practice of Philosophy,* but the important, indeed fundamental, thesis that different types of actual objects can be used as expressive devices is. This is the heuristic key to the elaboration of the idea of presentational forms.

Langer's root or seminal idea, which she formulates at the end of *The Practice of Philosophy,* concerns the centrality of meanings in philosophical analysis. "Meanings are the object of all philosophical research. The ability to construe them is the gift of understanding; and the swift, independent, clear-sighted appreciation of meaning—in nature, in life, in ritual and art—is wisdom, the goal of philosophy" (*PP* 221). This formulation aptly describes in programmatic fashion what the resolute and pathbreaking march of Langer's career of thought will be, whose first steps were taken in this genial and engaged work and presupposed in *An Introduction to Symbolic Logic.* In our later chapters we will see both the continuities in Langer's work and the revolutionary expansion and thickening that her classic works gave to her first, never repudiated, formulations of the tasks of philosophy undertaken in a "new key," with its broadening and deepening of the "logical" as symbolic.

2

Symbolic Transformation

Philosophy's New Key

Philosophy in a New Key, published twelve years after *The Practice of Philosophy*, remains the indispensable point of entry into Langer's mature philosophical project. It is central to our fuller understanding of her conception of what philosophy is, a position, we have seen, that is already staked out in her first book, but that is exemplified in more detail and with more substantial thickness in her classic work. Of especial importance is Langer's own self-reflection on her task as delineated in the three prefaces she wrote for successive editions of the book, which mirror in their own way her discussion of philosophical systems, focusing on their progressive exhaustion and their being overtaken by new problems and methods.

To begin with, in the 1942 preface, Langer, in quasi-reportorial mode, states her intention to demonstrate an "unrecognized fact" of the "new key" in philosophy and how to transpose the main themes of our thought into it (xiii). This will involve a changing of the questions of philosophy (xiii), away from the traditional "round up the usual suspects approach," to an investigation of the notion of *symbolic modes* and the "variable relationship of form and content" (xiii). What is one to study if one focuses on symbolic modes? Langer answers: myth, analogy, metaphorical thinking, art. They are all intellectual activities determined by these modes. That is, they are *forms of real thinking*, even if they are not themselves "philosophy." Readers familiar with the history of German Idealism, especially represented by Hegel and Schelling, will immediately recall that these subjects lay at the center of many of its concerns, but Langer will insist throughout all of her career that acknowledging these symbolic modes does not entail an idealistic interpretation of reality (xiv). All reality, however, must be accessed through "some adequate symbolism" (xiv), and it is to the study of these symbolic systems that she is going to devote her efforts.

Symbolic systems arise through processes of *symbolic transformation*, the key idea around which *Philosophy in a New Key* turns. Already in this book symbolic transformation is thought of as a *natural function*, as a "natural activity, a high form of nervous response, characteristic of man among animals" (xiv). This theme, we will see, marks a deep continuity in Langer's work, culminating in the *Mind* trilogy. It justifies her characterization of herself as a "sober naturalist." But even such a characterization could lead to confusion if "naturalist" be conflated with "reductionist." Langer herself triangulates her starting point as nonderivative from Cartesian, Humean, or Kantian premises. What, in spite of substantive differences, these philosophical projects share is a "subjectivist turn," a search for "ultimates" in consciousness. The Cartesian "thinking substance," the Humean "atomistic elements" of awareness, the Kantian universal "forms of intuition" and "categories of the understanding" are all tainted with various forms of "reductionism" or longing for metaphysical or epistemological ultimates. For Langer there is no thinking *substance*. Nor are there psychic atoms, mental building blocks, mysteriously compounding into objects without any ontological glue, and there are no trans-individual mental structures that a priori and universally shape and form the world. What is "ultimate" for Langer is a multiform *activity* that informs her "generative idea": "the essentially *transformational* nature of human understanding" (xiv). This idea is not a postulate, but a consequence of a set of converging discoveries in a multitude of disciplines, from psychology to anthropology to linguistics to literary criticism and theory and the history of religions and symbolic logic. In fact, Langer traces her focal concern back to logical rather than ethical or metaphysical interests (xiv). This is in full agreement with her early books. As the first chapter of *Philosophy in a New Key* makes abundantly clear, "respectable ancestors . . . are never to be despised" (xv). I would also add, neither are respectable parallels and contemporaries. This aspect of Langer's work is perhaps, on the philosophical side, not as developed as it could have been. One of the tasks of the present book is to indicate, where appropriate, how Langer's already fertile project could be further enriched and supported by being brought into closer dialogue with positions derived from the American philosophical tradition.

In the 1951 preface, Langer notes that the task of *Philosophy in a New Key* is really to develop a theory of mind that will acknowledge both science and art (ix). And indeed it is an oscillation between these poles that marks her work as a whole. Although Langer never developed a systematic philosophy of science, nevertheless she philosophized in light of an implicit one. In fact, it is mutual *illumination* of the phenomenon of mind by both science and art that will become one of the great themes of the *Mind* trilogy. It is the creative tension between these two exemplifying poles that gives such vitality to Langer's thought as a whole. Philosophy itself, she contends, and continued to maintain, moves from figuration to logical insight (x), expressed literally. Philosophy can, and often in fact does, begin in metaphor, but it aims toward a non-metaphorical account of its problems. We will, nevertheless, ask ourselves whether such a demand is able to be fully complied with in general and whether, in particular, Langer, in light of such concepts as "symbolic transformation," "living form," "logical pictures," and so forth, herself managed to do so. Lakoff and Johnson (1999) have shown with a wealth of historical examples how metaphor penetrates philosophy's deepest categories. The lesson they are teaching is that metaphor is not just an object of philosophical reflection but a medium for it. Philosophy arises and develops within systems of deep and pervasive metaphorical images and concepts, taken from the fundamental aspects of our existence as embodied beings, beings that are defined by being "enfleshed." Many of Langer's reflections intersect with these important themes.

Looking ahead, with ten years' distance between the first and second editions, Langer indicated that the concerns of *Philosophy in a New Key* will entail deeper and more systematic accounts of "creation," "abstraction," and "import," notions that will play pivotal roles in *Feeling and Form*, in *Problems of Art*, and later in *Mind*. The preface to the 1956 edition follows this up. Langer says that *Philosophy in a New Key* not only turned out to be a preface to *Feeling and Form*, but that it has opened to "a new philosophy of living form, living nature, mind, and some of the very deep problems of human society that we usually designate as ethical problems," themes that receive substantial treatment in *Mind* and have been focused upon especially, as I have noted, by Rolf Lachmann and Donald Dryden.

Characterizing *Philosophy in a New Key* as an "indispensable prologue" to an unfinished story (viii), Langer's non-dogmatic approach acknowledges that improvement, even if it means self-reversal, must be the guiding principle of philosophical reflection. Of especial, and enlightening, importance is Langer's naming together of Whitehead, Russell, Wittgenstein, Freud, and Cassirer as sharing a common task. While not exactly philosophical bedfellows, these thinkers for Langer slept in the same dormitory and exercised facing in the same direction. They "launched the attack on the formidable problem of symbol and meaning, and established the keynote of philosophical thought in our day" (viii). Their focal concerns play varying and differentially weighted roles in Langer's thought (especially Freud), and it should be noted that the Wittgenstein she refers to throughout her whole work is the Wittgenstein of the *Tractatus*, not of the *Philosophical Investigations*.

Symbolic Transformation: On Symbolic Need

How is Langer's core concept, "symbolic transformation," first developed in *Philosophy in a New Key*?

The central, and never repudiated, thesis of Langer's philosophical project is: "Symbol and meaning make man's world, far more than sensation" (*PNK* 28). Indeed, Langer provocatively asserts, *"our sense-data are primarily symbols"* (*PNK* 21). Human knowledge, the exploration of which is the task of epistemology—which is "really all that is left of a worn-out philosophical heritage" (*PNK* 21)—is for Langer, in a formulation whose meaning will become clear later, "a structure of *facts that are symbols* and *the laws that are their meanings*" (*PNK* 21). Already in *Philosophy in a New Key* Langer is going to continue to keep her eyes on the implications both of the key insights of modern logic—with its concerns for symbolic notation systems of all sorts, as we saw in the preceding chapter—and of the profound importance of certain strands of modern psychology, especially psychoanalysis and Gestalt theory. Langer will follow the lead of symbolism in two directions: (1) toward a broadened notion of logic, not so much the symbolism of logic but the *logic of symbolism* and (2) toward all those disciplines that encompass the study of emotions, religion, fantasy, what Langer calls, perhaps not aptly, "everything but knowledge" (*PNK* 24)—in the literal, discursive sense of the term. What is central to both directions is the notion that "the *human response* [is] a constructive, not a passive thing" (*PNK* 24). The human response is a symbolic response, and symbolization, as a "fundamental notion," is the "keynote of all humanistic problems," pointing toward a "new conception of 'mentality'"(*PNK* 25). It is clear that already at the beginning of what Langer described as her "lonely path" she was aware of the psychological and cultural dimensions and matrices of meaning-making. Indeed, she will develop in *Mind* a sort of biologically grounded cultural psychology with philosophical and semiotic intent, framing the "symbolic mind."

At the heart of Langer's conception of symbolic transformation is a decided movement away from foregrounding or focusing on impression, memory, and association as the ultimate conditions of sense or significance. The prime issue for her, properly understood, is no longer one of origins and acquisitions of faculties for dealing with sense data of all sorts, but with the *uses* of sense data, which Langer calls "the realm of conception and expression" (*PNK* 26). The main problem with relying philosophically on a genetic psychology, as Langer rather idiosyncratically understands the term, is its focusing on primitive needs (*PNK* 28). Later in her work Langer will also focus, admittedly on the level of philosophical interpretation, on genetic issues, but not in reductionistic fashion. Her genetic concern is the "functional genesis" of symbolization, which for her is a "tool." Indeed, symbol using is "presumably a highly integrated form of simpler animal activities" (*PNK* 29), and it enables humans to "synthesize, delay, and modify" their reactions (*PNK* 29). Animal mentality, Langer asserts, is "built up on a primitive semantic" (*PNK* 30). Non-human animals can receive only a variety of signals, they can make only a limited set of combinations of them, and their modes of reaction have a limited fixity or a limited adjustability of responses (*PNK* 30). In rather different terms, one could say that, on Langer's position, animal mentality is restricted to the realms of Peircean indexicality (or indication), based on "existential" connection, and iconicity, based on resemblance, a thesis that is also argued in Terrence Deacon's Peirce-inspired *The Symbolic Species* (1997). "Indication" and also "iconization" are to be distinguished from "representation" in the strict sense, which is dependent upon "symbolization," to which Langer and Peirce have slightly different verbal approaches. Animal mentality is described by Langer as fundamentally structured as a pragmatically oriented *transmitter,* a metaphor of mind that she will repudiate for humans. Indices for an animal belong to the class of symptoms, traces, and so forth, which are immediately wedded to the *perceptual context and situation* in which the animal is living and acting. Animals apprehend the world "iconically" or in the iconic mode to the degree that *sameness* plays a role in their experience. The denial of *representation* to animals, in the strict systematic sense, that is, as belonging to symbols and symbol systems, will be central to Langer's account of the distinctiveness of humanization, in spite of her insistence on nature not making ontological jumps. Representation, in the human symbolic sense, is to be seen as a semiotic emergence.

This means that although Langer maintains and defends a naturalist position, she still will draw a sharp contrast between human and non-human mentality. The traditional genetic conception of language—that language arose to fulfill "vital" or pragmatic needs—is still wedded to the practical schema, to, indeed, the schema of the transmitter, and therefore must operate under some principle of biological efficiency. Langer holds that even if, *per hypothesin,* language is to have primarily pragmatic value, it is, looked at from the biological point of view, still strangely prone to weird errors. How, from a pragmatic, genetic point of view, can we account for the tendency of language to confuse and inhibit, warp and misadapt actions, Langer asks? Such a biogenetic position can make no sense of what is intended or accomplished in word-magic, ritual, or even art. Already in the early part of *Philosophy in a New Key* Langer will foreground, in continuity with *The Practice of Philosophy,* the essentially symbolic character of art, that it is not "mere play." Langer will also challenge the utilitarian doctrine of symbolism when applied to *dreaming.* What practical function, Langer asks, do dreams perform, since they often present images that we certainly would not want to think about and that disturb our "balance"?

Langer proposes instead to think of *"characteristically human needs"* (*PNK* 38–39), not to rely on a generalized zoological, one-size-fits-all, model. Already in the second chapter of *Philosophy in a New Key* Langer engages with a biological model of mind, which will be a main theme in the *Mind* trilogy. For Langer, human beings are and remained substances "biologically organized" (*PNK* 40). This kind of organization brings with it "suffering and impulse and awareness" (*PNK* 40). They define a chemically active body, transmuted into a symbolic animal, to be sure. But Langer, while still remaining faithful to her commitment to the philosophical implications of biology, nevertheless thinks of symbolization as a *primary need* of humans, a point emphasized in a famous essay by Walker Percy, "Symbol as Need" (in Percy 1977: 288–297). "It is the fundamental process" of a human's mind, Langer writes, and it "goes on all the time" (*PNK* 41). Langer points out in a profound comment that symbolization is "an act *essential to thought,* and prior to it. Symbolization is the essential act of mind; and mind takes in more than what is commonly called thought" (*PNK* 41). This is a hint at the distinction, developed in a different way by Freud and other parallel thinkers, between the "canons of discursive reasoning" and the "enormous store of other symbolic material" that is put to divers uses or not put to use at all and that Langer had proposed in *The Practice of Philosophy* as proper objects of philosophical concern.

Already in *Philosophy in a New Key* Langer will insist that the brain is never quiescent, even in the absence of exogenous stimulation. It is "actively translating experience into symbols, in fulfillment of a basic need to do so. It carries on a constant process of ideation" (*PNK* 42–43). This is creation of a vast field of representations, in the broad sense, emerging from an extensive range of "symbolific activity," Langer referring here with such a phrase to Cassirer (*PNK* 43). The mind is "symbol-mongering" (43): it is a transformer, a fountain, spontaneous, given over to the "sheer expression of ideas" (43). One thinks of Philip Wheelwright's sorely neglected notion of "the burning fountain" (Wheelwright 1968). In this way Langer can, early in her intellectual journey, foreground sharply traits that humans do not have in common with animals: ritual, art, laughter, weeping, speech, superstition, and scientific genius (43). These activities are to be defined within the matrix of the primary activity of the *"symbolic transformation of experiences"* (44). An exemplification of this is Langer's pointing to how fundamental and primitive, for humans, the "sheer *symbolific* use of sounds is" (45) that arises prior to the mastery of conventional forms. *Meaning*-experience elicits this activity from the "vociferous little human animal" (45).

It is clear that Langer's real target in the second chapter of *Philosophy in a New Key* is the "psychogenetic" theory of mind, which, she points out, is simply bewildered by such a phenomenon as ritual. Langer is concerned to develop, I noted earlier, a notion of *symbolic need,* although she does not put it exactly that way. The need is an expressive need, and *does not have to end in overt action.* Ritual arises, according to Langer, as the desire to symbolize, and act out reactively, great conceptions. It enables us to "symbolize a Presence, to aid in the formulation of a religious universe" (49). Langer speaks of an interest stronger than the practical or manipulative interest, an interest in the *expressive* value of the mystic acts of ritual. (See Innis 2004 for more on ritual.)

While Langer's references to Freud are not frequent or even really substantial, in *Philosophy in a New Key* at least she recognized Freud's great contribution to the philosophy of mind: human behavior is (metaphorically) a language, "every *move* is at the same time a *gesture.*" Symbolization is both an *end* and an *instrument.* It is humans' primary interest (51). But to recognize the primacy of symbolization as such is to explode traditional theory of mind practiced as epistemology, or theory of *knowledge,* understood as discursive knowledge. Swastikas and genuflections are different kinds of symbols, with different types of meanings, from mathematical and linguistic symbols, but they are also both produced and *submitted to* by language animals.

So, we are led to the great question: What is it that makes a symbol out of anything, making something that is not a symbol into something *meaningful*? Meaning, Langer asserts, unsurprisingly in light of what we saw in the previous chapter, "rests upon a condition which is, in the last analysis, logical" (52). A logical analysis would deal with "what constitutes meaning, what characterizes symbols, and also the different kinds of symbolism and their logical distinctions" (52). These are the central topics of Langer's whole philosophical project.

The Logic of Signs and Symbols

Langer develops a general account of the "logic" of signs and symbols that functions as the background for her pivotal distinction between discursive and presentational forms, which runs like a permanent axis through her whole work, even if she does not always avail herself of exactly this terminology at every stage. This "logic" is part of Langer's explicitly philosophical contribution to general semiotics or a general theory of signs. While part of its general and initial terminological apparatus has not been taken up by other thinkers—indeed, Langer herself repudiated it or, at least, later acknowledged its inadequacy—the substantive insights are well taken once we do not quibble over extraneous verbal issues.

Langer's general reflections hang on two assumptions: an account of meaning must hold two intertwined aspects together, without, however, conflating the two. Meaning has (a) a logical aspect and (b) a psychological aspect. For something to be meaningful, to function as a sign, something must be "*capable* of conveying a meaning" (52). Such a notion points to the semiotic "carrying capacity" of a medium. Langer also points out that being capable is not enough. Something is not a sign in and of itself. Signs arise in use. They are employed or recognized by someone in order to articulate or grasp a meaning. This psychological side is "always present" (*PNK* 53). A sign is always a sign *to* someone, that is, to an interpreter.

Langer was not ignorant of Peirce's or Husserl's attempt to chart the logic of signs. But her summary judgment was that both accounts were too complicated. Calling Peirce's types of signs an "obstreperous flock" and the resultant order "terrifying," and arguing that Husserl ended up with as many theories as there are "meanings," Langer hoped to simplify the logic of signs and symbols. Although we may not be happy with such a summary dismissal of two mature and penetrating thinkers, we should not presume that Langer proposes to reinvent the semiotic wheel or to sidestep the issues that Peirce and Husserl strove to resolve. Indeed, much of what she says bears directly on their central concerns and in many cases is fully consonant with their generative insights, although Langer, independent thinker that she was, had no intention of showing that.

Langer thinks that the criterion for assembling various signs and sign systems into groups cannot be a shared quality or "family likeness" (55). Meaning is not a quality that some item functioning as a sign has in itself, although there are "qualitative meanings." Meaning is for her not a quality but a relation—and not only a two-term, or dyadic, relation. Meaning, as Langer conceives it, is a *function* of a term. We must, in order to grasp it, look at the term "in its total relation to the other terms about it" (55). Alluding to the example of the A-chord, Langer says that it must be seen as a "pattern surrounding and including A" (55). This is one of Langer's deepest insights: the functional account of what makes a term meaningful entails that meaningful terms rest on a pattern—and that *it is the pattern or whole that is primarily meaningful*. Semiosis, the production and interpretation of signs, involves at least three factors: (1) the "meaning"-term inserted in an appropriate relational matrix, (2) the object "meant," and (3) the subject using the term, the interpreter. Already one can see the *sign–object–interpretant–interpreter* factors of semiosis discriminated by Peirce, with, at the moment, the "ground," Peirce's fifth and rather enigmatic factor, not explicitly distinguished. But Langer is insistent upon the necessity of mind for semiosis (Peirce says, the necessity of a "quasi-mind"). This assertion of the necessity of mind for semiosis will take on another aspect later in Langer's work with her repudiation of Whitehead's universal organicism, which entails a kind of "experiencing" subjectivity "all the way down" in cosmic processes. Reality may be processional and relational all the way down, for Langer, but it is not mental or experiential, in any extended sense, all the way down.

Langer's axial distinction and focal concern in her general theory of signs, however, is first and foremost the "*relations of terms to their objects*" (57)—or to the "things-meant." This is fully consonant with one of Peirce's central foci: How *do* terms, that is, signs and sign-types, relate to their objects? What is the basis of their distinction? Langer in effect, as I have pointed out, draws the line between *indication* and *symbolization* as the two principal or axial modes in which signifying terms do their work. But, as we will see, *iconicity*, the third member of the famous Peircean triad, is also a core signifying mode, albeit functioning and placed differently in Langer's theory.

Indication comprises fundamentally the whole domain of "natural signs" or signs that have the same logical structure as natural signs. "A natural sign is a part of a greater event, or of a complex condition, and to an experienced observer it signifies the rest of that situation of which it is a notable feature. It is a *symptom* of a state of affairs" (*PNK* 57). This way of thinking about indication is fully consonant with Peirce's formulation. A term functioning in the mode of indication "indicates the existence—past, present, or future—of a thing, event, or condition" (*PNK* 57). Langer's examples illustrate this with the same scope and precision as Peirce's. Wet streets, patter on the roof, falling barometer or ring around the moon, smell of smoke, scar, lightening sky in the east, sleekness, all "point to" or are even "parts" of their meanings or objects. Indicative terms are *paired* with their objects in a one-to-one correlation, although it may take great effort to discover the correlation, since it involves empirical learning.

Who does the pairing? The experiencing and sign-reading organism, who is fundamentally related to the world as interpreter. Langer, just like Peirce, pushes interpretation "down" to the level of perception, which is governed first of all by indication and iconicity (felt, grasped resemblances) and relations of implication between terms functioning in a relational matrix. (See Innis 1994: 11–23.) While the paired polyvalent term-object correlation is attended to as a whole, one has predominance in being "more interesting" while the other is "more easily available" and hence able to make the other, which is more difficult to access, present at least to mind. As Langer puts it, thunder could just as well signify that there has been lightning. But in fact, we anticipate thunder by reason of our perception of lightning. For us, in the flux of perception, thunder follows lightning, and indeed we measure the distance of the lightning by reason of the interval between the visual perception and the auditory perception. This interval is a natural sign of distance. When we try to "read" future weather conditions in the configuration of clouds, we take an easily and readily accessible set of perceptual data and attempt to discern a future complicated and ambiguous pattern that is immanent in them. "Mares' tails" mean . . . x because they are not arbitrarily but also not fully unambiguously connected to or with . . . x, a connection that we have learned from experience and conceptualized. So, we can understand quite generally why Langer says, "The interpretation of signs is the basis of animal intelligence" (*PNK* 59), which is concerned with the guiding of their practical activities, including their practically ordered processes of perception. This is what Karl Bühler, within the context of his organon-model of language, called the "steering function" of sense data and also the focal point of von Uexküll's schematization of the functional circle, within which organisms construct and construe their "spaces of meaning." (See Bühler 1934, Innis 1994: 69–97, Innis 2002: 51–98.)

It is clear that the semiotic mode of indication, or indexicality, is not restricted to what we could call natural indexical signs. Many instances of indication, in language and in other domains, involve the production of arbitrary terms, whose connection with their objects is stipulated and by no means intrinsic. The whistle indicating the imminent start of a train, the gunshot indicating sunset, a black crêpe on a door indicating death—these are also indicative signs. They *lead* the interpreting subject to "what they mean." And what they mean is more important, existentially and practically weightier, than they themselves. They could easily be substituted for, since they are not connected with their object the way a symptom is with a disease. So, there is no limit to what terms functioning indexically can mean once we make the transition to arbitrary indices. The interpretive web becomes both more intricate and more ambiguous, making possible systematic error, mistake, or disappointment. Both the "simplest form of error" and the "simplest form of knowledge" arise from this level of the interpretation of signs (*PNK* 59).

Langer chose—and she admitted it later—an unfortunate set of terms for making her principal contrast, and perhaps even compounded the error later. Her principal contrast between signs and symbols, she later said, should have been between signals and symbols, with signs being the generic term of which signals and symbols were species. But I think that more sense could be made of Langer's real intention by foregrounding the notion of "ways of meaning" or "ways of signing" rather than what is in effect already a distinction between types of signs. This would enable us to avoid reification of signs, turning them into things. "Signals," as Langer uses the term, is not, I think, a felicitous choice, since the actual examples that Langer uses encompass both perception, *qua tale,* and effective action. While it is true that perception is embedded in an actional matrix, as Dewey (1896) so clearly showed, perceptual action and effective action are not identical, even if inextricably intertwined, as von Uexküll illustrated with his notion of the "functional circle" structuring the interactions between organisms and their "worlds" or "ambients."

Symbols, in Langer's original use of the term, are to be radically and firmly distinguished from "signs" or "signals." Note, however, that Langer speaks of a term being used "symbolically" or "signally," which certainly indicates that she is not reifying or substantifying terms. How does she draw the contrast between these two uses of terms?

Symbols, on Langer's position, are "not proxy for their objects, but are *vehicles for the conception of objects*" (*PNK* 60–61). Here Langer shows a sense of real complexity. Conceiving a thing or a situation, Langer observes, does not mean overt reaction or merely becoming aware of the thing's or the situation's presence, precisely the two intertwined dimensions, the perceptual and the actional, mentioned above. Symbols have to do with conceptions, primarily, and with things, secondarily. *Symbolic behavior is marked by behavior toward conceptions.* Indexical signs *announce* their objects to the subject, while symbolic signs lead the subject to *conceive* their object (*PNK* 61). Language involves the dual function of words (and sentences, to be sure). Linguistically mediated indexicality is also effected by, for example, tone of voice, a gesture (pointing or staring), "or the location of a placard bearing the word" (*PNK* 61). All these indexical uses are pointed out by Langer's predecessors and sources, Philipp Wegener, Karl Bühler, and Alan Gardiner, who in the course of *Philosophy in a New Key* are appropriately cited, and they are fully consonant with Peirce's approach, when applied to a semiotic analysis of language, which I have undertaken in part 1 of *Pragmatism and the Forms of Sense.*

But what, in more detail, does Langer mean by a concept, which arises in the process of symbolization? As she puts it, concepts are "abstract forms embodied in conceptions" (*PNK* 61n6), a distinction that is already present, though not fully exploited, in *An Introduction to Symbolic Logic.* There are no disembodied concepts; they always have various types of integuments (affective, imaginal, motoric), which make up a kind of envelope constituting the total sense of the symbol, including the image-schematic structures that Lakoff and Johnson have made a centerpiece of their work (see especially Lakoff and Johnson 2003, Johnson 1987). A proper name, for instance, has a symbolistic meaning and evokes a conception of something given as a unit, although it can clearly function, indexically, as a call name, and indeed proper names "have a different connotation for every denotation" (*PNK* 66). More generally, reflecting on the lessons of Helen Keller, Langer asserts that Keller's discovery that language signs could be instruments of thought and not just aids to association or tools for learning to expect or identify things in particular marked the breakthrough to recognizing *the point or principle of naming*. It was the discovery of the word (*PNK* 62), what Keller called in her *Story of My Life* "the living word" that "awakened my soul" (Keller 1936: 23–24; cited *PNK* 62). Langer speaks of this transition as a movement from a three-term relation (subject–term–object) to a four-term relation (subject–term–conception–object). In this way arises the pivotal distinction between *connotation* and *denotation*. Denotation applies connotations (the conceptual core as well as the conceptions a symbol bears) to the world. Application is needed, according to Langer, in fixing the connotations of things "whose properties are but vaguely known" (*PNK* 65). Peirce makes a similar point in his analysis of "vagueness." (See on this Potter 1996: chaps. 10–12; see also Liszka 1996: 92–98.)

When Langer speaks of the *logic* of terms, already her mode of speaking in *The Practice of Philosophy,* she has in mind the kind of syntactical dimension that Peirce also talked about and that was one of the formal foci of his semiotics. Philosophical grammar is the traditional name for what she has in mind. However, Langer also proposes a logic of discourse, for in her way of thinking a proposition, which arises from the synthesis of single terms, makes up a complex symbol with a complex sense or content (*PNK* 68). So, symbols are simple and complex, depending on whether we are speaking of constituent units or the wholes arising from their joining. Langer took over from the early Wittgenstein *a* (not *the*) picture theory of propositions, but very clearly went in a very different direction with it. Indeed, as I have noted, I think that it is for her really a metaphor or a model and does not constitute any claim to a strict identity or isomorphism. Her basic notion, yet to be explained, is that "the same sort of unity" binds a proposition and a picture together (*PNK* 68).

What do pictures and propositions have in common? A picture for her is a symbol, not a duplicate. It shares only "salient features" with what it is a symbol of (*PNK* 68), a "certain *proportion of parts*" (69). *Saliency* is contrasted with irrelevancy (for the purposes of pictorial representation) (*PNK* 69). *Detail* renders reference less equivocal, and Langer also recognizes *constancy of reference* through styles of presentation, as in portraits done at different times (cf. Rembrandt's self-portraits) or in different renderings of the crucifixion. A picture is a distinctive kind of symbol, and "the so-called 'medium' is a type of symbolism" (*PNK* 70), since there must be some correlation between distinctive features of the medium and distinctive features of the "object," which clearly does not have to be in the outside world. Reminiscent of Peirce's admittedly contentious but fundamental discussion of iconism—or of iconic signs—Langer is able to see both the continuity and difference between a stylized picture, weighty with qualities of its material medium (see also Meyer Schapiro's fundamental 1969 essay on the role of image-bearing matter, now in Schapiro 1994: 1–32), and a diagram, which involves a further distance from strict imitation and its putative fidelity. *"A diagram is a 'picture' only of a form"* (*PNK* 70). Langer's insightful example of a house presented in (a) a photograph, (b) a painting, (c) a pencil sketch, (d) an architect's elevation drawing, and (e) a builder's diagram illustrates what she considers key: the same relation of parts governs the different representations, which exemplify, in different formats and for different aims, a "fundamental pattern" (*PNK* 71). (Sebeok [2001: chapter 6] has engaged with a wide range of references the variety of issues attendant upon iconism.)

Such an observation is connected to the important distinction between a concept, which is "abstract," and a conception, which is more "concrete." We saw that Langer contended that "the same concept is embodied in a multitude of conceptions" (*PNK* 71). A concept for Langer is a form "that appears in all versions of thought or imagery that can connote the object in question, a form clothed in different integuments of sensation for every different mind" (*PNK* 71). This is a very important point for understanding the symbolic mind: sense organs, attention, imagery, feeling all differ, so no one has the same impressions (*PNK* 71), but the conceptual thread runs throughout the conceptional fabric/cable/web, which can exhibit or embody the same conceptual pattern. "Whenever we deal with a concept we must have some particular presentation of it, *through* which we grasp it" (*PNK* 72). Concepts are materially embodied, but are not to be identified with their material embodiments, a point made also by William James in his *Principles of Psychology*. This is Frege's point, too, when he distinguishes between *Vorstellung* (psychic presentation or representation) and *Begriff* (concept).

Concepts, Langer points out, with persistent emphasis, arise from the distinctive human power of *abstraction*. The foundation of human rationality is *abstractive seeing*. Such seeing actually operates on two levels. Langer has a kind of theoretical double vision here. She foregrounds, as she must, "the power of seeing *configurations* as symbols" (*PNK* 73). The reference here is first to a primary linguistico-symbolic fact, namely, our power of grasping *analogous configurations* as in the "temporal order of words" standing for the "relational order of things" (*PNK* 73). This clearly can also be seen as the generative principle of the development of cases and prefixes (see *PNK* 73n12, with reference to Wegener). But the notion of a configuration, structures and patterns in the experiential field, will become even more universally prominent as Langer's thought develops. The recognition and grasp of configurations is the paradigm of concept formation, bringing perception and conceptualization close together.

Language for Langer is a supremely powerful, supple, and adaptable symbolism (*PNK* 73). She is clearly no enemy of the discursive, seeing it in fact as a unique critical power of humans, though she does not favor it or give it "primacy" in any simple sense. Linguistic symbols name not only *things*, but *relations*. They do not have to *exhibit* or *illustrate* them, and in this respect they are more economical than pictures, gestures, or mnesic signs (*PNK* 74), while also being naturally and easily available semiotic tools, a point made by Bertrand Russell and followed by Langer. Linguistic symbols, as Langer sees them, are made up out of completely trivial and valueless materials—puffs of air or marks on a surface—and in this sense they are transparent or invisible (we pass through them to their sense and through the sense to the objects or states of affairs, often to our peril, as Abram [1996] has argued). For Langer the semantic power of a linguistic symbol, *as a symbol,* in her use of the term, is directly related to the physical barrenness and material indifference of the symbol (*PNK* 75), although clearly each symbol system has a distinctive "feel" or defining "quality." Conceptual activity flows *through* symbols. Furthermore, the combinatorial power of linguistic symbols makes possible the development of what Langer calls a *situation-concept,* that is, a descriptive phrase that joins individually named units into a web of relations that stands in the place of a shared perceptual situation, that is, as the context within which a novel predication will take place.

Since for her the distinction between connotation (sense and representation) and denotation (reference) is the seat of truth and falsity, not of meaning, Langer clearly sees the use of linguistic symbols as involving skill and necessitating application. If sentences, as complex symbolic structures, are *logical pictures* that are *exemplified* in things, *that* there is such an exemplification must be *seen* and the pictures *constructed. We* must see the analogy or analogous structures and we "read" both the symbolic configuration and the "world" together.

Summarizing her analysis, Langer details the "main lines of logical structure in all meaning-relations":

"(a) correlation of signs with their meanings by a selective mental process

(b) correlation of symbols with concepts and concepts with things, which gives rise to a 'short-cut' relation between names and things, known as denotation

(c) assignment of elaborately patterned symbols to certain analogues in experience, the basis of all interpretation and thought" (*PNK* 78)

On the basis of such a schematization Langer is able to develop and deepen one of her most famous distinctions, which we have already seen prelimned in *The Practice of Philosophy* under the rubric of "representative" and "presentative." The point is the same, but the terminology is different.

Discursive and Presentational Forms

The radical distinction between semiotic units separating indexicality from symbolicity is matched by, but by no means is identical with, another radical distinction that divides the domain of symbolicity into two irreducible classes. Langer in *Philosophy in a New Key* now calls the two classes discursive and presentational forms, a formulation she will retain. They make up two essentially different forms of symbolization, with different logics, tasks, and expressive powers. They constitute, in fact, two different dimensions of rationality, a theme Langer will foreground increasingly.

Langer wants to continue to sustain a central thesis: the limits of language, which so exercised the school of philosophy loosely connected with the early Wittgenstein, are not the limits of symbolic projectability. This became the cardinal principle of her whole philosophy of mind. Discursive projectability, which is due to and dependent upon language, is not adequate, Langer thinks, to "experiences that elude the discursive form" (*PNK* 86). Radically diverging from the early Wittgenstein, Carnap, and Russell, Langer speaks of an "unexplored possibility of a genuine semantic beyond the limits of discursive language" (*PNK* 86). This semantic would be carried by or embodied in a "highly intellectual" (*PNK* 87) symbolism at work in human experience that has a form and function very different from discursive symbolism. "The field of semantics," Langer contends, "is wider than that of language" (*PNK* 87). Langer's concern here is clearly epistemological, but goes far beyond the topics and issues usually treated from that point of view, since she is first of all concerned with the conditions of meaning and only then with the conditions of truth. For her the notion of a genuine semantic is connected with the very possibility of an adequate model of knowledge that recognizes a wide scope for what is to be included under that rubric. But language is not the only means of articulating thought, and everything that cannot be put into language is not mere feeling. While it is true, Langer will show, that the limits of an expressive medium are the limits of our conceptual powers, our conceptual powers are not restricted to one expressive medium. There are "things which do not fit the grammatical scheme of expression" and therefore need "some symbolistic scheme other than discursive language" (*PNK* 88). Such a scheme would be a "non-discursive pattern" (*PNK* 88), for "language is by no means our only articulate product" (*PNK* 89) and is, further, not to be taken as the primary model, either descriptively or normatively, for other symbolistic schemes. This is a position, first proposed in *The Practice of Philosophy* and now systematically explored in *Philosophy in a New Key,* that Langer will never abandon, but only deepen and expand.

What, Langer asks, are the "logical requirements for any symbolic structure whatever" (*PNK* 89)? Where does she look for an answer to this question—and does she continue to look in the same places in such a way that *Philosophy in a New Key* foreshadows later work? Although she does not avail herself of Peirce's semiotic terminology, Langer's investigations here take her deep into the whole domain of iconism, one of the most creative yet disputed areas of semiotics. What Langer does, and such a procedure is also followed by Terrence Deacon (1997), is in effect to push iconism down into the fundamental and most basic stratum of perceptual processes.

Without going into psychological details, Langer looks in sense-experience itself, conceived as "a process of formulation" (*PNK* 89), for the first glimmers of symbolic structure. This process of formulation involves the selection of "certain predominant forms" (*PNK* 89). For Langer a "form" and an "object," rightly understood, are in the last analysis synonymous. Objects are not mere givens. An object is "not a datum, but a form construed by the sensitive and intelligent organ" (*PNK* 89). What is fundamental for Langer's thought is the dual function of such a form: it is both (a) an individual thing, that is, a distinctive unit or configuration and (b) a symbol for the concept of it, "for *this sort of thing*" (*PNK* 89). Following up the lead of Gestalt theory, a permanent background to her thought from the very beginning, Langer foregrounds the selective power of our sense organs. The sensory field is organized into groups and patterns, or figures, not isolated Humean impressions. Our receptor apparatus, as she calls it, is engaged in an "unconscious appreciation of forms." Such an appreciation is "the primitive root of all abstraction" (*PNK* 89). As we have already seen and will see further confirmed in her later work, Langer wants to push meaning and rationality "down" to the distinctive type of body and perceptual systems humans have. "Mental life begins with our mere physiological constitution" (*PNK* 89). It is rooted in our ability to recognize analogous occurrences of experience rather than identical "repetitions," which do not occur. The abstraction of form is the essential condition for the grasp of "things." Langer's claim is that sense-data are actually "receptacles of meaning" (*PNK* 90). This powerful insight will take her far and in a number of different directions.

If there is any statement of Langer's that most epitomizes her work, it is the contention that meaning "accrues essentially to forms" and that "a mind that works primarily with meanings must have organs that supply it primarily with forms" (*PNK* 90). We will see that these organs of the mind are not just endosomatic but exosomatic, for humans are eminently endowed with symbolic organs existing *outside* our natural bodies. Note how Langer formulates her point, in full agreement with modern neuroscience in one of its key strands represented by the work of Antonio Damasio (1994, 1999). "The nervous system is the organ of the mind" (*PNK* 90), she writes, and "all sensitivity bears the stamp of mentality" (*PNK* 90). "'Seeing' is itself a process of formulation; our understanding of the visible world begins in the eye" (*PNK* 90). These are, Langer thinks, the far-reaching philosophical consequences of Gestalt theory, which was focused on "the real world construed by the abstractions which the sense-organs immediately furnish" (*PNK* 92), not those furnished by mathematical abstractions (*PNK* 92; see also the wide-ranging parallel explorations of Arnheim [1969 and 1974], Kanisza [1980], and others). Langer, however, consistent with her central focus, is concerned with what she called "sensuous conception," that is, "forms of direct perception" that furnish "genuine symbolic materials, media of understanding" (*PNK* 92). In the case of visual forms, they are capable of "articulation," that is, "complex combination" (*PNK* 93). As anyone who is fond of the visual arts knows, even if they cannot explain it, complex combinations of visual forms can express ideas or meanings "too subtle for speech," and in fact for Langer the whole visual world supplies the bases of a visual "non-discursive symbolism" (*PNK* 93). Nature, as the great poets and painters especially have shown, speaks to us through our senses in a vast array of "forms and qualities," which function as symbols, indeed prime symbols, of "entities which exceed and outlive our momentary experience" (*PNK* 93). Here we meet one of Langer's most important insights: visual forms exemplify not only "deep meanings" but also qualities, linear dimensions, volumes, rhythms that are "abstractable and combinatory" (*PNK* 94). But, as Langer's analysis of music will show, auditory forms also have powerful exemplifying functions that abstract and combine in a different sense modality.

There is, however, no "language" of vision or of music, and Langer does not want to use the linguistic analogy, in any strict sense, for other symbol systems. This is a distinctive mark of her work, which is still through and through semiotic. While presentational forms are defined by field values and context-dependency, something they share with language, they also have a unique feature: common total reference. They have, Langer asserts, a total structure, which is presented in a "simultaneous, integral presentation" (*PNK* 97). Throughout all of her work Langer will insist on this "all-at-onceness" of presentational symbols, even those symbolic forms that take time to come into existence for the interpreter or perceiver. Langer arrives at a truly fundamental insight, whose consequences she will exploit to the hilt: any perceptual "form"—visual, auditory, motoric, and so forth—can become a "symbol" and enter into combination with other symbols. This is once again a pushing down of meaning into the body's primary access structures to the world. So, presentational symbolism itself—*as a methodical and self-conscious exploitation of the semantic possibilities of the sensory system*—becomes a "normal and prevalent vehicle of meaning" (*PNK* 97). Each sense modality can correspond to a different type of symbolic mediation. Any visual experience, for example, can be raised to the level of a symbolic expression, for the units in the visual experience—water, wind, ice, mountains, deserts, fire—are forms, articulations, that have an immanent sense, what Cassirer called an expressive meaning, which is the "basis stratum" of the vortices of sense-functions. Dewey explored this stratum or dimension under the rubric of "qualitative" meaning (see Innis 1999). Visual forms in all their variety, then, for Langer are themselves *intrinsically meaningful* and hence potentially symbolic—and it is a central theme of Langer's work that "wherever a symbol operates, there is a meaning." As a result, different classes of experience will have an affinity with different types of symbolic mediation (*PNK* 97). Thus, using the senses as symbol systems, with all the consequences attendant upon material modality, allows a vast range of forms of logical formulation and conceptualizing beyond the realms of sayability. But rather than speaking of a specifiable "meaning" of a presentational form, Langer will speak of its "import," which is not separable from it. This will become an important difference between discursive symbolisms and presentational symbolisms—the latter cannot be translated into another idiom, but its import is resident in its form. This gives a distinctive *feel*, what Dewey, following Peirce, called a "quality," to presentational symbolisms that is present only in attenuated form in discursive symbolisms, though it is by necessity also there.

Langer aims to transform the Kantian epistemological project, moving from an epistemology of percept and concept to one of medium and meaning (*PNK* 98). Langer thinks that we have to regard "mind-engendered" forms not as *constitutive* of experience" but rather as "*interpretative* (as principles must be)" (*PNK* 98n14). The presentational order, as Langer calls it, furnishes "the elementary abstractions in terms of which ordinary sense-experience is understood" (*PNK* 98). As we have seen Langer insist, this order, the "order of perceptual forms," turns sense-experience into a "possible principle of symbolization" of the "impulsive, instinctive, and sentient life" (*PNK* 98). Such a non-discursive symbolism is not non-rational; it is eminently rational. Indeed, "rationality is the essence of mind, and symbolic transformation its elementary process" (*PNK* 99). This is the ground level of Langer's philosophical project.

Because for Langer rationality is "embodied in every mental act" (*PNK* 99), one could ask, as Langer does, "*just how* can feelings be conceived as possible ingredients of rationality" (*PNK* 100). Langer answers, "*feelings have definite forms, which become progressively articulated*" (*PNK* 100). Here the fateful notion of a *form of feeling*, which will become the focal point of Langer's aesthetics, makes a clear and strong entrance. Feelings, depending on the sense modality, have definite structures, qualities, or physiognomical properties. Langer shares this insight, we have seen, not just with Cassirer's philosophy of symbolic forms (Cassirer 1929 [1957]: 43–103) on the one side but with Dewey's pragmatic exploration of quality on the other (see Dewey 1931b). What Langer calls a "likeness" is really a "suchness." What, Langer asks, are the definite forms of feeling *like*? She answers, "For what these are *like* determines by what symbolism we might understand them" (*PNK* 100). Note the emphasis on understanding the feelings through a symbolism, which in this case involves the construction of a sensory analogue functioning as a symbolic projection, something that *exemplifies objectively* what the *feeling* is like *subjectively.* Indeed, as Langer puts it, presentational symbolism *explicates* "unspeakable" things, but it lacks denotation. As we have seen, it aims toward a *connotational semantic,* exemplified for Langer in *Philosophy in a New Key* paradigmatically by music, whose task is to explore and express, in all the dimensions carried by sound, the very movements of subjective, conscious existence *in their formal features.* It is the emphasis on formal features that has led some to call, mistakenly, Langer's approach a species of formalism. But this is not an accurate characterization. The role of the formal features is rather to convey an "unspeakable import," something beyond the realm of discursive logic. Presentational symbols do not name, they exemplify "what they are about."

The theoretical point, however, of Langer's distinction between discursive and presentational forms, its "main theme," is, as always, the integration of symbols in(to) human mentality (*PNK* 102). Symbolization, on Langer's account, goes "all the way down." It is present at the first formulation of a coherent world of things and events and their relational matrices. It is not restricted to language and language-like meaning-systems. Feeling itself, the perceived suchness of things, is a form of meaning-making, and forms of feeling can be *expressed* in material media, which give us true knowledge, although it cannot be "put into words." The kind of knowledge offered to us by presentational symbolism expands the reach of rationality. We can use symbols to *say* and we can use symbols to *show*. These are the two great natural divisions for Langer, and are "due to various ways of *using* symbols" (*PNK* 102) as well as to the internal logic of their makeup, that is, their semiotic "syntax."

So, we have now seen Langer establish a pair of axial divisions: (a) between indexicality and symbolicity, marking the major divide between non-human and human mentality, with iconicity mediating or straddling the fence, and (b) between discursive and presentational forms, marking the major division in the realm of symbolicity. They are the two semiotic tracks on which distinctively human rationality runs. These distinctions encompass both modes of meaning, quite generally, and modes of using symbols or terms. On the basis of these distinctions Langer is able to subject four modes of meaning-making to detailed analysis in *Philosophy in a New Key:* language, ritual, myth, and music. The first mode is the discursive form par excellence. The second three are paradigmatic presentational forms, the third of which furnished the generative insight for Langer into the essential symbolic nature of art. Such an assimilation is both the source of the main strength of Langer's mature aesthetic theory as well as the source of what is perhaps a puzzling, indeed perplexing, ambiguity in it.

In the next section we will analyze and evaluate Langer's still fertile and insightful model of language, with its nuanced use of sources that are still relatively neglected in current discussions. The realm of "meaning after language" will be the subject of the following chapter.

Language as a Discursive Form

Langer constructs the following list of the "salient characteristics of true language."

First, for some system of symbols to be classified as a language it must have a vocabulary and a syntax. There must be a repertoire of independent, or relatively free-standing, units of meaning that are combined according to the rules of syntax into "composite symbols with resultant new meaning" (*PNK* 94). This is the classical distinction between words and sentences or terms and propositions.

Second, in the case of language systems, of which there are many, one can, indeed must, at least in principle, be able to construct a dictionary. The single units of a language are able to be defined in terms of other units or combinations thereof. Language is an internally self-referring system where meanings are defined in terms of other meanings, although clearly there must be also a way in which meanings are "applied" to the world. The realm of language meanings is, by reason of the principle of the dictionary, a "world unto itself," but not exactly closed, since it has no greatest upper bound in the case of natural languages.

Third, language systems are defined by the possibility of translation from one language into another. Natural languages have a systematic correlation between units in the source and the target language, although it is clear that there is no strict isomorphism between any two languages. That is, while the correlations are systematic and often have complex historical roots, the relationships between languages are defined by overlappings rather than coincidence. But even this feature is not possible in the case of presentational forms, Langer holds. The search for equivalents between presentational forms, for example, visual equivalents of musical rhythms, is not a search for the "right word" as it is in language. In this language is *sui generis.*

Langer argues that none of the above-listed conditions holds for presentational forms. A picture, for instance, does not have any fundamental building blocks with independent meanings. Within a picture it is the gradation of elements within a field, not the "objects represented," that rules everywhere. There are no free-standing "basic units," although there are material *elements* that are combined in the construction of a visual artifact. And no basic units means no dictionary, for a dictionary implies definition of terms by other terms and some sort of fixed meaning, even if the meaning spaces are fuzzy around the edges, as they are in language. But a curve or a line in a picture, or a modulation of color, "has no fixed meaning apart from its context" (*PNK* 95). *Field values,* which clearly also are present in language, though in a rather different way, rule everywhere. It is the context or frame that turns an identical curve into the outline of an ear rather than the slope of a nose. Furthermore, while verbal symbolism has primarily a "*general* reference" (*PNK* 96), that is, the possibility of applying a symbol to multiple instances, a pictorial symbol has a kind of *total reference* that prevents, say, translating a sculpture into a painting or using either one of them to denote individuals or a class of things. Lacking intrinsic generality and speaking first and foremost directly to sense, we are confronted in the main with what Langer calls a "direct *presentation* of an individual object" (*PNK* 96). No two drawn triangles, as visual forms, are or can be absolutely identically the same. There will always be some minute difference, but the verbal label "triangle" will fit them all. Dream triangles can be "slack," "wobbly," or "monumental," but the concept "triangle" is none of these. In general, Langer holds, language's meaning unfolds or is presented successively, through a kind of process of discursive "gathering."

Presentational symbols, however, are composed of and presented as meanings in relation "within the total structure" (*PNK* 97), in a kind of "simultaneous, integral presentation" (*PNK* 97). It is the successiveness of discourse that gives it a singularly "linear" character, as Saussure so clearly foregrounded in his *Course in General Linguistics*. This is a linearity of constitutive structure, not only of creation but also of comprehension of the symbolic form, both of which "take time." In light of this Langer will also deny to music, in spite of its temporal nature, the character of linearity that is possessed by language. In discussing Langer's account of language, certainly one of the most substantial chapters in her book and of a rather different character than classic "philosophical" approaches that were current when she was originally composing it in the late 1930s and 1940s, we can make no pretense of touching on every important point she makes. This chapter is eminently synthetic in character, weaving together many strands of thought from a variety of disciplines. If we ever needed evidence of Langer's "non-disciplinary" approach to her intellectual work, this chapter, with its philosophical, psychological, linguistic, and biological sources, both exemplifies par excellence Langer's way of doing philosophy and points forward to its continuation in her later works.

What is the conceptual frame, the set of analytical concepts, Langer brings to bear on the account of language? Where do they come from? What is the relation between the conceptual and the empirical bases? And what is the status of these two bases in light of the subsequent explosion of research both in linguistic theory and in the psychological study of language and language acquisition?

Langer, while certainly no "human chauvinist," is concerned to foreground, once again, the human-animal contrast. Language is a distinctively "high" form of symbolism—and the general sense of symbolic pregnance, of intrinsic expressiveness, rooted in the iconic dimension, which makes possible on the human level the development of presentational forms, is "much lower" (*PNK* 110). Animals, Langer rightly and justly asserts, (a) express emotion, (b) indicate wishes, (c) control one another's behavior. These are certainly also aspects of human semiotic activity. But, as Langer emphasizes, animals have no tendency to babble spontaneously in the way human infants do. This tendency raises the problem of a language-making "instinct" as well as the much-researched problem of an optimal learning period for language. Langer's view of language is not really, however, dependent on any genetic hypotheses, although it clearly refers to them and tries to exploit their systematic import. The point is that human *vocalization* leads to systematic and controlled *verbalization*, something that is missing in the non-human realm.

Language, Langer asserts, following Edward Sapir, first and foremost grows out of the tendency to see reality symbolically. It is rooted in primitive forms of aesthetic attraction and mysterious fear, an originary "aesthetic sense of import" (*PNK* 110). Primates quite generally are grasped by a "mere sense of significance" (*PNK* 110), exemplified in such a phenomenon as the much-studied chimpanzee Gua's "aesthetic frights" and spontaneous withdrawings (*PNK* 112) when presented with toadstools. This primary stratum of felt significance is, I have already indicated, Cassirer's expressive domain as well as Dewey's "qualitative tones" of experience. Primates—and clearly on a high level humans—are sensitive to non-biological significance, an ability to react, by radical aversion or attraction, to the "sheer quality of a perception" (*PNK* 114). This quality is a kind of negative or positive charge, an *affective valence* that marks the object or situation the organism is confronted with. Objects themselves, encountered in the flux of experiencing, are significant, having what Michael Polanyi (1966: 11–12) called an existential or physiognomical meaning. This is, on the most basic level of world-building, a distinctive kind of order.

The roots of language, Langer holds, are to be found in this affect-laden or affect-drenched dimension of experience shared by both non-human animals and humans. Further, it is the ability, for example, to construct a symbolic gesture that leads to language as we know it. There is a difference in principle between an intentional genuflection and the emotional quaver of a suppliant's voice (*PNK* 114). Such a genuflection, or a curtsy, is a conventional expression of a feeling or attitude and is, Langer thinks, to be considered as the "lowest form of denotation" (*PNK* 114). The kiss of forgiveness "means" "forgiveness," and is *known to mean that.* This foreshadowing of representation does not, in the case of animals, cross the divide and pass over to language in any systematic or extensive sense. The great apes, Langer notes, remain essentially "mute." Their "natural proclivities," intimately connected with the ape's body, already indicated a genetic basis for speech. Bringing things into one's mind by means of language is not identical with bringing things into one's hands. The language of the body and the body of language are deeply intertwined, as Deacon (1997) and many others have shown.

Langer points out what she considers the important and pivotal consequences of the lalling instinct, the impulse to chatter (*PNK* 122). During the optimum period for language learning not only the lalling instinct, but also the imitative impulse, a natural interest in distinctive sounds, and a "great sensitivity to 'expressiveness' of any sort" (*PNK* 123) work together. The last feature is especially important for understanding what Langer is really getting at in her account of the roots of language. She speaks of the "child's tendency to read a vague sort of *meaning* into pure visual and auditory forms" (*PNK* 123). This is, once again, the *expres-*

sive stratum of experience. True to her deep commitment to the philosophical implications of Gestalt theory, Langer will develop the notion of pure gestalten that
have an expressive or physiognomical meaning, such as perceptual forms that
can carry the meaning of *indifference, dignity, ominousness,* and so forth. Cultural
anthropology, especially the cultural anthropology of religion, and cultural psychology have recognized how humans have the ability to take such perceptual
forms, in their unlimited variety, to symbolize moods and expressive qualities
(*PNK* 123), without, however, necessarily ascribing anthropomorphically such
moods to the objects themselves, which certainly played a role in the origin of
religion and the conception of vital powers that are beyond human control. For
Langer, "to project feelings into outer objects is the first way of symbolizing and
thus of *conceiving* those feelings" (*PNK* 124). Indeed, even our conception of "self"
is tied up with "this process of symbolically epitomizing our feelings" (*PNK* 124).
Certainly this applies to the development of a presentational symbolism, which
we will study in much more concrete detail in the next chapter, but how does
it apply to the case of discursive symbolization, exemplified in language, with
which we are presently concerned?

Language's entry into human life, as Langer pithily and helpfully characterizes it, involves the movement from a "diffuse awareness of vocalizing" to an "apparently delightful awareness of a vocable" (*PNK* 125). What is the significance
of this move? Well, Langer answers, "a new vocable is an outstanding *Gestalt*"
(*PNK* 125), a vocalized figure over against a vocalized ground. Such a Gestalt is
"an entirely *unattached* item, a purely phenomenal experience without externally
fixed relations. . . . It is the readiest thing in the world to become a symbol when a
symbol is wanted" (*PNK* 125). Although on the surface it looks as if Langer holds
to a kind of associationism (she speaks of fixing by association), she in the end
does not want to espouse any definite genetic hypothesis in the temporal sense.
What must be emphasized rather is the critical transition that takes place that involves the move to the *principle of symbolization.*

Whatever it is that ultimately fixes, at a point in time, the indissoluble connection between sound and object—perhaps still the great mystery—"the baby's
mind has hold of it [the object] through the word, and can invoke a conception of
it by uttering the word, which has thus become the *name* of the thing" (*PNK* 125).
This *need for a name* is not primarily, as Langer sees it, a socio-cultural or communicational need, although we do not have to follow her strict opposition here
to what she takes as Mead's and Dewey's mistaken emphasis on the social and
communicational function of language. For Langer the symbolic need is, and remained, biological in the sense that it is needed for the intrinsic development of
the mental life of not just the infant but the human person as such throughout

the course of life. Indeed, word-symbol and object, word-meaning and thing-meant, once fused, also become inseparable. This is one of the most fateful consequences of semiotic embodiment.

A central thesis for Langer is that "in a sense, language is conception, and conception is the frame of perception" (*PNK* 126). This is to be understood along the lines of a passage from a famous article of Edward Sapir, which Langer cites in full and which, indeed, encapsulates the central lines of her thought about language.

> Language is heuristic . . . in that its forms predetermine for us certain modes of observation and interpretation. . . . While it may be looked upon as a symbolic system which reports or refers or otherwise substitutes for direct experience, it does not as a matter of actual behavior stand apart from or run parallel to direct experience but completely interpenetrates with it. This is indicated by the widespread feeling, particularly among primitive people, of that virtual identity or close correspondence of word and thing which leads to the magic of spells. . . . Many lovers of nature, for instance, do not feel that they are truly in touch with it until they have mastered the names of a great many flowers and trees, as though the primary world of reality were a verbal one and as though one could not get close to nature unless one first mastered the terminology which somehow magically expresses it. (Sapir 1921: 57; cited *PNK* 126)

Langer thinks that the upshot of such a position is that "our primary world of reality *is* a verbal one" (*PNK* 126). Clearly, after we have spun ourselves, or been spun, into the web of language this is the case, even when our embodiment has become defective and regressive due to language loss or various forms of aphasia or alexia. Language, on Langer's account, which is certainly consonant with the results of later investigations, makes possible the retention of the world of distinct objects. It both makes and keeps the absent present and makes "the present" present in a new and permanent way. Rather than merely mirroring the world, which would be complete without it, language makes possible the transformation of experience into concepts. It is this process of transformation, not communication, that is, for Langer, the primary semiotic motor driving language. At the root of language is "formulative, abstractive experience . . . symbolic transformation and abstraction" (*PNK* 127).

Consistently, even if a bit stubbornly, Langer resists any putative primacy of the communicative dimension in delineating the constitutive matrix of language. It is not clear, however, that in light of her own sources there is, or even could be, such a sharp line between the formulative and the communicative dimensions. Karl Bühler, for instance, who is an important source for Langer's reflections, argued that the point of origin of expressed signs in social life comes from effected and lived-through participation in a cognitional surplus by a community of (potential) sign users in common situations. It is only when one member of the group has knowledge or an intention that is not shared that *the need for marking a difference in perception or in intended action* arises. In this way the cognitional and the communicative are completely intertwined. But we could also, following Peirce and Vološinov (1930), think of cognition itself in multiple dimensions as an intra-psychic communication involving two poles in the knowing subject. Thinking in this sense would be communicating novel knowledge to oneself, one of the central theses of Peirce's semiotic reconstruction of philosophy. This is a general theme that I have explored in more detail in my *Consciousness and the Play of Signs* and *Pragmatism and the Forms of Sense*.

Langer also, in spite of her normal caution, took over in *Philosophy in a New Key*, and repeated the procedure in *Mind*, a thesis on the origin of language first proposed by J. Donovan in 1891–92. This sticky topic was discussed by Donovan independently of any neurological hypotheses, which have marked later work such as Terrence Deacon's provocative analyses. I am not sure about its empirical verifiability, but, strangely enough, Langer is more interested in its theoretical lessons as a thought experiment and not just a "likely story." Briefly, Donovan's position, which hypothesizes a "festal" origin of speech, goes as follows. The hypothesis combines present observation with historical "ideal reconstruction." The basic principle that Donovan draws attention to is that sounds are the most suited to become free items without biological value. As we have already noted, this is rooted in their peculiar tendency toward a kind of free transparency. Donovan proposed that, in the case of "festal" occasions of variously motivated celebrations, rhythmic beating and hand-clapping can be (could be) used to emphasize various forms of play-mood and to keep it steady. Thus, in dancing around a captured enemy, or sacrificed lamb, or prospective wives, the group would engage in a complex play of rhythmic gestures, elaborated by the voice. Rhythmic groups of syllables would consequently get imposed, mainly tacitly and operatively, not stipulatively, on group dancing—structuring the various types of occasions and types of dances: "death-dances round a corpse, triumph-dances round a captive female, a bear, a treasure, or a chief" (*PNK* 131).

However, Langer's concern for the "original use" of language, it must be repeated, is not wedded to a specific genetic hypothesis. Langer thinks, admittedly a bit strangely, that the real lessons of Donovan's origin hypothesis are independent of its historical truth value. First of all, its fundamental assumption, which Langer herself held on philosophical grounds, is that language is marked by the central tasks of framing, fixating, conceiving, with explicitly intended communication being secondary. Secondly, Donovan's hypothesis also is committed to the claim that *metaphor* is a, perhaps *the,* semantic engine driving the evolution of language. Langer, reflecting upon the lessons of Donovan's hypothesis and other positions, thinks that the "first symbolic value of words is probably purely connotative, like that of ritual" (*PNK* 133). It creates a space of meaning in which to dwell but is not concerned with the domain of "aboutness." But for really human language to appear there is nevertheless needed the critical move to denotation, which, in Langer's view, is "the essence of language, because it frees the symbol from its original instinctive utterance and marks its deliberate *use,* outside the total situation that gave it birth" (*PNK* 133). A denotative word, or a word used denotatively, points in two directions: toward the conception, however vague it may be, which it often is, and toward a *thing-meant* (event, quality, person) that is "realistic and public" (*PNK* 133). This anchoring to and in real objects (*PNK* 134) involves words' carrying their "whole load of imagery and feeling" with them (*PNK* 134). Words are "semiotically thick," carrying multiple valences—iconic, indexical, and symbolic—together. They carry and evoke affects, elicit and steer actions, and direct and accomplish thought, the three functions that Karl Bühler delineated in his organon-model of language (see Bühler 1934).

Langer, in relying on Donovan's work, which she returns to in *Mind,* is attempting to construct a kind of ideal history of the genesis of language—starting at the level of the word, which has first a kind of "expressive" function. Word and object are "felt to belong together" (*PNK* 134), effecting the transition from sound to word. Langer admits, quite frankly, that what she is offering is "pure speculation" (*PNK* 134), but based on a "general study of symbolism." The goal is "at least a plausible theory" (*PNK* 134) and not a counsel of despair that is the fate of the linguists who have abandoned the search for language's origin.

But Langer is not just interested in language's symbolic and ideal genesis. She is also concerned to grasp and to give an account of the development of language's complex relational structure, for it is not just a "sheer conglomeration of symbols" (*PNK* 135). Language, Langer clearly saw, is essentially "an organic, functioning *system*" (*PNK* 135), which is composed of *symbols in relation.* By means of their internal ordering and relating they are able to differentiate and to order and relate what Plato called the "significant joints" of the world to one another. Although language may have begun by naming, it proceeds by relating. Naming allows an object to be held in focus. Being held, it can be seen as existing *with* something, whether "in contrast or in unison or in some other definite way" (*PNK* 135). Langer thinks, certainly rightly, that this phenomenon is of supreme importance in understanding language: *holding on to the object.* "A word fixes something in experience, and makes it the nucleus of memory, an available conception" (*PNK* 135). Furthermore, words exist in associative fields or contexts for both speaker and communication partner. But, following the lead of Karl Bühler, Langer saw that these fields or contexts did not have to be linguistic. What Bühler called the *empractic* use of language takes place purely in a diacritical manner, that is, to make a difference in an otherwise shared situation, such as giving an order to a waiter in a restaurant ("I'll have a cone" or "I'll have a cup," it being understood that you are not only ordering something but ordering ice cream). The notion of a *situation* here foregrounds the fact that in a speech-act or speech-event not everything has to be spelled out, but *only what is new*. Langer wants to show that this psychological commonplace is of fundamental importance for understanding the internal development of language.

Language indeed, it appears, proceeds according to the principles encapsulated in this formulation. Its use is marked by a principal difference between novel predication and the "merely qualifying situation, given by a visible and demonstrable circumstance" (*PNK* 136). In every utterance, therefore, there are put into play an *exposition* and a *novel comment*. The utterance cannot be understood without recourse to these two essential factors (although there are other factors, to be sure). But the "exposition" is itself embedded in a wide situation, mediated socially, which makes up a constitutive horizon for "verbal interaction."

Langer saw in this respect the critical value of the work of Philipp Wegener, which is still of the utmost importance. Wegener (1885 [1991]) contended that linguistic development, that is, the development of language as a system of forms and their combinations, is, on one level, due to the *principle of emendation*. This is the principal source of language's syntactical forms and the key to why language has the kind of structure that it does. Langer, following Wegener, and in spite of her downplaying of the communicative dimension of language, saw language developing in "situations" that are mutually understood, indeed that are presupposed and lived in, by the speech participants. As long as there is no misunderstanding, the surrounding situation supplies the complement of intelligibility to guarantee mutual understanding. The "empractic" use of language then embeds language in an actional matrix. The movement from the one-word sentence, no matter how long the "word," to the multi-word sentence is effected by the creation of linguistic elements that modify and make more precise and complex the original utterance and that not only bind it to the situation but internally differentiate it, that is, the situation and the utterance together. In this way the sentential structure, through the codification of the linguistic modifications that follow "quite closely the relational pattern of the situation that evokes it" (*PNK* 137), takes up the surrounding context into language. Modifiers and identifiers become attached to the original core predication. As Wegener put it, "appositives and relative clauses are subsequent corrections to our deficient presentations"

(Wegener 1885: 34, cited *PNK* 137). These additions make up the exposition of the original word, which is the locus of novelty in the utterance. We have, accordingly, a movement from a lived-through and shared situation to the articulation of verbal context. Wegener writes: "Only the development of speech as an art and science finally impresses on us the duty of rendering the exposition before the novel predication" (40, cited *PNK* 138).

Langer thinks that the lesson to be learned from Wegener's theory is that it "derives grammatical structure from the undifferentiated content of the one-word sentence, and the literal, fixed denotation of separate words from the total assertion by gradual crystallization, instead of trying to build the complexities of discursive speech out of supposed primitive 'words' with distinctly substantive or distinctly relational connotations" (*PNK* 138). This process is unconscious, based on humans' tendencies to form habits. Language, Langer thinks, could only have taken on the complex form that it has by "some such unconscious process as endless misunderstanding, modification, reduplication for emphasis and 'filling in' by force of formal feeling based on habits" (*PNK* 138). So, articulation evolves or proceeds by emendation. Understanding is the overcoming of misunderstanding or incomplete understanding or incomplete articulation.

One might ask, without undue skepticism, how one knows all this. It is certainly not just an "ideal history" dealing with the putative absolute origin of language, which turns out not to be so absolute. It is a kind of abductive inference to a set of generative rules governing a present structure, which we experience all the time in our verbal interactions. The main question is, What would have made it possible for language to arrive at its present structure, assuming that it did not spring full-blown from the heads and mouths of its first creators? Further, what in fact is the best way of describing language as it presently exists? And how general is the description? Does it fit all languages?

These are large and complicated questions, and they go beyond the scope and intention of Langer's own analysis, which is more structural than genetic, as I have been pointing out. But the theoretical points seem to have a kind of analytical and phenomenological accuracy. They correspond to our experience of using language and to the structural constants of language. And they cast a sharp and novel light on the complex whole that language is, considered as a structure. One could still ask, however, *at what level* this type of analysis proceeds. It appears to be meta-theoretical or meta-linguistic—or, rather, philosophico-semiotic, not linguistic.

Besides emendation, according to Langer, there is another general principle of language, *generality.* Langer thinks there exists a "more vital . . . principle of language (and perhaps of all symbolism): Metaphor" (*PNK* 139). Metaphor, in

Langer's view, is "an incomparable achievement" (*PNK* 139) and must be seen, perhaps paradoxically, within the framework of communication, which involves the two elements we have already seen, "the context (verbal or practical) and the novelty" (*PNK* 139). In order to express the novelty the speaker has to find an appropriate word that may be apt, new, or ambiguous, with the role of the context being to modify and determine just what it means. What happens when, in a slightly more than minimally developed language system, a precise word is lacking but there is still the need to find one that can be used? Langer, following Wegener, but in deepest continuity with her own "logical" position, has recourse to the "powers of *logical analogy*" (*PNK* 139). A word denoting something else is used as a "presentational symbol for the thing" meant (*PNK* 139). Something that is already named becomes a symbolic proxy for something that is nameless. When someone's anger "flares up," this expression, rooted in the presentational symbol of fire, "has acquired a wider meaning than its original use . . . it can be used metaphorically to describe whatever its *meaning* can symbolize" (*PNK* 139). It is the context that determines whether the meaning is to be taken literally or metaphorically. Here is the laconically formulated opening that Langer provides to, and the point of connection with, later discussions of metaphor, even of the most sophisticated and far-ranging sort. Without going into further detail, presentational symbolism encompasses the phenomena treated under the rubric of image-schemata by Lakoff and Johnson (2003 and 1999) and the main currents of cognitive linguistics.

But what, more specifically, is the exact mechanism of metaphor, as Langer construes it? "In a genuine metaphor, an image of the literal meaning is our symbol for the figurative meaning, the thing that has no name of its own" (*PNK* 139). This gives us generative or creative metaphor, novelty, emergence of sense, which then becomes sedimented in our conventional linguistic-conceptual frameworks (*PNK* 139). In a perspicuous analysis of "runs," Langer shows how it applies to brooks, fences, rumors, and persons and also how "constant figurative use has generalized" the sense of the word (*PNK* 140). Ultimately, "runs" is defined as "*describing a course*," a feature that is common to all its applications. The tendency, accordingly, is for metaphorical meanings to "fade" as they incline toward general meanings, even as they remain dependent on the image-schemata underlying them. I am not sure that Langer's position here is completely, or even coherently, formulated. For if general words are originally derived from "specific appellations, by metaphorical use" (*PNK* 140), why and how was there an original grouping to begin with, which clearly did not involve the generation of individual terms for every individual object? There must have been some type of generality, or at least deep affinity or shared quality, grasped by the perceiver. Deacon (1997) makes much of this, rightly connecting it with the theme of iconism. Or is Langer *really* saying that linguistic meaning is to a great extent grounded in presentational symbolism? Or could we, as I have been surmising, even go further and see a deep, that is, genetic, connection here with later work on image-schemata and the perceptual-motoric roots of linguistic meaning? Langer's insights would be wonderfully prophetic—which I think they are and which Donald Dryden has clearly and sharply shown (Dryden 2007).

A linguistic expression's meaning is defined, then, by an essential tension between the literal and the metaphorical, and between the context and the novel predication. The context must be literal, Langer thinks, since it is the literal that functions as the background to the metaphor's figure. If the context were itself structured metaphorically, we would need a further literal meta-context to define it. But there is no bad infinity at work here. This is the way successful language works. "Only the novel predication can be metaphorical" (*PNK* 140). The ability to disengage language from physical conditions, that is, to construct a discourse where the context is entirely expressed in language and not bound to "empractic" utterances, demands that we have at our disposal words with "fixed, general connotations, so that they may serve in a conventional, literal fashion, to render the *exposition* of the critical assertion" (*PNK* 140). Langer cites another pregnant passage from Wegener.

> All words, therefore, which may be logical subjects (of predications) and hence expository, have acquired this capacity only by virtue of their "fading" in predicational use. And before language had any faded words to denote logical subjects, it could not render a situation by any other means than a demonstrative indication of it in present experience. So the process of fading which we have here adduced represents the bridge from the first (one-word) . . . phase of language to the developed phase of a discursive exposition. (Wegener 1885: 54, cited *PNK* 141)

Langer glosses the whole issue in the following way, which lies at the very core of her philosophical project and which constitutes one of her most original and permanent insights. She sees metaphor as rooted in *abstractive seeing*. Such seeing is based on presentational symbolism, which expresses our ability to grasp, and be grasped by, an immanent significance, or originary significance, in the flux of experience. "It is in this elementary, presentational mode that our first adventures in conscious abstraction occur," exemplified in the grasp of similarities, but similarities that take a figurative form and appear publicly first in the spontaneous similes of language (or in publicly accessible images). Systematic construction of images arises only in beings already endowed with language. Metaphor, according to Langer, is not a conscious mechanism at the beginning but arises spontaneously out of our natural perception of a common form between separate domains of experience. One such form is hence able to be transformed into a linguistic symbol and to represent "a wide variety of conceptions" (*PNK* 141). Linguistic metaphor arises when there are gaps in our expression systems, when, that is, there is present a certain "poverty of language, need of emphasis, or need of circumlocution" (*PNK* 141). Karl Bühler speaks of an "*Ausdrucksnot*," an "expressive need," that metaphor fulfills. Maybe it is here that one of Langer's most insightful sources is to be found.

Metaphor is called by Langer the law of language's life. "It is the force that makes it essentially *relational*, intellectual, forever showing up new, abstractable *forms* in reality, forever laying down a deposit of old, abstracted concepts in an increasing treasury of general words" (*PNK* 141). Metaphor is accompanied by a further differentiation of language into mathematical, logical, and scientific terminologies, which seemingly, but not really, as many later studies have shown, leave metaphor behind. But the basic principle of symbolic transformation is operative there as well, and Langer warns us not to think of metaphorical speech as an embellishment with mere poetic intent.

Paralleling the question, Why metaphor? is the question, Why do all humans possess language? The answer Langer gives in *Philosophy in a New Key* is that human beings "all have the same psychological nature" (*PNK* 142). It is in *Mind* that Langer begins to explore the biological and neurological dimensions of this question in detail, but already in *Philosophy in a New Key* she speaks of a mutation, "perhaps even cerebral evolution" (*PNK* 142). This is a main theme in cognitive neuroscience, upon which Langer's later work casts a clear and burning light, a point made clearly and firmly by Donald Dryden (2007). But her own investigations are independent of scientific hypotheses and in fact do not so much deal with the empirical genesis of language as with *its semiotic genesis*, that is, what is achieved or what emerges in language. There was, Langer thinks, a profound generative insight, which could be "realized" without being "thematized." "The notion of giving something a name is the vastest generative idea that ever was conceived; its influence might well transform the entire mode of living and feeling, in the whole species, within a few generations" (*PNK* 142). Whatever the historical and anthropological evidence, it is clearly a fact that our entire mode of living and feeling is intrinsically tied up with language and with the symbolic matrices in which it arose.

Such are the first foundational steps in Langer's construction of a general theory of symbolism. There are two "symbolic modes," the discursive and the presentational, and both are intrinsic to fully functioning rational mental activity. Out of these modes arise imagination and dream, myth and ritual, and practical intelligence (*PNK* 143). Langer, following the lead of Cassirer, states the import of these two modes in the following manner. Discursive thought leads to scientific knowledge and to a theory of knowledge focused on a critique of science. But if we recognize the existence, nature, and scope of non-discursive thought we can construct a "theory of *understanding* that naturally culminates in a critique of art" (*PNK* 143). Langer's intellectual path will take her more and more toward art and art theory, and her final work, the great trilogy on mind, would have culminated in a critique of science and mathematics, but was ended abruptly due to the increasing blindness of its author. But, at any rate, what Langer calls "the parent stock" of both types of symbolic modes is the fundamental power of symbolic transformation, grounded in the fundamental distinction between indexicality and symbolicity. Such an identical root gives rise to two different flowers. In the next chapter we will investigate Langer's original examination of three non-discursive flowers: ritual, myth, and art, with a special focus on music and musical significance.

3

Meaning after Language

Ritual, Myth, and Art

Langer's account of symbolic transformation in the presentational mode, that is, "after language," in *Philosophy in a New Key* takes up and subjects to an especially illuminating analysis three central issues: (1) sacrament and ritual, comprising symbolic objects and symbolic acts that express the sacred, (2) the symbolic lessons of myth, which articulates human conceptions of divinity and the place of humans in a sacred or ultimate story or narrative, and (3) the symbolic prolegomena to the theory of art that Langer developed at length in her masterpiece, *Feeling and Form*. They come "after" language in the double sense that her discussion of them follows her analysis of language as a discursive form and also in the sense that these are forms of meaning that are authentic and that come "after" language, that is, they must be ascribed to beings that already have appropriated, or been appropriated to, language. Whatever the original relation was "at the beginning," which is at any rate inaccessible to us, language is now the enabling condition for the development of sign or symbol systems that do not follow the logic of language, but it is neither displaced by them nor is it able to encompass all their semantic or semiotic powers. Presentational symbolism, rooted in our imaginative powers, is for Langer an indispensable and exceedingly powerful means of meaning-making, and it broadens and deepens our notion of human rationality. Langer is fully consistent, both in *Philosophy in a New Key* and in all her work, in her repudiation of all forms of logocentrism.

It is important to understand what Langer is trying to do in the later chapters of *Philosophy in a New Key*. Her main goal is to present, with sufficient density, *exemplifications* of the "logic" of presentational symbolism and the type of "work" that such a symbolism is meant to do. Langer's purpose is not to give us a full phenomenology of presentational forms in their breadth and depth, nor is she giving a schematic history of the role such forms have played in historical and cultural life. By choosing paradigmatic examples of such symbolic forms Langer is able to deepen her formal and fundamental analysis undertaken earlier in *Philosophy in a New Key*, where the original lines between the two "tracks" on which human symbolic activity runs were drawn.

The leading questions she engages are the same as before, but now they are given a rich application and the answers are sought in a wide range of cultural phenomena. The pivotal concept is that of the *life-symbol*, or the pregnant symbolic image. It is the life-symbol that functions as the "root" both of sacrament and of myth, and indeed of the vital significance of art. So, Langer is concerned with a set of interlocking questions.

- Why does "life" embody itself in symbols?
- How is symbolization rooted in the human power of stabilizing the sensory flux by the creation of images?
- Why and how do images turn into symbols?

From Symbolic Images to the Sacred

The epistemological pivot of Langer's analysis of life-symbols is the difference between an image and a sensation (*PNK* 144). By "sensation" she means any sensory datum in its singleness of occurrence, its one-time-appearing. Since no individual sensory datum, however, can ever recur in its individuality, it is absolutely unique and particular. A sensory experience of a tree is unique at each moment and on each different occasion. The sensory datum exists in real time and in real space, that is, it has a set of coordinates that are unique and that define its ad hoc character. But, Langer notes, we would be unable to stabilize the world into objects if all we had access to were the flow of sensory particulars. Far below the level of the "articulation" of experience in speech there is involved a process of projection whereby sensory experience is accessed in image-schematic form. The perception of an individual thing, which is past beyond recall, gets itself embedded or embodied in a virtual dimension mediating between us and real objects. This is the dimension of the image *through which* we perceive the world. Between the sensation and the free image stands the perceptual *type,* a kind of original categorization in image-schematic form. Perception in this way is not just the grasp of things but of this *sort* of things. The work of Lakoff and Johnson and the studies of Rudolf Arnheim confirm Langer's approach here.

The image, however, as something we can recall and even construct at will, is not bound to an objectivistically conceived sensory order. Langer points out that we attend to images "only in their capacity of *meaning* things, being *images* of things—symbols whereby those things are conceived, remembered, considered, and not encountered" (*PNK* 144–145). The *symbolic* nature of images is primarily found in their "tendency to become metaphorical" (*PNK* 145). Langer wants, as we have seen, to push metaphor down to the level of "symbolic seeing," which is, in effect, prior in some senses to language—although the types of seeing are clearly those of the language animal and are also influenced by language. Metaphorical seeing, as Langer understands it, involves a "semantic displacement" *from* the primary *object-meaning*, which a symbolic image, or symbolically functioning image, has, *to* its transferred sense, a displacement based, she claims, on a "logical analogy" (*PNK* 145). The examples Langer gives here are by no means unusual, though her comment is certainly illuminating. The image of a rose, she says, symbolizes feminine beauty "so readily that it is actually harder to associate roses with vegetables than with girls" (*PNK* 145), although I suppose that to a starving scavenger the association could well go the other way. Fire, Langer notes, is "a natural symbol of life and passion, though it is the one element in which nothing can actually live" (*PNK* 145). What is it about fire that gives it its symbolic pregnance? It is its mobility and flare, its heat and color, which are distinctive and charged perceptual features. These features, Langer claims, make fire "an irresistible symbol of all that is living, feeling, and active" (*PNK* 145).

The central thesis and insight of Langer's—the claim that images are symbolic instruments for abstracting concepts "from the tumbling stream of actual impressions" (*PNK* 145)—is fundamental for her whole intellectual project. The achievement of images is to make a primitive abstraction that can later be elaborated in complex figures. Such primitive abstractions, symbolic images, are, on Langer's reckoning, "our spontaneous embodiments of general ideas" (*PNK* 145), though they are clothed in a variety of sensory garments. But while primitive, such symbolic images are subject to complex development, albeit in a way fundamentally different from language.

Symbolic images are not isolated units. According to Langer, image-making, while certainly the "mode of untutored thinking," is further the source of our mind's drive to construct "stories," or image-fantasies, the mind's "earliest product" (*PNK* 145). But such envisagement in images is not restricted to the visual domain: kinesthetic and aural elements, along with the visual, enter into the development of "fantasies" (*PNK* 146). Specific experiences, with a certain paradigmatic pregnancy, give rise to symbolic uses, since abstraction is something that happens spontaneously and quickly. In this sense any experience is not restricted to its original context, but can be used to "represent a whole *kind* of actual happening" (*PNK* 146). Certainly there is a Freudian connection here. The move to symbolically pregnant images is, on Langer's account, a move toward *general features*. The symbolic image has the task of *exemplification*. It possesses and displays the properties of a type of event or situation or action. Langer anticipates here a central concept later developed by Nelson Goodman within both an aesthetic and a general epistemological frame (see Goodman 1976 and 1978).

Using the example of the first impression of a train pulling into a station, Langer foregrounds the notion of a "general impression" (*PNK* 146), which is to be derived from, or built up out of, this singular event. It is an impression of "tone" or "quality." There is a fundamental grasp or perception of "*like*" and "*unlike*" operating in this process. "The fantasy which we call his conception of a halting train gradually builds itself up out of many impressions; but its framework was abstracted from the very first instance, and made the later ones 'familiar'" (*PNK* 147). We experience, or spontaneously construct an image or image-schema of, a train-pulling-into-a-station event. Here we have an "action-envisagement," not just the envisagement of an object. Words, images of things, and action-envisagements, Langer claims, follow "certain basic laws of symbols" (*PNK* 147), such as pregnance, good form, and so forth. But in the case we are examining here, the paradigm meaning of a train-pulling-into-a-station ("When George entered the room, he was a train pulling into a station"), there is not just a literal reference to something that can be formulated in concepts, but a tendency toward the conveyance of metaphorical meanings, indeed, the transformation of the modeling event itself into a metaphorical image. Metaphor, Langer shows once again, is pushed down here to a stratum that is not language-bound. In fact, language, as we have seen Langer insisting, is dependent upon this image, which functions as an image-schema, appearing in linguistic form. Hence, the great similarity-induced and similarity-inducing metaphorical transpositions that take place in language are also effected and operate non-linguistically. An arriving train, which we can recognize as a type of event on multiple occasions while standing on the platform, can mean not just itself—that is, an arriving train—but it "may have to embody nameless and imageless dangers coming with a rush to unload their problems before me" (*PNK* 147). The total complex of units making up the arriving train come to function as a "first symbol to shape my unborn thoughts" (*PNK* 147). The train, retained in memory as a specific event and a specific type of event, now transformed into symbol, leaves literal generality behind. The train can come to represent the approaching future, or the staged entry of a person into a room, through only certain selective features: "power, speed, inevitable direction (symbolized by the track), and so forth" (*PNK* 147). The example of the train, for Langer, shows how fantasy, working prosaically, turns into figure and then into a "metaphor of wordless cognition" (*PNK* 147).

But the theoretical point is entirely general—and what we are seeing Langer develop is a further illustration of her general thesis on presentational symbolism. "Metaphor," she writes, "is the law of growth of every semantic" (*PNK* 147). This principle applies no matter what the carrier or symbolic mode of the meaning-system is. While it is true that dreams manifest a "riotous symbolism," this is clearly not the only dimension where this semiotic riot occurs. While dreams may be "the lowest, completely unintentional products of the human brain," even the intentional products manifest the same logic. For the human mind on all levels and in all degrees of awareness is obsessed with finding the appropriate symbolism for conceiving all the dimensions of its existence, the first dimension clearly being that of "simply the experience of being alive" (*PNK* 147). This experience is, to be sure, a complicated web of intertwined desires, feelings, actions, images, and so forth.

On the most basic level Langer recognizes that our elementary conceptions are of "objects for desire" (*PNK* 148). Langer is deeply aware of the dimension of desire, without betraying any sense of an attachment to the strictly psychoanalytic domain, which she engages with more a glance than an examination. Speaking of an infant, Langer notes that "comfort and security, human nearness, light and motion—all these objects have neither substance nor fixed identity. The first images that sense impression begets in his mind have to serve for the whole gamut of his desires, for all things absent" (*PNK* 148). The infant, then, "reaches out" to the world through the constructive efforts of fantasy, understood in Langer's sense of that term not as "free fantasy" but as a kind of "bound fantasy." But, nevertheless, in this way "infantile symbols multiply" (*PNK* 148) as the symbolic images become "unbound." This is a process of "figuration," making up ultimately for the "poverty of everyday language" and lending it an imaginal matrix for its metaphorical expansion. This process of "spontaneous envisagement" involves the construction of "figurative images" in which the duality of form and content is abolished. The most primitive presentations, Langer follows Cassirer in holding, do not know such a distinction. Things get "fraught with intense value" or inspire terror without our reflective engagement. The dream level, for example, has no meta-level to make such a distinction. But the dream illustrates a fundamental principle: *meanings are embodied in symbolically pregnant objects.* In the original stratum of thought there is no thematic difference between object and meaning.

On Langer's reckoning, certain objects are emblematic of their "deeper meanings." These become "sacra" and lead to veneration by reason of their symbolic force, a theme explored in enlightening manner by Soltes, *Our Sacred Signs* (2005). Phallic symbols, death symbols, and other "bizarre holy articles" embody "the great themes of primitive religion" (*PNK* 150).

> Gods are at first merely emblems of the creative power; fetishes, trees, menhirs. Certain animals are natural symbols to mankind: the snake hidden in the earth, the bull strong in his passion, the mysterious long-lived crocodile who metes out unexpected death. When, with the advance of civilization, their images are set up in temples or borne in procession such images are designed to emphasize their symbolic force rather than their natural shapes. The snake may be horned or crowned or bearded, the bull may have wings or a human head. (*PNK* 150)

Natural symbols, Langer claims, have *import* rather than *meaning* in the linguistic sense. When a natural object takes on a symbolic value it generates in the perceiver "a peculiar emotion" (*PNK* 150), an affective (or emotional) interpretant in Peirce's sense of the term—that is, the proper significate effect of a sign, the equivalent sign that every interpreted sign gives rise to in the mind of the interpreter. This peculiar emotion gets connected with an "idea" presented in the object that transcends the functional sphere. It becomes the object of ritual contemplation, an object in which the human perceiver feels himself vested, although there is no explicit or thematized reason for the vesting. Rather, the sense of vesting comes from "our supreme and constant preoccupation with *ideas,* our spontaneous attention to expressive forms" that in the end fuses practical with symbolic values. Elicited contemplation of a *sacrum,* embodied in a symbolic object with a specific quality, generates excitement at the deepest levels of human existence, without operative action of our own, an excitement wedded to the *"realizing* of life and strength, manhood, contest, and death" (*PNK* 152). The "release" of powerful emotions or affects by the symbolic object goes over into an "expressed" objective form to *demonstrate* the feelings of individuals. This is an extremely powerful insight. But it flows directly from Langer's general semiotic framework.

Langer clearly sees here, in the origins of sacramental ritual, including sacramental contemplation, that expressive acts, including the selecting of appropriate emblems, go over from being *self-expressive* to being "expressive in the logical sense" (*PNK* 152). Expressive acts do not have to be identified with a present act of feeling or emotion, as an index or symptom would, but can denote, though not in the relatively unambiguous way linguistic symbols do, a feeling or type of feeling, indeed, bring it to mind, "even for the actor" (*PNK* 152). The expressive act and the expressive object then become *semiotic tools* with their own objectivity. In the case of actions, a genuine act, with its *functional* goal of achieving something, such as washing oneself clean, would have an intrinsic teleological need to be brought to completion, while an expressive act, as in ritual washing, would show only the "significant features" of the action. In this way an action can become an expressive form, or a true symbol. Ritual arises from "the formalization of overt behavior in the presence of the sacred objects" (*PNK* 153). Hence, sacrament, as Langer understands it, involves both sacred objects and ritual acts. The rites, spontaneous or contrived, enacted at the contemplation of sacred objects "formulate and record man's response" to the supreme realities that are expressed in them. *Articulation, contemplation, realization* are embodied in the ritualized gesture, which induces and maintains in the worshipper the "complex, permanent *attitude*" that is the "response to the insight given by the sacred symbols" (*PNK* 153). It stabilizes and gives the frame for "a disciplined rehearsal of 'right attitudes'" (*PNK* 153). Around sacred objects cluster memories of specific events and the definite feelings attendant upon these objects. *Mimetic* ritual seeks a deep existential participation, involving the body of the worshipper. The rhythmic logic of the ritual permeates the worshipper's body.

The narrative matrix of the mimetic rites, their dramatic framework of origin, rooted in *reenactment*, is complemented, however, by the framework of *supplication*. Corresponding to the "expressive virtue of sacra . . . conceived as physical virtue" is the "symbolic power of mimetic rites" able to be regarded as "causal efficacy" (*PNK* 154; note the Whitehead term here!), bordering on but not restricted to magic, which Langer thinks is not the beginning of religion, but rather the reverse. Religion, as Langer thinks of it, "is a gradual envisagement of the essential pattern of human life, and to this insight almost any object, act, or event may contribute" (*PNK* 155). But there need be nothing precious or rare that takes on religious significance. Sacred objects, formalized expressive gestures, mimetic gestures, these do not prior to their religious use have to be intrinsically weighty, although they do have "expressive weight," at least potentially and certainly not always on monumental scale, as Herbert Fingarette has shown in his *Confucius: The Secular as Sacred* (1972). Public religious use of an object or a gesture normally has had "a long career in a much homelier capacity" (*PNK* 155); its public religious use involves a *symbolic transformation*. Rites are rooted in play, indeed share the deep logic of play. And play involves the use of schematized actions or actions severely constrained by rules and modes of accomplishing. The physical and functional fullness of a practical act becomes schematized and radically diminished in its physical reality when it is incorporated into ritual. Ritual eating does not embody the full reality of eating, but *refers* to, or denotes, eating rather than trying to be a full *representation* of the activity. Ritual acts, schematized and reduced to their pertinent features, "are part of man's ceaseless quest for conception and orientation. . . . Ritual is the most primitive reflection of serious thought, a slow deposit, as it were, of people's imaginative insight into life" (*PNK* 157). There is no debunking here of the sacred and of the pertinence of ritual, although Langer will make it clear that the "religious worldview" is something that has no permanent values in terms of the realities projected in it. It is a realm of meaning, not of reality, for Langer, constituted by what Roy Rappaport (1999) has called Universal Sacred Postulates (see Innis 2004 and, for a rather different take, with many explicit references to Langer, van Roo 1981).

Fear, according to Langer, is the "driving force in human minds" (*PNK* 158). The overarching goal, then, is security, in the many senses of that term. Security entails the construction of a world picture that would ensure and effect "a definite *orientation* amid the terrifying forces of nature and society. Objects that embody such insights, and acts which express, preserve, and reiterate them, are indeed more spontaneously interesting, more serious than work" (*PNK* 158). Hence, the "universality of the concepts which religion tries to formulate draws all nature into the domain of ritual" (*PNK* 158). Using the example of a rain dance, Langer argues that the dance is meant to accompany the coming rain, to participate in it, to complete its coming. It is not principally a practical act, but a religious act. "Its real import—its power to articulate a relation between man and nature, vivid at the moment—can be recognized only in the metaphorical guise of a physical power to induce the rain" (*PNK* 159). But inducement is not the principal point. Mimetic ritual may give rise, Langer thinks, to sympathetic magic, which is a phenomenon of tribal, primitive religion. But religion's own teleology as it progresses is, it seems, to culminate, on one trajectory at least, with the *sacrament* (see, once again, van Roo 1981).

Sacraments have an overt form, usually in some act that is "essentially realistic and vital": washing, eating, drinking, slaughter, sexual union. Such commonplace events and actions are the point of origin of very profound and ancient symbolic forms (*PNK* 159–160), well known to the student of the history of religions. Behavior patterns can be formalized, and it is the formal element that "offers high possibilities to the symbol-seeking mind" (*PNK* 160). Langer's point is not empirical, but conceptual. It is meant to be an exemplification of her conceptual scheme. Washing away dirt, eating, bowing down before a superior, kissing, laying on of hands, and all the other acts that we are familiar with in everyday life are symbolically exploited in terms of their pertinent features. Eating an animal is not a matter of getting food, but we are absorbing its *animal characteristics*. Ritual slaughter and eating become symbolic acts, involving existential and semiotic participation. They are "exalted into sacred procedure" (*PNK* 161). The ritualization of eating charges or weights each detail with meaning.

> Every gesture signifies some step in the acquisition of animal virtue. According to the law of all primitive symbolization, this significance is felt not as such, but as genuine efficacy; the feast not only dramatizes, but actually negotiates the desired acquisition. Its performance is magical as well as expressive. And so we have the characteristic blend of power and meaning, mediation and presentation, that belongs to sacrament. (*PNK* 161)

Thus we find ritual to encompass "prescribed modes of participation and assent" (*PNK* 162).

What are these modes directed toward? Langer's answer is that it is impossible to continue directing them to a "nameless symbol" (*PNK* 162). Here is the great step from superstition to theology, the naming of the gods. Its first stage is not really anthropomorphic, Langer claims. No person actually dwells in an object. Rather, the object itself is conceived *as a personality* (*PNK* 163), "as an agent participating in the ritual." This is the movement from efficacy to ability, or power to act. Ability, embodied in a ritual image, in the long term becomes a "summary of a human ideal," the ideal of a tribe (*PNK* 163). Religious imagery, its active venerative performance in rites, involves the symbolic activity of *exemplification* and *typification*. Because of the complexity of human personalities, religious imagery has often, even predominantly in the cases of "primitive" religion, had recourse to the animal domain, for "animals run true to type" (*PNK* 163). "The man who sees his ideal in an animal calls himself by its name, because, exemplifying his highest aspirations as it does, it is his 'true self'" (*PNK* 164). In this way Langer attempts to define, on the basis of her philosophical principles, the genesis of totemism. "The primary conception of a totem must have sprung from some insight into the human significance of an animal form; perhaps some purely sexual significance, perhaps a sublimer notion of savage virtue" (*PNK* 164). Totemism, like all sacraments, Langer contends, echoing Durkheim, is "a form of *ideation*, an expression of concepts in purely presentational metaphor" (*PNK* 165). Such a presentational metaphor, powerful notion in itself, has a deep existential significance that we all recognize.

There is, Langer further claims, a passage from "such primitive sacramentalism to a real theology" (*PNK* 166), fantastic as it may seem. Langer thinks that the classic works of Jane Harrison and Gilbert Murray are essential supports and evidence for such a position. The clear Olympian Gods, Murray claims, in a pas-

sage cited by Langer, "are imposed upon a background strangely unlike themselves." It is a savage background, a "dark primaeval tangle of desires and fears
and dreams" rooted in "actual cult" (Murray 1925: 28, cited *PNK* 167). It was the
progressive giving of names to specific daimonic functions that led to the transition from ritual to theology. Zeus, Harrison and Murray claimed, followed by
Langer, usurped a ritualized focus and attained "perfect form, definite relations
to the heavens, the gods, and the human world" (*PNK* 169) by becoming a figure
"in something more than ritual; it is in the great realm of *myth* that human conceptions of divinity really become articulated" (*PNK* 169).

> A symbol may give identity to a god, a mimetic dance may express his favors, but
> what really fixes his character is the tradition of his origin, actions, and past adven-
> tures. Like the hero of a novel or a drama, he becomes a personality, not by his sheer
> appearance, but by his story. . . . Divinities are born of ritual, but theologies spring
> from myth. (*PNK* 169)

Langer cites, at the end of her chapter, a pregnant passage from Jane Harrison dealing with the origin of a *Korê*, or primitive earth goddess: "The May-
pole or harvest-sheaf is half-way to a harvest Maiden; it is thus . . . that a goddess
is made. A song is sung, a story told, and the very telling fixes the outline of the
personality. It is possible to worship long in the spirit, but as soon as the story-
telling and myth-making instinct awakes you have anthropomorphism and theology" (Harrison 1908: 80, cited *PNK* 170). She ends her chapter, however, with
a strong concluding thesis. The myth-making instinct not only has its own history, it has its own life-symbols, cognate with but different from those of sacrament and ritual. Myth for Langer has little function "below the level of dawning philosophic thought" (*PNK* 170). But for Langer, as she says in a controversial
and sharp passage, philosophical thought "is the last reach of genuine religion,
its consummation and also its dissolution" (*PNK* 170). Genuine religion, then, as
Langer conceives it, begins in ritual and sacrament, proceeds through mythical
elaboration, and is transformed in the interpretive activities of philosophical reflection, which have as their ultimate object the analysis of meaning. Philosophy,
in short, replaces participation with reflection. It replaces the lived-through character of meaning with analysis, not for the sake of mere destruction but for the
sake of living on a higher "rational" plane of a philosophical religion, perhaps
identical, though Langer does not say it, with a semiotically torqued Spinozistic
amor intellectualis Dei. Langer never quite puts it this way, though her claim to be a
sober naturalist points quite clearly in that direction and she makes no secret of
her repudiation of the "supernatural" world's literal reality and narratives, embodied in myths.

The Symbolic Lessons of Myth

Langer begins her analysis of myth by contrasting it more explicitly with ritual-istically informed religion. Myth for her culminates, after a distinctive develop-ment, in "permanent significant forms" (*PNK* 171). The focus on objects and acts in ritual, and the development of a complex, even if unthematized, sacramental-ism, is matched by the development of myth. "Ritual begins in motor attitudes, which, however personal, are at once externalized and so made public. Myth be-gins in fantasy, which may remain tacit for a long time; for the primary form of fantasy is the entirely subjective and private phenomenon of *dream*" (*PNK* 171). At the same time Langer thinks that even in the least developed stages of myth "the primitive story has some other than literal significance," that is, that it has a symbolic, that is, metaphorical, content (*PNK* 171). This is a firm and never re-pudiated principle of interpretation for Langer.

Langer's analysis of myth is more value-dependent, perhaps, than her treat-ment of rite and sacrament, which could, in fact, be extended out to the rise of "political liturgies" that mark the public order as a symbolic order—though they themselves are dependent on political myths, themes treated with great acu-men and depth, but with very different commitments, by Ernst Cassirer (1946) and Eric Voegelin (see especially his 1952). She speaks of some primitive forms of myths as being at a "very low stage of human imagination" (*PNK* 172). There is, Langer thinks, a kind of displacement taking place in many "primitive" myths, which are really "just" fantasies, where inanimate and fantastic objects seem to act in ways amazingly human and accordingly "out of character." But, Langer notes, "the act is not really proper to its agent, but to *someone its agent represents;* and even the action in the story may merely *represent* the deeds of such a symbolized personality" (*PNK* 173). She thinks that many fantastic mythical narratives have a "psychological basis" and that in fact many of the most remarkable stories are fabrications "out of subjective symbols, not out of observed folkways and nature-ways" (*PNK* 173). Fairy stories are, in her opinion, probably "an older form than myth," but myth is "not simply a higher development of the former" but rather a "thematic shift" takes place that separates the fairytale from the "true" form of myth. The fairytale, Langer thinks, is essentially a form of "wishful thinking," subject to a full explanation on Freudian terms, which show why such a form of thinking is "perennially attractive, yet never believed by adults even in the tell-ing" (*PNK* 175).

This is not the case with myth, between which and the fairytale Langer is clearly drawing a sharp and problematic contrast. The hero of myth, Langer claims, is not the hero of fairytale. Myth is taken with "religious seriousness," os-cillating between historic fact or "mystic" truth (*PNK* 175). The traditional myth is tragic, not utopian, Langer thinks, and mythic narratives have complex rela-tions with one another, unlike, in her opinion, fairytales. Myths and fairytales have "fundamentally different functions" and are "put to quite different uses" (*PNK* 176). Myth is a "recognition of natural conflicts" rather than personal conflicts. Langer asserts that myth "presents, however metaphorically, a world-picture, an insight into life generally" (*PNK* 177). Different myths do the same sort of thing, with close family resemblances, and thus myths enter into close and systematic relations with one another. Thus, mythical figures "with the same po-etic meaning are blended into one, and characters of quite separate origin enter into definite relations with each other" (*PNK* 177). The mythical hero is "a subject greater than any individual" (*PNK* 177). *It is what this hero symbolizes that is of impor-tance.* But the hero's function in the myth, as opposed to the fairytale, is to supply not vicarious experience but an understanding of "actual experience" (*PNK* 177). This is an important and substantial insight. While in individual cases there may be no clean dividing line between myth and fairytale, their *semiotic logic* is radi-cally different. The pivotal turn is a changed relationship toward "*realistic signifi-cance*" (*PNK* 178). Fairytales, with their plethora of ghosts, bogeys, ogres, corpses, skulls, and hideous idols pass over into spook-religion. But, most importantly for Langer, these figures of fairytale are not cosmological figures. They are symboli-zations of personal powers, fears, desires, and so forth, which are primarily so-cial and indeed super-personal. The demon, for example, is the "envisagement of a vital factor in life; that is why he is projected into reality by the symbolism of religion" (*PNK* 179).

What, then, really marks "the great step from fairytale to myth" (*PNK* 180)? Langer answers that it is the movement from the representation of *social* forces—"persons, customs, laws, traditions"—as the primary foci to *cosmic* forces. The "spontaneous metaphor of poetic fantasy" generates narratives of the relation-ships of an individual to nature and not just to society. Here nature itself sup-plies "permanent, obvious symbols" such as "the heavenly bodies, the changes of day and night, the seasons, and the tides" (*PNK* 180). It is the movement to a cosmic setting that is crucial. Gods and heroes, the agents in mythic fanta-sies, are interpreted as nature-symbols. How did this happen? Langer thinks that there is a transitional phase between the egocentric interest of folktale and the emergence of full-fledged nature-mythology, epitomized in the *legend* and its product, the "culture-hero" (*PNK* 181). It is the culture-hero who first medi-ates between fairytale and cosmological myth, for such a hero "interferes with the doings of nature rather than of men" (*PNK* 182). Thus, the fictional hero of legend is enhanced and exalted. The hero of fairytale is a "vehicle of human wishes" (*PNK* 185). The story-hero of fairytale overcomes personal opponents. The culture-hero of legend, standing in for Man, overcomes "*the superior forces that threaten him*" (*PNK* 185). The cosmic setting of these narratives with storm and night, deluge and death as foes and ordeals sets the task for the culture-hero: "His task is the control of nature—of earth and sky, vegetation, rivers, season—and the conquest of death" (*PNK* 185).

Consequently, "the culture-hero's story furnishes symbols of a less personal encircling reality. The hero's exploits are largely make-believe even to their inventors; but the forces that challenge him are apt to be taken seriously" (*PNK* 185). It is this movement to impersonal forces that marks the transition to a philosophically important mythic form of apprehension and expression. These nature symbols mean something beyond the often fantastic episodes or events in which they are expressed or embodied.

Langer attempts to exemplify these theoretical points through a set of selected examples. It is not hard to think of others, from religious as well as political realms. These examples are presented not for their own sake but for their power to illustrate Langer's hermeneutic and semiotic framework of analysis. It is not necessary to go into exact details here, for Langer's main point is a theoretical one: that a natural object (or, clearly, a person), with its various aspects and properties, can come to stand for something else. There is a sort of semiotic migration involved here. The moon, for example, can become a symbol of woman, as it does in the various roles played by the Hina figure in Polynesian mythology. "The moon, by reason of its spectacular changes, is a very expressive, adaptable, and striking symbol—far more so than the sun, with its simple career and unvarying form" (*PNK* 190). Be that as it may, given the rise of sun gods and its prelimning of the key symbol of monotheism, what Langer says about the semiotic fitness or aptness of the moon as a natural symbol is extraordinarily rich in its implications for an understanding of the symbolic mind. Because of the uncanny power the human mind has in recognizing "symbolic forms" (*PNK* 191), it will fasten on regularities and "the most insistent repetitions" in nature as symbolic materials for the work of articulating a fundamental relationship to the world.

The connection between woman and the moon exemplifies this structure for Langer. Woman, she thinks, is for the primitive mind "one of the basic mysteries of nature" (*PNK* 191). The deep and intimate connection with life's origins and its mysterious connection with sexual union turns woman into a potential "Great Mother, the symbol as well as the instrument of life" (*PNK* 191). But because of the slowness of the waxing and waning of the female body, it is itself hard to use as a symbol. In fact, *we need something to symbolize it and all it itself could symbolize.* As Langer puts it, "the actual process of human conception and gesta-tion is too slow to exhibit a pattern for easy apprehension" (*PNK* 191). How does one, then, facilitate or even effect such an apprehension? One *finds an appropriate symbol* in order to think "coherently" about it. Such an appropriate symbol is the moon, a "natural symbol" of waxing and waning, these processes themselves be-ing primary forms of manifestation of fertility, birth, and death. The moon in its phenomenal course telescopes and manifests a criterial feature of womanhood. Dream-symbolism, with its semiotic mechanism of condensation, does the same sort of thing. Presentational symbolism, no matter how "articulate" and struc-tured, is able to also condense a meaning-content in thick form. The moon be-comes, on this reckoning, a presentational symbol not only of woman, but of the phases of life itself. "But just as life grows to completeness with every waxing phase, so in the waning period one can see the old moon take possession, gradu-ally, of the brilliant parts; life is swallowed by death in a graphic process, and the swallowing monster was ancestor to the life that dies. The significance of the moon is irresistible" (*PNK* 192). Indeed, it functions as a *model* of the great cycle of life and death. Certainly, there is a deep insight and principle expressed here—with a scope and range far beyond Langer's own examples.

Langer rejects, rightly or wrongly is actually not the point here, the notion that nature-myths are "originally attempts to explain astronomical or meteorologi-cal events" (*PNK* 193). Nature-myths, she thinks, are concerned with figures that are felt to be more than human, superhuman, in fact, in the sense of a superman, "Mankind in a single human figure" (*PNK* 193). The superhuman hero, mascu-line or feminine, gets not only *represented* but *presented* in a natural symbol, *with-out explicit personification.* In Polynesian mythology the moon is not personified in the person of Hina. Rather Hina gets *lunarized.* The "savage," as Langer puts it, sees woman in the moon, not the moon in woman. "The lunar changes of light and form and place, nameless and difficult as mere empirical facts, acquire impor-tance and obviousness from their analogy to human relations and functions: con-ceiving, bearing, loving, and hating, devouring and being devoured" (*PNK* 194). The moon is a particularly apt symbol here "because it can present so many phases of womanhood" (*PNK* 194). The richness therefore of a presentational symbol is a semiotic richness, a presentational power that emerges from the crea-tive imagination's attempt to find an appropriate form to mediate conception.

The consciousness of a difference between the literal or metaphorical, or transferred, sense of a natural symbol does not occur to the "primitive" or "sav-age" mind, as Langer uses these terms. Only literal-mindedness raises the issue of belief and unbelief. Apollo for the Greeks was not the same Apollo for Milton. For the Greeks he was "one of the prime realities—the Sun, the God, the Spirit from which men received inspirations" (*PNK* 196). Apollo was not a figure of speech for the Greeks; he was a figure of thought, a way of apprehending the world in which there was no divide between figure and reality. *Reality was apprehended in the figure.* Apollo was a figured reality, a fate that also, perhaps, befell the central figure of the Christian myth or even the central figure of the Mosaic tradition. Langer sees the great mythologies as taking on stability by being fixed in poetic form, but poetic form is by no means the point of origin of the great mythologies. "The 'making' of mythology by creative bards is only a metamorphosis of world-old and universal ideas" (*PNK* 198). These universal ideas are not "free invention for the sake of the story" (*PNK* 198). The Finnish *Kalevala* and the great Greek myths both have at their base culture-heroes who are transformed in their poetic embodiments. Speaking of the Rainbow Maiden Aino, Langer writes:

> Every nature mythology treats the rainbow as an elusive maiden, but it requires the thoughtful formulation of poetry to see the rainbow's ephemeral beauty in a girl too wayward and beautiful for her aged lover, to put the human story first and incorporate the heavenly phenomena merely in her symbolic name. Here is the beginning of that higher mythology wherein the world is essentially the stage for human life, the setting of the true epic, which is human and social. (*PNK* 200)

The poetic frame supplies the "clarifying and unifying medium" for the elaboration of the original mythic impulse. Thus, the embodiment of mythology in poetry is "simply its perfected and final form," which we tend to see as its "true" form by reason of myths standing out as full symbolic forms, with a distinctive structure. The danger, however, of considering myths as poetic inventions is that we downgrade their true value: they are not pure fictions but rather *articulations* of "the supreme concepts of life which they really represent, and by which men orient themselves religiously in the cosmos" (*PNK* 200). This is a point that has been made by a wide range of thinkers such as Ananda Coomaraswamy, Mircea Eliade, and Joseph Campbell, to mention three quite different types of thinkers whose approaches have rather different conceptual bases.

Langer summarizes main points and results of her reflections on "meaning after language" in the following powerful paragraph.

> It is a peculiar fact that every major advance in thinking, every epoch-making new insight, springs from a new type of symbolic transformation. A higher level of thought is primarily a new activity; its course is opened up by a new departure in semantic. The step from mere sign-using to symbol-using marked the crossing of the line between animal and man; this initiated the natural growth of language. The birth of symbolic gesture from emotional and practical movement probably begot the whole order of ritual, as well as the discursive mode of pantomime.

> The recognition of vague, vital meanings in physical forms—perhaps the first dawn of symbolism—gave us our idols, emblems, and totems; the primitive function of dream permits our first envisagement of events. The momentous discovery of nature-symbolism, of the pattern of life reflected in natural phenomena, produced the first universal insights. Every mode of thought is bestowed on us, like a gift, with some new principle of symbolic expression. It has a logical development, which is simply the exploitation of all the uses to which that symbolism lends itself. (*PNK* 201)

When its uses have been exhausted, however, any particular symbolism can be superseded by "some more powerful symbolic mode which opens new avenues of thought" (*PNK* 201). The embodiment of discursive rationality in science and the mathematical domain will be given, at the end both of *Philosophy in a New Key* and of the third volume of *Mind*, a deep teleological significance and value as supreme achievements of human mentality.

Such a supersession has, however, happened in the case of myth, which reached its culmination in epic poetry, which is, nevertheless, no discursive form. While it can embody general ideas in the sense of exhibiting them, since it is a prime example of presentational symbolism, "it does not lend itself to analytic and genuinely abstractive techniques" (*PNK* 201). The mythical mode is not a fit instrument for the abstraction and manipulation of pure concepts. So, natural religion, in its mythic mode or form, gets superseded "by a discursive and more literal form of thought, namely philosophy" (*PNK* 201). This position on myth will be reprised and modified later in *Mind*. Indeed, the notion that a presentational form cannot engage in "analytic and genuinely abstractive techniques" is radically fine-tuned in *Mind*, where it is the paradigmatic presentational form of art and its distinctive abstractive techniques that give us the heuristic key to mind. While language certainly for Langer will also be the pivotal semiotic tool that effects the great transition to humanness, Langer's determination to avoid logocentrism and to validate art's distinctive cognitive role is already prefigured here in *Philosophy in a New Key*; indeed, it is one of its guiding motivations.

Langer describes language in *Philosophy in a New Key* as "a stiff and conventional medium" when used in its literal capacity (*PNK* 201), that is, purely and resolutely discursively. Language in its creative and generative phase operates by means of "some great and bewildering metaphor" (*PNK* 201), but in its discursive use it passes necessarily into a strictly analytical phase with its demand for precision, albeit if the demand, even on Langer's principles, cannot be satisfied. While myth is what Langer calls the "indispensable forerunner" of metaphysics, its inner trajectory is also toward metaphysics, and hence toward its own dissolution. But what does Langer mean by "metaphysics" here? Langer recapitulates in

Philosophy in a New Key the position of *The Practice of Philosophy*, namely that metaphysics is the "literal formulation of basic abstractions, on which our comprehension of sober facts is based" (*PNK* 201–202). Literal thought, as Langer is using the term, depends on an antecedent presentation of experience. Literal analyses operate on really new ideas, presented non-literally, and such ideas "have their own modes of appearance in the unpredictable creative mind" (*PNK* 202). Poetic significance and factual reference are not the same. But once the conflict between fantasy and fact has been raised to full and explicit consciousness, there is no going back. "There must be a rationalistic period from this point onward. Some day when the vision is totally rationalized, the ideas exploited and exhausted, there will be another vision, a new mythology" (*PNK* 202). This is a nuanced and complicated position, embroiled as it is with the seeming claim that there could be a metaphysics without metaphor. But if we attend to the findings of cognitive linguistics, it seems that we can never arrive at some sort of literal bedrock to our thinking. Metaphysics is itself a species of "vision," with both mythic and discursive dimensions. Loyal Rue, for example, has proposed a version of a new shared "vision" that could be built by "wising up to the epic of evolution" (Rue 2000).

Mythology, Langer asserts, as a passing phase in the evolution of human mentality, lives on in the epic, along with philosophy and science "and all the higher forms of thought" (*PNK* 203). The epic, however, while it may be filled with the content of the old myths, is a new symbolic form and "the first flower—or one of the first, let us say—of a new symbolic mode, the mode of *art*" (*PNK* 203). This new symbolic form is "ready to take meanings and express ideas that have had no vehicle before" (*PNK* 203). Langer is pointing here to a kind of internal history of symbolization, a history that can be charted in even the "higher" religions.

What are these new ideas and in what sense can art be thought of as "our first, and perhaps our only, access" to them (*PNK* 203)? How are we to think of these ideas and what can function as our best clue to them, since art does not belong to the discursive realm, and hence its meanings and ideas cannot be "said," but only "shown"? In order to answer this question Langer devotes two rich chapters in *Philosophy in a New Key* to the theme of "significance in music" and "the genesis of artistic import." Because, however, Langer stated that *Feeling and Form* should really be considered a sequel or volume 2 of the aesthetic theory presented in its nucleus or kernel in *Philosophy in a New Key*, I intend to treat her initial aesthetic theory in its *Philosophy in a New Key* form as an essential prolegomenon to the full and mature theory elaborated in *Feeling and Form*. This will enable us in the next two chapters to see whether and how *Feeling and Form* really is a coherent expansion of the key aesthetic insights and what it adds to the reflections presented in *Philosophy in a New Key,* where Langer is most concerned to establish the relations between, and relative autonomy of, the various symbolic forms that are the object of a semiotically torqued philosophical analysis: language, ritual, myth, art, and science.

Symbolic Prolegomena to a Theory of Art

We will focus our discussion on the following questions.

- What is the heuristic value of the notion of "significance" in music?
- Why would we look to music as a paradigm case of artistic significance?
- What is the relation between "significance" and "artistic import" as analytical categories?
- And where does artistic import come from?

It will become clear that Langer's characterization of *Feeling and Form* as in a sense volume 2 of or a sequel to *Philosophy in a New Key* does not refer merely to the chapters devoted to art as a symbolic form. It refers, as we will see, to the philosophical insights and categories developed in *Philosophy in a New Key* as a whole.

First of all, then, what can a reflection on the problem of "significance" in music tell us about how to think about art as a distinctive symbolic form?

The reference to "significance" is connected with Langer's own continuous reflection on the notion both of art as *a* "significant form" and of "significant form" as the key to art itself, both descriptively and evaluatively. Langer's approach to art is fundamentally "semiotic," in a way distinctive to her, and indeed without the terminological labyrinths of the Peircean analytical framework. It pivots around a central assertion: "great art is not a direct sensuous pleasure" (*PNK* 205). While there is no great art—indeed, no art at all—without sensuous symbolic embodiments, and while she supports, indeed validates, a psychological and even psychoanalytical approach to art, at least partially, Langer's concern is to try to establish the *semiotic autonomy of art.* Although she will certainly support the pleasure of artistic perception, such perception is defined not in terms of pleasure but in terms of *significance,* in a sense to be more and more determined. And while she will also clearly and unequivocally admit that art can emerge out of and reveal deep psychic conflicts, art is not defined by its points of origin or even its psychic motivations, real as they are with their hidden contents. The distinctiveness of artistic significance is not what the artwork as a sensuous construct is *about.* It is not the "aboutness" of the symbolic form of art that is determinative, its orientation toward an "object," but its "what-about-ness," its "mode of presentation" and not fundamentally its presented "subject-matter." In this sense, which has to be carefully attended to, Langer's approach to art is "formal."

Langer, in *Philosophy in a New Key* and *Feeling and Form,* makes music a paradigm case for purely artistic meaning for three key reasons. It is, in its highest achievements, preeminently non-representational; its reality consists in nothing but tonal structures; it has no obvious literal content. Langer thinks there are really only three options available to us when we are trying to define music's meaning. We can locate such meaning or significance either (1) in the musical effect evoked in the listener or (2) in the expression of a musical feeling undergone or being experienced by the composer/performer or (3) in the articulated musical symbol itself. This is the signal-symptom-symbol triad developed by Karl Bühler (1934), resulting in the distinguishing of the conative, expressive, and representational functions of language. Roman Jakobson (1960) later expanded these functions out to six, adding the poetic, the phatic, and the meta-lingual, issues that we need not go into in the present context.

The first option has been a constant theme and temptation of philosophical analysis from the time of Plato's severe critique of music and the poets. On this position the significance of music is to be found in its ability to affect the listener (and the performer, too) such that distinctive moods and forms of behavior are evoked or caused by music's various forms. This is a stimulus or causal theory, focused on behavior and the evocation of inner states, which is meant to be the main point of music. Without denying that music has distinct and distinctive effects on people (which it would be hard to deny), Langer does not think there is any real evidence that music has a lasting effect on character. It certainly has transient effects, and, in light of the human psychophysical constitution, it would be strange if it did not. But a direct emotional or affective effect, caused by a symbol, Langer thinks, is not the real meaning of such a symbol. The somatic (and psychological) influences seem, she says, to be a function of *sound* rather than of music as such. The belief in the affective power of music is not, however, absurd on its merits. C. P. E. Bach, son of the great J. S. Bach, himself endorsed such a position. "Since a musician cannot otherwise move people, but he be moved himself, so he must necessarily be able to induce in himself all those affects which he would arouse in his auditors; he conveys his feeling to them, and thus most readily moves them to sympathetic emotions" (cited *PNK* 215). Surely such an idea, perhaps purged of any simplistic notion of "inducing," has a certain validity and range of application.

The second option focuses on self-expression. Langer admits here, too, that there is an "undeniable connection of music with feeling," a mystery all the more compounded by the fact that music is an "art without ostensible subject-matter" (*PNK* 216). The major obstacle to thinking of music as a form of self-expression is the ineluctable fact that "the history of music has been a history of more and more integrated, disciplined, and articulated *forms*" (*PNK* 216) and "*sheer self-expression requires no artistic form*" (*PNK* 216). The emotional catharsis that would seemingly be attendant upon musical self-expression, Langer thinks, follows natural, not artistic laws. Musical self-expression, which certainly occurs, is not, however, even when based on the same piece of music, uniquely defined by it. To try to find the composer's self-expressive intention runs into the undeniable fact of multiple interpretations, and indeed the wild swings of mood of a sonata make it difficult to think that a performing artist would be expressing *himself*, as he presently is or was, in playing any piece of music.

The significance of music, whatever it in conceptual detail ultimately turns out to be, Langer claims, is *semantic, neither symptomatic nor a causal stimulus*. If music has an emotional content, she says, it has it the same way language has its conceptual content. It has it *symbolically*. This emotional content is "not usually derived *from* affects nor intended *for* them" (*PNK* 218). Music is neither the cause of nor the cure of feelings. It is, instead, their *logical expression* (*PNK* 218). Its logic makes it, however, incommensurable with language and also makes it incommensurable with other "presentational symbols like images, gestures, and rites" (*PNK* 218), although it, too, is a presentational symbol. Consequently, Langer thinks, rightly, that musical aesthetics will involve the whole logic of symbolism. While admitting that music does have a stimulus dimension as well as a symptomatic dimension, which in any case it would be hard to deny, Langer wants to explore just how the significance of music can *in some sense* belong to it as a symbolic form, though not as a "language." The "aboutness" of musical form is not the aboutness of language. There is an "ideational content" embodied in the "language of tones," although it is not transparent and certainly not wedded to any sort of "sound-painting." There is, as Langer says, an *"exposition* of feeling" that belongs to characters on a stage, characters in an opera, or "fictitious characters in a ballad" (*PNK 221*)—and, by extension, to "musical characters" or themes. But the reference to exposition indicates that for Langer we are dealing not with actual feelings, possessed by performer or composer, but with *knowledge of human feeling*, which is symbolically *embodied* in the music itself and *projected* symbolically in it.

Langer holds that the idea that music mediates knowledge, gives us knowledge "is the most persistent, plausible, and interesting doctrine of meaning in music" (*PNK* 221). Langer cites a passage from Wagner that clearly articulates such a position.

> What music expresses is eternal, infinite and ideal; it does not express the pas-
> sion, love, or longing of such-and-such an individual on such-and-such an occa-
> sion, but passion, love or longing in itself, and this it presents in that unlimited va-
> riety of motivations, which is the exclusive and particular characteristic of music,
> foreign and inexpressible to any other language. (Wagner, *Ein glücklicher Abend*, re-
> printed by Gatz, in *Musik-Aesthetik*, from the *Gazette Musicale*, nos. 56–58 (1841), cited
> *PNK* 222)

The lesson of such a passage is that music is, first and foremost, representation
and formulation, not self-expression. Musical forms are "logical pictures," Langer
claims, of emotions, moods, mental tensions and resolutions, the primary constituents of "sentient, responsive life" (*PNK* 222). Music has, therefore, heuristic
power and value. It is a "source of insight, not a plea for sympathy" (*PNK* 222),
even if such sympathy would flow from the achieved insight. So, we learn about
the structures of our "interior life" by encountering their *formalized and distanced*
presentations in the musical symbols.

Langer avails herself of Bullough's famous notion of psychic distance to under-
line the anti-self-expression thrust of her position. Confronted with a piece of
music, the listener and the performer have as their respective tasks the grasping
of and making conceivable a *content*. The content is resident in a symbol, it is a
"symbolized" content, and "what it invites is not emotional response, but *insight*.
'Psychical distance' is simply the experience of apprehending through a symbol
what was not articulated before" (*PNK* 223). This content—bearing upon the life
of feeling, impulse, and passion—is embodied in symbols that do not normally
express this content. A new symbolic form must be constructed that is *not intrinsically or existentially associated* with this content as a stimulus, symptom, or index.
Looking at music as a "symbolic form of some sort" turns the problem of music's
meaning or content into something to be investigated from the "purely logical
standpoint" (*PNK* 225).

This logical turn is a semiotic turn for Langer, and it constitutes one of her central claims about music in particular and art in general. Langer's claim, which
certainly has Peircean echoes, is that representations in the presentational mode
exhibit a *logical form* that they share with their objects. Musical figures, musical
structures, she claims, "logically resemble certain dynamic patterns of human
experience" (*PNK* 226). They are "iconic symbols." Notice the reference is to "patterns." Langer in her discussion of music has recourse, once again, to the lessons
of Gestalt psychology and what she considers its confirmation, in different terms,
by the work of Jean D'Udine. Consider the preliminary pertinence of this pregnant passage from Köhler's *Gestalt Psychology* (1947):

Quite generally the inner processes, whether emotional or intellectual, show types
of development which may be given names, usually applied to musical events, such
as: *crescendo* and *diminuendo, accelerando* and *ritardando*. As these qualities occur in the
world of acoustical experiences, they are found in the visual world too, and so they
can express *similar* dynamic traits of inner life in directly observable activity. . . . To
the increasing inner tempo and dynamical level there corresponds a *crescendo* and
accelerando in visible movement. Of course, the same inner development may express itself acoustically, as in the *accelerando* and *reforzando* of speech. . . . Hesitation
and lack of inner determination become visible . . . as *ritardando* of visible or audible
behavior (248–249, cited *PNK* 226)

Langer then cites a set of passages from D'Udine's *L'Art et le geste,* saying that
Köhler's description is "just the inverse" of D'Udine's description, where music is
treated as a kind of gesture, exemplified in the "mimic 'dance'" of the conductor:
"All the expressive gesticulations of the conductor is really a dance . . . all music
is dancing. . . . All melody is a series of attitudes. . . . Every feeling contributes, in
effect, certain special gestures which reveal to us, bit by bit, the essential characteristic of Life: movement. . . . All living creatures are constantly consummat-
ing their own internal rhythm" (D'Udine 1910: 6; cited *PNK* 227). Special articulations of feeling always occur against this steady rhythmic background. They
are rhythmic articulations themselves, emerging as breaks in the background
rhythms, that give a specific vitality to the perceiving organism. It is Langer's
contention that "these rhythms are the prototypes of musical structures, for all
art is but a projection of them from one domain of sense to another, a symbolic
transformation" (*PNK* 227). Köhler's use of the language of musical dynamics
to model psychological phenomena and D'Udine's use of movement itself as the
prototype of vital forms, as making all the arts a kind of dance, rest, Langer says,
on a *formal analogy.* Moreover, Langer also agrees with von Hoeslin's likening of
drama, plastic art, thought, and feeling to music "by reason of the same analogy"
(*PNK* 227). This analogy is based on music's resting on the foundation of *tensions
and resolutions* (*PNK* 227). These patterns, it is claimed, are "exemplified in all art,
and also in all emotive responses" (*PNK* 227), von Hoeslin's thesis that is both
reported and supported by Langer. It is an exemplification of formal properties
shared by music and "the inner life" (*PNK* 228). Langer was never to abandon this
position. It is a permanent component of her later reflections.

Logical form, in Langer's own peculiar way of using this notion, which is fully
consonant with its use in *The Practice of Philosophy,* is clearly rooted in the idea
of *similarity* between music and subjective experience. Music for Langer is, as I
have noted, a symbolism endowed with certain ("iconic") properties that make

it *symbolically apt* or fit for its specific task, not materially apt or fit in a physicalistic sense. Music as a tonal phenomenon satisfies "the purely structural requirements for a symbolism" (*PNK* 228). What are they? What properties do musical forms have?

(1) "they are composed of many separable items, easily produced, and easily combined in a great variety of ways"

(2) "in themselves they play no important practical role which would overshadow their semantic function"

(3) "they are readily distinguished, remembered, and repeated"

(4) "they have a remarkable tendency *to modify each other's characters in combination,* as words do, by all serving each as a context." (*PNK* 228)

Yet, Langer thinks, *while music is a symbolism it is not a language,* nor are any other art forms, for that matter. The tonal nature of music does not allow a strictly language-like structuring. Indeed, "the analogy between music and language breaks down if we carry it beyond the mere semantic function in general, which they are supposed to share" (*PNK* 232). But music has no fixed connotations, as language does. It has no literal meaning. But we must not fall into the trap, Langer warns, of thinking that nothing can be known that cannot be named. The strength of musical expressiveness is found in music's power to articulate forms that language cannot. There are many relations that language cannot set forth. "It is just because music has *not* the same terminology and pattern, that it lends itself to the revelation of non-scientific concepts" (*PNK* 233). It does not lend itself to any literal or exhaustive interpretation in any other terms than its own. Indeed, music itself is a constructive interpretation of experience that cannot itself be translated into another form. Music, on Langer's most considered position, which is also close to Wittgenstein's, gives expression to *the Unspeakable.* Music functions according to a "semantic of vital and emotional facts" (*PNK* 235). Langer, therefore, will think of music as essentially, and in principle, more congruent with the forms of human feeling than language is. This gives it its *revelatory* power. It does not reveal, however, any specific content that can be necessarily or exhaustively named. *"What music can actually reflect is only the morphology of feeling"* (*PNK* 238). Opposite forms of feeling, in fact, can have a "very similar morphology" (*PNK* 238), as in the melodic identity of drinking songs and sacred hymns. This is one of the great paradoxes of musical form.

There is consequently a temptation, which has to be fiercely resisted on Langerian terms, to see music as operating as a kind of abstract tonal algebra, with a kind of transparency attendant upon algebraic formulae. Music for Langer is no "high abstraction" (*PNK* 239). This comment for Langer has, it appears, both descriptive and a kind of admittedly problematic and controversial stipulative, normative force. Musical tone for Langer has an unmistakably *sensuous* value, its effect has a *vital* value, and it has deep *personal* import. "Its message is not an immutable abstraction, a bare, unambiguous, fixed concept, as a lesson in the higher mathematics of feeling should be. It is always new, no matter how well or how long we have known it, or it loses its meaning; it is not transparent but iridescent. Its values crowd each other, its symbols are inexhaustible" (*PNK* 239). Its inexhaustibility comes from its lack of *assigned connotation*. It has connotation, but its import is never fixed, in spite of music's power to articulate "emotive, vital, sentient experiences" (*PNK* 240). The power of music is due to its free forms that follow "inherent psychological laws of rightness" and—in a comment of deep and systematic importance that acknowledges the autonomous "sonic reality" of music—to our interest "in possible articulations suggested entirely by the musical material" (*PNK* 240). Just as language "grows in meaning by a process of articulation, not in articulate forms by a process of preconceived expression" (*PNK* 240), so music, too, has articulation as its innermost life. Its telos is not assertion or expression of a preconceived musical meaning; its telos is articulation and *expressiveness*, not "expression." The significance of a music symbolic form is implicit, not conventionally fixed (*PNK* 241). Indeed, Langer goes on to call music an "unconsummated symbol" (*PNK* 240). The notion of an unconsummated symbol, that is, a symbol without a fixed, conventional significance, accounts for the ambiguity of program music. Nothing prevents us, she argues, from assigning specific moods or spheres to program music, but such procedures do not touch the real essence of music, "which is unconventionalized, unverbalized freedom of thought" (*PNK* 243). The real power of music, and its distinction from language's power, is its ability to be "true" to the life of feeling, even at the highest levels of abstraction, in a very different way. Langer thinks that in contrast to language, music has an intrinsic "*ambivalence* of content" (*PNK* 243). Indeed, music does not just have a content, it has "a transient play of contents. It can articulate feelings without becoming wedded to them" (*PNK* 244).

Langer's discussion of music is extraordinarily rich and dense. The use of such terms as "sweet," or "rich," or "strident," something we are all familiar with, is rooted in a kind of physically mediated response to (not uniquely caused by) the physical character of a tone, transposed into metaphor. Key changes can carry a new *Weltgefühl* with them. There is a kaleidoscopic play of meanings, "probably below the threshold of consciousness, certainly outside the pale of discursive thinking" (*PNK* 244).

> The imagination that responds to music is personal and associative and logical, tinged with affect, tinged with bodily rhythm, tinged with dream, but *concerned* with a wealth of formulations for its wealth of wordless knowledge, its whole knowledge of emotional and organic experience, of vital impulse, balance, conflict, the *ways* of living and dying and feeling. Because no assignment of meaning is conventional, none is permanent beyond the sound that passes; yet the brief association was a flash of understanding. (*PNK* 244)

The task of music is to "*make things conceivable* rather than store up propositions" (*PNK* 244). Music brings us the gift of insight, "a knowledge of 'how feelings go'" (*PNK* 244). This is a powerful and challenging notion—and one that Langer will never relinquish but will extend to all the art genres in their different ways of meaning-making.

It is imperative, however, Langer warns, not to confuse the characteristics of the music with the emotions that they resemble. The auditory characters of music "merely *sound* the way moods *feel*" (Pratt 1931: 203, cited *PNK* 245). But symbol and feeling, while connected, are bound together not by a straight-forward natural resemblance that would at the limit confuse the symbol with the thing symbolized. As long as music is thought of, and experienced, as an implicit, not explicit, symbolism, the danger is there. "For until symbolic forms are consciously abstracted, they are regularly confused with the things they symbolize" (*PNK* 245), a "magical" point of view. This is the mark of "mythical consciousness," which operates with bound forms, where meaning is fundamentally implicit, not explicit, unthematized, not thematized. Strangely enough, indeed paradoxically, Langer calls music "our myth of the inner life" (*PNK* 245), which has not moved out of its "vegetative stage." This is a rather weird position, considering the deep and weighty importance that music plays in Langer's thought, and the actual history of music seems to contravene such a position. It is hard to think of the classical line through Haydn, Mozart, and Beethoven as a vegetative stage or of the supreme achievement of J. S. Bach as being in such a position. Perhaps the statement is not meant to be negative—it is hard to imagine that it is—but rather to situate music as a non-discursive presentational form that articulates by showing and not by saying and in this way plumbing the depths of our inner life as a kind of secular life-symbol to which we are deeply attached.

In chapter 9 of *Philosophy in a New Key* Langer deals more generally with the "genesis of artistic import." This issue is a constant theme in her later work. The problem here, as it was earlier, is just how "significance" is related to "import," and further with the relation of this significance and import to external, even extraneous, models and themes, which function both as motivations and as objects. At its point of origin music was not endowed with the capacity to use already abstracted tonal qualities and forms. Music appears to have been rooted in a pre-musical period where work and ritual were subjected to the discipline of rhythm, a category that plays a central role in the work of John Dewey (see the index to Dewey's *Art as Experience* and especially the chapter on the "organization of energies"). These tonal forms were, in Langer's view, not music but proto-musical elements, which get transformed. During the course of a day's work many sounds become fixed forms, and they can become music because they are "intrinsically expressive" (*PNK* 248). "They have not only associative value, but value as rhythms and intervals, exhibiting stress and release, progression, rise and fall, motion, limit, rest. It is in this musical capacity that they enter into art, not in their original capacity of signs, self-expressions, religious symbols, or parrot-like imitation of sounds" (*PNK* 248). We have to avoid both the genetic fallacy of reducing music to its origins or elevating "primitive emotional sounds, like bird-songs or the sing-song speech of sentimental persons, to the dignity of music. They are musical materials, but their unconscious use is not art" (*PNK* 249).

The movement from practical demands to conventional development of forms is not at the beginning artistic in any thematic way. But not just musical forms, but architectural, ceramic, and pictorial forms also arise "casually" (*PNK* 249). Consequently, the finding of musical models and prototypes in the rhythmically structured sound and work environment is matched by the plastic arts' finding natural models everywhere. The focus on natural models has both a benefit and a danger: it enables us, when molding clay or marking a figure in the sand with a finger, "to achieve organic unity in a design by making it *represent* something" (*PNK* 249). We see an object or figure "in" the constructed form. This is a productive instance of "seeing-in." The ability to see geometric forms is an achievement, not something given in normal perceptual circumstances, where it is the simple forms, if any, that come first to view. To see a geometric form as worthy of attention in itself, as a sensible *Gestalt*, requires "purely intellectual and original organization" (*PNK* 249). Natural objects, however, "carry a certain guarantee of unity and permanence, which lets us apprehend their forms, though these forms would be much too difficult to grasp as mere visual patterns without extraneous meaning" (*PNK* 249). Significant form is, then, at an early stage, wedded to natural models also in the realm of the plastic arts. "The profusion of natural models undoubtedly is responsible for the early development of plastic art" (*PNK* 249).

The danger in such a facilitation of the discovery of artistic form, however, is that the visual arts can very easily become "*model-bound*" (*PNK* 249). The visual arts, Langer claims, are not there to duplicate the world but to furnish an "abstractive vision" (*PNK* 250), a foregrounding of "pictorial interest" rather than in-

terest in an object as merely given. Langer admits the great temptation is toward
naïve representationalism and a concern for accuracy of representation, with a
value judgment about the worthiness of an object to be represented, and with a
judgment about whether the constructed work gives pleasure or displeasure. Accuracy, worthiness of the object or "subject," pleasure and displeasure, are, as
Langer says, "based on standards which have nothing to do with art" (*PNK* 250).
It is not its theme, nor its accuracy, nor the pleasurable fantasies evoked by it that
determine the significance of an artwork. The articulation of visual *forms* is the
root of significance, making up a visual "melody."

> We see significance *in* things long before we know what we are seeing, and it takes
> some other interest, practical or emotional or superstitious, to make us produce an
> object which turns out to have expressive virtue as well. We cannot conceive sig-
> nificant form *ex nihilo*; we can only *find* it, and create something in its image; but
> because a man has seen the "significant form" of the thing he copies, he will copy
> it with that emphasis, not by measure, but by the selective, interpretative power of
> his intelligent eye. (*PNK* 251)

This progression moves beyond any utilitarian focus; we move into a new state
when we can see "the 'dynamic' laws of life, power, and rhythm" in forms upon
which we are focused. The artist in us, the artist, quite paradigmatically, sees
things that cannot be named, "magical imports, rightness of line and mass," and
the artist's hands "unwittingly express and even overdraw what he sees, and the
product amazes and delights him and looks 'beautiful'" (*PNK* 252). Note here that
Langer puts "beautiful" in scare quotes—that is, beauty is assimilated to rightness, fitness.

It is clear, then, that in spite of the focus of "pictorial interest" as involving
symbolic transformation, not copying, of experience, the visual arts nevertheless have many natural models. But this is not the case with music. Referring
to a set of classical positions in the philosophical tradition, namely the Platonic
and the Aristotelian, with their differently valorized, but focally related, concerns with "copies" and "imitations," Langer clearly sees that pictures' reliance
on visual models, drama's dependence on prototypical action forms, and poetry's dependence on "story" or, I think, a "narrative" logic, have no direct parallels in music. Music has to rely upon "the indirect support of two non-musical
aids—*rhythm*, and *words*" (*PNK* 253). As to rhythms, they are "more fixed and
stable, more definite than intonations" (*PNK* 253). Rhythms can be exemplified
or embodied in multiple carriers, since it is "the same metric pattern, a general
dynamic form, that may be sung, danced, clapped, or drummed" (*PNK* 254). Because of this, rhythms offer us "the first logical frame, the skeletal structure of

the embryonic art of music" (*PNK* 254). As to words, they furnish the "most obvious tonal material," rooted as they are in the human voice. And indeed in *Feeling and Form* Langer will present an argument for the intrinsically *musical,* not poetic, character of song and vocal music. "The adjustment of speech-impulses to
the demands of rhythmic tonal figure is the natural source of all chanting, the beginning of vocal music" (*PNK* 254). There is a movement in music from "random
verbiage first dictated by rhythmic figures and tonal demands" to poetic sense.
The *poetic line* becomes the *choral verse* (*PNK* 254–255). Thus, "patterns of pitch follow patterns of word-emphasis, and melodic lines begin and end with propositional lines" (*PNK* 255). Dance and song then are considered by Langer to be the
two parents of music, a position she bases on a wide range of sources, copiously
cited in her rich and illuminating footnotes. These topics are insightfully taken
up and developed in *Feeling and Form.*

How does music separate itself as an independent symbolic form from these
two parents? What is the first independent *"musical* product" (*PNK* 255)? Langer
thinks that it is the "air," since such a musical form allows "any words in the
proper metrical pattern" to be sung to them (*PNK* 255). In this way music can free
itself both from word and from dance, from what she calls its poetic or terpsicho-
rean scaffolding. It becomes a tonal dynamic form, "an expressive medium with a
law and life of its own" (*PNK* 256), detached from its sources and roots in the real
world. It is the detachment from a strict representational temptation that makes
music distinctive. Comparing music and pictorial forms in terms of their abstractive nature, Langer says that "we can take the music and forget the dance far more
easily than we can take a painting and forget what it portrays" (*PNK* 256). It is
the freedom from object models that distinguishes music from painting. The *artistic* import of music is "easier to grasp" than that of "the older and more model-
bound arts" (*PNK* 257). Hence its paradigmatic importance for Langer's theory of
art as a whole.

What, then, are painters, sculptors, and poets trying to express *"through* their
depiction of objects and events" (*PNK* 257)? It is their *artistic import.* Plastic arts
are defined by a semantic determined by "the play of lines, masses, colors, textures," while the poetic arts pursue a semantic defined by "the play of images,
the tension and release of ideas, the speed and arrest, ring and rhyme of words"
(*PNK* 257). While avoiding premature and unnecessary dogmatism, Langer
opines that all the arts have the same import: "the verbally ineffable, yet not in-
expressible law of vital experience, the pattern of affective and sentient being"
(*PNK* 257). Such a pattern is conceived as something formal, though not "merely"
formal. It is a real content of the artwork, which is identical to a beautiful form,
though "beauty" plays scarcely a role in Langer's reflections, as we have been see-

ing. It takes, it is clear, a special effort to abstract *to* the artistic import of a non-musical work, but this effort on our part does not entail that music, in itself, is any higher on some scale than the other arts, in spite of Walter Pater's dictum in his *The Renaissance* that "All art aspires to the condition of music" (1908: 140, cited *PNK* 257).

In *Philosophy in a New Key* Langer hesitates to say flat-out that the subject matter or focal concern of all the arts is the same. She thinks the problem-space opened up by such a question cannot be answered within the analytical framework developed there. Different artistic mediums may be more appropriate for the expression of many special regions. "The medium in which we naturally conceive our ideas may restrict them not only to certain forms but to certain fields, howbeit they all lie within the verbally inaccessible field of vital experience and qualitative thought" (*PNK* 258). The erotic emotions, as Langer puts it, may be more suited to musical expression, while "our physical orientation in the world—our intuitive awareness of mass and motion, restraint and autonomy, and all characteristic feeling that goes with it—is the preeminent subject-matter of the dance, or of sculpture, rather than (say) poetry" (*PNK* 258). This hint will be explored and developed and made one of the central themes of *Feeling and Form*, which we will explore in the following two chapters.

Langer raises and rejects the possibility that the unity of the arts might be found, if not on the object side, on the side of the "aesthetic emotion," which would be common to all the arts and, on both the productive and receptive sides, would consist in the "comprehension of an unspoken idea" (*PNK* 259). But Langer does not accept any identification of "aesthetic emotion" with "emotional content" of an artwork. The source of aesthetic emotion derives from, or emerges out of and alongside of, an intellectual triumph. The barriers of word-bound thought are breached, and we achieve "insight into literally 'unspeakable' realities" (*PNK* 260). The emotive content goes beyond the intellectual level, it is deeper, "more essential, pre-rational, and vital, something of the life-rhythms we share with all growing, hungering, moving and fearing creatures: the ultimate realities themselves, the central facts of our brief, sentient existence" (*PNK* 260). Aesthetic pleasure, Langer thinks, does not stand apart in absolute distinction from the discovering of truth, but for her "truth is so intimately connected to symbolism that if we recognize two radically different types of symbolic expression we should logically look for two distinct meanings of truth" (*PNK* 260), a theme discussed with great acuity by John Gilmour (1986) in his *Picturing the World*. Both these symbolic modes are rational, and Langer rejects the dichotomy between objective truth and subjective truth just as strongly as she rejects the idea that the distinction between discursive and presentational symbols corresponds to the difference between literal and artistic meanings (*PNK* 260). Many only apparently presentational symbols—graphs, charts, maps—stand proxy for descriptions, indeed, could even be considered abbreviated descriptions. They certainly have expressive and logical power, but their content could be verbalized or put into discursive form, even if exceedingly clumsily. That is, their content is essentially translatable. But the symbols that make up art are, on Langer's reckoning, untranslatable. "Their sense is bound to the particular form which it has taken" (*PNK* 260), a sense which is always at its core implicit, having a surplus that remains after all discursive attempts to make it explicit have been exhausted. The verbal material of poetry, for example, and its literal import do not define it as an assertion. It is the mode, the way the assertion is made, that makes poetry an artistic form, including the "unifying, all-embracing artifice of rhythm" (*PNK* 261). Following up her musical analogy, Langer thinks of poetry's literal sense as a kind of "harmonic structure," while word-melody, which plays a distinctive role in literature, especially poetic literature, "is more akin to tone-color in music" (*PNK* 261). We will examine literature in more detail in a later chapter.

Developing further her fundamental idea that we cannot decompose a presentational form into independent signifying units according to the model of language, Langer thinks that the *import* of a drama, a painting, or a poem is a holistic feature of their semiotic architecture. Even if the material of poetry is discursive, "the product—the artistic phenomenon—is not" (*PNK* 261). In the case of a poem, the significance, such as it is, resides in the poem as a semiotic totality. Sound and suggestion, statement and reticence, as Langer says, can never be supplanted by a translation.

Following up the implications and significance of the great distinction between discursive and presentational forms, Langer goes further and asserts that in addition to these types of meanings there is another kind of meaning of an artwork: "its form as such, as sensory phenomenon, has what I have called 'implicit' meaning, like rite or myth, but of a more catholic sort" (*PNK* 262). Langer uses Reid's notion of "tertiary subject-matter," something that is beyond Coleridge's primary and secondary imagination. In the words of Reid, which Langer clearly accepts, "Tertiary subject-matter is subject-matter imaginatively experienced *in* the work of art . . . , something which cannot be apprehended apart from the work, though theoretically distinguishable from its expressiveness" (Reid 1929: 132, cited *PNK* 262; reprinted in Langer's *RA* 37–61).

It is at this point that Langer brings up the issue of "artistic truth." This is, as she puts it, "the truth of a symbol to the forms of feeling—nameless forms, but recognizable when they appear in sensuous replica" (*PNK* 262). This kind of truth is not propositional truth. Falsity does not belong to the sphere of negation, as it does in propositional contexts. Rather, falsity refers to a "complicated failing," to inexpressiveness, to an inadequateness to the "ideas they embody" (*PNK* 262). The severe consequences attendant upon error in the factual domain are not present in the artistic domain. "Art, on the other hand, has no consequences; it gives form to something that is simply there, as the intuitive organizing functions of sense give form to objects and spaces, colors and sound" (*PNK* 263). Langer, using a familiar expression, thinks that art gives us "'knowledge by acquaintance' of affective experience" (*PNK* 263). This is something below the level of belief. It belongs on the "deeper level of insight and attitude" (*PNK* 263). It avails itself of more or less adequate images, which Langer, as we have seen, considers "the primitive symbols of 'things'" (*PNK* 263). Here we see a real continuity between her analysis of the logic of presentational forms and their rootedness in the imaginative transformations of perception and art. The artistic image contains an "idea," the understanding of which is "more like *having a new experience* than like entertaining a proposition" (*PNK* 263). Langer further holds that the work—and its understanding, too—may be adequate "*to some degree*" (*PNK* 263). Although the artistic work has no literal truth, and so lacks this measure with its absoluteness, its artistic truth is really its significance, expressiveness, articulateness, which have degrees. Rather than being literally true or false, artworks are good or bad, and "each must be judged on our experience of its revelations" (*PNK* 263). But there is no "immutable law of artistic adequacy, because significance is always *for* a mind as well as *of* a form" (*PNK* 263). The perception of form, of a Gestalt, goes before the grasp of implicit meaning, and is itself dependent upon a certain familiarity, upon a trained and ready mind. Unfamiliarity of form leads to incomprehension. Creative artists, therefore, who are very often form-breakers, frequently are not accepted because their audiences do not have the proper mental versatility. This versatility is the *conditio sine qua non,* even if not fully sufficient, for grasping novel currents and creations in the artistic realm. The experienced mind can perhaps read the signs of novelty even if it is not quite adequate to confidently grasping or validating them. Aesthetic perception and judgment, then, are essentially open, without a greatest upper bound. This is one of Langer's most important lessons.

Langer also thinks that the artistic forms that are given to us are also "inexhaustible" (*PNK* 264). By this she means that we can, after we have exhausted the resources of a particular form or style, still produce another novel work. Indeed, "beauty," appropriately conceived, can be seen by "very catholic minds" in many different styles, a phenomenon perhaps easiest in music, with its freedom from literal references. For, as Langer puts it, "the worst enemy of artistic judgment is literal judgment" (*PNK* 264). The temptation in artistic perception is haste, premature judgment, rooted in hastiness of attention. Artistic, mythical, or sacred import are missed because of a *blindedness* rooted in the "glaring evidence of familiar things" (*PNK* 265). Langer comes close in such a comment to the fundamental idea that the function of art is a defamiliarization of the ordinary, a "making strange," that was foregrounded by the Russian and Prague School of aesthetics. It is the singular function and power of presentational forms to break the bounds of language's claim to be the "last limits of experience" (*PNK* 265). Langer remains always true to her central insight that "things inaccessible to language may have their own forms of conception, that is to say, their own symbolic devices" (*PNK* 265). Music's significance is undergirded by such symbolic devices, which are "charged with logical possibilities of meaning" (*PNK* 265). The recognition of such logical possibilities leads philosophical reflection "to the point of including not only the semantics of science, but a serious philosophy of art" (*PNK* 265) in its domain. This is a sign of the "catholicity" of Langer's philosophical vision.

It is this serious philosophy that Langer, building upon the insights of *Philosophy in a New Key,* will develop, with nuance, detail, and conceptual vigor, in what is perhaps her most substantial and lasting work, *Feeling and Form.* This work, of startling consistency and provocative scope, will be the focus of our discussion in the next two chapters.

4

Framing the Art Symbol

Forms of Feeling

What makes the object artistic . . . is where
philosophical art theory begins.

—(*FF* 34)

The *art symbol* constitutes the central, indeed culminating, focus of Langer's intellectual journey, although it is by no means her last major concern, which
is a comprehensive account of the "symbolic mind" embedded in the matrices
of "feeling." Like Rome, all paths lead to it and, perhaps, equally like Rome, if
we think of the eternal city as a model, all paths lead from it. Langer's general
philosophico-semiotic project, first limned in *The Practice of Philosophy*, while ostensibly concerned with the justification of a particular way of "doing" philosophy and hence with a schematization or characterization of its appropriate subject matter—*meaning-making and the systems of signs and symbols that make it
possible*—circled around aesthetic issues at practically every point. *Philosophy in a
New Key*, as we have seen, culminates in an attempt to generalize and extend the
lessons of the problem of "significance" in music, all the while placing art, as a
distinctive type of symbolic structure, in relation to ritual, sacrament, and myth
as symbolic forms that exceed the powers of discursive reason. But it is in *Feeling
and Form* that Langer gives a comprehensive account not just of the art symbol
in general but of its multifarious exemplifications in all the major art genres. All
the previously introduced key concepts are present, recapitulated, reconstructed,
and definitively configured in what many consider Langer's most lasting contribution to philosophy. At the same time, however, in the final work of Langer's
high maturity, the trilogy *Mind*, Langer puts the artwork, as a symbolic construct,

at the very center, not for its own sake but for its heuristic power to illuminate the fundamental features of the mind itself, focusing on the key phenomenon of artistic abstraction as the root power of the mind. We will see how the conclusion of Langer's *Feeling and Form* will leave open this "turn to abstraction" and its indispensability for enabling us to understand not just the phenomenon of art but also the phenomenon of mind itself.

The extensiveness of Langer's discussion of the art symbol makes a full or even an adequate analysis of it a daunting task. I will, accordingly, pursue a highly selective double-edged approach, corresponding, in fact, to Langer's own procedures, but not following Langer's own order in any strict sense. First, I will in the present chapter sketch three pivotal and interlinked theoretical concepts of Langer's aesthetic *theory:* (1) the symbol of feeling, (2) semblance, (3) the interlinking of expressiveness and interpretation. Langer thought of *Philosophy in a New Key* as a necessary prelude to *Feeling and Form,* so there is a certain amount of repetition involved in a discussion of the theoretical parts of this work. But the reformulations also expand the inner space of these concepts, and new dimensions, aspects, and contexts of their use become apparent. Second, in the following chapter, I will discuss how Langer schematizes various primary and distinctive "illusions" that each art form or genre creates, focusing selectively on the highlights of her analysis of (a) painting, sculpture, and architecture, (b) dance, and (c) literature, with only side glances at music, which we have examined in the last chapter. Our guiding question will always be, What is still living and what is dead in Langer's aesthetics? We will see that the answer to the first part of the question is, "a lot," and to the second part of the question, "not very much."

Aesthetic Theory and the Fundamental Features of the Art Symbol

Philosophy for Langer, she repeats once again, "deals primarily with meanings" (*FF* 3), exactly the thesis that informs *The Practice of Philosophy.* It is a "stocktaking of the ideas in terms of which one expresses facts and laws, beliefs and maxims and hypotheses" (*FF* 3). In its most general aspect and role philosophy deals with the "conceptual framework in which all our propositions, true or false, are made" (*FF* 3), including, clearly, the conceptual framework of an aesthetic theory. Langer laments, whether justifiably or not is not the issue, the nonexistence of an integrated or systematic theory of art that transcends the realm of "common sense." In place of common sense there is to be formulated an ordered set of key problems and the development of a "powerful terminology and principle of operation" (*FF* 4). To be avoided at all costs is the "fallacy of obvious abstraction" (*FF* 5). Langer conceives of philosophy as essentially "constructive," engaged in a "constant process of generalization" and in need of "logical technique, imagination, and ingenuity" (*FF* 5). But hasty generalization is to play no role here, for philosophy itself dictates the approach to art's problems, provided the philosophical framework is sufficiently comprehensive.

Philosophy's task with respect to art, Langer says, is the same as its task with respect to all other subject matters. Philosophy deals with, indeed constructs, interpretations. It is not concerned to discover new facts, which is an empirical matter. The function of these interpretations is "to increase not our knowledge of nature, but our understanding of what we know" (*FF* 6). In the case of art theory, systematic conception is what "makes some facts important and others trivial" (*FF* 6). As Langer sees it, art criticism—that is, for her, art *theory* in its philosophical form—does not rely on mere description or prediction. Indeed, "its whole aim is understanding" (*FF* 9), and in pursuit of this Langer proposes to pursue doggedly a single problem to its solution and perhaps in this way to "elicit a new logical vocabulary" with respect to art.

The problem that Langer foregrounds is the problem of *artistic creation*. Langer's guiding question is, What does the artist create? She will answer, "an expressive symbol" that is grasped in an act of "intuition," a notion that is to have a "single and unmysterious meaning" (*FF* 10). This, we have seen, is hardly the case. In order to deal directly with such issues, Langer proposes to take the point of view of the studio (*FF* 14) and in this way to avoid what she thinks is the "inveterate tendency to paradox" of current art theory, which results from false parallels, improper analogies, and hasty generalizations. The great polarity of feeling and form, the subjective and the objective, the Dionysian and the Apollonian, is itself a problem, she thinks, if we oppose them to one another. But the main issue that runs throughout Langer's whole art theory is that of a *feeling that is not subjective*. In her opinion, the great classic tangle of impression and expression, form and feeling, significance and sensation, if it is not sorted out, will impale art theory on the horns of a fatal dilemma. Langer asks, and attempts to answer the question, How can a "feeling" be "objective" and not "subjective"? How can we understand such a paradoxical notion?

Langer thinks that the "semiotic turn" or the "symbolic turn" is crucial for resolving the paradoxes of art and art theory. The principal tool is what she calls "the most powerful generative idea in humanistic thinking today" (*FF* 22), something that is not foreign to aesthetic theory, but "has never been used in its highest capacity and to its true purposes" (*FF* 22). This is the notion of "symbolic agency" (*FF* 22) that results in the artistic symbol. The symbol, qua artistic, "negotiates insight, not reference; it does not rest upon convention, but motivates and dictates conventions" (*FF* 22). It will be the peculiar cognitive, though not discursively conceptual, power of the art symbol to "acquaint the beholder with something he has not known before" (22). The art symbol, consequently, has a deep *heuristic* function and value, mediating insight. It is a semiotic tool of discovery. Applied to art, the notion of symbolic agency "is deeper than any semantic of accepted signs and their referents, more essential than any schema that may be heuristically read" (*FF* 22), that is, that functions as a mere transparent "pointer" or abstract model with no intrinsic interest or value of its own. The central question that Langer wants to face with all the conceptual apparatus attendant upon the focal notion of the symbol is, What is the type of "significance" in art that an artistic symbol has? The answer to such a question, elements of which we encountered already in *Philosophy in a New Key,* will involve finding a solution to the pressing problem of the possibility of "objective feelings, non-sensuous qualities invisibly seen" (*FF* 23) that Langer, relying on Otto Baensch, saw as lying at the heart of the key aesthetic paradox of the seemingly impossible fusion or inextricable intertwining of *subjective feeling* and *objective form.*

Langer reaffirms at almost every stage the continuity between *Philosophy in a New Key* and *Feeling and Form.* The original grounding of her reflections in the theory of music was meant to lead by a process of generalization to a putative unity of the arts. Such a unity was to be found not in external and facile parallels and analogies but in "the singleness of their characteristic import, the meaning of 'significance' with respect to any and each of them" (*FF* 24). The central thesis she will resolutely defend is that artistic significance is rooted in the expression of the *Idea* (*FF* 26), the semiotic core of the artwork.

Nevertheless, in *Feeling and Form* Langer still has not fully settled, by reference to other nomenclatures, the terminological issue of sign, signal, symbol. She still refers to Charles Morris's now discarded terminological schemata, but her main points, as we will see, are clear if we keep our eyes focused on substantive issues. These issues arise from her resolute adherence to the general notion of a *symbol,* in her use of that term, which, one cannot insist enough, is a distinctively cognitive tool. In the cases we will now be examining its aesthetic relevance and analytical power will be exploited to the full.

Langer's main thesis, and argument, then, which she promotes and pursues unceasingly, is that an artwork, in any genre, is essentially a "symbol of feeling." That is, it *means* a feeling, or makes a feeling known, articulates it in an objective form, or meaning-bearing matter. This is clearly a variation on and specification of, in the domain of art, the notion of a presentational symbol. Langer's use of the notion of a symbol, we have already noted and must keep always in mind, is not that of Saussure, which involves motivation, nor that of Peirce, which involves pure conventions, nor of the "symbolic" tradition, which looks for "higher," "deeper," "hidden," or "oblique" meanings. A "symbol" for her, as she puts it, following Whitehead, is any device by means of which we can make an abstraction (*FF* xi). For Langer a symbol mediates knowledge, giving us cognitive control, or insight, in one way or another. An aesthetic symbol, on Langer's conception, is an abstraction device that is meant to give us non-discursive "knowledge" of "feeling." Feeling, in Langer's use of the term, is clearly bipolar: it refers both to *anything that can be felt* and to *any way* anything can be felt, in the most general sense of that term. The aesthetic symbol is able to do this because it expresses, makes perceptible, in a constructed "semblance," the "morphology" of feeling, that is, it shares a "logical form" with what we have seen Langer call its "import," not its "meaning," in the traditional sense of that term. This sharing of a "logical form" is clearly one of the hard-core notions that Langer will attempt to, indeed have to, clarify and validate. The logical form is intrinsically connected to its "expressiveness." Langer repeats central theses already present in *Philosophy in a New Key:* the role and function of the aesthetic symbol is to "represent" the world not in the discursive mode but rather in the non-discursive, or presentational, mode. The non-discursive nature of the artwork gives it both a content, an import, and a certain ineffability, if that is meant to say that its import or content cannot be separated from its form. The artwork by itself does not "say" or "assert" anything and hence cannot be "true" or "false" by reason of its being measured by something outside of itself. As we have seen, the artwork exhibits or shows what it is about, but it is not subject to the laws of discourse even if it is constructed in the medium of discourse, that is, language, as the strictly "poetic" arts are. A literary work, for example, although it is made out of language as its materials, is not bound to a discursive logic. This fact makes the "interpretation" of a literary work run parallel to the interpretation of all other types of artworks, with specific differences, to be sure, as we will see in due course.

Langer's analysis of the different art genres exemplifies and clarifies the pivotal concepts of her aesthetic theory in a challenging and perspicuous way. Langer offers a kind of *propaedeutic* to and outline of a semiotic or symbolic theory of art as well as a set of concrete *illustrations* of its range and power. In *Feeling and Form* Langer attempted to develop a full philosophical position that covers all the arts and that is able to uncover what is particular, peculiar, to each major art genre, a topic we will engage in the following chapter. Consequently, her account of the distinctiveness of the various art forms operates on two intertwined levels: (1) the general aesthetic level, which is thematized "semiotically" or in terms of Langer's model of symbolization and (2) the level of distinctive art genres, where she frequently avails herself of "non-semiotic" or "non-symbolic" categories. Langer's aesthetic theory is "catholic" in its openness to insights from many different sources, even if the insights have undergone transformation.

With an eye on these two levels I will now focus schematically in this chapter on three pivotal and interlocked issues that will give a taste of Langer's distinctive, powerful, and at times contentious approach: (1) artworks as symbols of feeling, (2) artworks as constructed semblances, and (3) the expressive import of an artwork and the task of interpretation.

The Artwork as a Symbol of Feeling

Langer's permanent and fundamental position that all artworks are non-discursive or presentational symbols entails that as a constructed expression an artwork is not reducible to any subjective state of the creator of the expression nor to a "statement." Symbolic expression for Langer is the "articulation and presentation of *concepts*" (*FF* 26), although we cannot assimilate "concepts" to the discursive realm *tout court*. This is a point that must constantly be kept in mind. It is not, we have seen, a "signal" to elicit behavior nor a "mere" indexical sign that draws our attention to something, but has no interest of its own. There is an essential semiotic gap between an expression's making us notice something and an expression's enabling us to conceive an "idea." As Langer puts it, "a symbol is understood when we conceive the idea it presents" (*FF* 26). This applies also to a presentational symbol—and, *a fortiori*, to works of art.

The generative point of Langer's systematic reflections, we have seen, is her position on music. Music is, she claims, "a tonal analogue of emotive life." It remained an essential thesis for Langer that tonal structures bear "a close logical similarity to the forms of human feeling" (*FF* 27). "Logical similarity" and "feeling" are brought into conjunction. Langer uses "sentience" and "feeling" as comprehensive terms: they cover the total range of "movements" and "states" that mark human subjectivity and its organic embodiment. The forms of sentience, as Langer persistently notes, have distinctive patterns or logical forms (*FF* 27), which the artist has knowledge of or discovers, intentionally or even accidentally. Such patterns can be symbolically embodied—"iconically" embodied—when the artist can construct symbolic artifacts that share with their "object" "some common logical form" (*FF* 27). The closeness to Peirce's and Dewey's analysis of quality is patent here, as it is throughout the whole discussion (see Innis 1999). There is, Langer claims, a "formal analogy, or congruence of logical structures," some formal likeness between the symbolic artifact and the form of sentience it expresses. In general terms, Langer held the position, which transcends the discursive/non-discursive disjunction, that a "fairly adequate symbolism" is a condition for being able to think about something (*FF* 28). Art gives us symbolic structures that allow us think about what cannot be said, but only exhibited. This Wittgensteinian thesis, which also stands in close proximity to Peirce's position, is a permanent dimension of Langer's conceptual framework.

A symbol, as Langer is using the term throughout her work, can then be any "articulate form," whose "internal structure is given to our perception" (31), and this internal structure, with its reticulation of elements, carries the import of the articulate form. Not only, once again, is "music not a kind of language" (*FF* 29), but no work of art, no matter what the medium, is a kind of language. Langer repeatedly affirms that works of art lack "conventional reference" because they have no "conventional meaning." Langer is not using the notion of conventional reference that would obviously apply to iconographical conventions, the functioning of which she fully admits and validates throughout her various discussions. Musical "meaning" is really musical "import," and "this import is the pattern of sentience—the pattern of life itself, as it is felt and directly known" (*FF* 31) first by the artist and then by the interpreters. Works of art have significance, which can be complex indeed, but this significance is really a "vital import" (32), which corresponds, I have indicated, to C. S. Peirce's notion of an affective or emotional interpretant and to John Dewey's "felt quality," which is the core of his aesthetics that he developed extensively in his *Art as Experience.* Langer in *Feeling and Form* vigorously generalizes this notion, originally developed to account for music, to all the other art forms. "Vital" here involves "restricting the relevance of 'import' to the dynamism of subjective experience" (*FF* 32). The articulate but non-discursive form is no "symbol in the ordinary sense" (*FF* 32), with a Peircean logical interpretant or a mysterious "deeper" or "higher" meaning, ways of speaking that Langer does not use. It is, as Langer puts it in a pregnant statement, a "significant form . . . in which the factor of significance is not logically discriminated, but is felt as a quality rather than recognized as a function" (*FF* 32). This quality is the "reason" for our immediate recognition of "significant form" and is "the heart of the aesthetical problem" (*FF* 33). *Aesthetic quality,* which is not an evaluative notion, and *significant form* belong together.

This "quality" belongs to the artwork as a whole, permeating its elements or parts and holding them together in a unity. It is the felt presence of this quality that elicits the so-called aesthetic attitude, not the aesthetic attitude that establishes the quality—even if in the case of the aesthetics of nature we can take up such an attitude, which is itself informed by our encounters with works of art. Hans-Georg Gadamer, following Hegel, has made much of this, as has Nelson Goodman. The aesthetic attitude, Langer claims, is too closely connected with empiricism, psychologism, and "pragmatism," and hence infected with an in-eradicable subjectivism. The right approach, in Langer's conception, is "to look upon the art object as something in its own right, with properties independent of our prepared reactions, and make art the autonomous essential factor that it is in every human culture" (*FF* 39). At any rate, the artist, who is a "creator" of a form, has a skill as well as a knowledge of the dynamics of consciousness. It is this "affinity" between perception and form that Langer wants to foreground. Non-discursive symbols "articulate" by "exhibiting," and in this constructive ac-tivity on the part of artists we encounter radical novelty, each work of art having its own distinctive "feel." This deep Peircean position was also extensively de-veloped by Dewey, although Langer has only rather negative things to say about Dewey and pragmatism, and Peirce appears only obliquely in her discussions. (I am thinking of Dewey's two seminal essays, "Qualitative Thought" (1931b) and "Affective Thought" (1931a), and his indispensable *Art as Experience*.) In fact, Langer's position intersects with and complements Dewey's on many levels and in positive ways.

Speaking of the spirit of the work of art and claiming that "there is no name to be given to it," Dewey arrives at an insight that confirms Langer's deepest con-victions. About this "spirit" Dewey writes:

> It is the idiom in which the particular work is composed and expressed, that which stamps it with individuality. It is the background that is more than spatial because it enters into and qualifies everything in the focus, everything distinguished as part and member. . . . Things, objects, are only focal points of a here and now in a whole that stretches out indefinitely. This is the qualitative "background" which is de-fined and made definitely conscious in particular objects and specified properties and qualities. (Dewey 1934: 197)

Thus, in the case of an artwork, Dewey remarks that "the undefined pervasive quality of an experience is that which binds together all the defined elements, the objects of which we are focally aware, making them a whole" (1934: 198). Indeed, "the different elements and specific qualities of a work of art blend and fuse in a way which physical objects cannot emulate. This fusion is the felt pres-ence of the same qualitative unity in all of them" (196). This pervasive quality is apprehended right in the initial phases of our encounter with an artwork. Dewey writes:

> Even at the outset, the total and massive quality has its uniqueness; even when vague and undefined, it is just that which is and not something else. If the percep-tion continues, discrimination inevitably sets in. Attention must move, and, as it

moves, parts, members, emerge from the background. And if attention moves in a unified direction instead of wandering, it is controlled by the pervading unity; attention is controlled *by* it because it operates within it. (1934: 196)

Still, an artwork, on Langer's conception, does not involve a mere rearrangement of "given things,—even qualitative things" (*FF* 40). It is an achievement of the imagination, which Langer calls man's "utmost conceptual power" (*FF* 40). It is the artist's great ability to envisage *what it feels like to feel the world* and to construct a *symbolic image* that articulates and carries, that is, embodies, such a feeling or complex of feelings. Langer's notion of a symbol of feeling in *Feeling and Form* is clearly a reformulation and "torquing" of her central notion of a presentational form. Symbolization, we have been seeing, is rooted in the primary activity of perception, where it is "form" or "Gestalt" that is proximately apprehended. In spite of her criticism of positions such as Dewey's that are representative of what she calls the "continuity hypothesis" that charts the deep connections between ordinary experience and aesthetic experience, both actively and passively considered, Langer also pushes the artwork *down* into the field of perception or into the field of the vivid imagination. It is, moreover, essential to understand that Langer thinks of "presentational" in the strictest sense. The symbol of feeling, a symbolic *presentation* of the forms of feeling, is not a discussion of them. It is not so much "about" these forms, in the discursive mode, as it is a symbolic analogue of them, that is, it is iconic in Peirce's sense of that term. So, the artwork is a *symbol* of feeling and a symbol of *feeling*.

The Artwork as a Semblance of Feeling

An "iconic symbol," which seems on Peircean principles to be in some totally literal respects an oxymoron, is on Langer's reckoning to be further thought of as a *semblance*. This notion, along with that of the symbol, plays a central role in Langer's aesthetic theory as a whole. It is a central notion not just in Schiller but in Dewey. The different modes of semblance give rise to different "primary illusions," which are the *basic abstractions* effected by each art genre. Langer states that the semblance is what is "created," what comes into existence as a novel meaning-configuration carried by the materially embodied art symbol. Langer, with good reason, connects semblance with the "lure of the object" rather than the taking on of the "aesthetic attitude" (*FF* 45). In becoming a semblance the work detaches itself from, or is spontaneously perceived as detaching itself from, its surroundings (*FF* 45). We do not have to "do" something to get the process started. This production of a semblance is a process of dissociation from the ordinary, a form of "othering" or of producing otherness within the continuum of experiencing and felt life. In this sense the artwork is a "sheer image" (46) marked by "strangeness, separateness, otherness" (50). These notions are already present in *Philosophy in a New Key*. These phenomenologically apprehended properties put a real, experienced, gap between the image and its model, traffic between which is not central to art. Langer rejects, we have seen, the notion of art as copying, or even, it would appear, the centrality and criticality of the idea of mimesis, if we are to think of the purpose of art as rendering a model or making a model present—with the primary focus being on the model, on the "what" that appears in the artistic image. Langer, rather, continues in *Feeling and Form* to affirm the thesis that the purpose of art is to present a *way of accessing* a model. Art, in this sense, is an "access structure," but it is not the model that determines the access structure and therefore constitutes its value and significance. While the model may indeed, and in some cases must, be represented, *representation*, in the sense of *representation of an object* or even of an event, is not central to art or applicable to all the arts. Something can be an image without representing anything through "imitation," which is not "the essential power of images" (*FF* 47).

One must ask, then, where does the true power of the image lie? In the fact that it is "an abstraction, a symbol, the bearer of an idea" (*FF* 47). Images "abstract" the significance of appearances as well as the appearances of significance. A visible image "presents itself" to vision alone, including inner vision, "as a sheer visual form instead of a locally and practically related object" (47). The visible character of an image, for instance, is its "entire being" (48), and it is abstracted "from the physical and causal order" (*FF* 47). So, Langer points out, with phenomenological preciseness, in an image everything is "imaginary" (*FF* 49), and the image arises or emerges suddenly, a living form, a new appearance (*FF* 48). Even if there is no way of avoiding recognizing what the image is "of," because of our necessary background of world-knowledge, it is the factor of "of-ness" or "what-about-ness," not "about-what-ness," that is central. In this way we are freed from the tyranny of the object or subject matter.

Langer follows Friedrich Schiller's important, or rather essential, notion that a semblance "liberates perception" and "lets the mind dwell on the sheer appearance of things" (49), extracting us from all instrumental contexts. Artworks, then, are to be thought of as completely "virtual" objects that can arrest one sense (or multiple senses) and simply *be there* for it (*FF* 49). Now the semblance of something is, as Langer perspicuously claims, "its direct aesthetic quality" (*FF* 50). Although Langer continues to studiously avoid Dewey's Peirce-inspired (and Schiller-inspired) position in an almost perverse way, she is clearly delineating what Dewey calls a "consummatory experience," which is not an instrumental experience. Amazingly she uses an expression that Dewey employs in *Art as Experience:* artworks stand out "like peaks" (*FF* 53) from the flow of normal, everyday experiencing. Their function is to make "the forms of things" present (*FF* 51) by means of a specific type of abstraction. These forms are "abstracted only to be made clearly apparent" and "to be put to new uses: to act as symbols, to become expressive of human feeling" (*FF* 51). "Significance" for Langer is identical with "logical expression" (*FF* 50). Here is a crucial twist: art symbols express not "the world," but the *feeling* of a world. Langer notes that the artistic symbol is much more intricate than any traditional "form" (*FF* 51). The distinctive "quality, or essence" (*FF* 50) that makes up the art symbol is a constitutive element of the artistic form. But what are fused in the art symbol are "formal elements in the structure, not contents" (*FF* 52). Indeed, on Langer's reckoning, once again, the content of an artistic form is its *import* (*FF* 52), not its "subject matter." Import is the type of significance that a symbolic form has, and works of art are "essentially symbolic forms" (*FF* 52) that lie in a "different dimension from physical objects as such" (*FF* 52). They are emergent entities. They have this much in common with language, where verbalization emerges from vocalization, though they have a different logical form and a different function, as myth and dream.

In *Feeling and Form* Langer reaffirms the thesis that the *content* of an artwork is also not its *theme* nor its *motif,* no matter how "evident" that may seem. This thesis lies at the heart of Langer's aesthetic theory. The peculiarity of Langer's semiotic or symbol-based approach to art is that it sets up a kind of terminological equivalence: meaning, significance, content, vital import, emotional content of the symbolic form are embodied in the feelings that are logically presented (*FF* 52), *not evoked or caused* in the interpreter. Langer, once again, could have been helped here by a Peircean account of interpretants and of iconism, although she clearly, as we will see, deals with the "proper significate effects" of art symbols on the interpreter in her own way, but in a more global fashion. At any rate, the semiotic "strangeness" of the art symbol, which is paradoxically assimilated by Langer to a kind of "transparency," that is, being freed from reference to some "other," external to it, comes precisely from its liberation from the imitative impulse, from the demand for "objective" representation as its primary task. The import of the work of art is found totally *within* the art symbol. This import is *created,* not mirrored from an antecedent completed state of the artist or of the world. The import is not created *by* the object or subject matter. It is created *in* the subject matter. Langer can argue, therefore, that the work of art is "a hundred per cent symbolic" (*FF* 59). It does not express an actual feeling, but "ideas of feeling" (59), not an actual world, but a "virtual world."

Langer contrasts in an illuminating way the distinctiveness of her aesthetic

theory with that of David Prall (1936). Prall foregrounded not the symbolic nature of art but the role of what he called the *aesthetic surface*, which is resident in or
carried by the sensuous element in the arts. Prall, as Langer reads him, was concerned with the "natural departments of sense" (*FF* 55). Prall then attempted to
analyze the basic art forms in terms of the basic units of sensuous content, assuming as a matter of course that artworks were first and foremost sensuous objects.
Langer thinks that Prall's theory was "clearly applicable only to purely visual or
purely auditory arts—painting and music" (*FF* 57). It seems to her that we should
not limit the analysis of poetry to the temporal pattern of sound or "measure" nor
discuss dance in such a way that its analysis would also apply to mobile sculptures such as those created by Alexander Calder. It is clear, she rightly thinks, that
Prall's notion of "basic orders" can be accepted as heuristically fertile, but they are
not generalizable across all the arts, which are not universally defined by "scales
and spatio-temporal orders" (*FF* 57). Certainly each type of artwork is embedded in an order distinctive to it, and in the broad sense these orders are "perceptual." But, for Langer, the notion of sensuous orders does not adequately specify
the "dimensions underlying the various arts" or the "fundamental principles of
organization" (*FF* 57). This is an important qualification.

For Langer, as opposed to Prall, the proper starting point of aesthetic theory as
a general theory of the arts is not perceptual accessibility. It is rather the "problem
of created form (which is not always sensuous) and its significance, the phenomenology of feeling" (*FF* 57). What is *created* is Langer's constant concern. For her
both the *elements* and the *wholes* (not the *materials,* which are in the last analysis
Prall's concerns) are "created, not adopted" (*FF* 57). Scales and geometries certainly, Langer notes in a pregnant comment, can be adopted, but what is created
and exemplified are "continua of existence, the spaces and durations and fields
of force" (*FF* 57n). *Spaces* play their role in the primary illusion of visual art, *durations* in the primary forms of musical art, and *fields of force* in the primary forms
of balletic art, that is, dance. Painting and the visual arts, music, and dance, indeed, make a kind of permanent, though not exclusive, focal point of Langer's
reflections, which also throw a powerful and sober light on the literary arts. For
Langer, no matter what the material embodiment of a work of art may be, the
work of art itself is not an "arrangement" of previously given sensuous elements.
It is a *created symbol,* and in this respect it transcends the physical order altogether
and is not bound to its creator the way a symptom is. Art does not express actual
feeling, but, functioning as a symbol, "ideas of feeling" (*FF* 59). It involves abstraction, plastic freedom, and expressiveness (see *FF* 59–60).

There is, nevertheless, a permanent tension in Langer's account of art due to
the role the non-representational arts, especially music and dance, play in her

theory. They have, in fact, a deep connection with what Langer calls "pure de-sign," which she discusses in mainly visual terms. What does the notion of *pure design* bring to the discussion? Basically the ideas of fitness, decorum, formaliza-tion, the ability to make a visible (or auditory) surface more visible (or auditory), the concentration and holding of vision (*FF* 61). Pure design, Langer claims, is not dependent on its "object." Indeed, it clearly does not have to have an object. Furthermore, it is removed from all instrumental contexts and concerns. While pure design is clearly rooted instinctively in the principles of perception, effecting what Barnes called a "liberation of the senses," Langer also sees it as a paradigm of expressiveness, as a "basic artistic form with an emotional import" (*FF* 62). Its task is to "impregnate and transform" perception (*FF* 62) and to educate the plas-tic imagination. The very "logic of vision" itself is exemplified in decorative de-sign (*FF* 62).

In the case of the decorative arts of pure design, then, we can recognize the validity of the metaphor of carving out a figure from the "amorphous sensory chaos," since we can see in the resulting figure the appearing of "basic vital rhythms," which conform to "biological feeling and its emotional efflorescence, 'life' on the human level" (*FF* 62). Basic vital rhythms are expressed in plastic forms, and pure decorative design is indeed a paradigm of "direct projection of vital feeling into visible shape and color," with "motion and rest, rhythmic unity, wholeness" (*FF* 63). The decorative design "expresses life," with its qualities of emanation, repetition, balancing (*FF* 63). "Motion" in art is "growth" and what characterizes motion is "continuity, directedness" (*FF* 64). The line of design, however, Langer points out, does not "really" grow and move. Its growth and movement is a "semblance" with an intrinsically "symbolic import" (*FF* 65).

In this way, Langer thinks, echoing both Cassirer and Paul Klee, a line can exhibit "what is the essence of life—incessant change, or process, articulating a permanent form," where permanence refers to "a pattern of changes" (*FF* 66) that is retained and sustained. A line can be seen as the embodiment of the ab-stract principle of direction, which is something that is "non-discursively ex-hibited and perceived" (*FF* 65). A line can be "charged with the idea of motion" and in this way be perceived as a "living form" (*FF* 65). This is the "constant aim of living matter" (*FF* 66), to be seen as, as well as to be, a living form. Motion in art is *"change made perceivable,* i.e., *imaginable,* in any way whatever" (*FF* 66), cer-tainly a genre-transcending notion if there ever was one. At this point Langer makes interesting use of the contrast between "exemplification" and "symboliza-tion," concepts that in other cases she conflates. A line, or a delimited space, is a fixed form, on Langer's reckoning, and in this way, since it does not "change," *ex-emplifies* permanence. Yet, Langer holds, a line can *symbolize* motion and thereby carry with it the concept of growth. The goal of the decorative arts, then, can offer a key heuristic clue to art quite generally and to its concrete instances: art is *symbolic exemplification*. The sense of "life" expressed by a line, for example, with its opposing principles of permanence and growth, is due to the *illusionary nature* (semblance nature) of the form and its dynamic pattern. The movement of the line is situated within a "framework of felt stability" (*FF* 67), giving us a kind of "duality of motion-in-permanence" (*FF* 67), a true "semblance," a mode of appearing apart from the physical order. This is the phenomenon Paul Klee was referring to in his remark about "letting a line wander."

A semblance, in this sense, is then both the medium and the object of perception. It is *the* artistic expression, and expression, as Langer repeats, is the "presentation of an idea through an articulate symbol" (*FF* 67). For Langer all art symbols have one unifying feature: they create a "semblance" and articulate a "vital form within its scaffold" (*FF* 68). This focus allows us, Langer thinks, to situate "all further problems of art—the ways of imagination, the nature of abstraction, the phenomena of talent and genius, etc.—" (*FF* 68). The issue is, what light, *by implication*, can the central idea throw on these themes, for implications, that is, true generalizations, are "the philosophical strength and pragmatic value of concepts" (*FF* 68). These topics will reappear constantly as our discussion proceeds.

Interpretation and the Expressive Import of an Artwork

For Langer every work of art, no matter what the genre or material carrier, is "a single, indivisible symbol, although a highly articulate one" (*FF* 369). But it is a *prime symbol*, not a symbolism, since its elements play their roles in a "total form" and have no independent standing (*FF* 369). The prime symbol that is a work of art is articulated by reason of the various *elements* in it, not its *materials*. In the "Expressiveness" chapter, which strangely enough follows her close examination of the great dimensions of art, Langer says that there is not only "an epistemological challenge to be met," but also many psychological questions "that naturally arise, some of which might lead right to the heart of anthropology and even biology" (*FF* 390). This is the path that Langer will take in *Mind*. It is another indication of the "nested" nature of Langer's whole philosophical project.

The total form that is the work of art is marked by tensions that arise from interacting elements. In the case of plastic art space-tensions are united by space-resolution (*FF* 370), but the space-tension belongs to virtual space where *esse est percipi* (*FF* 371). Indeed, the tension presented in an artwork engenders, without "causing," what Langer calls a total organic awareness (*FF* 371), which is effected in the body of the percipient (or reader) *and is itself a form of interpretation*. As Langer puts it, "every smallest shift of awareness calls out a readjustment" (*FF* 371). Readjustment can also be transformed into a total shift of consciousness when the intellectual and imaginative functions that "have a controlling share of influence on waking activity" (*FF* 361) are maximally put into play. Dewey speaks of the union of "sense, need, impulse and action characteristic of the live creature" (1934: 31) that is rooted in the body and in motor dispositions. For him, aesthetic perception, just as normal perception, demands "an organized body of activities, including the motor elements necessary for full perception" (1934: 261). The full body of the interpreter is brought into play.

> It is not just the visual apparatus but the whole organism that interacts with the environment in all but routine action. The eye, ear, or whatever, is only the channel *through* which the total response takes place. A color as seen is always qualified by implicit reactions of many organs, those of the sympathetic system as well as of touch. It is a funnel for the total energy put forth, not its well-spring. Colors are sumptuous and rich just because a total organic resonance is deeply implicated in them. (1934: 127)

The mental activity and sensitivity that "determines the way a person meets his surrounding world" (*FF* 372) is also, Langer thinks, "molded by imagination" (*FF* 372) and gives rise to, as Peircean "proper significate effects," "attitudes with distinct feeling tones" (*FF* 372). This important, indeed critical, reference to feeling tones is an echo of Whitehead's philosophical position. It is also a central feature of Langer's notion of the "life of feeling," which is "a stream of tensions and resolutions" that are iconically embodied, and interpretively recognized, in the "appearance of life, growth, and functional unity" that give works of art an organic appearance, although they are not organisms, a theme Langer develops extensively in *Mind*, as we shall see in a later chapter.

The emphasis on a stream of tensions and resolutions, which Langer first developed thematically in her analysis of music or the "musical matrix," with its revelation of the inner life, is asserted by Langer to be carried over to the nontemporal projection of the plastic arts, which manifest the "same sort of pattern" (*FF* 372). Langer goes so far as to say, rather astoundingly, that "painting, sculpture, architecture, and all kindred arts do the same thing as music" (*FF* 372). The temporal image and the timeless image both exhibit "tension and resolution simultaneously" (*FF* 373). It is Langer's major aesthetic concern—and achievement—to make sense of such a phenomenon, but always with the proviso that works of art are *not* organisms; they only present "the appearance of life, growth, and functional unity" (*FF* 373); that is, a work of art is *a semblance*.

This organic, and hence holistic, appearance is the perceptual and affective root of Langer's constantly repeated assertion that what a work of art "sets forth . . . has no counterpart in any vocabulary" (*FF* 374). The work of art—no matter what the medium—effects the conveyance of "one nameless passage of 'felt life,' knowable through its incarnation in the art symbol even if the beholder has never felt it in his own flesh" (*FF* 374). Indeed, the artist often *discovers* through his elements possibilities of feeling that surprise. The artwork objectifies the life of feeling in a complex symbol that is not subject to a discursive logic. The import of such a symbol is known by the "basic intellectual act of *intuition*" (*FF* 375). This notion, which Langer has wrestled with from the beginning, is now set in relation to Croce's position that intuition is "an act of perception whereby the content is *formed,* which means, for him *turned into form*" (*FF* 375). Croce identifies intuition with expression (*FF* 375), but according to Langer, Croce also had a "false conception of the relation of intuition to symbolism" (*FF* 376). This is due to Croce's equating "intellectual" with "discursive." But the deep connection of intuition with expression entails for Langer that expressive activity be thought of as "the process of elementary symbol-making" (*FF* 376). Since, however, for Langer, "the basic symbols of human thought are images," which function as symbols, "no human impression is only a signal from the outer world; it always is *also* an image in which possible impressions are formulated, that is, a symbol for the conception of *such* experience" (*FF* 376). This is a position already defended in *Philosophy in a New Key.* It is essential to understanding Langer's central insight. Symbolic images "mean" both past and future impressions that "exemplify the same form" (*FF* 376). The notion of *suchness,* which Peirce also foregrounded, is rooted in this recognition of sameness of form. This notion of *such,* Langer adds in a statement rich with implications, "bespeaks an elementary abstraction, or awareness of form" (*FF* 376)—which does not have to be thematic or explicit. Such an abstraction takes place on the "lowest stratum" of our apprehension of the world. So, Langer, once again, has pushed meaning down to the very stratum where perceptual unities are first grasped, even if dimly. Grasping, or "being grasped," is a form of formulation, which goes over, or can go over, into "representation" and "abstraction," and these are "the characteristic function of symbols" (*FF* 377). The bottom line for Langer is, once again, that there is "no formulation without symbolic projection" (*FF* 377). This is a central thesis of her whole philosophical project.

Cassirer, Langer claimed, returning to the theme of "intuition," "furnished the propaedeutic to a study of intuition" (*FF* 378), and indeed showed that there was more than one kind of intuition or intellectual act that grasped or constituted form. For Cassirer, Langer reports, "all cognition of form is intuitive" (*FF* 378). But what are the proper objects of such intuitive acts? Langer lists *relatedness, dis-*

tinctness, congruence, correspondence of forms, contrasts, and synthesis in a total Gestalt. All these, she claims, can be known only by "direct insight, which is intuition" (*FF* 378). Cassirer, as Langer notes, wants to uncover "the basic symbolic value which probably precedes and prepares verbal meaning" (*FF* 378), something that Cassirer calls "symbolic pregnance" and that is close to, but not identical with, Langer's notion of formal significance or import. But the connection of symbolic pregnance with Langer's root notion is even closer. For symbolic pregnance in its deepest sense is the inseparable intertwining of symbol and meaning, their indissoluble unity and the untranslatability that marks a presentational form. Langer's aesthetic theory, especially as developed in *Feeling and Form,* grows out of this fundamental Cassirerian insight.

We have to see that the intuitive act by which a symbolically pregnant form is grasped is for Langer both an act of abstraction and an act of interpretation. *Abstraction,* on Langer's view, is a spontaneous and natural "comprehension of form itself, through its exemplification in informed perceptions or 'intuitions'" (*FF* 378). *Interpretation* is the recognition of the metaphorical value of "some intuitions, which springs from the perception of their forms" (*FF* 378). This is an insight that is already present and developed in *Philosophy in a New Key.* Even the literary work, in spite of being constructed "in sentences" which have to be grasped sequentially and developmentally, with the meaning gradually emerging at a certain moment in the process, is really grasped in an "intuition of *a whole presented feeling and its import*" (*FF* 379). Langer wants, in the case of the art symbol, to drive a wedge in general between synthetic construal in language by a "succession of intuitions" (379) and the seeing or anticipation in art of "the complex whole" (*FF* 379). The radical difference between verbal meaning, even in verbal art, and artistic import is that import, "unlike verbal meaning, can only be exhibited, not demonstrated to any one to whom the art symbol is not lucid" (*FF* 379). The hermeneutic task, then, is to "make lucid," to "envisage" the "commanding form" of a more or less permanent symbol.

This inseparability of the sense and the artistic symbol is, as we have repeatedly seen, central to Langer's whole project. "A symbol that cannot be separated from its sense cannot really be said to refer to something outside itself" (*FF* 380). "Refer" is not the right word for what it does. The expressive content is intrinsically wedded to the expressive form. The "imaginative envisagement," in Collingwood's sense, is inseparable from its expression. When Collingwood speaks about art as the "language of consciousness," Langer understands "language" as the equivalent of her "symbol." The danger, according to her, is to transform "symbol" into "symbolism." This implies an articulate system, and while the symbol is certainly articulate, it just as certainly does not belong to any symbol system along any linguistic or mathematical model. This, we have seen, is a constant theme in Langer's reflections.

In *Feeling and Form* Langer puts unswervingly and emphatically at the center of her work "the concept of the *created* thing as non-actual, i.e., illusory, but imaginatively and even sensuously present, functioning as a symbol but not always as a physical datum" (*FF* 386). Non-actual here really means "ideal," and Langer is close to Karl Bühler's notion of the principle of abstractive relevance, which points out that only pertinent features of sign-bearing matter carry its meaning, exemplified in the distinction between phonetics and phonology. Art is the creation of virtual objects—complexes of pertinent features—that are expressive forms. The creation of these virtual objects involves technique, to be sure, but it is an imaginative technique. Technique and imagination develop together. Langer speaks, with phenomenological acuity, of indivisible acts of hearing and composing, hearing and playing or singing. As she puts it, "painting and seeing are all of a piece when a person is creating a picture" (*FF* 387; see Wentworth, *The Phenomenology of Painting* [2004]). This is a process of what I would call *symbolic materialization*, advertence to which clearly and strongly makes an epistemological and semiotic point: "It is hard to hold an envisagement without a more or less permanent symbol" (*FF* 387). The construction of the "permanent symbol" is a *conditio sine qua non* of the artist's being able to know and to express the vital import. Langer's grounding insight is that *the artist cannot know this import before expressing it.* At the same time in seeking the appropriate symbol the artist is guided by "the envisagement of the 'commanding form,' the fundamental feeling to be explored and expressed. *This is 'the work of art in the artist's head,'*" which Collingwood so insistently refers to (*FF* 389). Langer's point is that this "inner work of art" is already bound to a material form, which is the carrier of the *total import* of the artwork. The work is a "free symbol" (*FF* 390), whose cognitive value overflows both the creator's and the interpreter's immediate subjective experience and intention. The artist "learns from the perceptible reality before him possibilities of subjective experience that he has not known in his personal life" (*FF* 390). In this way, mental scope and growth and expansion of personality are deeply involved in the creation of the artwork.

Langer is a kind of semiotic empiricist. She admits that "all knowledge goes back to experience" and that we "cannot know anything that *bears no relation* to our experience" (*FF* 390). Consequently, what an artist envisages, she claims, is "like" his own subjectivity, connected with his "ways of feeling" (*FF* 391), but not restricted to them. The work of art, as an expressive form, effects a "symbolic revelation" that emerges out of the "funded imagination" (*FF* 391), an idea that is very close to one of Dewey's major insights. But in the construction of the art symbol, the artist transcends his own personal subjectivity toward a "much greater vision," which includes "knowledge of his own subjectivity" but is not restricted to it, though it does remain at the center of his greater vision. Indeed, the artist's knowledge of life "goes as far as his art can reach" (*FF* 391). And it is in reaching for, and finding, the appropriate symbol that the artist reaches a knowledge that is beyond words.

One of Langer's most critical observations is that the public function of the art symbol imposes on it "a standard of complete objectivity. It has to be entirely given; what is left to imagination being implied, not missing. But the implication may be subtle" (*FF* 393). Imaginative implication is the presence of an absence, not a lack. Indeed, it may be so subtle that the ideal audience or ideal beholder or ideal interpreter "may come into actual existence only after many years of its career" (*FF* 393). Recognizing such a situation, and perhaps even being able to identify instances of it in our own lives, we are faced with a question that Langer, certainly innocent of the complexities of contemporary interpretation theory, nevertheless poses in all directness: "How do we know that we have understood the artist's message?" (*FF* 393).

First of all, as might be expected, Langer denies the legitimacy of the notion of a "message." The art symbol is not a discourse nor a comment, she claims, which is a very deceptive "working model" (*FF* 394). A work of art's import is "not separable from the form (the picture, poem, dance, etc.) that expresses it" (*FF* 394). Once again, Langer has recourse to the fundamental Wittgensteinian distinction between *saying* and *showing,* which grounds her work from the very beginning. The work of art is not a "mere sign." The artist is "showing us the appearance of a feeling, in a perceptible symbolic projection" (*FF* 394). The feeling—the vital import—is "always bound to its symbol" (*FF* 394). The work offers to the beholder or to the reader "a way of conceiving emotion" (*FF* 394), rather than merely making judgments about it. The reader—and the art lover quite generally—responds to the *work* as he or she would to a *natural symbol.* The created form *has* the feeling *revealed,* which is *in* it. But the "actual emotion," as opposed to the "virtual emotion," is induced by the contemplation of the art symbol, and this actual emotion "belongs to the percipient" (*FF* 395). It is, Langer thinks in a psychologically astute comment, "a pervasive feeling of *exhilaration,* directly inspired by the perception of good art" (*FF* 395). "Good" here obviously means "successful." This feeling of exhilaration, however, is not necessarily an instance of "pleasure," nor is it the "aesthetic emotion" spoken of by Clive Bell (*FF* 395). While they could be considered *indices* of good art, they are not especially powerful concepts of the theory of art, Langer thinks.

Indeed, the feeling of exhilaration, which we have all experienced in our interpretive activities, is not "objectless" or "empty." The intrinsic expressiveness of a work of art is due to its being "designed to abstract and present forms for perception—forms of life and feeling, activity, suffering, selfhood" (*FF* 395–396). Beauty, in the last analysis, on Langer's reckoning, "is expressive form" (*FF* 396), but it is not identical with charm and sense appeal, though they are or can be ingredients in it. This means that the art symbol gives us *knowledge,* in the form of virtual experience, of what it *means* to act, to suffer, to be or become a self, *to feel the world in a certain way,* in various and diverse media. Understanding a work of art, or reading and interpreting a text, entails one whole and entire qualification: responsiveness (*FF* 396). While art in all its forms certainly "does something to us," exhilarates us, as Langer says, its job is not to give us in a causal manner "emotions and moods," though that certainly can happen. Its principal goal—its overarching determinative goal—is to formulate, as Langer puts it in a ringing passage, "our conceptions of feelings and our conceptions of visual, factual, and audible reality together. It gives us *forms of imagination* and *forms of feeling,* inseparably; that is to say, it clarifies and organizes intuition itself. That is why it has the force of a revelation and inspires a feeling of deep intellectual satisfaction, though it elicits no conscious intellectual work (reasoning)" (*FF* 397).

Langer parallels John Dewey in a most important way with her claim that "in art, it is the impact of the whole, the immediate revelation of vital import, that acts as the psychological lure to long contemplation" (*FF* 397). The *lure of feeling* of an artwork must accordingly be "established almost at once" if the artwork is to be successful or interesting. Langer insightfully calls this "intuitive anticipation" (*FF* 398). This intuitive anticipation engages us in a process not only of making a revelation of our inner life, mediating self-understanding, but of shaping "our imagination of external reality according to the rhythmic forms of life and sentience" and in this way impregnating the world with aesthetic values (*FF* 399). Art and language shape seeing, acting, and feeling (*FF* 399). Just as, for example, painting "affects visual imagination," so poetry "affects one's conception of events" (*FF* 400). Because "life is incoherent unless we give it form" (*FF* 400), we construct *scenes* in which we can *enact* important moments of the life of feeling. So, as Langer sees it, the interpretation of a work of art is a process of *performative envisagement.* The labor of interpretation allows art to penetrate deep "into personal life because in giving form to the world, it articulates human nature: sensibility, energy, passion, and mortality. More than anything else in experience, the arts mold our actual life of feeling" (*FF* 401). Note the reference to "molding." Texts are themselves "symbols of feeling," and we "give ourselves up to their contemplation spontaneously" (*FF* 405), indeed *integrate ourselves into them,* as Michael Polanyi has so perspicuously shown and argued. This is due to their expressive power, which imposes them upon us and steers our modes of attending.

Langer argues that "art does not affect the viability of life so much as its quality" (*FF* 402). This makes it "akin to religion, which also, at least in its pristine, vigorous, spontaneous phase, defines and develops human feelings" (*FF* 402).

> When religious imagination is the dominant force in society, art is scarcely sepa-
> rable from it; for a great wealth of actual emotion attends religious experience, and
> unspoiled, unjaded minds wrestle joyfully for its objective expression, and are car-
> ried beyond the occasion that launched their efforts, to pursue the furthest possibili-
> ties of the expressions they have found. In an age when art is said to serve religion,
> religion is really feeding art. Whatever is holy to people inspires artistic conception.
> (*FF* 402; see also Soltes 2005)

The forms of art that flourished with religion are not, however, inseparably bound to "ritual or morals or sacred myth, but flourished freely in sacred realms as long as the human spirit was concentrated there. As soon as religion becomes prosaic or perfunctory, art appears somewhere else" (*FF* 402). Although Langer was by no means conventionally religious, what she says has a sharp and ring-ing tone. "Bad music, bad statues and pictures are irreligious, because everything corrupt is irreligious. Indifference to art is the most serious sign of decay in any institution; nothing bespeaks its own age more eloquently than that art, under its patronage, becomes literal and self-imitating" (*FF* 403). When art exits from the religious context it begins to draw on "unrestricted feeling somewhere else" (*FF* 403). In short, it becomes free and self-determining, according to its own cri-teria and demands.

The recognition and thematization of the autonomy of art, which is still not the same as "art for art's sake," gives Langer's aesthetic theory an important critical edge. The rise of the museum, which Dewey also discussed, is connected with the clear and irrefutable fact that "people do not naturally and constantly see works of art," and hence both the museum with walls and the museum without walls are, from one point of view, impoverishing. Church or temple as locus for art allowed artworks to "loom up before one in their greatness, as altar-pieces and splendid windows and statues do. The plastic arts have become es-tranged from their public" (*FF* 403)—by being collected in a new place or deposi-tory. The original "sacred precinct," which was the matrix of art, has migrated to another secular realm, but nevertheless, Langer qualifies, has not for that reason lost its seriousness or weightiness. They constitute a domain of "entertain-ment," not "amusement," which is, on Langer's reckoning, essentially frivolous

(*FF* 404). Entertainment, as Langer sees it, is "any activity without direct practical aim, anything people attend to simply because it interests them" (*FF* 404).
Langer does not think that the category of entertainment is in itself a "value category" (*FF* 404). "It includes both pastime and the satisfaction of imperious mental
needs; but, trivial or serious, it is always the work of the mind. Whitehead has
defined it as 'what people do with their freedom'" (cited *FF* 404). Not, note, with
their "leisure" in the traditional sense of that term. For Langer the mental energy
and emotional strength of individuals is "shown in what interests them," not in
what amuses them, which certainly can show degrees of refinement.

An important consequence of Langer's development of the notion of entertainment is that art is—or at least can be—just as much at home "there" as in its
religious context. The pivotal idea is that of "envisagement." In the case of tragic
drama, for instance, we have the "envisagement of individual existence as a
whole, and of its complete development to the limits of action and passion. This
envisagement, first presented in sacred art, is a necessity to people who have attained a mature self-consciousness" (*FF* 405). Such a self-consciousness is absorbed in "the joy of revelation, the vision of a whole wholly significant, of life
spending itself and death the signature of its completion. It is simply the joy of
great art, which is the perception of created form wholly expressive, that is to
say, beautiful" (*FF* 405). It is to such art that we spontaneously give ourselves
up in contemplation, "without any other intent than to hear and see and be en-
thralled" (*FF* 405). We are caught up in its "play," a point emphasized by Schiller
in his "aesthetic letters" and taken up and exploited by Dewey in *Art as Experience*
and by Hans-Georg Gadamer in his hermeneutical theory, where the category of
play does a lot of heavy lifting (Gadamer 1986: 1–53 and 123–130). This aesthetic
need, Langer notes, "used to be assuaged more surely and more often by sacred
objects and offices" (*FF* 405). The need is now satisfied by "good art," the criterion
of which "is its power to command one's contemplation and reveal a feeling that
one recognizes as real, with the same 'click of recognition' with which an artist knows that a form is true. All the forms of feeling are important, and the joy-
ous pulse of life needs to be made apparent quite as much as the most involved
passions, if we are to value it" (*FF* 405). The perceiver and the creative artist are
here brought into close correlation with one another, and the existential import
of art's power is foregrounded.

The reference to the problem of a criterion, to aesthetic power, brings us,
quite clearly, to the problem of a standard of comparison. Langer denies there
is a certain way of defining a standard in art, there being no "sure principle of
selection" (*FF* 406). In fact, however, Langer makes a comment that resonates
with a position that we have seen developed and defended by John Dewey:

"Appreciation—being impressed or left cold—comes first; but the recognition of how the illusion was made and organized and how the sense of import is immediately given by a strong piece, even though the critic himself may be nonplussed by its strange feeling—that recognition is a product of analysis, reached by discursive reasoning about the work and its effects" (FF 406). The actual judgments of success or failure, but not the subsequent analyses, are "intuitively known or not at all" (FF 407). These arise, we have seen, quasi-spontaneously. No theory, indeed no "mere" theory, is able, Langer thinks, to establish beforehand a stable set of criteria of expressiveness that would function as standards of beauty. The measure of the success or failure of a work is the presence of the "commanding form" or Deweyan "permeating quality," which is open to the critical perception of the perceiver or interpreter. The commanding form is the "matrix of envisaged feeling" that will be articulated in the work. So, there is a double talent, on the side of the artist and on the side of the critic. As Langer illuminatingly and astutely points out, adverting to the embodied state of the artist and the interpreter, this talent "seems to be closely linked with body-feeling, sensitivity, muscular control, verbal or tonal memory, as well as the one great mental requirement, aesthetic responsiveness" (FF 407). But, when all is said and done, Langer and Kant are in agreement: talent is not genius. Langer binds talent to the power of execution, and genius is not a degree of talent. Genius is the power of conception, and it does not have to be wedded to great technical skill, which does not always accompany it, or which appears later in the development of the artist, or which is already at its highest level but is then exploited by even deeper creations, as in Beethoven, Shakespeare, or Cézanne. In short, genius is "not superlative talent, but the power to conceive invisible realities—sentience, vitality, emotion—in a new symbolic projection that reveals something of their nature for the first time. . . . [I]t does not admit of degrees; and a small amount of genius is not a rare endowment" (FF 409).

So, as Langer contends, just as we saw that there is no theory that "can set up criteria of expressiveness (i.e. standards of beauty)" (FF 407), so there are no methods that will automatically guarantee either the creation or the proper interpretive access to the symbolic form. Here Langer once again approaches central issues of Kant's aesthetics and its later developments both inside and outside philosophy, without engaging them directly or thematically.

Langer is eminently aware of the cultural importance of art, although the social dimension is not as dominant in her work as in Dewey's. Art is the school of feeling of a culture, Langer writes, because it formulates the "felt life" that is its heart and in this way "molds the objective world for the people" (FF 409). It is a "defense against outer and inner chaos" (FF 409)—but not an impregnable one as

the history of high-civilizational disorder shows. The semiotic tool here for molding or ordering the world is the art symbol, pivot and core of Langer's reflections.
Its conceptual hinge is the theory of expressive form. The peculiarity of Langer's
model is the wedding of expression with an objective symbol such that the symbol does not reflect or mirror the actual experience of the artist or creator but formulates an objective idea in the non-discursive mode. This conceptual framework is in direct continuity with Cassirer's great philosophical project, which
was, as Langer states, developed with no systematic aesthetics in mind. While
he "hewed the keystone" of such a structurally rich aesthetic theory, Langer described her role as putting that stone in place.

For understanding Langer's aesthetic theory in its deepest sense, then, the
paradoxical notion of an "intuitive symbol" is crucial. It encompasses perception,
interpretation, semiosis as interpenetrating "dimensional planes" of the total
phenomenon of our encounter with an artwork as a distinctively structured symbolic form, a topic I have treated extensively elsewhere (Innis 2001 and 2007).

Langer highlights the intertwining of dimensions in an important way:

> The comprehension of form itself, through its exemplification in formed perceptions
> or "intuitions," is spontaneous and natural *abstraction;* but the recognition of a meta-
> phorical value of some intuitions, which springs from the perception of their forms,
> is spontaneous and natural *interpretation.* Both abstraction and interpretation are in-
> tuitive, and may deal with non-discursive forms. They lie at the base of all human
> mentality, and are the roots from which both language and art take rise. (*FF* 378)

Langer points out that the logical, that is, semiotic, distinction between discursive and presentational forms accounts in a pivotal fashion for the different ways
meaning emerges and is "symbolized" in our experience of any form. Discourse,
she asserts, "aims at building up, cumulatively, more and more complex logical
intuitions" (*FF* 379). The sudden emergence of meaning that marks discourse is
"always a logical intuition or insight" (*FF* 379). However, the art symbol, even the
linguistic work of art, Langer contends,

> cannot be built up like the meaning of a discourse, but must be seen *in toto* first; that
> is, the "understanding" of a work of art begins with the intuition of the whole pre-
> sented feeling. Contemplation then gradually reveals the complexities of the piece,
> and of its import. In discourse, meaning is synthetically construed by a succession of
> intuitions; but in art the complex whole is seen or anticipated first. (*FF* 379)

Such is the challenge Langer issues to a semiotically construed aesthetics:
to hold to a general semiotic framework that brings all the art genres under the
general rubric of *symbols of feeling* yet respects the primary illusions of each art

genre and the severe tasks they place upon the interpreter. Interpretation is then not defined by a "primary reading" but by a hermeneutic "ex-plication" or "un-folding" of the content of an intuitive insight into a symbolic whole (see Innis 2001). Absent this insight, this dialectically charged holding-in-view of all the elements that make up the formed feeling that is the import of the work, the work is a "mere sign" without power to affect us and release the train of interpretants that mark the presentational order as opposed to the discursive order. Langer's whole approach to the artwork is to maintain this pivotal distinction, the key to her semiotic theory of knowing and mind as a whole.

5

Art Forms

The Logic of Primary Illusions

The deep divisions among the arts are those that set apart their
very worlds, namely the differences in what the various arts
create, or differences of primary illusion. . . . I also believe that
art is essentially one, that the symbolic function is the same in
every kind of artistic expression, all kinds are equally great, and
their logic is all of a piece, the logic of non-discursive form (which
governs literary as well as all other created form). But the way to
establish these articles of faith as reasonable propositions is not
just to say them emphatically and often and deprecate evidence
to the contrary; it is, rather, to examine the differences, and trace
the distinctions among the arts as far as they can be allowed.
They go deeper than, offhand, one would suppose. But there
is a definite level at which no more distinctions can be made;
everything one can say of any single art can be said of any other
as well. *There lies the unity.* All the divisions end at that depth,
which is the philosophical foundation of art theory.

—(*FF* 103)

Langer subjects the major art forms to analysis in the central part of *Feeling and
Form*. Her substantive positions are developed in intense dialogue with a wealth
of sources and resources, many of which she rehabilitates and situates in the context of her own systematic framework. Our principal task, as always, is to make
as visible as possible the "figure" of Langer's analytical model that appears over
against the background of her assumptions, her sources, and her distinctive aesthetic theory. Our focal point will always be to examine Langer's view just of
how concretely art forms *exemplify* forms of feeling, the specific "work" that they
do. This "work," Langer holds, is the construction of a "primary illusion," which

is projected in and by the work of art. What makes Langer's analysis so rich, indeed fascinating, is the tension between common principles, organized around the category of a primary illusion, and the specific symbolic "logic" of each form of art, which is uncovered by a twofold process of "stipulative derivation" and of phenomenological description.

By "stipulative derivation" I mean "instructions for perceiving." Langer thinks that her conceptual framework teaches us what we should look for each art genre as trying to accomplish. In this way her approach is thoroughly informed by philosophical principles and has deep normative implications. It is a fusion of the analytical, the critical, and the phenomenological. Phenomenologically, Langer's analysis of the various genres of art displays both a nuanced taste and a keen sense for the theoretically essential. In what follows, three major domains will be subjected to analysis, all the while omitting a more extensive confrontation with music, which nevertheless, as we saw in the preceding chapter, plays a large heuristic role in Langer's work. Langer's position on musical issues has been extensively discussed and applied elsewhere in a number of very different contexts, ranging from music education (Reimer 1970), the problem of an unconsummated symbol (Budd 1985: chapter 6), the relations between representation, music, and the emotions (Addiss 1999), the ineffability of musical knowledge (Raffman 1993), and musical meaning and expressiveness (Davies 1994), to her theory's place in a general philosophy of music (Kivy 2002). But the "lessons of a musical aesthetics" will, nevertheless, clearly inform much of what follows, especially with respect to the "irrelevance of representation" in the traditional sense of that term.

Virtual Space: Pictorial and Visual Arts

Langer deals with the three major forms of the visual arts—painting, sculpture, and architecture—in two stimulating chapters of *Feeling and Form*. The aesthetic lessons here are most interesting, especially since her original reflections on art theory were, as we saw, motivated by music, which is distinctively and resolutely non-representational. Langer begins her discussion by noting that the fundamental forms that appear in the decorative arts function as *motifs* of design. This is a point we have seen her making already in *Philosophy in a New Key*. Motifs are "organizing devices that give the artist's imagination a start, and so 'motivate' the work in a perfectly naïve sense. They drive it forward, and guide its progress" (*FF* 69). While such a notion clearly has musical application, Langer has in mind in the present context such motifs as circles, triangles, spirals, parallel lines, and so forth. The "basic shapes" can suggest "forms of familiar things" such as flowers and the paradigmatic floral rosette, which Langer considers "one of the old-est and most widespread of these ornamental designs with obvious representa-tional reference" (*FF* 69). The exploitation of these motifs allows a new effect to spring into being, something truly novel—"a representation, the illusion of an object" (*FF* 69). Langer's main thesis, which she will return to time and again, is that "*form is first,* and the representational function accrues to it" (70), although the decorative motif, with its deep geometrical strata, is still recognizable after multiple complex transformations, just as musical motifs are. Moreover, "the use of color, like that of forms, is *first* ornamental and *afterwards* representative of natural attributes" (*FF* 70). Langer speaks, in ways confirmed by the later work of Gombrich on the sense of order (Gombrich 1979) and of Arnheim on the psy-chological dimensions of the perception of expressive symbols (Arnheim 1966 and 1986), of decoration, "based on quasi-geometric shapes that are 'congenial' to our spatial intuition, and guided by interest in felt continuities, rhythms, and emotional dynamics," as being a "simple but pure and abstract order of expres-sive form" (*FF* 70). The combination of *design* with *pictorial* elements allows a com-plex tension to exist at the heart of visual art that makes art never a mere copying of direct visual impressions. Visual art is "symbolizing from the outset," a pro-cess of formulation, shaping, defining of "the impressions themselves according to the principles of expressiveness" (*FF* 71). But in this process "the representa-tive interest makes art transcend its elementary motifs" (*FF* 71). The systematic depiction of objects absorbs and transforms the old decorative devices. In time, in fact, the objects pictured will themselves become "motifs," adding another level of complexity.

It is nevertheless axiomatic for Langer that "imitation is never the main de-vice in organization" (*FF* 71). Plastic art has as its purpose the articulation of visual form in such a way that the work itself, "so immediately expressive of hu-man feeling that it seems to be charged with feeling," becomes the sole or para-mount object of perception. Think of van Gogh's cosmic vortex of "Starry Night," the "torqued" "Room at Arles," or "Wheatfield with Crows." The work effects a "shaping *of* space," not just the creation of a shape *in* space. The space, which is a created space, leads to the more general and universal question, "What is created, and how is anything created, by the process of deploying colors on a ground?" (*FF* 71). This created space is not the space of science, which has a logical form, nor of everyday life, which Langer rather problematically thinks of as amorphous (see Heelan 1983 for groundbreaking studies of the relation of various spatial log-ics to one another, including the relation of space perception in art to the space of science). The space of visual art, she thinks, not uncontroversially, is "an en-tirely visual affair" (*FF* 72), with no direct involvement of the other senses. Pictorial space is a "virtual space," and it gives rise to "an intangible image" (72), with no intrinsic connection to other spaces. It exists in a completely different order. "The created virtual space is entirely self-contained and independent" and this space is "the primary illusion of all plastic art" (*FF* 72). If the other sense or perceptual modalities appear in the virtual space they appear by virtue of "*visual substitutes* for the things that are normally known by touch, movement or inference" (*FF* 73). Tactile values, which have been foregrounded in aesthetic theory by others such as Berenson and Cézanne, are hence devalued at the very start, seemingly on principle, but they are not, strictly speaking, excluded.

Following in her own way the hints and analyses of Adolf Hildebrand, Langer holds that the architectonic process of creation is "*the construction and ordering of forms in space in such a way that they define and organize the space.* But a perceptually defined space is a shape: so the complete shaping of a given visual field is a work of pictorial art" (*FF* 74). In this way we are presented with a certain primacy of the visual field, or picture plane. This plane is multi-planar, for the visual field is made up of "several planes, or layers of design" (*FF* 74). The virtual space of pictorial art is "entirely independent and not a local area in actual space" (*FF* 75). It is a "self-contained, total system" (*FF* 75), whether in two or three dimensions. "In any work of art, the dimensionality of its space and the continuous character of it are always implicitly assured. Perceptual forms are carved out of it and must appear to be still related to it despite their most definite boundaries" (*FF* 75). Thus, following Hildebrand, Langer thinks of the role of visual artists as defining volumes of space by the "sinking" of objects into it, although clearly modern abstract art was more concerned with "forces" and "fields" than with objects. Visual values arise from the role of the various semblances of objects, people, landscapes, and so on in shaping portions of perceptual space. To illustrate what she means by a visual value Langer cites a passage from Hildebrand.

> By the visual values of space we mean those values of an object which issue only in purely spatial perceptions tending toward the general conception of a segment of space. By purely spatial perceptions we mean perceptions independent of the organization or functioning of the object involved. Let us take a form which is given visual expression by contrasts of light and shade. Through their particular relations and respective positions, these different degrees of brightness and darkness affect the spectator as if it were actually modeling the object—a concerted effect is produced existing only for the eye, by factors which otherwise are not necessarily connected. (Hildebrand 1932: 55, cited *FF* 75)

Langer in this way, following her own theoretical principles, for which she is always looking for confirmation, commits herself to the Hildebrandian position that *representation is secondary.* Its role is really "for the sake of creating individual forms in relation to one another" (*FF* 76). This includes not just forms of objects but forms of colors, forms of color planes, and so forth. The artist's real *goal,* as Langer sees it, is to construct a semblance of an object, "the look of it, and the emotional import of its form," not the actuality of the object that we can read like a label. It is not the "pictured thing" that the artist is concerned with, something "in" nature. Rather, "the factors which the artist presents are those which make us aware of related forms in the continuum of perceptual space" (*FF* 77). It is not the actual form of the object that is at issue, but *"making space visible and its continuity sensible.* The space itself is a projected image, and everything pictured serves to define and organize it. Even representation of familiar objects, if it occurs, is a means to this end" (*FF* 77). Such a position straddles the fence between description and stipulation. It clearly involves a theory-informed critical decision.

The artist, Langer holds, is not trying to re-create anything. Virtual space is created, not re-created. In the case of Cézanne, for example, Langer observes, perhaps without the necessary qualification, "the transformation of natural objects into pictorial elements took place *in his seeing,* in the act of looking, not the act of painting" (*FF* 78). For him "attentive sight and spatial composition were the same thing. Virtual space was his mind's habitat" (*FF* 78). It resulted in the abstraction of new forms "in which the glow of feeling and the sense of vital process are visibly articulated" (*FF* 79)—certainly a precise and sensitive remark. Virtual space is the space in which the created symbolic form exists. It attains full reality only by degrees, for, as Langer is at pains to point out, "expressiveness has endless degrees," whose culminating point would be "perfect livingness of the work" (*FF* 79). This notion of livingness has monumental importance for Langer, and it will play a central role in the discussions in *Mind.*

> "Living form" is the most indubitable product of all good art, be it painting, architecture, or pottery. Such form is "living" in the same way that a border or a spiral is intrinsically "growing": that is, it *expresses* life—feeling, growth, movement, emotion, and everything that characterizes vital existence. This expression, moreover, is not symbolization in the usual sense of conventional or assigned meaning, but a presentation of a highly articulated form wherein the beholder recognizes, without conscious comparison and judgment but rather by direct recognition, the forms of human feeling: emotions, moods, even sensations in their characteristic passage. (*FF* 82)

What Langer will persistently—some might say contentiously, or even stubbornly—call "living form" is "the symbolism that conveys the idea of vital reality; and the emotive import belongs to the form itself, not to anything it represents or suggests" (*FF* 82). So, in a remark of exceptional epistemological acuity Langer asserts that the "emotion in the work is the thought in the work. Just as the content of discourse is the discursive concept, so the content of a work of art is the non-discursive concept of feeling; and it is directly expressed by the form, the appearance before us" (*FF* 82). As John Dewey might put it, feeling or the meaning-quality is in the work the way a pattern is in a carpet. This "concept," it is crucial to remember, is not the "subject matter." It is the "sentiment" that radiates from a symbolic form and that is "instinct" in every feature of it, imposing itself upon the perceiver, even in spite of himself. Dewey, along with many others, makes a practically identical remark about the "magical accord" of a work of art. This magical accord, the root of a work's livingness, is immanent in the creation of virtual space and its organization by forms "that reflect the patterns of sentience and emotion" (*FF* 83). The creation is of a symbolic form, and a symbol exists in a symbolic, not a physical, order. This is Langer's version of the "framing" effect that separates the semiotic from the physical order.

Langer's discussion of virtual space, I have already said, oscillates between her arguing for a thesis and its exemplification in a range of sources, along with what can only be called a "phenomenological" procedure, which brings her analysis into close proximity to the actual activities of artistic creation that Wentworth (2004) has explored with great success under the tutelage of Maurice Merleau-Ponty's own phenomenological approach. It gives her presentation a certain thickness and richness that bring it close to the actual practices of artistic creation and perception. The creation of the primary illusion of virtual space comes with the "first stroke of brush or pencil that concentrates the mind entirely on the picture plane and neutralizes the actual limits of vision. . . . Just establish one line in virtual space, and at once we are in the realm of symbolic forms" (*FF* 84). This is distant echo and extension, once again, of Cassirer's example of a *Linienzug*, a drawn line, that is "pregnant" with various forms of meaning or significance. The physically and actually visual is turned into the virtual. Just as our hearing is transformed by our making out a word in a complex auditory environment, so our vision is transformed by such an act of "marking" a surface. "The image, be it a representation or a mere design, stands before us in its expressiveness: significant form" (*FF* 84). This "whole organized semblance" that draws us into sustained contemplation should, ideally, make the return to the actual environment difficult to keep up. And when we do "return," we return with a perception "impregnated" with new visual values, a point also made by Nelson Goodman on many occasions (see especially his 1978: 1–22 for a readily accessible discussion).

In the analysis of virtual space, therefore, Langer takes a first, big step in delineating the concrete heuristic power of the pivotal concepts of her theory of art. The first is the concept of an art genre's *primary illusion*. Langer defines this as "the basic creation wherein all its elements exist; and they, in turn, produce and support it" (*FF* 84). The primary illusion does not exist by itself, nor does it mean "first-established," but rather *always* established when the "elements" of a work are given. *Elements,* we repeat, are not, as Langer pointedly insists, the same as *materials,* a distinction that also plays a role in Wentworth's phenomenology.

What are, in Langer's conception, *elements*? "Elements are factors in the semblance; and as such they are virtual themselves, direct components of the total form" (*FF* 84). *Materials* in a visual creation are, for example, paints and the colors the paints have in the tube or on the palette. However, "the colors in a picture are elements, determined by their environment. They are warm or cold, they advance or recede, enhance or soften or dominate other colors; they create tensions and distribute weight in a picture. Colors in a paintbox don't do such things. They are materials, and lie side by side in their actual, undialectical materialism" (*FF* 85). Thus, painted *wood* and painted *glass* differ as to materials, but not as to elements. The visual artist clearly works with both elements and with materials, and it is his or her mastery of both that gives rise to the effectiveness of the created semblance, whose whole being is geared toward the creation and maintaining of the primary illusion.

> All the discernible elements in a picture support the primary illusion, which is invariant, while the forms that articulate it may vary indefinitely. The primary illusion is a substrate of the realm of virtual forms; it is involved in their occurrence. (*FF* 85)

In an extremely important footnote to this difficult, but crucial, passage Langer recognizes the possibility, indeed the actuality, of secondary illusions, "certain non-visual created effects such as 'a sense of time,' what Malraux calls 'holiness,' 'dramatic feeling,' 'powers,' etc., that support the plastic intent" (*FF* 85n14). Moreover, the perhaps unfortunate use of the term "substrate" does not really entail something "lying under" to which other elements are added, since Langer thinks of the elements as actually "supporting" the primary illusion. A better analogy might be "invariant constitutive matrix." Reichling (1995) has grappled with this notion with good examples and range of reference.

While recognizing the primacy of the primary illusion, Langer admits that there are different modes of it as well as diverse ways of constructing it. So, there exist "quite distinct realms of plastic art" (*FF* 85). We are not confronted with a night in which all the cows are black, with hasty generalizations or facile identifications of things that are clearly different. The universal elementary function—

the creation of a primary illusion—is differentiated into different modes. In the chapter on "The Modes of Virtual Space" Langer will make a perspicuous and valuable distinction between painting, sculpture, and architecture. Pictorial art will give rise to a *virtual scene*. Sculpture will give rise to *virtual kinetic volume*. Architecture will give rise to a *virtual ethnic domain*. These are the primary "abstractions" effected by these three modes of creating virtual space. So, virtual space differentiates into *scene, volume,* and *ethnic domain*.

Let us take a closer look at these notions in light of Langer's fundamental distinctions and categories.

The illusion that is created in pictorial art Langer calls a *virtual scene*. Scene, as Langer uses the term, means *"a space opposite the eye and related directly and essentially to the eye"* (*FF* 86). Sculpture, for its part, "even when wedded to a background as in true relief, is essentially *volume*, not *scene*" (*FF* 88). The volume is not "a cubic measure, like a space in a box. It is more than the bulk of the figure; it is a space made visible, and is more than the area which the figure actually occupies. . . . The figure itself seems to have a sort of continuity with the emptiness around it, however much its solid masses may assert themselves as such. The void enfolds it, and the enfolding space has vital form as a continuation of the figure" (*FF* 88). The goal of sculpture is to arrive at "the semblance of organism" (*FF* 88), a sense of inevitable form, necessary form, inviolable form. What makes such a figure to have these properties is *"vital function*. Living organisms maintain themselves, resist change, strive to restore their structure when it has been forcibly interfered with" (*FF* 88). The sculptural work is not itself an organism. It is through and through dead matter. Langer's thesis is that it is its *form* that has the semblance of being organic. "Only its form is the form of life, and the space it makes visible is vitalized as it would be by organic activity at its center. It is *virtual kinetic volume*, created by—and with—the semblance of living form" (*FF* 89). This semblance of living form, Langer's central analytical notion, is not tied to the representation of natural organisms. Boccioni's bottles and Moore's baskets and birdcages, along with monoliths, screens, urns, and so forth, can express biological feeling without suggesting biological function. Sculpture torques, at least ideally when it is successful, the primary illusion of virtual space into the modality of volume. This is an equally visual space, "but not a space of direct vision; for volume is really given originally to touch, both haptic touch and contact limiting bodily movement, and the business of sculpture is to translate its data into entirely visual terms, i.e. *to make tactual space visible*" (*FF* 90).

From the side of the perceiver, Langer points out, fully aware of the phenomenological dimension of her project, although she does not call it that, the sculptural form engenders complex sensory reactions, fusing touch and sight, with an innate temptation to want to "handle" the sculptural form. We clearly want to touch sculptures in a way we do not want to touch paintings, or most paintings. Sculptural form "is a powerful abstraction from actual objects and the three-dimensional space which we construe by means of them, through touch and sight. It makes its own construction in three dimensions, namely the *semblance* of kinetic space" (*FF* 90). This kinetic space speaks to, maybe even grows out of, each person's own spatial environment, whose center point is the person's own body, the person's own kinetic volume. In this way Langer is able to follow Bruno Adriani in his comparison of sculptural space to the subjective construction of the world as a realm centering in one's own kinetic volume (*FF* 90). Just as one's body is the center of a three-dimensional space, so is a piece of sculpture. "It is a virtual kinetic volume, which dominates a surrounding space, and this environment derives all proportions and relations from it, as the actual environment does from one's self. The work is the semblance of a self, and creates the semblance of a tactual space—and, moreover, a visual semblance. It effects the objectification of self and environment for the sense of sight. Sculpture is literally the image of kinetic volume in sensory space" (*FF* 92). It is the imaginal nature of the sculpture that turns it into an abstraction. In this sense the sculpture is not treated as "an object." Rather, as Langer puts it, "we see it as a center of a space all its own; but its kinetic volume and the environment it creates are illusory—they exist for our vision alone, a semblance of the self and its world" (*FF* 92). Thus, even when and if we lay our hands on a piece of sculpture, we often find that we are more appreciative of the abstractive power of the piece. For the felt contradiction between what we see and what we touch "checks the anthropomorphic fancy, and heightens the abstractive power of the work. Yet handling a figure, no matter what it gives us, is always a mere interlude in our perception of the form. We have to step back, and see it unmolested by our hands, that break into the sphere of its spatial influence" (*FF* 92). One of the most exemplary instances of this phenomenon is Bernini's *Apollo and Daphne.*

Architecture for Langer is a third mode of creating virtual space, which she remarkably and insightfully says is "more subtle than the construction of illusory scene or even illusory organism" (*FF* 92). It is, she says, "commandingly artistic, and in its scope the most ambitious of all" (*FF* 92). Indeed, it is in architecture that we most directly come face to face with the problem of "appearance and reality" (*FF* 93). Architecture, Langer claims rather contentiously, but certainly pertinently, is not defined intrinsically by functionality, and functionality is not the measure of beauty (*FF* 93). A correct view of the distinctiveness of architecture must avoid interchanging the two notions of *arrangement in space* and *creation of space,* a theme also pursued by Bruno Zevi in his *Architecture as Space* (1957).

Architecture, too, has its primary illusion and it is not to be confused with a primary actuality, with the "real" world. For Langer, architecture is a plastic art, just as painting and sculpture are. Its first achievement "is always, unconsciously and inevitably, an illusion; something purely imaginary or conceptual translated into visual impressions" (*FF* 93). The architect is concerned with a *"created space, a virtual entity: the primary illusion of plastic art effected by a basic abstraction peculiar to architecture" (FF* 94). This "basic abstraction" Langer calls *an ethnic domain,* which is "the sphere of influence of a function, or functions" not necessarily an actual physical place. Langer enlighteningly remarks that a Gypsy or Indian camp may literally be *in* a place, but culturally "it *is* a place. A Gypsy camp is a different place from an Indian camp, though it may be geographically where the Indian camp used to be" (*FF* 95). So, "a place, in this non-geographical sense, is a created thing, an ethnic domain made visible, tangible, sensible. . . . [I]t is . . . an illusion. Like any other plastic symbol, it is primarily an illusion of self-contained, self-sufficient, perceptual space. But the principle of organization is its own: for it is organized as a functional realm made visible—the center of a virtual world, the "ethnic domain," and itself a geographical semblance" (*FF* 95). Note, then, the following summary, schematic paragraph:

> Painting creates planes of vision, or "scene" confronting our eyes, on an actual, two-dimensional surface; sculpture makes virtual "kinetic volume" out of actual three-dimensional material, i.e. actual volume; architecture articulates the "ethnic domain," or virtual "place," by treatment of an actual place. (*FF* 95)

This virtual place can range from the monumental to the absolutely minimal. Stonehenge, a simple column or pillar, the Temple of Poseidon at Sounion, tombs carved out of solid rock, all can sever "holiness from the profane. The outside world, even though not physically shut out, is dominated by the sanctum and becomes its visible context; the horizon, its frame" (*FF* 95) in the case of the temple or sacred sanctuary, while the tomb would in itself have no outside, all its proportions being "internally derived" (*FF* 95). All of these structures are semblances, and "whatever effects that semblance is architecturally relevant" (*FF* 95). The job of the architect is "monumental," then, in more ways than one. The architect must be so very aware of the complex factors that make up a culture in order to create its image: "a physically present human environment that expresses the characteristic rhythmic functional patterns which constitute a culture" (*FF* 96). Such a task is accomplished by "the spatial *semblance* of a world," something with its "own center and periphery, not dividing one place from all others, but limiting from within whatever there is to be. That is the image of an ethnic domain, the primary illusion in architecture" (*FF* 97).

While, Langer admits, "the most familiar product of architecture is . . . the *house*," the great architectural ideas "have rarely, if ever, arisen from domestic needs. They grew as the temple, the tomb, the fortress, the hall, the theatre" (*FF* 97), paradigmatic exemplifications of "ethnic domains." This is due to the public nature of tribal culture out of which these structures arose, and indeed to its essentially religious matrix and the paradigmatic creation of a religious space, which is a virtual realm. But the import of the early religious structures was cosmic. "The heavenly bodies could be seen to rise and set in the frame" each defined. Indeed, in its presentation of this space to what Langer calls popular thought "it unified earth and heaven, men and gods" (*FF* 98). This last statement echoes one of the main theses of Heidegger's reflections on the origin of the work of art, where the "temple" plays a paradigmatic role in "opening a world horizon" (in Heidegger 1960), and is explored in wonderful detail by Vincent Scully in his classic *The Earth, the Temple, and the Gods* (1979).

Langer is exceedingly insightful about the deep symbolic import of architecture. "Religion, though no longer the whole of life, is the confluence of all ideas" (*FF* 98). The sanctuary is deeply separated from the outside world; it is "a holy world, that one cannot live in, because it is too pure and moving, but that one enters for conscious communion with God and man" (*FF* 98). These thoughts are paralleled by those of Emerson and Philip Larkin and bear upon the future of "ritual spaces" in a desacralized world, a topic I have discussed in a different context (see Innis 2004 and all the studies in Handelman and Lindquist 2004). The tomb likewise becomes an image of an Underworld. Tombs are "intended for silence and the reign of Death," while still retaining a "tense quietness" (*FF* 98). Tombs are, in a wide range of cultural variations, "the Realm of the Dead envisaged" (*FF* 98). This is both a descriptive and a prescriptive comment, exemplifying once again the kind of "double vision" that informs Langer's discussion of art.

Architecture, as Langer conceives it at the deepest level, "creates the semblance of that World which is the counterpart of a Self. It is a total environment made visible" (*FF* 98). The form of this semblance can be personal or collective, focused on the home or on the communal space. Langer here makes a distinction between an actual environment and a functional environment to the effect that the first is a "system of functional relations" while the second, the created space of architecture, is "a symbol of functional existence" (*FF* 98). Note the contrast between a functional system and a symbol. The essential function of architecture, on Langer's conception, is symbolic expression, which is "something miles removed from provident planning or good arrangement. It does not suggest things to do, but embodies the feeling, the rhythm, the passion or sobriety, frivolity or fear with which any things at all are done. That is the image of life which is cre-ated in buildings; it is the visible semblance of an 'ethnic domain,' the symbol of humanity to be found in the strength and interplay of forms" (*FF* 99). For Langer, once again, this is not merely a descriptive issue. It is *plainly normative*, furnishing a "measure" for criticism as well as a focusing lens for analysis.

Langer already in *Feeling and Form*, we have seen, insists upon and utilizes the great organic analogy, which plays such a role in *Mind*. "Because we are organ-isms, all our actions develop in organic fashion, and our feelings as well as our physical acts have an essentially metabolic pattern. Systole, diastole; making, un-making; crescendo, diminuendo. Sustaining, sometimes, but never for indefinite lengths; life, death" (*FF* 99). This notion will be much further developed in *Mind*, supported by a generalization of the concept of an *act*, which builds a bridge be-tween the physical and the psychical, or at least encompasses both of them. As a result of this organic structure Langer thinks of the human environment as "the complementary organic form" (*FF* 99). This environment "holds the imprint of a functional pattern" (*FF* 99). Any building, whose task is to "create the illusion of an ethnic world," which is a "'place' articulated by the imprint of human life" (*FF* 99), has to be perceived as an organic form. Architecture, to be "good" ar-chitecture, must be "organized," in the literal sense of that term. A successful building must preserve the architectural illusion of an ethnic totality, or virtual place (*FF* 100). The loss of such virtual places, the loss of a vision of an ethnic to-tality, is the price one pays for a built world devoid of organic form. Langer's posi-tion points toward the comprehensive analyses of Christopher Alexander's great tetralogy (Alexander 2002a and 2002b, 2004, 2005) and is confirmed by the marvelous and phenomenologically rich investigations of Yi-Fu Tuan, especially his *Space and Place* (1977) and his *Passing Strange and Wonderful* (1995).

Langer's intent is not to give us a complete theory of architecture, but rather to frame its distinctiveness in light of her unified and internally differentiated aes-thetic framework. Her goal is fundamentally theoretical and philosophical. It is to place architecture in the system of plastic forms and its primary illusion of virtual space, which appears in the mode of *"envisagement of an ethnic domain"* (*FF* 100). The first consequence of such a notion is the freeing of architecture from merely technical considerations, a temptation to which many architects in the age of modern technically enabled architecture have succumbed. The second conse-quence is that architecture should proceed "from the inside to the outside of a building" (*FF* 100). The outside, Langer thinks, is, indeed ought to be, defined by the extremes of opaqueness and transparency, depending on the factors of pro-tection or interaction as carrying more weight. The third consequence is that we establish a criterion for distinguishing between essentials, variables, and auxiliaries in architecture. Roofs and rooms convertible into summer or winter rooms are variables, furniture is clearly an auxiliary; steam or hot-water heat, on the other hand, affects "the utility of a building, but not its semblance—not even its functional semblance." They are material factors, but not architectural elements" (*FF* 101).

What about the relation of architecture to sculpture? While the earliest sculpture, such as the primitive "Venuses," was entirely in the round, sculpture itself, she observes, rapidly got assimilated to architecture. Relief and free figures get supported by the buildings they are associated with. But Langer claims that great sculpture is not an architectural element. Indeed, it takes a "very strong, self-sufficient" interior to accommodate sculpture. An architectural space and a piece of sculpture are "each other's exact complements; the one, an illusion of kinetic volume, symbolizing the Self, or center of life—the other, an illusion of ethnic domain, or the environment created by Selfhood. Each articulates one half of the life-symbol directly and the other by implication; whichever we start with, the other is its background" (*FF* 102). Sculpture can articulate the clear meaning of a building when it would otherwise be over the heads of its possessors. Such a situation was found in the case of the medieval cathedrals, though the statuary did not create the architecture. "The cathedral is a place created for life-symbols rather than for actual life, which falls too far short of the architectural idea. In highly ideal creations sculpture and architecture often have to supplement each other" (*FF* 102). The most perfect cultures are in fact characterized by mental reaches that are "far beyond actual human grasps," and it is in these contexts that we have such supplementation. Langer has in mind here Egypt, Greece, medieval Europe, China, Japan, and so forth in their highest and greatest periods. Sculpture becomes once again independent when the concept of the social environment "falls emotionally into confusion" and "life" is understood "only from *within* the individual" and then painting also, as the "semblance of objective visual *scene*," comes "into its own as the paramount art of our day" (*FF* 102).

Such in outline is Langer's insightful and engaging treatment of the arts of the visual from her symbolic-logical perspective. It displays both a persistent unity of vision and a recognition of the critical and normative implications of a coherent point of view. It is a set of instructions for perception as well as a theoretical establishing of limits. But the heuristic power, if not completeness, of Langer's approach is also confirmed when we turn to one of the "poor sisters" of philosophical aesthetics, namely, dance, an art form that Langer was deeply attached to.

Virtual Powers: Dance

Langer's aesthetic theory, and her instructions for perceiving, is deepened and extended by her discussion of the art of dancing. The question, as she sees it, is to determine just what dancing is—"what it expresses, what it creates, and how it is related to the other arts, to the artist, and to the actual world" (*FF* 169). Langer asks the same two questions about dance that she asks about the other arts: What is the "primary illusion" created by dance and what is the "basic abstraction" by means of which the illusion is "created and shaped" (*FF* 169)? The problem is to determine just what it is that dancers do and "what the doing signifies" (*FF* 169). Although the perception of a dance is "just as direct and natural as the enjoyment of any other art" (*FF* 169), dance, Langer thinks, is subject to many misunderstandings. For Langer dance is not "a gestural rendering of musical forms" (*FF* 169), nor one of the essentially plastic arts, using physical movement as its medium (*FF* 172), nor is it fundamentally pantomimic or dramatic (*FF* 173). Langer once again distinguishes between materials and elements. "Pantomime, like pure motion patterns, plastic images, and musical forms, is dance material, something that may become a balletic element, but the dance itself is something else" (*FF* 173).

What does Langer think it is? If it is to be an autonomous art form, on Langer's account, it must have its primary illusion and its basic abstraction. Langer resolutely insists that the primary illusion of any art form "is something created, and created at the first touch" (*FF* 174). In the case of dance a *motion* is transformed into a *gesture*. For Langer "all dance motion is gesture, or an element in the exhibition of gesture— . . . always motivated by the semblance of an expressive movement" (*FF* 174). Dance has an essentially "gestic character," for gesture is "the basic abstraction whereby the dance illusion is made and organized" (*FF* 174). Note, once again, that Langer consistently uses the concept of a "basic abstraction."

But what is a gesture, one asks, as opposed to a physical movement? A gesture is a vital movement, with "subjective and objective, personal and public, willed (or evoked) and perceived" dimensions or aspects (*FF* 174). The performer of a gesture accesses it directly as a kinetic experience and in a vague way also by sight, "as an effect" (*FF* 174). From the side of the observer the gesture is "*seen and understood* as vital movement" (*FF* 174), not as a "motion of things, sliding or waving or rolling around" (*FF* 174). For Langer it is the *form* of the gesture that is responsible for its being always spontaneously expressive. What Langer includes under "form" here encompasses the expressive qualities of being "free and big, or nervous and tight, quick or leisurely, etc., according to the psychological condition of the person who makes it. This self-expressive aspect is akin to the tone of voice in speech" (*FF* 175)—but in the dance it is controlled. In the case of dance—indeed, in the case of the "dance" of human life—gestures that in actual life would function as signals or symptoms are transformed into symbols, a system composed of assigned and combinable elements or units. *A dance gesture is not gesticulation.* Gesture in art, on Langer's position, is something *imagined* apart from the situation or mentality in which it was first rooted. In this way a gesture becomes a "free symbolic form, which may be used to convey *ideas* of emotion, of awareness and premonition, or may be combined with or incorporated in other virtual gestures, to express other physical and mental tensions" (*FF* 175). So, *tensions,* and their "logic," can also be expressed in dance, which, while rooted in the concrete body of the dancer, nevertheless is fully "abstract."

The pivot of Langer's analysis is, once again, the semiotic distinction between signals and symbols, between indices (symptoms) and symbols, in Peircean terms, and between the actual and the virtual. Virtual gestures, which make up the elements of dance, "are not signals, they are symbols of will" (*FF* 175). While natural gestures well up from living beings as actual centers of vital force, virtual gestures create an illusion, and the vital force they express is itself illusory: "the 'powers' (i.e. centers of vital force) in dance are created being—created by the semblance gesture" (*FF* 175). In this way we arrive at one of the central theses of Langer's account of dance: "The primary illusion of dance is a virtual realm of Power—not actual, physically exerted power, but appearances of influence and agency created by virtual gesture" (*FF* 175). There is a fertile tension in Langer's account. The gestures not only create a sense of powers but seem to be a place where they appear, the motion of the dances seeming "to spring from powers beyond the performers" (*FF* 175). These powers or forces, however, are purely virtual, not physical, although the medium in which they appear is clearly physical. The virtuality is rooted in "the subjective experience of volition and free agency, and of reluctance to alien, compelling wills" (*FF* 176). We are confronted in the dance with a feeling of power, but the power is not "physical," in an objectivistic sense, but involves *a play of "felt" energies.* Felt energies and felt powers take on form in the dance gesture. The dancer by means of the dance, in which he or she is embodied, presents us with a *conception* of a power. The dance is a symbolic form that presents such a conception or idea. The dance is not symptom, not physiological effect or outpouring of a surplus of emotion or feeling, but *a constructed image or objective symbol.*

What governs the dance, as it does other forms of art symbols, is *imagined feeling,* "not real emotional conditions" (*FF* 177). Langer constantly hammers home the thesis that the dance gesture is not real gesture, but virtual gesture. "It is *actual movement,* but *virtual self-expression*" (*FF* 178). Actual movements can, of course, be the "first ingredients" or "models" for the virtual gestures of the dance, which are gestic forms, not actual gestures, naturalistically and purposively understood. A gesture, on Langer's principles, can be either "self-expressive" or "logically expressive" (*FF* 180). "It may indicate demands and intentions"—signaling behavior—"or it may be conventionally symbolic," or clearly it can be both, but not from the same point of view. This is Bühler's principle of abstractive relevance once again, based on pertinentization. The same movement is or can be both symptom and symbol, depending on the framework of analysis, which determines to which features and relations we are to attend. While human language has clearly developed in unique ways the symbolic side of language, gesture is clearly more fit for "self-expression" than for functioning as "word." A word is expressive when it "formulates an idea clearly and aptly, but a highly expressive gesture is usually taken to be one that reveals feeling or emotion. It is *spontaneous* movement" (*FF* 180). In the dance, however, as we have repeatedly seen, we must always make a distinction between actual gestures and virtual gestures. This is a kind of semiotic *pons asinorum.* "The dancer's actual gestures are used to create a semblance of self-expression, and are thereby transformed into virtual spontaneous movement, or virtual gesture" (*FF* 180). We see clearly here the continuing central role of the notion of "semblance."

Langer's analysis further points to crucial somatic, kinesthetic, dimensions not just to dance but to the other arts of performance. The actual movement in a dance, she remarks, is controlled by "an actual body-feeling, akin to that which controls the production of tones in musical performance—the final articulation of *imagined* feeling in its appropriate physical form. The conception of feeling disposes the dancer's body to symbolize it" (*FF* 181). With such a comment Langer clearly shows her phenomenological perspicuity. The performance arts of music and dance are rooted in the lived body, which phenomenological aesthetics has foregrounded. Hence, "Virtual gesture may create the semblance of self-expression without anchoring it in the actual personality, which, as the source only of the actual (non-spontaneous) gestures, disappears as they do in the dance. In its place is the created personality, a dance element which figures simply as a psychical, human or superhuman Being. It is this that is expressing itself" (*FF* 181). A philosophical analysis of dance, and not just dance, must, in spite of its intrinsic difficulty, "keep virtual elements and actual materials separate" (*FF* 181). The formulation of feeling in a perceptible symbol creates an imagined feeling or emotion. It is not the "expression" of an actually felt emotion on the part either of the artist or of the performer.

The dance gesture is a symbol that expresses, as we have seen in the case of all art symbols, as Langer claims, a *vital import*. This import itself is not illusory. It is "something actual that is revealed, articulated, made manifest by the symbol" (*FF* 182). The symbolic form, which is the dance itself and all its constituents, must be supported by every imagined factor, but "the feeling of the whole work is the 'meaning' of the symbol, the reality which the artist has found in the world and of which he wants to give his fellow men a clear conception" (*FF* 182). This symbol, we must never forget, belongs to a different order of reality than actuality. It is *not* what it *is*. The basic abstraction of dance—the basic abstraction of all the arts—involves a *Scheingefühl*, the semblance of a feeling. The constitutive gesture that makes up dance is not a real gesture, expressing "real" feeling, but the semblance of a gesture. The dance movement only "*seems* to spring from feeling" (*FF* 183). The feeling implied in such a gesture does not have to be attributed to the dancer but can be attributed to "some natural or supernatural power expressing itself through him" (*FF* 183). The dancer can be a receptacle through which a power passes. But a sharp line separates actual feeling *shown* and feeling *represented*, symptom and symbol, motif and created image. If these are confused, insight into the distinctive nature of an artwork is blocked.

Dance creates a "true artistic illusion, a realm of 'Powers,' wherein purely imaginary beings from whom the vital force emanates shape a whole world of dynamic forms by their magnet-like, psycho-physical actions" (*FF* 184). These powers can be of many sorts and indeed are and have been intimately connected with "religion, terror, mysticism and madness" (*FF* 184). The anthropological literature, to which Langer refers but which does not have to be examined here, is replete with analyses that connect dance, in all forms, including the dance of "ritual" and "liturgy," with these psychic and affective states. Still, dance can perform the function of art "in worship as in play" (*FF* 184); indeed, it can turn worship itself into a kind of play, a theme pursued with scholarly details by Bernhard Lang in his illuminating *Sacred Games* (1997). In all these instances we have the setting up of "dance forces, virtual tensions, virtual centers or 'poles' of energy" (*FF* 185). The dance elements emerge "from the interplay of virtual forces of 'space tensions' and 'body tensions' and even less specific 'dance tensions' created by music, lights, décor, poetic suggestion, and what not" (*FF* 186). The connection of religion with art and the aesthetic dimension is clearly once again adumbrated here, a theme pursued by many others in different formats such as Gerardus van der Leeuw (1963), F. David Martin (1972), Thomas Martland (1981), and James A. Martin (1990). It also becomes clear that the "powers" made manifest by the dance/dancer *need not be personalized*. They can be impersonal, cosmic powers.

The primal sin of aesthetic theory is, and remains, for Langer to fail to distinguish between the actual and the virtual and between the virtual symbol and its import, "which refers us back to reality" (*FF* 186). Langer refers to Cassirer's analysis of mythical consciousness here, which Cassirer shows, in Langer's words, is marked by a "telescoping of symbols and meanings, word and world, into one metaphysical entity" (*FF* 186). Mythical consciousness is *"structurally the same as the artistic consciousness. It is metaphorical almost from first to last"* (*FF* 186). Dance, accordingly, produces "semblances of physical or magical forces" (*FF* 186). A proper understanding of dance (and even by extension a ritual) as virtual "lets one conceive the entire world of dance as a field of virtual powers—there are no actualities left in it at all, no untransformed materials, but only elements, living Beings, centers of force, and their interplay" (*FF* 187). The key notion of "virtual spontaneous gesture" carries, then, enormous weight for Langer. This is the primary illusion of dance, in which the play of Powers is made visible. It establishes dance as a "complete and autonomous art, the creation and organization of a realm of virtual Powers" (*FF* 187).

This realm comes into existence in sets of objects that are "complexes of intersecting forces in balletic space" (*FF* 187). These objects, as Rudolf von Laban wrote and Langer cited, are marked by tension (*Spannung*) and nucleation (*Ballung*). A complex, maybe even at times cosmic, field of tensions is nucleated in the dance, coming into existence and passing away. "This nucleation arises, endures, expires and begets by this play of tension the impressions of Time, Space, Power, and the like," Laban writes, in a passage that Langer cites approvingly and helpfully.

Langer deepens her analysis of dance—and shows its relevance far beyond dance proper, too—in a second chapter devoted to "the magic circle," which is also dependent upon Cassirer, as is her framework as a whole. The magic circle is the circle of myth, which is founded on one key idea: "the idea of the Spirit World" (*FF* 188), which is also a field of forces that escape the net of scientific investigation. Langer refers explicitly to Cassirer's analysis of mythic powers, to which are ascribed an "objective" reality even if they are rooted in "subjectivity," ultimately in the sense of bodily power and of the body as an originating center of force. Mythic consciousness, on this conception, is defined by "the feelings of power that serve as symbols" which "are attributed to the reality symbolized, and the world appears as a realm of potent Beings" (*FF* 189). Dancing, perhaps the most archaic of all the "authentic" arts, "creates an image of nameless and even bodiless Powers filling a complete, autonomous realm, a 'world.' It is the first presentation of the world as a realm of mystic forces" (*FF* 190). But "original" dancing, embedded in mythic consciousness, does not distinguish between the symbolic dance and the "realities" it makes us participate in. Religious thinking "begets the conception of 'Powers' as it symbolizes them," and these realities, made present in the dance, are not perceived as "merely symbolic" of something else. "The symbol of the world, the balletic realm of forces, *is* the world, and dancing is the human spirit's participation in it" (*FF* 190; see all of part 1 of van der Leeuw 1963 which treats "beautiful motion").

Langer, following Curt Sachs, foregrounds the circle dance, the locus of the sacred realm, as the original magic circle. It is not a spontaneous expression of *joi de vivre*, a kind of prancing defined by an overflow of vitality. Rather "it fulfills a holy office, perhaps the *first* holy office of the dance—it divides the sphere of holiness from that of profane existence. In this way it creates the stage of the dance, which centers naturally in the altar or its equivalent—the totem, the priest, the fire— or perhaps the slain bear, the dead chieftain, to be consecrated" (*FF* 191). Such a dance is "ecstatic" in the sense of decentering, since the center of concern is displaced to the realm of virtual Powers. These powers are not strictly speaking *imitated*. It is true that an *image* is created, but the image is "of a world of vital forces, embodied or disembodied" and the constructive function of the dance elements is oriented toward establishing, maintaining, and articulating the play of Powers that make up the original realm of holiness. Whatever mimetic elements, in the sense of motifs, there are to be found in the dance are transformed. They do not refer to themselves, but rather are taken up into the magic circle wherein the dancer becomes an apparition, or at least the locus of apparition, of something— personal or impersonal—beyond the dancer. This is a "remote, rationally indescribable world in which forces seem to become visible. But what makes them visible is not itself always visual; hearing and kinesthesia support the rhythmic, moving image, to such an extent that the dance illusion exists for the dancer as well as for the spectators" (*FF* 195). Dance is in a sense the first *Gesamtkunstwerk*.

Still, dance, according to Langer, is, and remains, an essentially visual phenomenon, exploiting a given illumination, while, paradoxically, its basic abstraction is virtual gesture. The gesture is seen, indeed must be seen, as well as felt. "Conscious gesture is essentially communication, like language," but it loses its communicative character when the exchange of gestures takes place in total darkness. As a result, Langer will hold to a most nuanced position: "Our most direct knowledge of gestic expression is muscular feeling, but its purpose is to be seen" (*FF* 196).

> Every dancer *sees* the dance sufficiently to let his imagination grasp it as a whole; and with his own body-feeling he understands the gestic forms that are its interwoven, basic elements. He cannot see his own form as such, but he *knows* his appearance— the lines described by his body are implied in the shifts of his vision, even if he is

> dancing alone, and are guaranteed by the rhythmic play of his muscles, the freedom
> with which his impulses spend themselves in complete and intended movements.
> He sees *the world in which his body dances,* and that is the primary illusion of his work;
> in this closed realm he develops his ideas. (*FF* 197)

Langer argues that the musical and pictorial effects that always universally accompany dance are contributory to its primary illusion, the appearance of Power
(*FF* 198). Langer's position, nevertheless, seems to involve a paradox: space and
time enter constitutively, but not necessarily essentially, into dance. Langer quotes
a provocative, indeed profound, passage from Rudolf Sonner's *Musik und Tanz:*

> On lower cultural levels, dance is a typical symbol of space, and begets an intense
> space-experience. For there is, as yet, no place of worship save possibly a plotted
> field (sacred grove), a holy ground. But from the moment when, by the building of
> temples, a new, deep space-experience is created in terms of another symbolism,
> dance as a [spatial] cult ceremony seems to be superseded by the forces of architec-
> ture.(1930: 76, cited in *FF* 198)

As to time, dance, Langer notes, "always moves in *musical time*" (*FF* 198) and
between music and time there is a "universal affinity" (*FF* 198). Both dance and
music take us out of ourselves. They are essentially *ecstatic.* But the dance as an
ecstatic experience, wherein the dancer dances *with* the world, goes over into the
dance as spectacle (*FF* 199). Being addressed to an audience allows the dance to
become essentially a spectacle and thus to find "its true creative aim—to make
the world of Powers visible" (*FF* 199) and not just to evoke this world. The form
and continuity of the dance is no longer dictated "from within" (*FF* 199), as
drive toward mythic participation. The kinesthetic elements "must be replaced
by visual, audible, or histrionic elements to create a comparable ecstatic illusion
for an audience" (*FF* 199–200)—and for the dancer who now sees himself from
the outside, in effect objectifying himself for himself, instituting a kind of double
vision. This breaks the focus on actuality and "sets up the virtual image of a different world; to create a play of forces that *confronts* the percipient, instead of en-
gulfing him, as it does when he is dancing, and his own activity is a major factor in making the dance illusion" (*FF* 200). Thus the rise of the passive audience
separates the dance as spectacle from the dance as activity, a crucial event in
the history of the balletic art. Indeed, dance as activity is a more primitive form,
which could even be subject to regressive tendencies, a return to "primitivism"
in various forms and contexts, including, Langer notes, with ominous astuteness,
"a strong tendency to myth and cult activity in political life" (*FF* 201). Cassirer
wrote a remarkable book, *The Myth of the State,* about precisely this phenomenon
and turn of events. Indeed, the staging of the great Nazi rallies illustrated, in the

twentieth century, the great temptation toward ritualistic enthusiasm where a kind of "dance" supplanted reasoned discourse and persuasion in making "political reality" visible. Leni Riefenstahl's *Triumph of the Will* immortalized this regression to the demonically primitive under the guise of high sophistication.

Secularization, to which Langer, in spite of her very ambiguous relation to religion, if, however, not to the "religious" and the "holy," ascribes the infliction of a great trauma on all the arts, has affected deeply the separation of stage dancing from ecstatic dancing (*FF* 201). It leads one to ask why people continue to dance at all, if dance has lost its mythico-religious context and if there are no effective motives of worship or magic-making. Langer's answer is that the image of Powers is still vital and active as a world image, even if there is a profound shift from religious to romantic uses of the dance, wherein a dream world of erotic forces comes to effective presence. However, from the balletic standpoint, as Langer notes, there is effected a "sense of freedom from gravity" (*FF* 292). This is the type of ingredient or component that is not affected by any change in the external context of dance. There is a "direct and forceful effect of rhythmicized gesture" (*FF* 203) such that there is produced

> a new body-feeling, in which every muscular tension registers itself as something kinesthetically new, peculiar to the dance. In a body so disposed, no movement is automatic; if any action goes forward spontaneously, it is induced by the *rhythm* set up in imagination, and prefigured in the first, intentional act, and not by practical habit. In a person with a penchant for the dance, this body-feeling is intense and complete, involving every voluntary muscle, to the fingertips, the throat, the eyelids. It is the sense of virtuosity, akin to the sense of articulation that marks the talented performer of music. The dancer's body is *ready for rhythm.* (*FF* 202–203)

This is another instance of Langer's phenomenological acuity and range as well as a consequence of her constant awareness of the "studio standpoint" in aesthetic analyses.

How is a dance made into a work of art? Through the "translation of kinesthetic experience into visual and audible elements. . . . The dancer, or dancers, must transform the stage for the audience as well as for themselves into an autonomous, complete, virtual realm, and all motions into a play of visible forces in unbroken, virtual time, without effecting either a work of plastic art or of 'melos'" (*FF* 204). Dance is autonomous and *sui generis,* absorbing music, space, time, and all supporting components into itself. This makes dance an exceedingly "thick" art form.

> The primary illusion of dance is a peculiarly rich experience, just as immediate as that of music or of the plastic arts, but more complex. Both space and time are im-

plicitly created with it. Story runs through it like a thread, without linking it at all to literature; impersonation and miming are often systematically involved in its basic abstraction, virtual gesture, but dance pantomime is not drama; the mummery of masks and costumes, to which its thematic gestures belong, is depersonalizing rather than humanly interesting. Dance, the art of the Stone Age, the art of primitive life par excellence, holds a hegemony over all art materials.

Yet like all art it can harbor no raw material, no things or facts, in its illusory world. The virtual form must be organic and autonomous and divorced from actuality. Whatever enters into it does so in radical artistic transformation: its space is plastic, its time is musical, its themes are fantasy, its actions symbolic. (*FF* 204)

But in spite of these powerful secondary illusions, Langer holds steadfastly to the distinctiveness of dance. Indeed, for Langer the orders of art, which are radically distinct, never really merge, any more than all the various symbolic forms merge upon a "common reality" existing independently of them. The secondary illusions and their supporting facts "serve to make the semblance of psychic and mystic Powers an image of the 'powers' directly felt in all organic life, physical or mental, active or passive" (*FF* 206). This enables the dance form to grow organically, since it springs from "an idea of feeling, a matrix of symbolic form" (*FF* 206). Langer will return to these themes in a different, epistemological context in *Mind*, pinpointing in the later sections of the book the gradual process of disenchantment or secularization. But in spite of the fact that "the realm of magic around the altar" has been broken, "inevitably and properly," human beings still "dance with high seriousness and fervor; the temple dance and the rain dance were never more reverent than the work of our devout artists" (*FF* 207). The *form* of the "magic circle" remains.

Langer ends her discussion of dance by noting that while *serious* dance is very ancient, dance *as art* is relatively new. "And as art it creates the image of that pulsating organic life which it was formerly expected to give and sustain" (*FF* 207). As a conclusion to the chapter Langer cites a long passage from Mary Wigman's essay "The New German Dance." It is a fitting conclusion to her own involuted and profound argument.

> The image which has assumed form gives evidence of the primary vision conceived through the inner experience. That creation will ever be the most pure and forceful in its effect, in which the most minute detail speaks of the vibrating, animating unity which called forth the idea. The shape of the individual's inner experience . . . will also have the unique, magnetic power of transmission which makes it possible to draw other persons, the participating spectators, into the magic circle of creation. (Wigman 1935, cited in *FF* 207)

Symbolic *objectification* and existential, indeed cosmic, *participation* stand in a permanent tensive relationship to one another. Here is a challenge for us to engage dance at the deepest levels of our bodily existence.

Virtual Experience and Virtual Memory: Literature

Turning now to Langer's treatment of literature, one of the most discussed of all forms of art, is both illuminating and at the same time rather perplexing. Langer's main assertion is that the *"illusion of life* is the primary illusion of all poetic art" (*FF* 213), just as the illusion of space is the primary illusion of plastic art, the illusion of time the primary illusion of the musical arts, the illusion of a field of forces or power the primary illusion of the balletic arts, and so forth. Indeed, when Langer claims that the poet has made an illusion she refers directly to the visual arts, and the poetic illusion is "as complete as the illusion of space created by a few strokes on paper" (*FF* 211). It is an illusion "by means of words," and words are the *materials "out of which* he makes his poetic elements. The *elements* are what he deploys and balances, spreads out or intensifies or builds up, to make a poem" (*FF* 211). *Materials*, once again, then, are to be distinguished from *elements*, a distinction that runs through Langer's whole theory. Now every successful poem, Langer claims, referring to one of her root concepts, must have "organic character" (*FF* 214). Its task is to create the "semblance of experienced events . . . a virtual order of experiences" (*FF* 214). But the import of the poem is not, indeed cannot be, "literal," in any sense of that term. It is, like all the other art genres, a self-contained world, purely virtual, not actual, a "presented 'world'" (*FF* 217). It is this world that the poem—or novel—is "about." This world is purely experiential, immanent to the poem. It is this feature that "makes the 'world' of a poetic world more intensely significant than the actual world" (*FF* 216), whose significance it can, nevertheless, profoundly and sharply illuminate, but not directly. The virtual world of literature parallels the virtual space of a picture. "For the primary illusion of literature, the semblance of life, is abstracted from immediate, personal life, as the primary illusions of the other arts—virtual space, time, and power—are images of perceived space, vital time, felt power" (*FF* 217). So, the primary illusion of literature arises from its primary abstraction—virtual events embodied in a text, a web of words.

In spite of her attempt to generalize the aesthetic lessons of music and of the plastic arts, which are treated in *Feeling and Form* before she turns to literature, Langer resolutely holds to the centrality of language in world building. "Meditation," she writes, is "inseparable from ways of speaking" and "discursive thought . . . is in turn the mold of our individual experience" (*FF* 220). There is, for the language animal, no realm of "brute fact," a topic Langer had already broached in her first works and given a thematic treatment of in the epistemologically focused last chapter of *Philosophy in a New Key*. Here, consequently, Langer is content to simply assert that "whatever brute fact may be, our experience of it bears the stamp of language" (*FF* 220), including the language of science, that is, number. The consequence of this for literature is that "in poetic events, the element of brute fact is illusory; the stamp of language makes the whole thing, it creates the 'fact'" (*FF* 220), just as "scientific facts," in some of their forms, are created by the numerical symbolism that was expressly invented or developed to deal with them. "Facts" and "symbolic" formulations grow together. Langer, totally in line with a Deweyan approach, which she nevertheless persistently refuses to seriously engage, claims that "virtual events are qualitative in their very constitution—the 'facts' have no existence apart from values; their emotional import is part of their appearance; they cannot, therefore, be stated and then 're-acted to.' They occur only as they seem—they are *poetic facts,* not neutral facts toward which we are invited to take a poetic attitude" (*FF* 223). In this passage, once again, we have Langer opposing the notion of an "aesthetic attitude."

As a result, literature—in whatever its mode—is not propositional and does not produce a discourse "about" facts that exist independently of their qualitatively defined formulations, although a literary work is filled with what seem to be propositions, that is, language in statement form (see Innis 2001 and 2007 for an exemplification of this in the analysis of a text from a novel of Iris Murdoch, *The Sacred and Profane Love Machine*). "It was a dark and stormy night" is not a report on weather conditions *tout court* and cannot be verified by independent evidence or by an alternative empirical description. Propositions are "only materials of poetry" (*FF* 227). A poem, and *a fortiori* a novel or short story, is not a set of statements, even if it includes language in statement form, but a "created appearance, a fabric of virtual events" (*FF* 228). Yet, it is also not an "escape from reality" (*FF* 228). When direct statements are found in a poem or another form of literary "fiction," when, that is, we seem to be dealing with a discursive form, their "directness is a means of creating a virtual experience, a non-discursive form expressing a special sort of emotion or sensibility; that is to say, their *use* is poetic, even if they are bald assertions of fact" (*FF* 228). Their role is to function as a "symbol of a feeling" (*FF* 230). This role is "iconic," in the Peircean sense, or qualitative in the Deweyan sense, even if they are clearly linguistic forms. The peculiarity of Langer's approach here, in the case of the poetic arts, is to claim that the art symbol, in her sense of that term, can iconically, but not in instrumental or "pointing" fashion, embody the feeling, "not by recalling objects that would elicit the feeling itself, but by weaving a pattern of words—words charged with meaning and colored by literary associations—akin to the dynamic pattern of the feeling (the word 'feeling' here covers more than a 'state'; for feeling is a process, and may have not only successive phases, but several simultaneous developments; it is complex and its articulations are elusive)" (*FF* 230). So, in Nelson Goodman's terms, once again, the symbol *exemplifies* the properties of what it is "about," that is, it possesses, albeit metaphorically, the properties. (See Goodman 1976, 1978; Innis 1977.) These properties can clearly be the properties of "appearing" to be straightforward discourse. A novel in the form of a "memoir" can appear to be such a report of "real" events while all the while being entirely virtual. James Joyce's *Ulysses* is a veritable encyclopedia of rhetorical modes and exercises within the framework of a "novel."

No form of poetic art, then, follows, or can follow, the laws of a "discursive logic" (*FF* 233), for every "poem" is a "non-discursive symbolic form" that follows its own laws of thought, which "*never apply to scientific or pseudo-scientific (practical) reasoning*" (*FF* 234). The effective laws here are the laws of the imagination, not the laws of discourse. The use of verbal statement in the poetic arts hides, by reason of its obviousness, "the characteristic forms of verbal figment" (*FF* 234). Consequently, Langer draws, in the case of literature as in the other arts, a sharp dividing line between *actual* experience and *virtual* experience, which defines the sharp separation, in her opinion, between art and life in general and between fact and fiction, literature and life, in particular.

For Langer a work of poetic art is not only an *image* of life but also an image of *life*. Following Cassirer, Langer continues to assimilate the poetic art to a kind of mythic thinking, which does not follow the laws of discourse but mingles, as primitive man did, abstraction with fabrication, fuses symbolic reference and power, and, out of an emotional excitement, initiates a complex naming process that "created entities not only for sense perception but for memory, speculation, and dream" (*FF* 237). These entities are isomorphic with the literary image, subject to a logic of multiple meanings and employing "representative figures instead of classes" (*FF* 237). But while mythic thinking may have arisen spontaneously and without self-conscious control of the abstraction process, the literary image is for Langer a patent construct. In weaving its verbal web it exploits the full meaning of words, which are "flashing, iridescent shapes like flames—ever-flickering vestiges of the slowly-evolving consciousness beneath them" (*FF* 238). Cassirer and Owen Barfield, upon whom Langer relies, hold, in ways still relevant, a "theory of multiple meanings and fusion of symbol and sense" (*FF* 239). When the symbol and the sense are fused, what Cassirer calls "symbolic pregnance," we have a "non-discursive form," no matter what its material embodiment may be. Mythic and aesthetic forms, however, while closely related, are not to be identified, though they share common deep features. These forms, Langer insistently holds, "articulate knowledge that cannot be rendered discursively because it concerns experiences that are not *formally* amenable to the discursive projection" (*FF* 240–241).

What are these experiences?

Langer answers that they are "the rhythms of life, organic, emotional, mental (the rhythm of attention is an interesting link among them all), which are not simply periodic, but endlessly complex, and sensitive to every sort of influence. All together they compose the dynamic pattern of feeling. It is this pattern that only non-discursive symbolic forms can present, and that is the point of artistic construction" (*FF* 241). These forms are marked by three great semantic principles, which are not unique to Langer: *over-determination, ambivalence,* and *condensation,* which are well known to literary scholars and to all workers in the human sciences, including those who work in the realm of dream and neurosis, which for Langer is distinctly not the realm of art. A poem, she says, is meant to be "always emotionally transparent" (*FF* 244), which does not mean "obvious." It is meant to be an "*illusion of experience*" (*FF* 245), which is the "poetic primary illusion" (*FF* 245). The virtual world of the poem—of the literary work, quite generally—has an "emotional significance above the suggested emotions which are elements in it" (*FF* 245). In this virtual world comes to expression what Langer calls "the morphology of real human feeling" (*FF* 253). This morphology is rooted in our intellectual and biological being: "we are driven to the symbolization and articulation of feeling when we *must* understand it to keep ourselves oriented in society and nature" (*FF* 253).

But the principle of poesis is that "everything actual must be transformed by imagination into something purely experiential" (*FF* 258). So, the literary work, too, is a form of experiencing, a symbolic experiencing that arises out of "biological unities of thought and feeling which are entirely unexplored as yet" (*FF* 259)—or so Langer thought at the time she was writing *Feeling and Form.* (See now, however, the works of Antonio Damasio and Gerald Edelman and others that are throwing new light on these biological unities. Donald Dryden [2007] is a valuable and compact resource here, as is Evan Thompson [2007], who resolutely pursues the theme of the "continuity of life and mind. Where there is life there is mind, and mind in its most articulated forms belongs to life" [ix]). The subjectivity, however, that is embodied in the literary work is an *impersonal subjectivity* (*FF* 261). And just as the *objects* in a painting are not its import, so the *motif* or subject matter of a poem is not its import. The subjectivity present in a literary work and the consequent virtual experience do not really belong to anyone outside of the text. While, to be sure, narrative is a "major organizing device" and "is as important to literature as representation to painting and sculpture" (*FF* 261), it is clear that Langer does not think it is indispensable or even necessary. While it is clearly a widely used "structural basis on which most works are designed," the narrative is not the artistic import, which does not, in itself, point outside of the work to something else. The virtual life that is presented in literature is "always a self-contained form, a unit of experience" (*FF* 262), having a closed form that actual experience does not have. The virtual experience, virtual history, and virtual memory of a literary work, Langer holds, must give us the illusion of a life that is experiential through and through, wherein "all its connections are *lived* connections" (*FF* 265). What Langer says about the poet, whose paradigmatic product is the lyric, is also apt to characterize the writer of narrative, whose paradigmatic product is prose fiction: "The poet makes a semblance of events that is *experience-like*, but universally accessible; an objectified, depersonalized 'memory,' entirely homogeneous, no matter how much is explicit and how much implicit" (*FF* 265). The job of the critic or of the interpreter is then to discover "the intricacies of real memory through the artistic devices that achieve its semblance" (*FF* 266), with all the complications of the "play of tenses" that may be involved.

Langer denies a sharp divide between the various literary forms. Speaking of the novel, Langer contends, in a contentious manner, to be sure, that it is not discursive at all. It performs no *essential,* as opposed to subsidiary, discursive function such as informing, commenting, inquiring, confessing, and so forth. The goal of the novelist is to "create a virtual experience, wholly formed, wholly expressive of something more fundamental than any 'modern' problem: human feeling, the nature of human life itself" (*FF* 289). The "representational features" of the novel, no matter how weighty, are, Langer claims, not determinative of its nature. The novel aims at attaining "a completely virtual, vital (i.e. organic) form, emerging with the advance of the art itself" (*FF* 289). The "air of reality" must always be maintained while we keep the literary work's fictional or virtual quality. We do this by "the simplification and manipulation of life's image that makes it essentially different from its prototype" (*FF* 292). Thus literature operates totally in the "experiential mode" (*FF* 293), which is *created, not recorded.* While, to be sure, the *material* of literature is "discursive language, not even modified and distinguished from ordinary speech by the conventions of verse, yet the product is not discourse, but the illusion of life directly lived, a world in which thinking and conversation may occur" (*FF* 297).

In general, it is clear, Langer's approach to the "semblance" character of literature follows rather traditional lines. But she embeds the traditional position in her theory of virtuality. This foregrounding of "virtual" experience detaches the literary work from "reality" or "real reference." While the "given" can certainly be a motif for a literary work, the work itself is designed to express not the "object, the fact" as such but their "emotional significance" (*FF* 301). The emotional significance is the expressive quality of the literary work, which adheres to the *form* of the expression and also to the forms and relations of the objects and events appearing in it, which may or may not have their analogues in the "real" world. But even discursive forms have a distinctive feel and can be used as a "vehicle of feeling" (*FF* 302) to display the "significant form" of argumentative thinking and reasoning, which have a distinctively phasal structure culminating in

> the cadential feeling of solution, and the expansion of consciousness in new knowledge. If all these phases merge in one configured passage, the thought, however hard, is natural; and the height of discursive style is the embodiment of such a feeling pattern, modeled, word by word, on the progressing argument. The argument is the writer's motif, and absolutely nothing else may enter in. As soon as he leads away from the motivating thought to (say) mystical or moral reaction, he is not supporting the process of understanding. (*FF* 302)

This is, to say the least, an astounding, indeed marvelous, comment. It shows the universality of feeling in Langer and also the deep parallel to Peirce's and Dewey's account of affective or qualitative thought. The message is clear: *every expressive form has a distinctive feel.* Expressiveness is the defining feature of an artwork in any genre or medium. And it is its expressiveness, in Langer's sense of that term, that is the proper object of interpretation, not the matching of the artwork with a world external to it.

So, now, we have had a taste of the actual analyses of the distinctive art forms in light of Langer's general aesthetic theory. It is, I have noted, a kind of "deduction" from her symbol theory, modified and shaped by a keen phenomenological sense for the experientially concrete. It is also a sophisticated fusion of the descriptive and the prescriptive, an attempt to apply a coherent and unified conceptual framework to the whole continuum of art genres and to submit them to a unified description and interpretation. It is not necessary to accept everything that Langer proposes, but while one need not accept her account as the whole story, she has certainly managed to uncover essential features of the various genres and to provoke us to confront what she *really* says with positions developed from quite different starting points.

6

The Mind of Feeling

Langer's intellectual adventure culminated in her massive trilogy, *Mind: An Essay on Human Feeling*. This astounding work defies easy summarization and critical evaluation, although in one way it is a clear continuation of Langer's engagement with a permanent set of concerns that also, in some important respects, vex the main currents of the cognitive science quite generally, although Langer's themes go rather far beyond its normal scope:

- the nature of philosophical reflection in relation to non-philosophical methods
- symbolization, or symbolic transformation, as the central activity of human mentation
- the development of a comprehensive concept of *feeling* to cover the total mental field
- the centrality of art as the heuristic key to mind
- the nature of abstraction as the pivotal act of mind
- the role of images in the development of mind
- the evolution and implications, both epistemological and cultural, of the great symbolic forms of language, myth, ritual, art, science

At the same time Langer turns more explicitly to issues that can only be characterized as "metaphysical," especially as dealing with the "metaphysics of mind."

Mind is a kind of philosophical tour de force, a complex web of semiotic, phenomenological, psychological, metaphysical, and meta-philosophical reflections.
Its sources range from the introspective and personal to the most arcane researches in neurochemistry and neurobiology in multiple languages, comprising pivotal neglected materials from the past as well as, at least when Langer was
writing, up-to-date work in a wide variety of scientific disciplines. But her conclusions are conceptual and constructive and have not been superseded by later
"discoveries" of an empirical nature.

In one sense Langer's *Mind* is more a deepening than a revolutionary advance
or radical break with her previous work. It is, however, certainly and fundamentally novel, in both format, method, and tone. Langer wanted to develop "a philosophical theory of mind" that "can serve the mental and social sciences" (*M-I* 52),
a topic that lies at the center of John Powers's and Lloyd Sandelands's interests in
Langer (see Powers 2006 and Sandelands 1998). How? "It means going back to
the beginnings of thought about mental phenomena and starting with different
ideas, different expectations, without concern for experiments or statistics or formalized language" (*M-I* 52). In a sense this is exactly what Langer does, although
her sources are at times extremely technical and specialized, not easily accessible
areas of biology and psychology.

Langer defines the central problem of *Mind* as "the nature and origin of the
veritable gulf that divides human from animal mentality, in a perfectly continuous course of development of life on earth that has no breaks" (*M-I* xvi).
The gulf is found in the human power, indeed need, to produce symbolic images. Images have a unique power to make us "originally aware of the wholeness and over-all form of entities, acts and facts in the world; and little though we
may know it, only an image can hold us to a conception of a total phenomenon,
against which we measure the adequacy of the scientific terms wherewith we describe it" (*M-I* xviii). Consequently, Langer wants to find an adequate image, not
model, of mind, which for her is a distinctive biological phenomenon. Where?

> It was the discovery that works of art are images of the forms of feeling, and that
> their expressiveness can rise to the presentation of all aspects of mind and human
> personality, which led me to the present undertaking of constructing a biological
> theory of feeling that should logically lead to an adequate concept of mind, with all
> that the possession of mind implies. (*M-I* xviii)

Works of art, as we have clearly seen in the last two chapters, are for Langer "expressive forms," manifesting every type and way that vitality and feeling, deliberately vague but rich terms, can be structured and appear. These forms can cover
the whole of life and can reveal the continuous shifts, without metaphysical gaps

and breaks, between physical and mental realities, while still pinpointing crucial thresholds "where mentality begins, and especially where human mentality transcends the animal level, and mind, *sensu stricto*, emerges" (*M-I* xix).

Langer distinguishes firmly, in this context, between an image and a model. They serve different purposes. "Briefly stated, an image shows how something appears; a model shows how something works. The art symbol, therefore, sets forth in symbolic projection how vital and emotional and intellectual tensions appear, i.e., how they feel" (*M-I* xix). This gives the art symbol an enormous heuristic fertility for Langer. In a mode of speaking that harks back to *Feeling and Form*, Langer says that art symbols make up a realm of "pure semblances" (*M-I* xix), a field of holistic symbols, that give us the key to how to conceive life itself. "Under the aegis of a holistic symbol, the concept of life builds up even in entirely scientific terms very much like the vital image in art, with no break between somatic and mental events, no 'addition' of feeling or consciousness to physical machinery, and especially, no difference of attitude, point of view, working notions, or 'logical language' dividing physics and chemistry from biology, or physiology from psychology" (*M-I* xx). What Langer wants to do on the philosophical plane is to expand, generalize, and systematize some literally meant scientific terms and observations, and in this way to develop a comprehensive theory or account of mind. The key philosophical and methodological notion is that of generalization, proceeding stepwise toward a synoptic view that has metaphysical import and value. Surprisingly, in spite of its bulk, Langer makes no claim in the trilogy to prove "the sole rightness" of her approach to her central problem: "the problem of conceiving mind as a natural phenomenon, a 'natural wonder,' and to us the greatest of all such wonders of nature" (*M-I* xxii). Langer is certainly right in this genuinely modest claim, even if her investigations are, in fact, indispensable for a refined and nuanced semiotic naturalism. She makes a more restrained claim for "serviceability." In spite of her sovereign mastery of a vast panorama of materials and her ingrained habit of working alone, Langer in effect pleads for collaboration and extension.

My procedure in this and the following chapters has by necessity to be conceptual and philosophical. I want to situate and evaluate Langer's conceptual framework and the distinctive methodology she follows. In one sense I want to take a conceptual X-ray of her theory of mind, indicating its essential distinctions, some perspicuous exemplifications, and its points of intersection with, as well as parallels to, other projects. The contexts will be methodological, semiotic, epistemological, aesthetic, cultural, and moral. The present chapter will be concerned with "subjective mind," the "mind of feeling." The following two chapters will be concerned with "objective mind," that is, mind as emerging out of a matrix of acts and mind as embodied in cultural and symbolic artifacts. In these chapters we will see how Langer once again reformulated, recapitulated, and deepened central themes of her earlier work on myth, ritual, the origin of language, the rise of science, and so forth, with the addition of an explicit ethical or moral dimension, epitomized in the fateful discovery of death.

Feeling and the Image of Mind

Langer's mature and definitive concept of mind, just as her aesthetic theory, is based on the concept of *feeling*. Feeling is, quite generally, "whatever is felt in any way, as sensory stimulus or inward tension, pain, emotion or intent." It is *the* "mark of mentality" (*M-I* 4). Feeling, on Langer's conception, characterizes physiological systems, not as an additional "reality" but as a dimension or phase of the system. In the cases of physiology and psychology, as understood by Langer, the "overlapping of the two fields is patent" (*M-I* 4). Psychology, on her conception, is "oriented toward the aspects of sensibility, awareness, excitement, gratification or suffering which belong" to physiological events, which are clearly material, when they reach a certain level of complexity (*M-I* 4). Mentality and feeling, for Langer, are synonymous. Mentality is a field of "felt impingements and activities" (*M-I* 9) and covers feeling, thought, sensation, and dream (*M-I* 9). A science of mind needs, Langer thinks, in a way paralleling the work of William James, not so much a "definitive concept of mind, as a conceptual frame in which to lodge our observations of mental phenomena" (*M-I* 17). And this is what the conceptual frame of "feeling" is meant to supply. It is, Langer would like to think, not altogether unproblematically, a generic term that is meant to be deliberately open, not freighted with a vast range of conceptual baggage from the philosophical tradition in which one particular kind of mental event is chosen to represent or norm all the rest. For Langer, mentality, in whatever form, is present when there is "feeling" of any sort or grade. The phenomenological task is to sort out its varieties.

But to speak of "feeling" is not to say there are "feelings" as distinctive reified entities. We have above all to avoid a basic misconception, that is, "the assumption of feelings (sensations, emotions, etc.) as items or entities of *any* kind" (*M-I* 19). This is a "genuine metaphysical fallacy" (*M-I* 19). For Langer, "to feel is to do something, not to have something" (*M-I* 20). Langer proposes, accordingly, to reconstruct the concept of feeling, which she calls "the modulus of psychological conception" (*M-I* 21). Assuming a world of vital processes, Langer asserts, in accordance with her philosophical naturalism, that "being felt is a phase of the process itself. A phase is a mode of appearance, and not an added factor"

(*M-I* 21). It is a becoming aware of processes, in which processes enter into their psychical phase, "the phase of being felt" (*M-I* 21). This does not create another order of reality, for "the phase of being felt is strictly intraorganic" (*M-I* 21). While, as we will see, such processes can give rise to extraorganic structures that make up the objective semiosphere, they are thoroughly "natural." Moreover, they are aspects of, modifications and transformations of, the normal substrate of a universal *feeling tone* or *tonus* that marks organic life. There is, to be sure, a "fabric of totally unfelt activities" that Freud, according to Langer, reified as "the 'Unconscious,'" though Langer considers "the theoretical basis of classical psychoanalysis" as "overassumptive" (*M-I* 22–23), a topic that we can safely pass by in the present context. This fabric of unfelt activities is made up of a web of *acts*, some of which become felt in their psychical phase, although Langer will resolutely repudiate all forms of panpsychism, which are not, at any rate, irretrievably romantic or philosophically unsophisticated (see Clarke 2003). Feeling, in the last analysis, is to be strictly regarded as "a phase of physiological process" (*M-I* 23), and the category of feeling allows the "paradox of the physical and the psychical" to disappear (*M-I* 23). They are not two different levels of "reality." They are two different ways in which natural processes occur. There is a Spinozistic parallel here, though clearly no isomorphism based on Cartesian assumptions.

Langer's chief thesis is then the following. "The entire psychological field—including human conception, responsible action, rationality, knowledge—is a vast and branching development of feeling" (*M-I* 23). And, furthermore, "there is not some primitive form of feeling which is its 'real' form" (*M-I* 9). No form of feeling is more "basic" or "fundamental" than any other, nor can one manifestation or form be "reduced" to any other form. In this sense Langer operates according to the principle of "semiotic parity," paralleling Justus Buchler's concept of "ontological parity" (Buchler 1990). This is not only a conceptual decision on Langer's part. It is also based on a commitment to a kind of semiotic phenomenology, which she in fact carries out in the course of her work as a whole, and especially in the three volumes of *Mind*. So, her project is both constructive, governed by a systematic intent, and descriptive, in search of "authentic instances" of feeling. It imposes on her the task of drawing the lines between the "significant joints" in the plenum of feeling. The "forms of feeling" have to be "natural" in the sense of being able to be marked off from one another. But by being marked off they have also to be related in some systematic context, since we need to avoid both the rigidity of distinctiveness as well as the "night in which all the cows are black" approach. Hence, it is imperative for Langer to be able to uncover both the general structures that characterize feeling as such, as a quality that permeates all its forms, and to determine what is specific to each of its forms.

Feeling, therefore, is an activity (or quality of an activity) rather than a "thing" or "entity." Activities in general can be felt in many ways, we will see, but there is a clear divide, in principle, between the feeling of impact, of something intersecting with us "from outside," and the feeling of autogenic action, that is, of something felt as action. So, we have here a distinction between *exogenous* feeling and *autogenous* feeling, even if there are rarely any completely pure or unmixed cases. This distinction will appear throughout the analyses in *Mind*. Any organism embedded in an environment is a center of receptivity and of activity; indeed, the organism is a kind of system that is subject to various degrees of fine control. The relation between the environment and the organism is asymmetrical in that the environment has a kind of gross control over the organism, but the organism has a fine control over itself and its engagements with the environment. The organism is by no means a passive medium upon which the environment writes its messages. The organism is rather "a continuous dynamism, a pattern of activity" (*M-I* 26), that is, essentially an "open system." Speaking in a quasi-pragmatist mode, Langer says that all vital action is "interaction, transaction," (*M-I* 26), intrinsically reciprocal, but while the environment determines what is *given*, the organism determines what is *taken* (*M-I* 27).

For Langer the organism as an open system is a locus of creativity or "creative advance," in Whitehead's sense of the term (*M-I* 27). The immediate and permanent task of the organism is "keeping going" and developing structures and skills that respond appropriately to the "exigencies of contact with the plenum of external events" (*M-I* 27). The organism is structured by both need and demand: need for external stimuli and the demand the external field places upon it. Because the organism is in constant "motion" it is imperative that it develop, as the occasion demands, a "transitional dynamic pattern" of adjustments, systems of intercalations. The organism clearly must deal with "qualitatively different kinds of impact" (*M-I* 28). Sensibility, which Langer with full justification calls "a major department of feeling," is certainly constituted by these different kinds and, indeed, "more typically the sources of sensations are peripheral" (*M-I* 28), and come from the outside. To be a sensing organism is to be open to "irritation." At the same time Langer points out with phenomenological acuity that there is a "background of general body feelings and a texture of emotive tensions" (*M-I* 28) that not only pre-structures the organism's receptivity to the aforementioned plenum of external events but also functions as background for the vital rhythm of autogenic acts (*M-I* 29), that is, acts that arise from the center of the organism itself.

Langer maintains resolutely a kind of metaphysical monism with respect to feeling as the most comprehensive term for consciousness and for mental phenomena of all levels and types. A mental phenomenon, in any mode whatsoever, is for Langer, in an admittedly deeply enigmatic remark, not a "product of neural impulses, but . . . an aspect of their occurrence" (*M-I* 30). Feeling is "not an adjunct to natural events, but a turning point in them" (*M-I* 32). It is Langer's constant position that it is bipolar, with a subjective and an objective pole. The subjective side is "whatever is felt as action" (*M-I* 31). The objective side is "whatever is felt as impact" (*M-I* 31). This distinction clearly corresponds to the autogenic/exogenic (sense of impact) distinction and even, in one way, to the distinction between emotivity or affectivity, which defines a "state" of the organism and is itself "felt," and sensibility, which is oriented toward the external world. Hence, "subjective" and "objective" "denote functional properties" (*M-I* 31), not realities. They are "two possible modes of feeling, i.e., of psychical phases of activity" (*M-I* 31). Note here that "activity" is taken as an even more comprehensive term than "feeling," although it is clear that feeling itself is a form of activity. The influence of Whitehead is implicit and muted, but real, although Langer does not fully ascribe to the range and scope of the Whiteheadian categorial scheme. Langer's universe, like Whitehead's, is one not of substances but of centers of activity, all the way down. These centers are self-assembling and not permanent, even if they are relatively stable. But they are not built on or into a permanent substrate. In this sense Langer's universe is a process universe, and the controversial notion of an "act," which is a complex analogical notion, will play a major role in her reflections.

Langer, however, though clearly a kind of monist, will reject a whole set of what she calls "idols of the laboratory": physicalism, methodolatry, jargon, the cult of "objectivity," and mathematization, which attend scientistic and crudely materialistic forms of monism. For Langer, in fact, and as her own practice shows, the study of mental and social phenomena is "more akin to history" (*M-I* 53), that is, as we will see, a kind of natural history or even a semiotic history. Repudiating "some primitive, scientifically useless entity—soul, entelechy, metaphysical subject or vital essence" (*M-I* 51), Langer proposes to supply "a sounder substructure" for the understanding of mental phenomena. "Feeling," then, occupies a middle position between biological structure and process and the "purely human sphere known as 'culture'" (*M-I* 32). Feeling, accordingly, points "down" as well as "up." Biological processes are more universal than psychological processes, and therefore psychology is less extensive than biology, but nevertheless Langer holds that its domain is "still inestimably great" (*M-I* 32). This is why, in effect, Langer is not developing a philosophy of biology but a kind of semiotic psychology that is not cut off from its biological roots. It is not the origin and structure of life that lies at the forefront of Langer's concern, although she engages even this issue, but the origin and structure of the "psychical." "An adequate concept of the 'psychical'

should serve all psychological purposes" (*M-I* 32), ranging from the first glimmers of sensibility to "the first genuinely symbolic utterances, speech, which
marked the advent of man" (*M-I* 32).

Langer's procedures rest upon an important observation, which for the un-
suspecting might sound strange considering the massive research and technical
base upon which *Mind* is constructed and by which it is supported. Langer claims
that "we all have direct knowledge of feeling" (*M-I* 56). But what would one
thereby have, more concretely, direct knowledge of? Feeling, in Langer's conception, "includes . . . the whole realm of human awareness and thought, the sense
of absurdity, the sense of justice, the perception of meaning, as well as emotion
and sensation" (*M-I* 55). This perhaps on the surface bewildering choice of speci-
fied domains is not meant to be exhaustive, nor is it systematically named. But
Langer is insistent on the role of prescientific knowledge of feeling.

> Builders may know the basics of mechanics, cooks find out chemical properties, and
> sailors map the sky; but who has any such naïve yet expert knowledge of psychical
> phenomena? Who knows the essentials of feeling? . . . The real patterns of feeling—
> how a small fright, or "startle," terminates, how the tensions of boredom increase
> or give way to self-entertainment, how daydreaming weaves in and out of realistic
> thought, how the feeling of a place, a time of day, an ordinary situation is built up—
> these felt events, which compose the fabric of mental life, usually pass unobserved,
> unrecorded and therefore essentially unknown to the average person. (*M-I* 56–57)

Such a situation is paradoxical, to say the least. For how are we to raise to explicit awareness the "real patterns of feeling?" We need some conceptual knowledge and some way of making present the full range of feeling. Conceptual
knowledge is needed for the study of mind "because the dynamic forms of felt experiences are a major exhibit of the rhythms and integrations, and ultimately the
sources, of mental activity" (*M-I* 58). The role of feeling is found in "the constant,
systematic, but private display of what is going on in our own systems, the index
of much that goes on below the limen of sentience, and ultimately of the whole
organic process, or life, that feeds and uses the sensory and cerebral system"
(*M-I* 58). It is at this point that Langer makes one of her most revolutionary and
fateful proposals. It is not sufficient, she thinks, to be able to construct a *model* of
feeling. We need a comprehensive *image* of feeling. A model, on Langer's conception, we have seen, differs essentially from an image. A model "always illustrates
a principle of construction or operation; it is a symbolic projection of its object
which need not resemble it in appearance at all, but must permit one to match
the factors of the model with respective factors of the object, according to some
convention" (*M-I* 59). An image, however, as Langer understands the term, is not

a model at all. It is governed by the principle of resemblance, as Langer understands the term, although, on Peirce's account, a model is also a species of icons,
based on a broad notion of resemblance, which is clearly not Langer's. An image
"is a rendering of the appearance of its object in one perspective out of many possible ones. It sets forth what the object looks or seems like, and according to its
own style it emphasizes separations or continuities, contrasts or gradations, details, complexities or simple masses" (*M-I* 59).

So, Langer wants, in this way, to try to find a domain that can function as the
heuristic key to feeling, something that both embodies and resembles feeling. She
finds it in the realm of images, *specifically art images.*

> An image does not exemplify the same principles of construction as the object it
> symbolizes but abstracts its phenomenal character, its immediate effect on our sen-
> sibility or the way it presents itself as something of importance, magnitude, strength
> or fragility, permanence or transience, etc. It organizes and enhances the impres-
> sion directly received. And as most of our awareness of the world is a continual play
> of impressions, our primitive intellectual equipment is largely a fund of images,
> not necessarily visual, but often gestic, kinesthetic, verbal or what I can only call
> "situational." The materials of imagination which I crudely designate here as "im-
> ages" will be discussed at length in later parts of the book. Suffice it now to point
> out that we apprehend everything which comes to us as impact from the world by
> imposing some image on it that stresses its salient features and shapes it for recog-
> nition and memory. (*M-I* 59)

Because we "tend to see the form of one thing in another" (*M-I* 60), it is crucial, Langer thinks, to be able to present objectively the form of feeling if the objective image indeed can function as an image of mind. If images can exist in an
almost unlimited number of forms they can then be taken to exemplify an unlimited number of forms of feeling. An image may fit many different impressions, but in the end, Langer thinks, "it permits their interpretation in terms of
the conception which the image expresses" (*M-I* 60). In the case of mentality, as
a distinctive form of feeling, we are consequently looking for paradigmatic exemplifications in imaginal form. Where are we to look? Who, Langer asks, has
the requisite prescientific knowledge of feeling that can function as the foundation for a more conceptual modeling?

Langer answers, it is artists who have an "intimate and expert knowledge
of feeling" (*M-I* 64). In an expression echoing the central thesis of *Feeling and
Form,* Langer states that artistic form is "always the form of felt life" (*M-I* 64).
What does the artist do? The artist, Langer responds, "simply creates an image of
that phase of events which only the organism wherein they occur ever knows"
(*M-I* 64)—and in this way makes possible a form of cognitive participation. The

image, then, is a cognitive tool. The art image, furthermore, has an "import" that is directly perceived, but its production is not "systematic" in the sense of being manipulated or produced according to any rule or method. Such an import is "intuitive, immediate, and its deliverances are ineffable" (*M-I* 65), in the sense of not discursively projectable. Indeed, the perceptiveness of the artist does not give rise to a distinctively conceptual schema but precisely to an image, a symbolic image, in Langer's way of thinking. It is Langer's deepest held belief that because feeling is "a dynamic pattern of tremendous complexity" (*M-I* 67) it is best identified and engaged through very special types of images, that is, through works of art. The "extraorganic structure" (*M-I* 67) of works of art turns them into created semblances, images of the inner life of feeling that confront us like phenomena in the so-called external world. Feelings are, therefore, for Langer to be strictly speaking *embodied* in works of art—but primarily in terms of their "forms." A work of art "only presents a form which is subtly but entirely congruent with forms of mentality and vital experience, which we recognize intuitively as something very much like feeling; and this abstract likeness to feeling teaches me, without effort or explicit awareness, what feeling is like" (*M-I* 67). We are here, with the reference to "abstract likeness," at the very center of the tangled problem of iconism, which Langer is attempting, without explicitly saying so or referring to Peirce, to throw a sharp light on. The issue, as Langer sees it, is of "recognizing vital patterns in pure art which may be keys to essential relations in the life of feeling" (*M-I* 69). What Langer calls "a student of actual sentience," who recognizes that psychology's "first inspiration" is and ought to be the prescientific knowledge present in art, will recognize that the artistic image will project an empirical datum "with a degree of precision and detail" that eludes or transcends introspection (*M-I* 69). The empirical datum is not actually or primarily the object upon which the image bears, but *the form of feeling in which the object is accessed*. In this sense the form of feeling, objectified in the artistic image, is a projection.

Projection, as Langer uses the term, which is clearly metaphorical, is the way the artist's idea becomes perceptible (*M-I* 74). Projection gives an idea "enhanced perceptibility" (*M-I* 75), in that projection functions in art as "a principle of presentation" (*M-I* 75). Presentation of what? Presentation, Langer repeats, of a "form of feeling" or of "the morphology of feeling" (*M-I* 75). The type of presentation gives us "new empirical knowledge" of feeling, a kind of experiential knowledge not available in any other way. Langer works, we have seen, throughout her philosophical project from the very beginning on the principle, or maybe the assumption, that feelings have a distinctive "logical form" (*M-I* 77). In the case of the construction of an artistic image, consequently, "the process of projection rests on the recognition of one and the same logical form in different exemplifications, which are, therefore, different expressions of it" (*M-I* 75–76). This idea was already formulated, we saw, in *The Practice of Philosophy*. Such a comment is in fact a revisiting of the pivotal notion, definitively developed in *Philosophy in a New Key*, of a presentational form and its distinction from a discursive form. A presentational form, we saw, contains its sense in an inseparable and irreducible way, which Cassirer (1929) explored under the rubric of "expression" and "symbolic pregnance." The sort of significance that such a form has makes it "more than a symbol," that is, an arbitrary and conventional expression of meaning or sense. Rather, such a form contains its sense "as a being contains its life" (*M-I* 77). It is, Langer always held, untranslatable into another form. Symbolic expression in the presentational mode is "primarily the formulation of perceptual experience, and the constant reformulation of the conceptual frames which the cumulative symbolizing techniques—conscious or unconscious, but rarely altogether absent—establish, one upon another, one in another, one by negation of another" (*M-I* 80).

One of Langer's most important insights is that the choice of a mode of presentation, in the most general sense, is not indifferent, but rather fateful. Langer admits, with reference to Cassirer, "the dependence of different modes of thought on respectively different symbolic forms" (*M-I* 80). The mode of thought practiced by the artist, however, is not a transitional phase of mental evolution, like mythical ideation and dream (*M-I* 81). While in one sense myth has been, or maybe should be, "transcended" for Langer, *art will never be.* It is an autonomous form of thought and meaning-making, that, while it has an evolution and a history, will never reach an "end-point" where it is transformed or transmuted into something else. It is for Langer a "final symbolic form making revelation of truths about actual life" (*M-I* 81). The artistic image has a wondrous power, rich in ways and means. The sphere of art is the sphere where "diverse means and very subtle ways of projecting ideas force themselves on one's attention" (*M-I* 81). The reason for the diverse means and subtle ways is due to the fact "art has no ready-made symbols or rules of their combination, it is not a symbolism, but forever problematical, every work being a new and, normally, entire expressive form" (*M-I* 81). Langer formulates in this context one of her most important theses, which bears upon the semiotics of art at the deepest analytical level.

> A work of art is a single symbol, not a system of significant elements which may be variously compounded. Its elements have no symbolic values in isolation. They take their expressive character from their functions in the perceptual whole.
>
> Art has a logic of its own (and by "a logic" I mean a relational structure), which is very complex; it is largely by virtue of its complexity that it can present us with images of our even more complex subjective activity. (*M-I* 84)

Subjective activity is even more complex than the image, but it is the image, that is, the universe of all images, that gives us privileged access to the realm of subjectivity, of felt life as lived.

Indeed, Langer points out, the whole universe, as experienced, becomes the source of the artist's activity.

> [T]he artist's eye sees in nature, and even in human nature betraying itself in action, an inexhaustible wealth of tensions, rhythms, continuities and contrasts which can be rendered in line and color; and those are the "internal forms" which the "external forms"—paintings, musical or poetic compositions or any other works of art—express for us. The connection with the natural world is close, and easy to understand; for the essential function of art has the dual character of almost all life functions, which are usually dialectical. Art is the objectification of feeling; and in developing our intuition, teaching eye and ear to perceive expressive form, it makes form expressive for us wherever we confront it, in actuality as well as in art. Natural forms become articulate and seem like projections of the "inner forms" of feeling, as people influenced (whether consciously or not) by all the art that surrounds them develop something of the artist's vision. Art is the objectification of feeling, and the subjectification of nature. (*M-I* 87)

It is in this context that Langer, in spite of her "formalism" and her opposition to "mimesis," only apparently asserts the ultimate primacy of representation, claiming that "our present cultivation of non-representational art . . . is episodic in history" (*M-I* 87). While one can clearly pursue "sheer perceptual values" in art, that is, purely non-objective formal values, in the end there will always be a return to "nature" or to the realm of "objects and events." This is clearly a shift in emphasis in Langer's approach to art, but not an essential change, if it is looked at within the context of her whole project, which does not sever feeling from "the world."

Langer wants to draw attention to the highest importance of the intuition of artistic import for both psychology and epistemology. The roots of such intuition, she claims, "lie at the same depth as those of discursive reason, and are, indeed, largely the same" (*M-I* 89). This brilliant insight will become clearer as our discussion proceeds and we arrive at Langer's conception of the artist's idea and of the central mental act of abstraction. It is important to realize that, on Langer's reckoning, the artistic import is not something that is directly, or rather actually, felt by the artist. It is, rather, something "contemplated and imaginatively grasped" (*M-I* 89) in an act of personal insight. The import of art is what is objectively projected in the artwork; "what the created form expresses is the nature of feelings conceived, imaginatively realized, and rendered by a labor of formulation and abstractive vision" (*M-I* 41–42). The form does not arise out of a stable system of pre-

existing defined units, a notion that has been proposed by the tradition of reflection on art stemming from a generalization of Saussure's structural linguistics.
Langer reiterates at almost every turn one of the central theses of her philosophy
of art: "There is . . . no basic vocabulary of lines and colors, or elementary tonal
structures, or poetic phrases, with conventional emotive meanings, from which
complex expressive forms, i.e., works of art, can be composed by rules of manipulation" (*M-I* 90). Art is symbolic without being a symbolism. How, then, in light
of such assertion, are we to understand what is definitive of the type of symbolic
projection of feeling made in art? What answer does Langer give in *Mind*?

Langer has recourse again and again to the central principle that "different
modes of thought derive from different principles of presentation," that is, "with
different projections of their subject matter" (*M-I* 90). In the case of art the projection is through images, and the primary function of images is broadly "representation," that is, symbolic, and the formation of these images is "a living process, and therefore as complex as all living processes are" (*M-I* 94). If the work
of art is a constructed image, Langer argues, referring here to the work of Jean
Philippe (1903), it "should reflect the basic structure of the primitive and spontaneous image; if that structure is determined by the elementary function of
representation, it must express first and always the natural laws of representation" (*M-I* 94). These laws are, in the case of vision, not the laws of optics but "of
visual interpretation, which begins with the act of looking" (*M-I* 95). The work
of art, says Langer, following Philippe, is the "plastic 'realization' of a mental image," and the laws of imagination can be read off of, because they are reflected
in, "the laws of plastic expression whereby the art symbol takes its perceptible
form" (*M-I* 95). This is a process of "building up" by means of a set of visual conceptions: figure and ground, direction and change of direction, opposition, proportion, differentiation of color, interaction of colors within a field of general col-
oration, volume, and visual changes of volume with torsion (*M-I* 95). This list is
strikingly similar to the types of issues discussed by Arnheim in his *Art and Visual
Perception* (1974)—and, *mutatis mutandis,* these issues are also central in other artistic genres than the visual. But, as Langer points out, these conceptions, or
what could be called "representational tools," cannot be utilized or combined me-
chanically or by rule. Doing so results in a dead or empty or unfelt image, Langer
notes (*M-I* 96), no matter what its medium is. The art image, in fact and necessarily, if it is at all successful, "has an irresistible appearance of livingness and
feeling, though it may not represent anything living" (*M-I* 96). Langer identifies
in one sense the livingness and vitality of the art image with its import, not with
its objective reference, and, in a pivotal observation that one must never forget, "it
is conveyed entirely by artistic techniques, not by what is represented" (*M-I* 97).

Representation of objects, to be sure, is a powerful and practically universal device, clearly parasitic on "real objects," in some sense of that term, but the "space" is not a pure "geometric" space, an actual space or the space of our actions, but a "virtual space" (*M-I* 97), created with and by the artistic image. It is, in short, an abstraction. The continuity with the discussion in *Feeling and Form* is patent.

Langer accordingly thinks, perhaps drawing too sharp a contrast, that the "process of creating an art symbol is entirely different from that of making a model of an object. It is guided by imagination, and imagination is fed by perception; there lies the reason for all drawing from nature, as for all Aristotle's poetic 'imitation'" (*M-I* 97). But it is not specifically object-orientation that marks the art image. "The techniques of art are intricate, subtle and manifold beyond any prevision or accounting" and the "forming of a mental image is an act, a vital process as ramified and complex as all functions of living things are" (*M-I* 98). The product, the art image, and the act by which it is produced bear the stamp of both cerebral process and the deepest levels of the "whole vital substructure" of our lives. In the artistic image we have presented to us paradigmatically and objectively "the feeling of activities interplaying with the moments of envisagement" (*M-I* 99)—truly an astounding observation. Nevertheless, artistic images are not "natural occurrences," a kind of spontaneous overflow, although they are marked by spontaneity and emergent properties. "They are constructed symbols, made in the mode of imagination, because imagination reflects the forms of feeling from which it springs, and the principles of representation by which human sensibility records itself. If a piece of art is to express the pulse of life that underlies and pervades every passage of feeling, some semblance of that vital pulse has to be created by artistic means" (*M-I* 99). Note here, once again, Langer's use of the notion of "semblance."

Langer avails herself also of the work of Philippe Fauré-Fremiet (1934 and 1940), who spoke of the "realization" of an image under the rubric of "re-creation." For him, and for Langer, "all conscious experience is symbolically conceived experience; otherwise it passes 'unrealized'" (*M-I* 100). But the difference between a spontaneous symbolic projection and an artistic symbolic projection lies in the way the elements are situated vis-à-vis one another. Different principles of very diverse sorts can be mixed in spontaneous envisagement, because all that is important are their deliverances and not their organic unity. The elements are only used instrumentally. But in art, Langer continues, the multiplicity of different forms of symbolic projection must be subjected to a kind of overarching unity that will encompass all the image's elements. One of Langer's central insights—and theses—is that it is precisely this specific type of unity-in-multiplicity that makes it impossible to capture the image's import in a single discursive projection, even metaphorically—a thesis defended by a significant part of the tradition of philosophical aesthetics that has not given in to reductionism or radical subjectivism. Verbal statement *in the discursive mode* cannot form and convey conceptions of feeling, although it clearly can in the presentational mode. Discursivity in linguistic form is a single projection or principle of projection, with elements subordinate to, or ingredient in, discursivity—interrogative, imperative, and vocative elements—as auxiliary forms. For Langer, "the essence of language is statement" (*M-I* 102)—its systematic presentational use in art has added to it a new, conscious, power. But it is precisely statement in the discursive mode that constitutes both the power and the limitation of language as a symbolic projection. Language is clearly for many reasons "the paradigm of symbolisms" (*M-I* 102), but as Langer has insisted at every point, art is not a symbolism, in the sense defined. Both art and language can be subjected to certain types of semiotic or semantic control to moderate various degrees of vagueness and equivocality, but such control is strictly context-dependent, albeit in different ways.

The power of language, which Langer locates in its atomistic structure and its singleness of projection, is matched by its limitation by the same two factors. "It is clumsy and all but useless for rendering the forms of awareness that are not essentially recognition of facts, though facts may have some connection with them. They are perceptions of our own sensitive reactions to things inside and outside of ourselves, and of the fabric of tensions which constitutes the so-called 'inner-life' of a conscious being" (*M-I* 103). The only adequate symbolic projection of this inner-life is artistic expression, the material for which "is furnished by the natural resources of imagination" (*M-I* 104). These resources, we have seen in preceding chapters, are clearly not exhausted by visual forms, but are comprised of forms of sound, bodily movement, "and even envisagements of purposeful action" (*M-I* 104). The great orders of art arise out of the exploitation and transformation of these various forms. "The potentialities of the imaginative mode seem to be endless" (*M-I* 104). These potentialities are combined and structured in novel ways, without general rules of manipulation, and give rise to "created appearances which reflect the patterns of our organic and emotional tensions. The illusion of tensions is the stuff of art" (*M-I* 104).

Langer deepens and confirms her central theses in the chapter on projection in art, foregrounding the universal features of an artistic image, which arises through a combination of many projective techniques, "mingling several principles of presentation" (*M-I* 104). Indeed, in a remark that resonates with a major theme of contemporary reflections on meaning, and which echoes our discussion of interpretation in chapter 4, "a work of art is like a metaphor, to be understood without translation or comparison of ideas; it exhibits its form, and the import is immediately perceived in it. One might well call it a metaphorical symbol" (*M-I* 104). Such a symbol does not merely mirror or transmit or transpose, but rather it transforms by a process of abstraction. The artistic image abstracts a form by making apparent "the sameness of logical structure in experientially different loci" (*M-I* 105). Langer then has a remarkable passage that clearly and forcefully continues the analyses of *Feeling and Form,* mixing semiotic and other terms in a nuanced and perspicuous way: convention, semantic function, symbol, image, index, virtual, perceptual form, feeling, and quality. In order to do this work of "making apparent," the art symbol, specifically as a symbol and not a symbolism,

> does not rest on convention. There are conventions in art, and they do change, but they govern only the ways of creating the symbol, and not its semantic function. . . . The import of art inheres in the symbol, which has no dispensable or changeable physical character at all, because it is an image, not an index; its substance is virtual, and the reality it conveys has been transformed by a purely natural process into the only perceptual form it can take. Feeling is projected in art as quality. (*M-I* 105–106)

What, importantly, does Langer mean by "quality" in this context, which certainly and insightfully calls to mind, as we have seen, one of the chief concepts of John Dewey's aesthetics and of Peirce's semiotics? Repudiating any British empiricist notion of quality, Langer writes: "There is a kind of quality that different colors, or even a tonal form and a visual form, may have in common; even events may have the same quality, say of mystery, of portentousness, of breeziness; and a word like 'breeziness' bespeaks the qualitative similarity of some moods and some weathers" (*M-I* 106). Peirce also thinks that every object, perceptual or otherwise, is defined by a qualitative unity: "the color of magenta, the odor of attar, the sound of a railway whistle, the taste of quinine, the quality of emotion upon contemplating a fine mathematical demonstration, the quality of feeling of love, etc." (*CP-I* 304). For Langer, likewise, a work of art is permeated by quality. It is

> the resultant of all its virtual tensions and resolutions, its motion or stillness, its format, its palette, or in music, its pace, and every other created element. This quality is the projected feeling; artists refer to it as the "feeling" of the work as often as they call it "quality." The image of feeling is inseparable from its import; therefore, in contemplating how the image is constructed, we should gain at least a first insight into the life of feeling it projects. (*M-I* 106)

This is one of the central tasks Langer set herself to accomplish in *Mind*. The path to mind is through art, and Langer is a consummately knowledgeable trail guide.

The Artist's Idea

Langer makes more precise, within the framework of a discussion of "the artist's idea," her distinctive and powerful notion of a "quality" and of how it is both conceived and known. The "idea" that comes to expression in an artistic image is, we have repeatedly seen, not the "theme" or the "subject matter," no matter how important or weighty. It is, in fact, not defined by anything antecedent to the artistic symbol itself, although it can be *motivated* by it, as in paradigmatic forms of sacred art. The art symbol, the expressive form or the work, is "created, not found and used" (*M-I* 117). In spite of Langer's highly nuanced and hedged recognition of the primacy of "representation," at least in visual art and certainly to a great degree in certain genres of literature, what she calls the *poetic import* of the artistic composition "is not represented—it is presented, as the perceptible quality of the created image" (*M-I* 117). This perceptible quality arises from the artist's attempt to create what Langer calls an *apparition* (*M-I* 118), which in *Feeling and Form*, one recalls, is a *semblance*. Although the reality presented in the art image is virtual, as we have seen, the artwork itself, as a constructed symbolic image, is a symbolic "actuality" that has been colored by the artist's "way of feeling" (*M-I* 118). The goal of the artist is to create an image of "the way things appear to his imagination under the influence of his highly developed emotional life" (*M-I* 118). The artist, Langer claims, attempts to re-create a quality he has "once known" (*M-I* 118), not to express an emotional state presently, or antecedently, felt. The emotional value is rooted in the fact that when a "theme" excites an artist the artist tries "to abstract its quality" (*M-I* 119) and to embody it in an objective form. But, Langer notes, in an exquisitely precise phrasing, the artist does not think abstractly, "he thinks abstractively" (*M-I* 119). Indeed, what pulls the activity of the artist forward, eliciting from him or her the work, is "the quality he wants this particular piece of his to have" (*M-I* 119). This is the central aim of the artist's work: to achieve artistic quality. This consists in presenting the idea "of some mode of feeling in the nameless but sensible quality which shall pervade his nascent creation" (*M-I* 124). Thus the artist generates a "virtual field in which forms arise for pure perception" (*M-I* 124), an important general point that Langer, contra Peter Kivy (2002: 30), does admit.

Langer returns in this way in *Mind* to a theme found in *Feeling and Form*, the effect of formal design. Its primary job, for example, in the case of vision, but with appropriate modifications of key notions applicable to other art forms, is "to animate a surface" (*M-I* 124) and to establish "symmetry, or correlation of counterparts, which creates the axis as a structural element" (*M-I* 125). In Langer's view the perceiver, as a wholly embodied being, even embodied in the "seamless web of language" (see Burnshaw 1970), responds to such animated surfaces from a sort of still center, or "resting tonus of the whole organism" (*M-I* 125). The response is intuitive. Intuition, Langer says, is a "hominid specialty," a kind of "natural light," that "lies at the base of all specifically human mental functions" (*M-I* 130). (The notion of natural light is given further discussion in *Problems of Art*, chapter 5, "Artistic Perception and 'Natural Light.'") Intuitive acts, according to Langer, are entirely natural (*M-I* 130). Ordinary intuitive acts involve the "recognitions of similar formal structures in sensuously dissimilar things" and the consequent reception of one as symbolic of the other (*M-I* 57). A "dancing" flame, for example, can become symbolic of joy as well as the course of a fit of anger. This powerful thesis Langer already explored and defended in *Feeling and Form*, and it was broached in her earlier works, too. What we are dealing with is the fundamental phenomenon of the appreciation of expressive form, something that "seems to be primitive and immediate in man" (*M-I* 130). What this involves, Langer notes, is akin to what Cassirer called "physiognomic seeing" (*M-I* 133) in which qualities of fearfulness, friendliness, serenity, awe, and so forth are projected onto and into experience, thus giving rise to "the spontaneous production of new perceptible entities" and visible forms (*M-I* 130) or at least visualized forms. Indeed, "symbolic projection and interpretation are spontaneous responses" and can be accomplished as a completely unconscious process (*M-I* 130). The roots of art, at least the originary domain of visual art, are to be found here, at the "lowest" stratum of significance—and perhaps the roots of religion, too (Guthrie 1993).

Art is present when we have the "expression of conceived feeling," not the presentation of any determining or defining subject matter or theme, no matter how embedded they are in the form. This is a constant refrain in Langer's philosophical project. Moreover, in spite of our being "language animals," Langer resolutely holds that artistic activity and expression, if they are really intuitive, "may occur without any verbalized intention, without preconceived standards" (*M-I* 140). The only real criterion of art is the presence or absence of vital import. Vital import is immanent in the created form and it is never "object-bound," that is, essentially dependent on something "outside" the form, even if it may be the "form" of the object that becomes symbolic. While, to be sure, as Langer always holds, art images may, indeed often do, have recourse to and utilize natural motifs that are represented in the image, and although humans for the most part have a need for "an arresting and organizing subject matter" (*M-I* 145), the subject matter does not define the import, which is found in "those inward tensions that compose our life of feeling" (*M-I* 146)—even if oriented toward the object. It is clear that non-representational as well as representational forms of art are able to express these tensions. But rather than insisting on a kind of aesthetic formalism, with practically exclusive focus on formal features and aggressive repudiation of the tyranny of subject matter or theme, which would result in art being concerned with the "form of the form" and hence in an assertion, in the case of painting, of the superiority of non-representational or "abstract" art, Langer will stick to the primacy, if not the absolute indispensability, of the representational component at least in the visual, poetic, and dramatic arts. At the same time art is concerned with "the perception of the formal aspects of concrete realities" (*M-I* 146), rooted in our "intuition of significance as such" (*M-I* 147). This intuition can be "realized," that is, made real, in the creation of an image, by giving the envisaged form "a locus in our universe" (*M-I* 146). Because we have an intuition of significance as such, rooted in a kind of sense of rightness and wrongness of forms, "symbolic activity begets its own data for constant interpretation and reinterpretation, and its characteristic feelings" (*M-I* 147).

Mental acts quite generally for Langer are deeply embedded in a matrix of sense and emotion, understood, I think, here as a bipolar structure, echoing the exogenic/autogenic distinction, which, I have said, is constant in *Mind*. This bipolar structure is unitary in that "orientation toward the other" and "felt attunement" belong together. This is an important, indeed, indispensable, insight. What Langer calls "primeval feeling" (*M-I* 150) is itself bipolar. And even on the highest level Langer insists that the "wide discrepancy between reason and feeling may be unreal" (*M-I* 149), a thesis defended vigorously by Antonio Damasio. Symbolization, and concatenation of symbols, is constant and apparently is a spontaneous activity of the human brain. But it carries its own deepest roots with it. Intellect, Langer opines, should be seen as "a high form of feeling—a specialized, intensive feeling about intuitions" (*M-I* 149).

The work of intellect for Langer, then, is paradigmatically exemplified in the production of art symbols, art images. It is one of her strongest and permanent contributions to philosophy. Art images are, even more than the products of science and discursive reason, of the highest heuristic value. "That image seems to be capable of encompassing the whole mind of man, including its highest rational activities" (*M-I* 150). Once again, Langer has recourse to the same point about the import of art: "[T]he import of art is one vast phenomenon of 'felt life,' stretching from the elementary tonus of vital existence to the furthest reaches of mind. All psychical phases of human nature may furnish the 'ideas' of art" (*M-I* 151). The reason is that unfelt activities are reflected in the art symbol, and the highly articulated nature of the symbolic projection makes them available for "immediate intuitive apprehension" (*M-I* 151). What is intuitively apprehended, according to Langer, is the livingness of the image, and this gives us an image of mind that appears as a living process (*M-I* 151). Human experience is this living process, "a dialectic of symbolic objectification and interpretive subjectification" (*M-I* 152). This is the process of art itself. The basic transformation in art is "from felt activity to perceptible quality; so it is a 'quality of life' that is meant by 'livingness' in art" (*M-I* 152). This quality is a virtual quality, and there are innumerable ways to achieve it. These ways arise out the processes of spontaneous ideation that is "the matrix of human nature, the mind" (*M-I* 152). Art, or at least the possibility of art, and human mentation are in this sense co-originary. So, such a way of thinking about the mind entails a "shift from a concept of human mentality built up in terms of sensation and association to a concept built . . . on principles of symbol and meaning, expression and interpretation, perception of form and import" (*M-I* 108). This is a repetition and confirmation of the core theses and insights, bearing upon epistemology and the philosophy of mind, of *The Practice of Philosophy* and *Philosophy in a New Key*.

Abstraction

Langer insightfully connects symbolization with abstraction. Her thick and precise discussion of abstraction is one of the most rewarding parts of *Mind*.

Langer claims, rather incautiously perhaps, that "the problems of abstraction in art have never been philosophically surveyed and analyzed" (*M-I* 153). This is true as far as it goes, since Langer's scope is to all intents and purposes universal, or "philosophical" in her sense of the term. Scientific abstraction, which Langer certainly is no enemy of, proceeds, on her account, by a sequence of widening generalizations. Hence, its procedures are governed by what Langer calls "generalizing abstraction" (*M-I* 153), which is not to be misconstrued as "abduction" in the Peircean sense. But artistic abstraction is of a different sort, indeed, of many sorts (*M-I* 154). In an important way artistic abstraction is deeply connected with what Langer calls "semantic intuition" (*M-I* 154). Langer, as we have seen already in our discussion of the perceptual roots of significance in *Philosophy in a New Key*, not only pushes abstraction deep down into the originary stratum of perception, but makes the further claim that there are "at least four or five independent sources of abstractive techniques" utilized by artists. It is these techniques that give such a distinctive feel to the artistic images. They do not belong to the discursive realm, which is the domain par excellence of generalizing abstraction. It is the realm of art, where a different kind of abstraction is at work and which is the foundation of the artistic image in all its rich complexity. Langer, unsurprisingly, calls this kind of abstraction "presentational" abstraction. It is "logical" in the relational, cognitive sense that it effects "the process of perceiving and rendering the forms of feeling which are not amenable to generalizing abstraction" (*M-I* 155). It is the function of the semblance of objects "to objectify the total expressive form" (*M-I* 169). That is, presentational abstraction takes a perceptual image, no matter what the sense modality, and makes it "stand for" or "display" a distinctive kind of meaning. It is Langer's great contribution, then, to see that abstraction does not always generalize, but that there is a kind of *abstraction through symbolic exemplification*.

Presentational abstraction in art for Langer is difficult to achieve, paralleling the difficulties of discursive abstraction. It is neither spontaneous nor can it be accomplished by a fixed set of rules or a stable methodology, any more than generalizing abstraction can. Because Langer holds that presentational abstraction is "capable of expressing the entire range and complexity of human experience" (*M-I* 157), it uses a wide variety of means, which Langer will chart in the chapter on abstraction, but there is "no series of successive levels of abstractness to be reached by all elements in the complex of a symbolic projection at the same time" (*M-I* 156). The principle of succession is not a governing principle in presentational abstraction. The artist at the beginning is faced with a fundamental and elementary problem, which is unavoidable: how to transform *subjectively known realities* into objective semblances "that are immediately recognized as their expression in sensory appearances" (*M-I* 157). This process and act of transformation aims to produce the primary illusion that governs each type of artistic projection. The vital image that results then is developed further by a kind of internal logic, composed of "indirect and subtle orders of abstraction: isolating, metaphorical, secondary, transcending and perhaps others for which one could invent suggestive names" (*M-I* 157).

It is a central thesis of Langer's that every art form, no matter what the genre, seems to be defined by the general characteristic of tension and resolution (*M-I* 158). The first element in the creative process, whether line, gesture, tone, opening phrase, and so forth, creates an anticipatory and at times universally determinative range of tensions. This is the basic technique of artists in any medium. So, a work of art is first and foremost generated by a pattern of tensions, which "reflects feeling predominantly as subjective, originating within us, like the felt activity of muscles and the stirring of emotions" (*M-I* 164), a point made long ago by Schiller and Shelley. Art is an isomorphic construct, "an image of human experience, which means an objective presentation" (*M-I* 164). The process of objectification, which is initiated by the recognition or creation of "tensions," must nevertheless effect a closure in the perceptual field. Such a closure, or tendency to closure of form, is due to the gestalt principle, which, as we have seen, plays a great role in Langer's thought practically from the beginning.

Langer's argument runs as follows. Our core ability is being able to compose "distinct retainable images" and even being able to use interpretively single instances of a perception, such as a visual form, to stand symbolically for other actualities. This process of "imposing" an abstracted form onto the experiential flux arises from our power of abstractive seeing and hearing. This power "deeply affects the potentialities of art" (*M-I* 165). The movement toward "closure" involves the creation of "pre-eminent bounded shapes, carved out of the total virtual space of the work. What is said here in terms of space holds for all other virtual dimensions" (*M-I* 165). The principle of closure, therefore, intersects with "isolating abstraction" (*M-I* 166), which emphasizes the intended form through a process of suppressing and canceling. This process of isolation makes it possible for a visual form, say, to come with a "single impact" (*M-I* 169) and to be able to be the objectified carrier of an expressive form. This is the place of resemblance in art, which is based on principles of relevance and pertinence.

Abstraction of gestalt, a common gestalt, enables us to use one object for thinking of another, a theme now developed extensively in cognitive linguistics by George Lakoff and Mark Johnson (see their 2003 for a first orientation). This applies not just to shapes but also to "nameless characteristics" (*M-I* 170). In this sense the artistic image can be thought of as an "instrument of envisagement," functioning as a kind of scaffolding for envisaging something that it is not. "The resulting gestalt 'is and is not' its avowed object" (*M-I* 170). But while the religious symbol-user would give the gestalt a profusion of meanings, connected with the holy and with a participatory involvement in "another world," Langer claims that the artist "sees the gestalt emerge as something in its own right," interpretively developing it, when appropriate and needed, "until it yields elements of pure design," which can be completely independent of "any representational intent" (*M-I* 171–172)—or ontological or religious commitments. So, the "principle of gestalt or articulation of forms has intimate relations with the principle of dynamic structure or tensive design in all the arts" (*M-I* 173). With a gesture toward a kind of conceptual ultimacy, Langer adds that "the life of every design springs from some interaction of these two creative processes" (*M-I* 173), one focusing on structure, the other on dynamism. Their interaction, Langer claims, sets up a kind of "permanent tonicity" (*M-I* 175) that is the source of a work's "livingness." Gestalten, in short, have not only a clearly abstractive function, but also a kind of dialectical function due to their interplay with dynamic elements, and also a "physiognomic" function, an ability to present "a primitive sort of 'intrinsic expressiveness.' Some percepts convey ideas of internal feeling, without being cathected by association with any emotive experiences" (*M-I* 175).

Langer's discussion of this physiognomical dimension is extremely important and insightful. In one way, she thinks, this type of perception is non-social, and it often "precedes or even replaces perceptions of physically describable sensory forms" (*M-I* 177). Perception is initially "global," with certain physiognomical qualities dominating "the structural qualities" (*M-I* 177, quoting Conrad 1954). In the case of adults there has been a clear passage from this "primary" form of perception to the division between primary and secondary qualities, one of the great themes of traditional epistemology. But initially autogenic and exogenic activities are merged together, and there is no sharp divide between subjective and objective. What happens, in the case of art, Langer thinks, is that expressive features of a perceptual datum are "transformed into a presentational datum, which 'mirrors' their dynamism and appears as its expression" (*M-I* 177). The result is the "transformation" and "projection" of an expressive datum or of a feeling as "the most obvious quality of a perceived gestalt" (*M-I* 178). This "obvious quality" of a perceived gestalt is the emotive import that is the object of a natural propensity of childhood perception and becomes "the source of artistic vision" (*M-I* 178). The job of the artist is to "translate feeling into perceivable quality" (*M-I* 178)—a statement that could have been made by John Dewey. Its point of origin is a kind of "bud" in gestalt form, a *vorgestalt* that is transformed into an *endgestalt,* to use the formulation of Klaus Conrad, which Langer takes over (*M-I* 178–179).

Langer is interested in the ability, as well as the necessity, of an *endgestalt,* the finished artwork or art image, to hold "all the phases of the evolving vision" (*M-I* 179). "The artist's 'realized' form has to retain all these experiential aspects which an ordinary perceptual datum gives up as it reaches its full objective status; because the ordinary percept becomes a thing for the percipient, but the artist's creation becomes a symbol" (*M-I* 179), that is, it becomes a presentational symbol, which can enfold every aspect of life, including even the discursive aspect, which is there not for its own sake but for the sake of its physiognomical function, to "appear" as discourse. Langer's phenomenological acuity is manifest in the following comment. "Everything that enters into a work has some physiognomy or at least the seed of physiognomic value. . . . There is a reflection of inner feeling in the most typically outward, objective data of sensation. . . . Their character is never as fixed and simple as the distillations our conventional store of qualifying adjectives has made from them" (*M-I* 179). These physiognomical qualities, however, do not retain their autonomy in being taken up into the finished artwork, being merely combined in an external fashion. Combination of sense data does not give us a work of art, for which quite different principles are needed. One of these is "the principle of sensuous metaphor, the symbolic equivalence of sensations that have an emotive character in common" (*M-I* 186). This central principle of Langer's thought is perspicuously illustrated in the case of language and the metaphorical uses to which it is put, reflecting a world of "natural symbols" in which, for example, light, smoothness, and especially movement become natural symbols of "life, freedom and joy, as darkness and immobility, roughness and hardness are the symbols of death and frustration" (*M-I* 193). Symbolically deep perceptual impressions, then, can be "intuitively received as expressive" and thus can be encapsulated in language, constituting in this way the roots of the "poetic."

While the gestalt engenders the primary illusion of the artwork, the sensuous metaphor aspect of the image intensifies the impression and gives rise to a realm of secondary illusions, a notion that Langer employed in *Feeling and Form* and that makes a return in *Mind* (and is helpfully explored by Mary Reichling [1995] with great sensitivity to music). These illusions "are products of the composition, not given with its material, but created by the development of the material" (*M-I* 195). Langer continues in this way her focus on creativity, on the "creation" of meaning, which Vincent Colapietro has put at the very center of her philosophical project, seeing her investigations of human symbolization as "also an exploration of both human creativity and the irreducibly different unique forms of human creation" (1997: 10). Behind such metaphorical extensions, which clearly are illustrated in language and the realm of words, and which are based on a kind of recognition of "deep resemblance" and "semantic transfer," is the phenomenon of words ending up meaning their exact opposite. Langer points to, among others, such examples as the derivation of "gloom" from "glow" and of "wan," meaning "colorless, languid, pale," from Anglo-Saxon *wann* or *wonn*, meaning "dark, black." Referring to Webster's account of "lurid," she remarks that it lists the word's meaning as (1) "deathly pale," (2) "glowing through a haze," and (3) "vivid in a harsh or shocking way." So, as she puts it, "from deathly to vivid" (*M-I* 195–196). The systematic point she wants to make is that what makes possible such a transposition of meaning is that "every primitive concept arises and exists in an area of relevance," which clearly has two extreme semantic poles that mark in fact a continuum. "In every sensory experience there is the threat of evanescence and the threat of intolerability, and the precarious balance between them is implicit in every moment of perfection. A sensible quality, therefore, gives into the artist's hand the whole range of feeling it can express, even the existence of that range itself" (*M-I* 197). Every perceived quality carries within it-self the imminent possibility of the appearance of its opposite.

What is at issue in this dialectical junction of qualities is the "making of vir-tual living form" (*M-I* 197), many examples of which, even if seemingly small and simple, as in decorative design, can have a kind of "astonishing complexity" (*M-I* 197). Not only do artworks, as pregnant images, arise out of a rich reservoir of mental complexity, but they display, in their inner logic, life and the mind it-self. Abstraction and creation are not always separable, and their inner drive is the uncovering of "living form," which is operative both in nature and in art. This is one of Langer's central notions, which has, as many of her concepts do, a flexible range of application due to what I would call, in Peircean mode, their "rich vagueness."

Living Form

What, Langer asks repeatedly, is the point of introducing the art symbol into a philosophy of mind? The answer, we have seen, is that *the art symbol projects a spe-cific and distinctive image of mind*. The artistic projection makes mentality, which is its generative source, appear "as a highly organized, intricate fabric of mental acts emanating more or less constantly from the deeper activities, themselves nor-mally unfelt that constitute the life of the individual" (*M-I* 200). Acts, as Langer understands the notion, "have characteristic dynamic forms," and so do works of art. Acts both in the mind and in the artwork are defined by the organizing ma-trix. And in both instances an act is, as defined by Langer, "any unit of activity" (*M-I* 202). While this is clearly so in the case of mentality, it is perhaps surprising that Langer ascribes the same structure to artworks. But precisely in this lies the significance of her deeply insightful reflections. Her chief, and difficult, thesis is that the *logical form* of acts is projected in the art symbol, though the projection does not entail that the artistic elements themselves appear as acts. It is that the elements have formal properties "which, in nature, characterize acts" (*M-I* 204), such as inviolability, fusability, and the revivable retention of past phases. The elements exist in a relational matrix. The art symbol is in this sense a system of internal relations—a perceptual-semiotic system—and every element in the art symbol, whether tension, gestalt, contrast, accent, rhythm, and so forth, "seems to emanate from the context in which it exists" (*M-I* 204). The artwork paradoxi-cally both is made up of the internal system of these elements and is the source of them, not their result, just as "an organism is made up of its own acts, and at the same time is the source of all its acts" (*M-I* 204). In Deweyan terms (1934:

168–193), an artwork both effects and is the exemplar of the "organization of energies."

The artwork, consequently, in Langer's conception is governed by a phase principle that encompasses the dialectical interdependence of its elements and their pattern of relations (*M-I* 204). This pattern, Langer points out, is intrinsically rhythmic, a notion that is central also to the pragmatist aesthetics of Dewey. In the virtual object that is the work of art, and in human perception itself, this dialectical structure is the "main source of its unity" (*M-I* 205). This unity gives the artwork a kind of substantive character, a kind of basic presence, giving it the appearance of being a plenum in which and over against which the secondary illusions emerge and develop, though they are never completed in their own right, the primary illusion being precisely the plenum itself. This plenum "seems like a negative background," supplying the complementary forms of the secondary illusions. "And since secondary illusions may be of many kinds, that background has to have a protean character, which gives it an air of indefinite potentiality" (*M-I* 206). Langer, in metaphysical mode, will make much of this parallelism of acts in art and nature. "In nature, such indefinite potentiality is the essence of bodily existence, which feeds the continuous burgeoning of life" (*M-I* 206), while the artwork "seems to have a core from which all its elements emerge—figurations and rhythms and all the qualities to which these give rise" (*M-I* 206). There thus arises "an effect of constant becoming" (*M-I* 206). Such a comment clearly derives from a kind of phenomenological attentiveness that marks Langer's analytical and constructive approach to philosophy. Once again, we see the intimate union of description and prescription in Langer's analytical procedures.

A central point that Langer makes, and strongly insists upon, is that the artwork can be organic without really being an organism in any natural or literal sense. Consider how Langer exploits this most helpful distinction. Just like an organism, the artwork, in its total qualitative dimension, gives the appearance of "springing out of a matrix or body of potentialities" and in fact gives "the illusion of bodily existence" (*M-I* 207). Here is the root of the "tangibility" of art, as if the artwork is bodying itself forth. But because the artwork is a system of internal relations it also manifests complexity, and this complexity gives it not just a semblance of bodily existence but the ability to reflect, implicitly or explicitly, "all levels of feeling" (*M-I* 208). The ability to manifest depth "is a matter of logical structure" (*M-I* 208) and is not, in itself, mysterious and unknowable. Depth, like other features of the work, is understood through the ways in which it is achieved (*M-I* 208). What appears in the artwork are created semblances: substantiality, depth, unity, individuality or "uniqueness." While, to be sure, the artwork has the "inviolable unity of a total form" and presents itself as a "matrix" for the articulation of its sensuously given articulations, it also is marked by a unique individuality. This individuality is a created quality, "as virtual as all other artistic qualities" (*M-I* 209). The sense of a work's being "alive" or "expressive" derives from its "uniqueness."

Langer points out that another source as well as manifestation of a work's livingness is the fact that the artistic elements that it both exploits and embodies are made up of "gradients." This extremely important, indeed indispensable, notion points to the fact that competing potential forms and elements are not all equally present or balanced off against one another. It is this differential development that makes a work interesting and engaging. Langer's discussion of gradients is most enlightening and exemplifies the phenomenological richness of her account. "Gradients of all sorts—of relative clarity, complexity, tempo, intensity of feeling, interest, not to mention geometric gradations (the concept of 'gradient' is a generalization from relations of height)—permeate all artistic structure" (*M-I* 211). This illuminating notion of a gradient Langer takes from D'Arcy Thompson's morphological study, *On Growth and Form* (1942), where the focal concern was plants and animals. Langer will take over three points from Thompson's researches: (1) organic structure is a record of the processes of growth, a kind of logical projection; (2) "phase-beauty" introduces a temporal factor into the spatial character of living forms; and (3) the same logical pattern can appear in both static and dynamic projections (*M-I* 211).

Langer draws deep and fundamental aesthetic consequences or applications from these three notions. First, "the sense of becoming" that marks an artwork is "symbolically rendered very largely by gradients of apparent completeness" (*M-I* 212). These gradients give rise, she says, to the "impression of evolution from the slightest to the richest articulation of volume, line, surface and implied structural tensions . . . gradients of all sorts run through every artistic structure and make its rhythmic quality" (*M-I* 212). Second, "phase-beauty" accounts for the sense of successive phases, what Dewey in *Art as Experience* calls "cumulation," and Langer sees "advance" as present in a typical form, allowing the interchangeability of the spatial and the temporal. Speaking of the level of "natural symbols" or "the spontaneous interpretation of visual data," Langer wants to draw attention to "the naturalness of the symbolic projection of vitality, especially growth and rhythmical activities, in essentially spatial as well as essentially temporal arts" (*M-I* 213). Visual objects can be seen as retaining the phases of their own development and thus appearing to be in a kind of "motion," as in Leonardo's drawing of flowers or van Gogh's cypresses. Third, Langer points out, with a kind of phenomenological stipulation for prescribing what to look for, that "in art all motion is growth, although the lines and volumes and tensions that seem to grow never reach any increased dimensions" (*M-I* 213). Growth is therefore "virtual," belonging to the art symbol as a semblance, not an actuality, a continuation of Langer's mature aesthetic insights. But Langer wants to make an even more universal and comprehensive point, that ascribes a kind of metaphysical revelation to the artwork. In the artwork comes to expression "the all-inclusive 'greatest rhythm' of life," a kind of universal cadential rise and fall, growth and decay, and so forth. It is such a perception that in even essentially static forms elicits "our intuition of 'living form' without any conscious judgment" (*M-I* 213). In the artwork life speaks to life.

Gradients, a notion that Langer shows to be of the utmost importance, clearly raise the whole issue of degrees within a perceived continuum, a sense of "more" or "less" in the qualitative dimension. For Langer, as for Dewey in his profound article, "Qualitative Thought," "the tacit recognition of . . . qualitative continua, which is inherent in human perception itself, is the intuitive basis of our concepts of degree" (*M-I* 214). Articulation, whether visual, audial, or some other mode, deploys sensory materials by degree. "Sensations, like emotions, like living bodies, like articulated forms, have gradients of growth and development" (*M-I* 214). Langer continues in the phenomenological mode:

> The rhythm of acts which characterizes organic forms pervades even the world of color and light, sheer sound, warmth, odor and taste. The implicit existence of gradients in all sensation reinforces our appreciation of living form by giving it an echo or reiteration, in sense, which is always charged with feeling and consequently tends to subjectify the form, to make its import felt yet hold that import to the projective medium. This is probably the greatest single means artists have of "animating" their work. (*M-I* 214)

This process of animation, it is clear, is complex and involved, utilizing many procedures and sensory modalities. But the recognition of what Langer calls "gamuts in the realm of sense," that is, simultaneous existence of qualities and their opposite, is the great source of qualitative gradients. The "implicit interplay of extremes" reinforces the other elements in the creation of a living form. Indeed, it is precisely such an interplay that also allows strictly subordinate features to take over roles when the whole form has been mutilated. This is one of the reasons why fragments can give us a sense of the whole. They have an intrinsic orientation toward completion, since they carry within themselves a kind of "sense of preparation" for a whole symbolic projection.

Langer recognizes that the Kantian aesthetic project anticipated, without either developing or being fully conscious of the implications of, this set of notions, specifically the concepts of "telic form without purpose and perceptible rationality without discursive logic" (*M-I* 218). Langer thinks that the main weakness in Kant's reflections, however, was that his epistemological theme was perception rather than significance, which is clearly her main focus. But, Langer says, surely rightly, that Kant recognized a kind of presentational abstraction and had an idea of formal intuition that was not dependent on concepts, although, in Langer's view, Kant did not have a sufficiently developed concept of expressiveness.

"The semblance of motivation," Langer continues, "is another powerful factor in making artistic elements similar to acts rather than to things" (*M-I* 220). Motivation is logically connected with the notion of acts, in the sense that Langer uses these terms. For her, life is motivated activity, even if it does not have to be the pursuit of conscious or thematic purpose. Acts can be telic without being purposive, and that entails that in the case of art *telic patterns* can appear in the artist's image of life. These telic patterns have about them a sense of inevitability. This sense is "created by the fittingness of forms, the build-up of tensions and the logic of their resolutions, the exact degrees to which the elements are articulated, etc.; the idea is completely abstracted from actual life, transformed into quality, projected in sensuous terms" (*M-I* 221). This process of projection is also a process of *individuation.* What is individuated in any concrete case of a work of art is an expression of an artistic idea, a "personal conception of the ways of feeling" (*M-I* 225). The realization of the work is not something merely typical or foreseeable. "Where the semblance of growing individuation is paramount, it makes a radical shift in the image of living form. It effects the humanization of artistic import" (*M-I* 228). The "commanding form" is the germ out of the which the artwork emerges and develops. The internal complexity of the artwork raises it "to a level of complexity that reflects not only universal vital rhythms, but particularly human ones" (*M-I* 229). As we have seen and will see in greater detail later, Langer thinks that human mentality has a unique characteristic that marks it off as different in kind from animal mentality.

It consists, Langer says, in a "constant stream of cerebral activities which are essentially subjective, having no perceptible overt phases, but terminate as images, thoughts, recollections, often elaborate figments, entirely within the organism in which they take rise" (*M-I* 229). That is, human mental acts have "intraorganic climaxes" (*M-I* 229). The artwork, as an art symbol, Langer says in a remarkable formulation, "reflects the nature of mind as a culmination of life, and what it directly exhibits, first of all, is the mysterious quality of intangible elements which arise from the growth and activity of the organism, yet do not seem entirely of its substance" (*M-I* 230). The work, that is, has a substance of its own, due to the presence of multiple secondary illusions, such as "color" in music, "eloquence" in the lines of a sculpture, "musicality" in the play of colors, "movement" in the plastic arts, and so forth. "The effect is a sublimation of the expressive form" (*M-I* 230). Generalizing on notions already sketched in *Feeling and Form,* Langer claims: "In all advanced artistic creations there is some such play of secondary illusions over the unfailing, all-supporting primary illusion, with various effects, ranging from the expression of elementary feeling as a transient phase emerging from the organic matrix (as in rhythmic designs) to the appearance of acts that seem to depart from their somatic source, and form a separate, essentially mental pattern" (*M-I* 230).

Secondary illusions give a sense of *livingness* to the art symbol. Langer gives in this context a musical example, that of "harmonic space." Harmonic space as a principle of artistic construction has made European music something unsurpassable, even if music cannot be static and even if the harmony is directed forward toward cadence. Indeed, with a keen musical and phenomenological sense, Langer points out that "melodic motion abstracts the feeling of locomotion" even if there is absolutely no displacement of anything. And, further, at a higher level of abstraction, "harmonic progression makes a further abstraction, for it does not even create any semblance of locomotion. It makes a direct and very pure abstraction of a feeling of pure temporal change, which is its outstanding quality" (*M-I* 236). Consequently, secondary illusions have a kind of quality of disembodiment in the sense that they have no substantial content but rather appear suddenly as properties of a form whose primary illusion is entirely different. "Space" applied to music, which is essentially temporal, or a "plastic appearance" in the culminating part of a drama, or a "musical effect" in painting, as already mentioned, are all secondary illusions. In one of her most important observations, Langer states that "the possibility of their occurrence makes the art symbol capable of reflecting the many-dimensional and incalculable character of experience" (*M-I* 238). The function of a secondary illusion is to make itself be perceived as "an act of transition from one level of feeling to another. It is transition made perceptible" (*M-I* 239), the emergence of a sense of strangeness or magic. The sudden appearance of a secondary illusion makes an artwork exciting. "A powerful secondary illusion usually carries the virtual life beyond that brink and makes the impression of a real shift from one order of existence to another" (*M-I* 239).

> All secondary illusions, whether they serve primarily to intensify the expressiveness of a piece or whether they create a quintessential moment, have the same character of suddenly coming into existence from nowhere, apart from the virtual substance of the work (which is anchored in the primary illusion according to its proper mode), and fading again into nothing. In their very nature, therefore, they project

the outstanding attribute of human mentality, the termination of autonomous acts in psychical phases that resemble those of perceptual acts in many respects; that is to say, the occurrence of images. Like fantasies, secondary illusions seem to have no somatic being; they are disembodied, yet they come out of the created form and heighten its livingness, even to a degree where the form in its entirety seems to be changed. (*M-I* 240)

For Langer the monumental philosophical point, which she holds to be phenomenologically grounded, is that the appearance of secondary illusions is an image of mental life itself. It reveals the dynamic pattern of conceptual acts, "the strangeness and 'otherness' and bodilessness of symbolic imagery" that is projected in great art. This symbolic projection is essentially, as we have seen, bipolar. It is the objectification of feeling, resulting in the "building up of a whole objective world of perceptible things," and the subjectification of nature, which involves "the symbolic use of natural forms to envisage feeling, i.e., the endowment of such forms with emotional import, mystical and mythical and moral" (*M-I* 241). Langer then adds both her conclusion and her thesis: "The dialectic of these two functions is, I think, the process of human experience" (*M-I* 241). Read off the art image or art symbol, this process is deeply intertwined with the creation of secondary illusions, which offer a central "key to the mystery of art as an image of mind" (*M-I* 242). Langer here appeals to phenomenological more than analytical aspects of the topic. Speaking of the way "different perceptual realms seem to intersect" in the creation of secondary illusions, she remarks on the phenomenological property of the illusion seeming to "transcend the sensory vehicle altogether and make an almost pure presentation of the 'Idea'" (*M-I* 242). Once again she refers to the "magical" effects of the created form, as well as a sense of "sublimation" and of "quite sudden and unaccountable simplification" in which prior factors are taken up into an encompassing whole. Clearly, Langer is attempting to give a conceptual label to an experience that we can all recognize.

At the end of her chapter, the last chapter dealing with "the import of art," Langer states that her goal, in spite of appearances, is not to "penetrate the mysteries of art" with the help of biological categories, but the reverse, that is, "to gain some biological and psychological insights through the suggestiveness of artistic forms."

A symbol always presents its import in simplified form, which is exactly what makes that import accessible for us. No matter how complex, profound and fecund a work of art—or even the whole realm of art—may be, it is incomparably simpler than life. So the theory of art is really a prolegomenon to the much greater undertaking of constructing a concept of mind adequate to the living actuality. (*M-I* 244)

Strange as it may seem, Langer considered the types of biologically influenced re-flections on the import of art to be a mere prelude to her real interest, to which the bulk of *Mind* is devoted. In the rest of her trilogy she will make a heroic attempt to develop the heuristic fertility of the concept of an act, chart the "great shift" from animal to a symbolically conceived human mentality, and attempt to delineate the contours of the "moral structure" in which mind operates at its highest pow-ers. Let us first trace in outline this great movement from act to symbolization.

7

From Acts to Symbolization

The second stage in Langer's mature strategic attempt to construct a comprehensive account of mind is two-pronged. The first prong, which is a kind of descriptive metaphysics of mind, not a substitute neurobiology, develops, under the Spinozist rubric of *natura naturans,* a naturalistic theory of "acts," whose role we have already seen in the previous chapter, as the essential constituent of the human mind as a distinctive phenomenon. The second prong, more explicitly semiotic and understood against the background of the account of acts and the organisms that they constitute, argues for the reality, distinctiveness, and revolutionary importance of the "great shift" to human mentality. Langer's controversial analysis and defense of acts is relatively novel and extremely intricate, involving a constant oscillation between the empirical, the conceptual, and the phenomenological-semiotic. Her substantive analysis of the "great shift" does not differ greatly from the point of view of conclusions from much of her previous work, although the empirical or "scientific" support is rather different and the socio-cultural focus is more explicit here than previously. It is this complicated combination of different procedures that makes a crisp summary of Langer's theses and their proper theoretical "placement" so difficult. Consequently, our discussion here has to be even more selective and schematic. Our major interest will be as always to determine, that is, bring into focus, just what is central and novel in Langer's project, what is living and what is dead, and what she really intends to accomplish.

Langer issues a set of strong challenges to our interpretive frameworks for the great shift without trying to supplant empirical results by an a priori philosophical prescription. She has added rather a *further analytical level* that functions above the level of the empirical-biological. Thus, her contribution is at the level of ultimate categories, belonging to the "metaphysics of mind." It is in this context that we are to understand her generalization of the notion of act to cover such a wide range of phenomena.

The Concept of an Act

In dealing with "acts" as an ultimate analytical notion Langer states that "we are not dealing here with material parts of a living thing, but with elements in the continuum of life" (*M-I* 261). Once again the material-element dichotomy, which is pivotal in her analysis of art genres, appears. This continuum Langer describes as a web, indeed a web of acts that progressively develops. Acts expand and are elaborated into wholes, and organisms are marked by the matrix of acts that make them up. But Langer goes further and lays her descriptive metaphysical cards on the table.

> The act concept is a fecund and elastic concept. It applies to natural events, of a form characteristic of living things, though not absolutely peculiar to them. Such events arise where there is already some fairly constant movement going on. They normally show a phase of acceleration, or intensification of a distinguishable dynamic pattern, then reach a point at which the pattern changes, whereupon the movement subsides. The point of general change is the consummation of the act. The subsequent phase, the conclusion or cadence, is the most variable aspect of the total process. It may be gradual or abrupt, run a clearly identifiable course or merge almost at once into other acts, or sink smoothly, imperceptibly back into the minutely structured general flow of events from which the act took rise. (*M-I* 261)

An "act" for Langer encompasses such phenomena as the twitch of a horse's skin to throw off a fly, the processes of digestion and excretion, and the human construction of a symbolic form. It is to be found in the physical order, the vital order, and the mental or ideational order, including the psychic order. It refers to a "generic trait" of existence, in Dewey's sense of that term.

Langer had pointed out earlier, as we have seen, that an analysis of the artwork can and must focus on articulated *elements* within the dynamic whole that is the artwork. These elements, she proposes, are "act-like" (*M-I* 273), related to one another as mutually and even progressively motivating. The artwork is not just a web of relations but also a dynamically charged field that directs, motivates, and elicits the elements that constitute it. Thus, Langer can say, using ourselves as a putative locus of acts, that "every act arises from a situation. The situation is a constellation of other acts in progress, often including some which develop with the acute initial phases of peripherally originating acts, such as we feel as impact if they are intense enough to develop a psychical phase" (*M-I* 281). What for an organism is an *ambient*, Langer's translation of von Uexküll's *Umwelt*, becomes for the analysis of the artwork a kind of immanent, generative matrix, in which is found a constellation of self-organizing systems of acts or act-like elements. But in her technical definition of an act Langer only occasionally appeals to art, where in fact she first uses it. The proximate context and support is biological and, at times, physical, by extension, although Langer will proceed very cautiously in this murky metaphysical swamp. This is one of the places where she keeps the more grandiose claims of "process philosophy" at arm's length.

Act is for Langer a "formal unit, or modulus, of living processes" (*M-I* 288). Her thesis is that it, not the organism, nor the organ, nor the cell, is the basic unit of biological thinking (*M-I* 305). But they can be of what seem to be radically different types and orders, as a cursory listing of Langer's examples show. Acts for her encompass the following types of events: aggression against a father-surrogate, a sudden increase in saliva flow, a heartbeat, a twitch of a horse's skin, the tensing of a muscle in vocalization, the firing of a single neuron in the brain. What all these events, or spatio-temporal occurrences, have in common is the "act form itself" (*M-I* 288) with its phase-structure. All these events are marked by sequence from incipience, to acceleration, consummation, and finally cadence (*M-I* 288–289). A stimulus of some sort, that is, some antecedent condition, activates a process, understood as a drive, which marks the organism, and thus functions as a motivation. Behavioral acts are thus "terminations of 'drives'" (*M-I* 290) and consequently can be thought of in terms of an "intraorganic dynamism" rather than a "billiard ball" type of connection. For Langer's core vision, then, it is the dynamism of life, but not reified into some sort of *élan vital*, that functions as the model of mind, governed as it is by an incipient impulse. While the artwork may reveal heuristically salient features of this dynamism, Langer's main concern, which is philosophical, is really—and rather paradoxically—to model the mind conceptually and not produce just an image of it. While art itself produces the fertile images of mind, we attend to them in order, on the philosophical plane, to construct our model. Note, among other things, the operative analytical terms in the following descriptively rich passage.

> An impulse is usually conceived to be a homogeneous discharge of energy, the equivalent in animate nature of a force, or impetus, in the inorganic realm. But an impulse, or nascent act, is an offshoot of a fluid situation which, because of its unstable character from one moment to another, is probably never altogether determinable. Within the active organism, the very matter which is implementing an act may undergo dissolution in the process and be transformed, so that it enters into another mechanism that functions in another situation. The first really identifiable element is the impulse; and this is already an articulated process. (*M-I* 291)

The total act, consequently, is the realization of a dynamic pattern, the resolution of a generative tension resulting from an accumulation of energies, a notion reminiscent of Dewey's mode of analysis. The act is defined by a basic unity, which Langer grounds in "the singleness of an over-all tension" (*M-I* 294), by its development from some sort of functional "center," "some sort of intraorganic starting point" (*M-I* 294), which Langer considers to be an "impulse," and by the influence of a situation on the act that passes through the act tendency. For Langer, then, an impulse functions as a potential act, and opens up the possibility of defining a whole set of consequent notions: actualization, inhibition, intention, opportunity, choice, and effects of decision (*M-I* 299).

Any organism as a center or matrix of acts "has to select its course" (*M-I* 304). This process of selection is a "play of impulses" that forms "the dynamic matrix of life, a plexus even more involuted and compounded than the metabolizing, differentiating, ever-changing structure that is the material organism, because the latter consists only of actualized events, but the life comprises also all the potential acts which exist only for milliseconds or less. Perhaps that is why we feel that life is 'in' the body and pervades its actuality. Out of this matrix all mental and behavioral acts arise" (*M-I* 304). On the basis of such penetrating considerations Langer is able to distinguish between *acts, actions,* and *activity* in a precise and illuminating fashion. An act, we have seen, is "an event, a spatio-temporal occurrence" (*M-I* 304). But such an event has itself a "form," which Langer calls "action." This is the formal aspect of acts. "It is action that living and non-living mechanisms may have in common" (*M-I* 304), such as pumping, filing, filtering, and so forth. These are causal patterns, or operative principles, that can be realized in different materials and by different mechanisms. Besides acts and actions Langer wants to use also the concept of activity. "The constant events of life, such as circulation and breathing, are generally called 'activities'" (*M-I* 306). So, for example, ciliary or flagellate movements, heartbeat, gill or lung breathing, which are acts usually "concatenated into series, wherein the same general form is discernible over and over again," are examples of activities on the deep biological level that Langer is concerned with in her initial reflections on the act concept. Activities can be examined from the point of view of their rhythm, their dialectical relations to one another, their tendencies toward self-continuation, and indeed in terms of their being activities of an agent, which is to be defined in terms of acts. So, we see, once again, how a central concept is employed by Langer by exploiting its rich, in the Peircean sense, analogical vagueness. Just as one strand of metaphysics developed an "analogy of being," so Langer's metaphysics of mind develops an "analogy of acts."

A second main step in Langer's discussion of *natura naturans* and the development of a conceptual frame for the biological foundations of mind utilizes the analytical pair of *individuation* and *involvement*. What is going on here? And what is the connection with the analysis of acts?

Individuation, not individualization, Langer holds, "is a process consisting of acts; every act is motivated by a vital situation, a moment in the vital advance of antecedent acts composed of more and more closely linked elements, ultimately a texture of activities" (*M-I* 311). Each act has a unique situation, and such a situation is a "phase of the total life, the matrix, from which motivation constantly arises" (*M-I* 311). The principle of individuation, Langer claims, is "exemplified everywhere in animate nature, in processes that eventuate in the existence of self-identical organisms" (*M-I* 310), ranging from proto-organisms to Beethoven and Winston Churchill. There is an arc from cytological differentiation to the development of the deepest human personality, exemplifying individuation, matched by a converse concept, and process, of "involvement," which characterizes the "integration" of the organism, or parts of the organism, with "the other." Here the arc runs from the mutual control of cells in a tissue all the way up to processes of human communication in society (*M-I* 311–314). Mind, which is the human version of "mentality," arises out of the mutual functioning and interaction of these two principles. Mind, as Langer is most concerned to show, belongs to agents. "Nature" has no mind; only agents within nature do. An agent is a "self-continuing system of actions proliferating and differentiating in more and more centralized and interdependent ways. . . . An agent is a complex of actions, and all actions that belong to that complex are acts of that agent" (*M-I* 314). Acts are self-involving, also on the level of subacts and superacts, this being the "basic dynamism of life," making up the domain of "motivation" (*M-I* 315).

Langer connects her phenomenologically fertile discussion of individuation and involvement with an account of the origin of life, the details of which we cannot go into, since we (and ultimately she) are interested in the conceptual lessons of the very problem itself. The first lesson, which really defines the problem, is that life is bound up with a formation of patterned activities and their more and more perfect integration until they constitute a matrix in which their own form becomes modified or even entirely blurred, so that it can only be found again by analytic abstraction. Such living matrices may have various degrees of coherence and persistence; but they are systems, self-sustaining, and (as we know them) self-propagating, wherein every event is prepared by progressively changing conditions of the integral whole. Every distinguishable change, therefore, arises out of the matrix, and emerges as an act of an agent; for such a vital matrix is an agent. (*M-I* 322)

Interdependence is the rule here at the beginning or earliest stages of life, and interdependence leads to, indeed demands, the establishment of rhythms. "Rhythmic concatenation is what really holds an organism together from moment to moment" (*M-I* 323). Langer points out that vital rhythms are essentially superior to the non-vital rhythms of inanimate nature. They are not strictly periodic, as most non-vital rhythms are, and there is, moreover, a rhythm that belongs to the act overall (*M-I* 323). Langer speaks of rhythm, once again, in ways remarkably reminiscent of Dewey's formulations in his *Art as Experience,* especially in the chapter on "The Organization of Energies." She thinks of the essence of rhythm as consisting in "the alternation of tension building up to a crisis, and ebbing away in a graduated course of relaxation whereby a new build-up of tension is prepared and driven to the next crisis, which necessitates the next cadence" (*M-I* 324). Rhythms, on this conception, which we all find exemplified in our own experience, have differential durations, not strict metronomic periodicity. Change of rhythmic pulsing takes place over against a fundamental "tonus of living tissues" (*M-I* 327) and also over against a matrix of pre-given acts. The prior state is a kind of "self-inducing and self-limiting dialectic ground base" without which no new act and rhythm could ever occur. For Langer, an organism "is made entirely by processes which are vital acts" (*M-I* 327) and "the body, throughout life, is the 'dynamic equilibrium' itself, growing and differentiating into articulate forms" (*M-I* 329). It has a material substrate, Langer points out, a material matrix, "which is the counterpart of the functional matrix of activities, and indeed the product, and therefore the exact reflection, of the latter" (*M-I* 329). This astounding assertion, rooted in a non-monistic, or at least non-reductive, naturalism, of the ontological and conceptual primacy of acts is part of Langer's attack on "substantialist" metaphysics, making, in fact, the types of bodies we have be dependent on the types of acts that make up their living matrix, and not the other way around. That bodies grow out of acts and act-matrices is a very strong claim in the philosophy of biology. In fact, in one sense, for Langer the body is a material translation of acts, not the material "expression" of its genes. Dynamic patterns of rhythm and of rhythmic acts inscribe themselves into bodies. This is a deep and provocative claim and assertion, but it may be questioned whether it is a biological assertion. It belongs, once again, to Langer's metaphysical, even imaginative, vision, to her descriptive metaphysics of mind, or what Vincent Colapietro called her "evolutionary naturalism" (1998: 64). It cannot be "verified" in any factual sense, but must be validated in terms of its descriptive and interpretive power, its range of use and application.

At the same time, Langer points out, in a way paralleling the work of von Uexküll (1940) and Hans Jonas (1966), that the boundaries between organism and ambient are constantly shifting, subject to ambiguities, both through exploitation and interiorization and through "extrusion," as in the spider's web or in a bird's carrying of gravel in its crop to grind up hard-coated grains. Ultimately, in such processes of involvement, and at times integration, Langer will espy the roots of human technology and of human language, paralleling, here too, the approach of Hans Jonas to a philosophy of biology and a philosophy of life and culture built on top of it. Life's trajectory, which is never foreseeable in detail, proceeds in an "ever-mounting advance of devouring, integrating, self-maintaining activities" (*M-I* 354). Individuation and involvement proceed together.

> The gradients of individuation might appear as strong lines in a swirling flow of ecological involvement of species with species, life with life, wherein every impulse to individuation sets up its own course, that may be long and become spectacular on the way, or may come to a stop very soon. Individuation goes on all the time, but it can proceed only in a framework of active involvements with the generating stock and the nourishing substrate of an ambient that is a small detail in the whole biosphere. (*M-I* 354)

There is in many cases an increase of repertoire that is not often paralleled with a loss of individuation, as in the social insects. There is a dialectical relationship between corporate acts and the degree of individuation that becomes especially critical in the case of humans, where the balancing becomes more and more comprehensive and delicate, and where the serious frustration of individuation leads to the organism's falling apart. Such, Langer thinks, is the fate of mind in the biosphere, which is permanently perilous. Symbolic power does not guarantee survival.

The physical, non-vital world does not furnish us with a model of "this endless rhythm of individuation and involvement," but, unsurprisingly, Langer once again points out that we do have such an image in the world of art, "and most purely in the dance" (*M-I* 354), and "in the highest musical form that has yet been developed, the sonata" (*M-I* 354). Here we see that even in the midst of technical biological discussions the import of art is never far away for Langer. So, individuation and involvement, which make up the extremes of "the great rhythm of evolution" (*M-I* 354), also are the extremes of the evolution of the inner structure of art forms. The rhythm of evolution moves between the extremes, just as art does, the inner trajectory being "always toward more intense activity and gradually increasing ambients of the generic lines that survive" (*M-I* 354). Loss and gain engage in a complicated dance of life, mirrored in the proliferation of art forms and open-ended vitality and fertility.

Furthermore, according to Langer, acts both *evolve* and *grow.* Langer devotes two chapters to these two related, but different, concepts. What are the philosophical points we can extract from these two notions, which are given a rather different conceptual weight and range than normal?

Langer develops, while still remaining within a thoroughly naturalist framework, a philosophical critique of the Darwinian conceptual scheme as an ultimate interpretive framework. In her opinion, it ultimately and irretrievably assigns the organism a passive role in evolution. In its place is to be put a "reformulation of the basic conceptual scheme" that would "let the organism count for what it is, i.e., as the agent" (*M-I* 369). Looking at the higher forms of feeling through the conceptual lens of her "act concept," Langer thinks that the

> act concept erects a different scaffolding. . . . The basic terms it logically provides are act and situation, motivation and actualization; in these terms potentiality, impulse, activity, rhythm, dialectic, entrainment and other essentially biological notions may be defined. . . . And just as the beginnings of life on earth fall within the compass of that conceptual structure, so does the whole evolutionary pattern of generation and differential survival, which underlies the phenomena of mind for which the framework is constructed. (*M-I* 369–370)

Langer introduces the concept of "pression" for the "class of relations which obtain between situations and acts" (*M-I* 370). These "pressive relations" mediate and automatically adjust the elements of the complex dynamism of life to one another. Pression is matched, even superseded, in importance by another relation between acts and situations, which Langer calls "implementation" (*M-I* 370). "Every act requires some support from its environment, be it intraorganic or extraorganic" (*M-I* 370). This structure of support is made up of the conditions of implementation. Breathing is implemented by a constant availability of oxygen, just as metabolism has to be fed continually. "[N]ormally acts of hearing, vision, tactual perception or of manipulation require a relatively great and constant implementation" (*M-I* 371), while mitosis, or cell division, may need only one outside act in order to be triggered.

Langer's startling meta-theoretical thesis is that motivation, implementation, and the many forms of pression "are the influences that produce and shape the evolving system of acts which we see as a life, and in larger extent as the life of a stock" (*M-I* 371). Langer places the locus of evolution in acts, first of all, and then, secondly, in taxons. "The evolutionary pattern is inherent in acts, and in all the complexes they form: lives, populations, stocks, and finally the whole history of life on earth that we usually mean by 'evolution'" (*M-I* 371). So, Langer asserts, "the so-called 'mechanisms' of evolution have their prototypes in the processes that beget and regulate all acts. The continuity of the vital matrix rests on the rhythmic self-renewal of its activities" (*M-I* 371). Thus, Langer says, "in the fight for survival the tendency to continuous elaboration of started activities is always there" (*M-I* 383), a statement, she claims, that is clear of all charges of "orthogeneticism," "teleologism," or "Lamarckism." As a result, Langer thinks, "'natural selection' is a historical pattern, not a mechanism; it is the pattern of the natural history of life" (*M-I* 394). "Each germ of life is a packet of potential impulses; each moment of its development is a configuration of occurring impulses seeking actualization among the basic acts already in process of realization" (*M-I* 400). There is a deep continuity of impulse underlying the vital order: "The continuity of impulse patterns through geologic ages of unbroken life, through alternate contractions into infinitesimal germs and expansions into new individuations, operates in phylogenetic as in ontogenetic progression. The causes of evolution lie in the dynamic properties of acts and act-engendered entities" (*M-I* 408).

Clearly, this statement involves an interpretation at the meta-level of Langer's descriptive metaphysics. It belongs not to biology but to the philosophy of biology. For Langer "evolution" is, or rather is to be interpreted as, "essentially an evolution of acts. It is acts that grow and continue and rejuvenate, and that may come to an end, from which there is no rebirth—extinction" (*M-I* 413). Not only are the patterns of acts subject to shifts of function "from old means to new and readier ones" (*M-I* 413), but there are also "extremely rare and intrinsically unpredictable changes, not in patterns, but in the quality of events" (*M-I* 413). It is to this type of change that Langer ascribes great heuristic fertility for the understanding of mental phenomena, where there is a radical qualitative shift involving the emergence of genuine novelty.

It is at this point that Langer introduces the topic of the "growth" of acts as following upon the topic of the "evolution" of acts. What are the chief theses here?

Acts are not only the ultimate "units" that evolve, according to Langer's contentious and provocative descriptive metaphysical theory; they also "grow." Langer says that acts grow in scope, complexity, and intensity. They do so according to (1) their chances of implementation; (2) their organizing propensities, which depend largely on the opportunities they create for subacts to develop, and for lesser acts in progress to become entrained; and (3) the energy of their original motivation, which may be greatly enhanced by confluent impulses in the course of actualization. Each of these modes of increase may reach its own kind of limit, where it can develop no further in the same pattern, so a crisis occurs; the creature's activity undergoes a radical change, as the same essential impulse finds a different road to consummation. (*M-I* 416)

A pivotal qualitative change is the development of a membrane that is so perforated that it has pores that generate inward and outward termini of interactions between the living unit and the "outside" world. This becomes critical in the higher animals, where their outer surfaces, functioning as an *integumentum commune*, keep the organism separate from its environment while, by mediating their exchanges, they join the two together. This development of the skin has great philosophical import for Langer, as it did for Arthur Bentley. "Often the skin as a whole seems to be a highly multipotential organ" (*M-I* 422). By "skin" here we are to understand "living membrane," as opposed to "mere surface," as in a water droplet. The water droplet does not have an increase in qualitative intensity by being heated, for example, although it can certainly change state, by turning into steam. But the peripheral surfaces of animals engender acts of "such intensity that they enter a psychical phase, a moment of intraorganic appearance as sensation" (*M-I* 424). Such a rise of "inner intensity" can be exceedingly fleeting and lack any determinate qualitative character, although, Langer hypothesizes, there is "some faint little gleam of feeling" (*M-I* 424). While this "event" may have no clear or even perceptible effect on the organism's behavior, Langer thinks that the organism, precisely because of it, "would be prone to prepare its own repetitions, so that psychical phases might become more frequent and finally common in some kinds of situation" (*M-I* 424).

Such repetitions lead to the emergence of true novelties that do not involve a *saltus naturae*. Langer remains firmly on the ground of her sober naturalism. The emergence of sensibility as a novelty Langer characterizes, in a striking phrase, as an "emergent presentation" (*M-I* 424). Sensibility is the earliest kind of feeling, although the distinction between internal and external is not originary. It is something that itself emerges when the psychical phase becomes permanent and stable, leading to behavioral actions. Then such actions "fall under the influence of its felt encounters and become organized to anticipate repetitions of such episodes; more and more, then, behavior—the acts of an organism as a whole in relation to extraorganic conditions—comes to be guided and developed by feeling, which at this level had best be termed 'awareness'" (*M-I* 425), which Langer thinks of as momentary states without continuity. The psychical level is reached when there occurs "a basic division of felt action," manifested in the distinction between "what is felt as impact and what is felt as autonomous act" (*M-I* 425), a pivotal phenomenological distinction that, we have seen, runs throughout Langer's reflections and that becomes most significant on the human level, where all levels of felt passage are in play, many of which already play a role in the realm of subhuman motivations but are rarely attended to on the more mature level of humans. The growth of behavior in humans involves an orientation of acts toward the external. Behavioral acts arise out of a matrix, in which they are found, and "no external event can cause them except through its influence on the situation of the agent, in which external and internal elements intersect and interact" (*M-I* 427). What is primary is not a "response" to a "stimulus," but rather a configuration of acts and motivating situations. These motivating situations, we will see, are ultimately, in the case of humans, defined in terms of *meaning*. These theses are also proposed and defended by Jakob von Uexküll in his *Theory of Meaning* and by John Dewey in his seminal article, "The Unit of Behavior," from 1896, which functioned as a kind of permanent core to all his later work. Here is another point of intersection between Langer's and parallel projects with respect to both a biologically based semiotics and a kind of biologically aware pragmatism, which Dewey exemplifies.

Thus arises what Langer, once again, calls the "act form" (*M-I* 428), which for her, under the guise of "organic form," appears "in nature as it appears in art" (*M-I* 159), that is, as "tension patterns expressed in substance, which hold their form by a staggering complex of rhythmicized acts. Such dynamic patterns are not parts, but elements. Down to the structure of protein molecules, they determine the nature and potentialities of living matter" (*M-I* 428). This is the same distinction we saw in Langer's analysis of art. These potentialities are actualized in situations by a process of adaptation. Adaptability refers both to "genetic adaptability" and to "functional adaptability" (*M-I* 430n24). Functional adaptability—and such adaptability can be phenomenologically charted—refers to "active adjustment" possibilities, which ultimately involves a complex layering of acts upon acts in the internal system of the organism.

Active adjustment is first and foremost mediated through the skin, which, as mentioned, has extraordinary importance for Langer. Langer remarks on the presence of "muscle tonus," embodied in minute acts of "muscle contraction," which forms a kind of background for another system of "contractile acts," which manifest themselves as acute motions in the *milieu externe* of the organism and constitute, strictly speaking, its behavior. Humans, like other "higher animals," in Langer's conception, are marked by a "progressive increase and organization of contractile tissues" (*M-I* 434) and hence the increase of internal tensions point-ing "outward." The skin is a kind of early warning system, which in higher ani-mals allows the development of "a proportionate awareness of imminent situa-tions" (*M-I* 434). In humans the concomitant development of nervous structures removes to the interior the central locus of behavioral control. But these struc-tures are themselves constituted of acts and systems of acts, competing for control and actualization. Where there is actualization, Langer claims, there has been an option selected, for the act systems are in competition with one another, and thus potential conflicts are everywhere. For Langer "options belong to the very nature of acts. The optional character of life is so pervasive that it presents not as a structural feature but as a quality," which appears, as we have seen, projected in works of art as "vitality" (*M-I* 436). Behavioral acts arise out of a flood of un-felt options. The foundation of behavior is to be found in the interplay of the two impulse patterns of felt impact and autonomous acts, a distinction, we once again see, that is constant in Langer's descriptively rich reflections on mind.

Langer has this picture of the organism as a unified system of acts that ap-pear in feeling as having the two different characters just mentioned. The up-shot of the functioning of these systems is that "the organism as a whole performs all the acts its situation permits, fitting them into the conditions of its ambient" (*M-I* 438). As she describes it, there is a process of hierarchical entrainment of systems of acts by other acts, so that automatic acts such as respiration and the respiratory cycle, which normally goes on of its own accord, can be entrained by the power of vocalization, which clearly builds on it. Vocalization is, in fact, embodied in "highly elaborate acts" that are "synthetic products of the instinc-tive repertoire, formed under the pressions or implementations, encouragements or discouragements of the outside world" (*M-I* 439). In general, Langer notes in a comment ripe with metaphysical implications, new situations can cause or-ganisms to "realize some quite unforeshadowed potentiality" (*M-I* 440). While the primitive eye, for example, may have been defined by non-visual activities, with light perception and propagation being actually connected with metabolic and trophic processes, it is clear that there has been a radical transformation in function, a further "interiorization" of vision that has turned it into a "distance sense." There is a marked difference between original "vision" and the vision in-volved in "reading." Vision has clearly grown in "extent, diversity and intensity" (*M-I* 442), opening a wider and wider ambient for human and other "higher" ani-mals. As a result, Langer says, "growth is the perpetual trend of life; the mate-rial self-enlargement of organisms is only one manifestation of it. Acts and am-bients grow and diversify, reintegrate and shift to higher levels, together. That is the course of evolution. The power to negotiate a larger and more 'difficult' ambient is often taken as the measure of evolutionary advance" (*M-I* 442). "Advance" here is clearly an evaluative notion, but not dependent on any form of intrinsic teleology or finality. There is nothing, Langer thinks, "necessary" in the creative advance of novelty-producing nature (see Crosby 2005).

Growth is not always oriented outward. There can be growth in intensity, in the quality of "being felt," a deep Whiteheadian theme that has been explored by Judith Jones (1998) and clearly lurks everywhere in the background of Langer's reflections. Life is a paradigmatic instance of this, for life in other than a physical sense arises with the quality of "being felt." Life is the realm of *value,* and there is no value without consciousness. "Where nothing ever is felt, nothing matters" (*M-I* 444). The movement of evolution, in the case of the hominid stock, seems to have tended without necessity, Langer holds, "in one general direction, which was toward cerebral activity" (*M-I* 444). Within this tendency there occurred a "great shift." This "great shift" is the shift from animal to human estate, that initiated the development of mind (*M-I* 444). Langer proposes in part 4 of *Mind* to attempt a kind of rational reconstruction of this shift, without in any way implying that it was necessary or predictable.

What, then, is the philosophical upshot of her philosophical and metatheoretical narrative, which is of the utmost interest and complexity?

The Great Shift

In what follows we will be dealing with a series of expanding questions.

- What does Langer mean by "great shift"?
- What has to be "explained," or at least talked about, to chart the rise of the distinctively human mind or human mentality?
- What is the relative weight to be assigned to the vast empirical and scientific underpinnings of Langer's reflections and her conceptual and analytical framework?

Langer states that "the most important concepts to bear in mind in dealing with the problematical issues of animal behavior are (1) the wholeness and typical form of acts, (2) the advance of situations, and (3) the fact that an organism always does everything it can do" (*M-II* 3). Intraorganic activity and behavior are both composed of acts, but the main difference between the two is that "the decisive conditions controlling behavior are external, the somatic elements being largely permissive" (*M-II* 3). For Langer, as we have seen, the organism is a matrix of activities, an array of options that involve the choice and configuration of alternative acts. Animals develop a repertoire of behavioral acts, some of which are "prepared, if not actually exercised, *in ovo* or *in utero*," while others are found in adaptive behaviors that ultimately furnish "the elements from which instinctive acts are formed" (*M-II* 7). Langer is of the controversial opinion that "all animal behavior below the level of concept formation is instinctive; and the conceptual level is very high on the evolutionary ladder, not far short of human mentation, if short of it at all" (*M-II* 16). It should be noted that Langer does not *eo ipso* deny "concept formation" to animals. Instincts, for their part, are stereo-typic actions, "sometimes of considerable complexity, that show very little varia-tion from one individual to another within a species, but great interspecific dif-ferences" (*M-II* 17). An "instinct" differs from organic behavior in that

> the former is fitted to external conditions and requires extraorganic substrates or means. Its distinction from reflex action is that it is prepared by related acts, or "ap-petitive behavior" which culminates in the consummation of the total act, i.e., in a subact, quite properly called the "consummatory act." . . . Consummatory acts are the most stereotypic movements, but also least peculiar to any taxonomic division below the largest, e.g., class or even phylum. It is mainly "appetitive behavior," and the less noticed cadence which follows consummation, that are species-specific, and provide the defining characteristics of the various "instincts." (*M-II* 17–18)

Instinctual behavior is a "response" to a distinct "stimulus." What is the con-ceptual scaffolding, Langer asks, needed for dealing with species-specific acts and act complexes? These acts are hereditary, rooted in the organism. They are of sev-eral kinds:

> (1) pure reflexes, elicited by particular acute stimuli, and requiring no conscious intent; (2) autogenous acts motivated by changes of internal situation, prenatal or postnatal; (3) direct responses to opportunities for action offered by the ambient, which are made in characteristic ways by different species—the typical movements generally recognized as examples of instinct; (4) special proclivities, such as a rac-coon's to dip its food into water, the cat's to bury its feces; and (5) apparently pur-poseful, elaborate acts, like the sunfish's fanning his brood, the nesting and feed-ing habits of many birds, the astounding performances of sea otters, dolphins and apes. (*M-II* 30–31)

Langer then states that "these acts are all instinctive in animals" (*M-II* 31), though this does not mean that they are not intelligent (or not "rational") or are done un-consciously. While the environment might be exploited in a most clever fashion to implement the animal's impulses, "I submit that their acts are all made out of elements in the agent's native repertoire and steered by the current advance of the motivating situation, organic and ambient, from move to move" (*M-II* 31). All the behavioral acts of animals, Langer continues later, arise "from a texture of

activity which is full of gradients, summations, urgencies, inadequacies and ab-
normal substitutions" (*M-II* 33). What she calls "true instinctive acts" are "made
by gradual integration, maturation and the molding forces of pressions from
within and without. Instinctual elements, rather than a collection of 'instincts,'
compose a creature's basic behavioral repertoire" (*M-II* 37). Such a thesis results
from Langer's most fundamental, and repeated, principle for biological interpretation: "an organism always does everything it can do at the time" (*M-II* 41). The
situation—or the ambient—is made up of all the pervading opportunities that
the organism avails itself of or selects from. Organisms will go to fantastic lengths
to exploit these opportunities. This is the process of transition from impulse to
behavior, for "no living mechanism is ever doing absolutely nothing" (*M-II* 30).
Langer perceptively notes that even "waiting is a physiological activity" (*M-II* 30),
part of the "automatic trend of impulses toward implementation of their active
expressions" (*M-II* 42).

Continuing in her line of conceptual reconstruction, Langer thinks that it is
the evolution of ecosystems, and not the mechanical adaptation of elements to
one another, that is primary. What must be attended to is "the scope of individuation and aberration, the freedom of action permitted by a creature's place in the
ecosystem which frames its existence" (*M-II* 43). Not all ecosystems are equally
exploitable, but those that are "encourage the enlargement of at least some of the
Umwelten they comprise" (*M-II* 43). Langer speaks here of "this leeway of life" as
the condition of possibility for the emergence of novelties. It also "in some respects certainly underlies the growth of instinctive behavioral acts and the ambients that expand with their growth" (*M-II* 43).

Langer is deeply concerned with the differences between animal ambients, or
Umwelten, and human worlds. Animals, it is known, clearly have different sensory worlds and sensory fields. These are not merely more or less reduced or enhanced forms of a common perceptual apparatus that they share with humans.
Langer's primary contention is the following: "[T]he primary characteristics
which animals see are values, and all the qualities of form, color, shape, sound,
warmth, and even smell, by which we would naturally expect them to recognize
things, enter into their perceptual acts only as they enter into their overt behavior
as values for action" (*M-II* 55). Perception, then, is intrinsically tied to values and
to possible action. Space, for example, is not pure perceptual space but action-
space, involving bodily engagement. There is a consequent extension of actual
into potential movement based on "feelings of direction, distance, contact and
progression" (*M-II* 60). Langer follows then familiar empirical research in claiming that what animals perceive is "above all a qualitative character, a 'complex-
quality' of a total situation" (*M-II* 62). This quality engages the animal in all its

various dimensions, motor, visceral, and emotive, and previous qualitative complexes are carried forward as lived schemata or "reactive schemes" by the animal when it is confronted with novel situations. Langer thinks, rather problematically, to be sure, that the literature shows no power of perceptual constancy in the human thematizing sense in the animal realm. While this may or may not be true, in some sense of the term, the point Langer is making is clear, and her argument does not stand or fall with how the matter here falls out in certain instances.

Consequently, Langer's main point is that trying to figure out just what it is an animal perceives should first of all involve study of the animal's acts, both behavioral and organic. Non-reflex behavioral acts, which are clearly publicly observable, should first be studied with an eye on their total form, which we must think of as continuous with "internal preparatory acts" (*M-II* 64). Only then can we hope to infer anything about their "covert, psychical phases" (*M-II* 64). The phenomenological or descriptive task is to discern the characteristic phases of these acts. Langer thinks that one conclusion supported by the empirical materials is that "adaptation to external conditions is made chiefly at the commencement of the act" (*M-II* 64). The act is then expanded "into a sequence of perception, conative posturing, and finally the strike," say, in the case of predation or hunting. This expansion is rooted in the ability of "quite massive impulses" to generate and sustain tensions over long periods. "It is the nature of these large impulses, motor and locomotor, that really shapes the ambient of an instinctively enacted life" (*M-II* 77). The domain of instinctive impulses, Langer thinks, frames a way for animal percepts to function that is very different from the human sphere.

> If we would speculate on what an animal sees or fails to see in its environment, we must start from what it is doing; for it sees whatever will implement or frustrate its acts. Their implementations may be materials, special places, and above all vistas and avenues permitting an act in progress to continue, unfold from one move to another; that is, the creature has an eye for enticements, openings and options, perhaps not far ahead, but arising as they become relevant. In this serpentine, ever-developing ambient, impending frustrations of acts, ranging from small obstacles to threats of instant death, appear with the same continual emergence as the successive opportunities. (*M-II* 77)

In Langer's view animals act in these ways without the benefits of concepts or symbols in the strict sense, and yet they function just as effectively in these situations in which they find themselves as humans would. To what is such a success due? Langer thinks that the major instinctive acts of animals are "highly articulated, phylogenetically developed units, unconfused by any awareness of merely possible exigencies, possible errors, or thought of other possible acts" (*M-II* 77). These units compose types of complete patterns "not found in human lives" (*M-II* 77). Higher animals make their ambients by their acts, and their places "are created largely by instinctive activities, and reflect those behavioral patterns" (*M-II* 78). Their places, she argues, are marked by a sense of familiarity, which does not involve any explicit and articulate cognitive mapping. In a comment reminiscent of Whitehead and Dewey (and Bachelard), Langer continues: "'Places' are not geographical regions, but pragmatic entities, locations of felt events; as such, they may expand or contract with the expansion or contraction of the life to which they belong, which may have several places—feeding, nesting, hiding, courting places—each with its unique, inherent feeling tone, and its own special sense of familiarity when it is revisited" (*M-II* 80). Clearly such a notion will be potentiated on a much higher level in the human sphere, perspicuously explored in a series of insightful books by Yi-Fu Tuan (esp. 1977 and 1995). Places are not just seen. Even the well-known case of chicks following inanimate objects is interpreted by Langer to involve much more than visual fixation. A fixated point, if it moves, functions as a lure, and the movement generates an action-space that is existentially vital for the chick. Indeed, she infers that "muscular feeling seems to enter crucially into the space experience" (*M-II* 84). Perception and action in these cases, she thinks, are intertwined, and the space in which they occur is not thematic or objectified space. Langer in effect thinks that the evidence from empirical research, which she supplies in great abundance but which we cannot reproduce here, shows that animal space is "built up by non-conceptual acts . . . and is essentially a complex of paths and actively evolved places" (*M-II* 90).

There is, Langer says, a certain "melodic" character to the sensory guidance of animals. "Each movement furthers the motivating situation for the next, so the implementing situation advances from chance to chance, the creature progressing as its need is met" (*M-II* 101). Langer cites a fantastic passage from Volkelt in which this melodic metaphor is provocatively used to explain why animals possess no "representations," in one importantly qualified sense of that term:

> According to our view, the landscape which a carrier pigeon sees beneath it does not resemble a "map," but appears to the pigeon relatively unarticulated and diffuse. . . . The successive impressions do not compose an internally ordered series of mutually limited, distinct images, but present something like an optical melody. And likewise, what the carrier pigeon's memory contains is not . . . a vast sum of isolated impressions; but melody-like qualitative complexes, that will unroll at the touch of sensory impressions, constitute its available stores. By these optical melodies it finds

its way from landscape to landscape, as a person reproducing a song finds his way from one tone to the next. (Volkelt 1912: 126, cited in *M-II* 101)

Langer admits that we are on very dangerous ground here in trying to construe animal acts in their interior or covert dimensions in non-conceptual terms. But the question would then follow: How are we to maintain consistency in the framework of interpretation to make possible systematic observation? We cannot simply transfer such terms as "social," "rational," and "ceremonial" to the animal world *tout court*. We need a way of interpreting animal practices "as acts formed in impulses and guided by the melody-like passage and growth of sensible and emotive feeling, to consummation or failure" (*M-II* 101). This is, she proposes, a more animalian way.

How does she propose to do this? By means of a discussion of "animal values." What does Langer mean by this loaded expression, and what does she hope to accomplish by using it as an analytical tool?

Langer's idea, however, is not to reform biology but to find "biological concepts on which to base any indirect methods for the study of psychical phases in animal life" (*M-II* 104–105). Without such concepts we will not be able to determine the critical difference, which she wants to establish, between feeling in animals and the type of feeling that marks human mentality. "If the psychical moments of animal acts are different from ours, it means that the acts are different, perhaps from their very impulses to their consummations" (*M-II* 105). If the space perception of animals is not geometric but melodic, and if indeed, almost as a consequence, for them there are no permanently self-identical objects, that is, simple substances with variable and thematizable attributes, even though animals successfully deal with objects, "how do they know what to do with them, when to seek and when to avoid them? There must be differences between their object perception and ours, as great as between their ways and ours of possessing space" (*M-II* 106). What is the nature of these differences that led to "the fateful evolutionary shift that has taken place in the hominid stock" (*M-II* 108)?

Langer proposes to reject the great variety of explanatory and descriptive categories either in terms of neurology or in terms of the psychological categories of stimulus and response or the use of terms such as "mechanisms," and so forth. Langer is especially hard on the habit of carrying over to ethology words and concepts that have their home in anthropology and ethnology, such as "symbol," "ritual," and "ceremony." This is the way of anthropomorphic psychologizing, and Langer resolutely wants to avoid going down this path, wanting instead to interpret the ethological data "as strictly and consistently as possible in non-human terms, up to the point where the 'great shift' becomes imminent" (*M-II* 113). If we stick to the act-form, and what follows from this form, we start from the fundamental notion that the basic properties of acts "produce the patterns of tensions which constitute the continuous lives of organisms" (*M-II* 113). This pattern is a "progressing matrix" (*M-II* 113). This advancing act matrix in the case of animals must not be pre-judged in human laboratory terms, which are set up ultimately based on humanly conceived values and are conditioned by tests we want the animals to undergo.

How, then, does one begin to access the domain of properly animal values, that is, just how and to what do animals really attend? And how do we know that?

Langer develops some hints about human perception that are to be applied to the interpretation of the perceptual field of animals but without the ascription of human values to the animals. Langer starts with an interesting phenomenon discovered through tachistoscopic presentations: there is often a premonition of positive or negative value in the process of recognition of words even before the word is fully identified. Such a finding raises a fundamental question. How can something, whether word, image, or any other presentation, be evaluated before it has been recognized? This seems against common sense. Recognition, one would think, must precede evaluative reaction. But Langer thinks there is a deep heuristic clue here to the perceptual world of animals. The perceptual act actually seems to start as

> a deep, complex, gradually gathering enactment of a total sensory impulse; an impulse elicited from the peripheral receptor organ by the impact of some ambient event, but propagated through the brain via many paths, and entraining all sorts of impulses—defensive, conative, or more vaguely emotive—as elements of itself along the way. Its psychical phase develops gradually, however fast its completion may seem; perception is not an instantaneous act followed by discrimination and evaluation, each of which imposes some value on the ultimate form. (*M-II* 115)

The lesson to be learned here, which ultimately Langer will connect with the phenomenon of "subception," is that "value may be adumbrated before perception of forms is complete" (*M-II* 115). There is what Langer calls an expectant, covert anticipation of the full percept that we normally miss, since it is so transitory. But the human perceptual act is complex. Such complexity "allows earlier phases to be felt in other than cognitive ways, either as an uneasiness about the coming presentation or an eager expectation of it, growing as the percept emerges" (*M-II* 116).

Langer's hypothesis or tentative "rational reconstruction" of animal perception is that this prior phase, prior to a descriptively conceived perceptual judgment of recognition, is elaborated in and definitive for animal perception. Animal perception may not be primarily a matter of recognizing and relating objects by their attributes of color, shape, size, and so forth. Maybe, she opines, it is normally "a matter of locating situations for action, in which a center of highest value draws the agent's interest" (*M-II* 116). Indeed, the animal clearly does recognize that the "object" has sensory properties, but they are not thematized or "objectified." What is primary or fundamental is the emergence and consummation of acts and the sense of satisfaction and of facilitation attendant upon them. Facilitation, progressive sensitization, abbreviation, more rapid consummation are the directly experienced outcomes of perceptual acts.

Langer offers a number of illustrations of this thesis or notion. She interprets the gull's rolling of a displaced egg back to the nest with the underside of its beak as rooted in the need for and seeking of contact with the egg, precisely where the famous red spot is. While from one point of view this is clearly inefficient, we must not assume that "labor-saving" is one of the gull's values. "[T]he practical results of acts are not motivating ideas, but . . . bodily feeling and immediate desire, fear and a medley of other fleeting emotions control instinctive performances, rather than any humanly acceptable 'goals' or purposes. That is a basic insight gained by the observation of a relatively small deviation from rational behavior" (*M-II* 120). Likewise female pigeons will not lay in solitude, but must have some sort of visual contact, and not merely auditory contact, with another pigeon.

Langer has an extremely interesting—but hedged and tentative—discussion of sound and hearing that is directly opposed to the notion that their function is primarily communicative in animals. "The first important relation between utterance and hearing may be that the animal hears itself" (*M-II* 121). Audition "clearly served originally for information of general ambient conditions, and was preceded by vibratory sensations with which it still merges, for human sensibility, at the lower end of the audible frequency range" (*M-II* 121). As for vocalization, Langer thinks, they are "originally expressive acts of inward excitation, and it is quite conceivable that their basic motivation is self-expansion, enlargement of the act in its noisy consummation" (*M-II* 121). She cites erotic and angry excitement as instances of such expressive acts. Langer's *interpretation,* or hypothesis, is that these instances of overt excitement, "which normally evoke the responses of a partner, were probably not purposive in their origin, but purely autistic, spontaneous acts of self-enlargement, enhanced by the hearing of the agent's own resounding accompaniment" (*M-II* 122). Indeed, autogenic vocal activity, which has its own distinctive feeling tone, is "more allied to kinesthesis than to peripheral perception" (*M-II* 122). The "peculiar emotive character" of hearing makes it fundamentally empathic, with objective and subjective feelings being easily mixed, Langer thinks, because animals have no "conceptual functions to define the subject-object boundary" (*M-II* 123), although there clearly is an operative or functioning sense of self and other. Accordingly, empathic hearing is always ego-centric even if it guides an outwardly oriented response. It can wax and wane just as the protracted acts that make up the procreative cycle can.

Langer thinks that all the great hereditary behavior patterns are under the control of two internal mechanisms: the nervous system and the endocrine system (*M-II* 127f.). The nervous system is the locus for central and peripheral stimulation. The endocrine system works to sensitize differentially the perceptual systems to ambient conditions, indeed, imposing "special values on perceptual objects in harmony with the growth of impulses" (*M-II* 127). In one sense, then, the hormonal system, Langer claims, is the primary locus of values, governing the interest structures of the animal. "The currently prevailing chemical balance is a general condition underlying the play of perceptions, and as these are essentially emotive perceptions of momentary values the animal's total awareness is governed by the inward pattern of sensitization" (*M-II* 128). Thus Langer can speak of "the act-determined sensitization of a receptor organ to special percepts," something we share with most animals, as "one of the physio-psychological substructures of all mentality" (*M-II* 128–129). From that common organic groundwork there diverge the different paths of development taken by man and beast (*M-II* 129). Hence the role of the limbic system in humans, with its deep affective undertones, giving us a matrix of "the feeling of what happens," explored so insightfully by Antonio Damasio in a set of interconnected but differently focused works (1994, 1999, 2003).

Langer claims that further prime determinants of behavior for animals, though not for us, are the functions of empathy and suggestion as elementary feelings. They are communal rather than social. Empathy is "an involuntary breach of individual separateness," exemplified in such phenomena as tendencies to vomit when seeing or hearing vomiting, experiencing vertigo when observing a steeplejack, and so forth. Langer thinks that "in human life, where conception and imagination pervade the whole fabric of sensory reception and its immediate uses, empathy is largely replaced by sympathy or some other semi-intellectual response; but in animal life it exists unrecognized, unchallenged and operative at all possible levels and to all degrees" (*M-II* 129). Suggestion is a universal motivating power for animals, much more so than for humans. Langer interprets the behavior, for example, of flocking birds and schooling fish not in terms of signaling, which in her opinion implies intention, although this may be too restrictive from a comprehensive semiotic point of view. Suggestion motivates an impulse to flee. Animals, as she sees it, are immensely excitable and are not in-clined to "watch each other objectively; they see the act a companion is engaged in, and at once have an impulse to do the same thing themselves, but they may do it by a different method" (*M-II* 131). Some animals are so sensitive to other ani-mals' impulses "that the first 'intention movement' runs through a whole drove of individuals" (*M-II* 131), as in a group of feeding starlings, or a herd of deer and antelope, a school of fish, and so forth.

Langer, without committing the "fallacy of false contrasts," adamantly re-fuses to think that animal perception is "simply an impoverished version of hu-man perception" (*M-II* 137). It can be, with respect to our perceptual powers, lim-ited or extended, or it can contain "possible sensitivities to impingements that we cannot feel" (*M-II* 137). But, on Langer's account, the determining principle of their perception is their values. That something is physically perceptible does not mean that it is attended to or utilized. This clearly obtains also for us, and its application to the animal's sensory field seems justified. But Langer goes fur-ther and insists that signals, especially communicative signals, which *sensu stricto* must be intended and interpreted, "play a very minor part among even the high-est non-human beings, if such devices occur at all; and that directly felt inward and outward acts, springing from impulse and ambient pressions and opportu-nities, are sufficient for all animal needs" (*M-II* 138). This is a startling thesis, to say the least, especially in light of a semiotic account of animal communication, a constant theme in the work of Thomas Sebeok. Animals do communicate, to be sure, but Langer does not want to put the pivotal point in the "exchange of signs and signals." Rather, animal life, as well as human life, she sees as a "great texture of impulses and enactments" (*M-II* 140). Instinctive life "is pushing from the ma-trix of impulsive organic activities all the time" (*M-II* 140), and in the case of ani-mals, Langer persistently and resolutely thinks, we have no need of looking for "the specialized human functions of concept formation and symbolic expression" (*M-II* 140). The "higher" animals are marked by "a great increase in emotionality, which entails a corresponding increase of perceptive functions, not necessarily by virtue of better receptor organs, but of increasing values imposed on what an-ciently developed senses convey" (*M-II* 140).

Instinctive action, then, is rich and complete, within the space of its own "logic," and it can reach veritable heights of discriminate sensibility and emo-tional reaction, but there is, Langer proposes, a critical point that marks the diver-gence of animals and humans. This is found in what Langer calls an "overcharged system of mental operations" that "breaks over into imagery and symbolic con-ception, and the great shift from animal mentality to mind begins" (*M-II* 140).

Langer, it is clear, is trying to offer a radically different framework of interpretation of animal behavior and mentality that both recognizes the radical distinctiveness of animals and humans while at the same time refusing to break the unity of nature and introduce some non-natural *salto mortale* into the explanatory mix to account for the clear and definitive characteristics of the human mind. In a startling chapter, "Interpretations," Langer attempts to work out the assumption that overt animal action is guided constantly by feeling, "both peripheral and central, i.e., perceptual and emotive" (*M-II* 141). This means, she thinks, that the often extremely complex behavior of animals should be interpreted "in terms of direct individual impression and equally immediate expression," not in terms of "'social' usefulness or prevision of future conditions" (*M-II* 141). It is the agent's own feeling that controls the fully elaborated act. "The motivation of a behavioral act has to be conceived as a felt element in the situation from which it arises, that is, as something with a luring or driving value for the performing organism, not only as an inherited reaction established by 'natural selection' for the good of the species" (*M-II* 141).

Langer then attempts alternative interpretations of some paradigmatic behavioral episodes that have become famous in the ethological literature. They illustrate her interpretive conjectures without, strictly speaking, being "proofs" of them. They clearly exemplify her permanent contention, already proposed in her *The Practice of Philosophy,* that philosophy deals not with the discovery of facts but with their interpretations.

Take first the case of fighting wolves. What is the meaning of the "surrender gesture" on the part of the defeated wolf? And what is the meaning of the urination act afterward? As to the first, Langer claims that "a wolf's yielding to superior strength is not a gesture, but an actual collapse, in which the loser can still use mouth and feet in purely defensive action but gives up all aggressive tactics, so the casual fight is really over, and the victor gives up the encounter, too" (*M-II* 144). Langer does not think there is any indication that the defeated animal intends to expose its throat or any other vulnerable part, since it even in defeat continues to closely watch the winner. It is not "registering humility in its attitude" (*M-II* 144). This is, she claims, an "arbitrary 'in-reading' of symbolic human values" (*M-II* 144). Likewise, the top wolf's aggression is clearly suddenly inhibited, but just precisely why? Not by an explicit recognition of an "appeal" from the cringing underwolf, but because the groveling posture of the defeated wolf evokes "an empathic sharing of the animal's emotional tensions in the victor, as though he himself were wholly overcome and suffering what is happening to his victim" (*M-II* 145). There is no longer a fight. "There is only this cringing underdog" (*M-II* 145), with which the superior wolf feels a strong affinity. Affinity and existential participation are intimately fused here. The winner is not "magnanimous" or "merciful"—characteristics that play no role in the animal realm, being anthropomorphisms—but rather the inhibition of the aggression seems to be bound "so closely to the despairing partner's active expression that it seems to spring from the sight and feeling of the latter's yielding body and probably the smell of his terror, as though these all melted into one overweening dread that communicated itself . . . to the top wolf" (*M-II* 147). Such an inhibition seems to be operative only within species, and not between them. This is a challenging and powerful observation and clearly an interpretation.

As to urination, Langer thinks the first act of micturition is a completely natural one. Most animals urinate after an exciting episode. It is not a celebration on the part of the winner of his or her victory. It could "mark the spot" of the fight, giving it a specific "place character," but this does not necessarily involve, Langer claims, intention. Subsequent use of the post that has been urinated on is motivated by the principle of suggestion, not by marking of dominance: "the smell of genus-specific urine is enough to evoke micturition especially in male dogs, and, according to the few available accounts, other canines" (*M-II* 148). The scent post is of extreme interest—it has a *value,* a perceptual value—and enacts "the inward focusing of feeling on an external object overtly in a self-expressive gesture" (*M-II* 149), a directed response, "an extension of the organism in the form of a shot of urine" (*M-II* 149). It appears, indeed, that there are physiological and anatomical reasons why this behavioral complex of directed micturition developed primarily in males. The interaction between the wolves is governed, then, by two impulses: empathy and suggestion. Empathy governs the inhibition of further aggression. Suggestion governs the habit of directed micturition.

Another example from the ethological literature. Langer thinks that howler monkeys' habits of breaking off and throwing dead limbs and defecating on intruders are also governed by two impulses: aggressive advance toward the intruder and the visceral response to general excitation. "The motivation of the 'attack' is evidently not simply hostile, nor is it entirely momentary excitement" (*M-II* 151). What is it, then? What is really going on here? Taking a clue from deer mice's learning to control a running wheel or lights in their cages, where the immediate satisfaction is control of environment, namely, the "opportunity to initiate a perceptible change in the external situation, . . . a change which completes the consummation of a novel kind of act" (*M-II* 152), Langer applies the same explanation to the howlers. What they are turning on and off is their experimental observer, Dr. Carpenter. Langer ascribes defecating on the person underneath to an overwhelming feeling of excitement and satisfaction of doing something for control. Indeed, "all their feeling seems to be for action" (*M-II* 155).

One of the main thrusts of the theoretical point that Langer is making concerning the interpretation of animal behavior is that many observers' interpretations involve the imputation of intentions, as if human-like intentions could simply be transferred to or projected onto animals. Animals, just like humans, can be overwhelmed by circumstances. Direct reaction to immediate conditions can lead to terror and collapse, to a sense of helplessness. So, Langer argues, the cowering dog or the turkey dragging its wing or the wildly gyrating courting bird are not "signing" in any explicit or thematic sense. They are overwhelmed by the emotion of the instant. Their behavior develops from feelings that engage the entire organism. Distraction display, courtship rituals, cowering and bowing are not explicit sign and signal systems. A behavior that to us seems to be one of decoying is not that, Langer argues. In fact, she goes even further. We have a deep tendency to impute characteristically human mental acts to animals, such as imagining how we must appear to others. "Short of such conceptual powers, intentional deception is impossible; consequently, I hold that no animal can deliberately feign, deceive, distort evidence, or invent any ruse to trick an antagonist" (*M-II* 163; see Rue 1994). Langer wants at all costs to avoid the notion that our analytical concepts, such as "rank," "dominance orders," "leadership," "submission," "group cohesion and loyalty," and so forth, are actually operative concepts in the animal world itself. What governs this world, Langer proposes, is not social aims but an animal's "own felt tensions and constantly emerging perceptions" (*M-II* 167). Langer thinks that the analytical categories used in ethological research impose "the image of human society on the activities of animals, and not even only on gregarious ones" (*M-II* 171). Allo-grooming is given a psychological explanation by Langer: "what induces and guides the act of examining and handling another animal's skin is primarily an impulse on the part of the groomer, not the recipient of the service" (*M-II* 168). Baboons' tendency "to approach a threatening individual rather than flee from it may require far-reaching systematic interpretation" such as, Langer holds, self-enlargement (*M*-II 172).

But what about what seem to be clear cases of cooperation and communication in the animal world? Does Langer really want to attack these concepts, too?

As to cooperation, Langer wants to take up some typical examples and "try to account for them in terms of impulse and immediate feeling" (*M-II* 172). The key question is, Langer holds, do animals *intend* to cooperate? Taking first the so-called division of roles in a group pursuit of a quarry, Langer asks how it was or could be planned and roles assigned. She makes the observation that the fact that animals run in circles when pursuing a prey gives those on the inside of the circle an automatic advantage. It is not something planned, to put the fastest on the inside. Likewise, that howling monkey mothers wait at key points between trees so that the trailing youngsters can use her body as a bridge can be explained by the motivating situation itself. There is no need for a plan or for directive communication. There is an immediate operative and felt empathy between adult mother and young monkey, rooted in the mother's past experience of feeling the youngster as intimate parts of themselves. Is this not Polanyi's notion of "conviviality," developed at length in a monumental chapter in *Personal Knowledge* (1958)? Even dog teams cooperate without watching one another's moves. Seemingly cooperative behavior among dolphins Langer thinks should be examined not in terms of "intelligence," "problem solving," or "learning," but first in terms of animal feeling, "as an expression of impulse, steered by the perception of opportunities and the felt fluctuations of ambient conditions, and developing from within by a constant generation of reinforcing or competing impulses" (*M-II* 181). Dolphins not only transfer companionship to remote species but function as nurses to sick dolphins, the peculiarity of their breathing patterns falling into synchronization by some two-way adjustment, involving "some fusing of felt somatic tensions to implement the cooperative activity" (*M-II* 182). This is a close empathic relationship. "Now, empathy is a typically animalian form of communion; so it is a supreme development of non-human capacities, rather than an approach to human intellect, that is strongly indicated in the dolphin's care for its sick" (*M-II* 182). This is a strong and controversial reinterpretation, which is clearly not incredible in any obvious sense. But it is fully consonant with Langer's non-reductionist naturalism.

Animals, as opposed to humans, Langer thinks, seem to be under the necessity to give expression to every subact that makes up an overt act. Animals are not able, in her interpretation, to break off an act prior to a total impulse running its course. "Animals do not attempt such rational control of their impulses, but seek the most complete actualization of them even if their central drive was quickly consummated" (*M-II* 186). When a cat continues to "play" with a mouse by letting it go and capturing it again, what is really happening, Langer claims, is that it is protracting the hunt until the impulse to hunt and capture the mouse, with its whole panoply of impulse-driven subacts, is spent (*M-II* 187). We must not ascribe an anthropomorphized motivation to the cat's behavior. Its situation is peculiar to itself. We cannot immediately think that an externally similar overt act has the same underlying emotional tension patterns as ours, even if it is exceedingly difficult to refrain from doing so. In her interpretation of dolphin behavior as instinctive Langer has recourse to two guiding principles: "the constant development of new motivating situations from minute to minute in the course of a life" and "the rise and decline of values, the slow or sudden change of cathexis which an object may undergo as it enters or leaves an agent's transient 'world'" (*M-II* 199). Their world is transient, Langer holds, by reason of the absence of clear, that is, thematized, relational concepts. They feel relationships only "in moments of their acute changes, i.e., abrupt emergence of a new relation or sudden break of an old one" (*M-II* 199). The conclusion that Langer's whole discussion up to now of animal behavior has been driving to show is that "animal ways may be viewed as acts based on self-centered impulses and courses of immediate feeling" (*M-II* 200).

When, however, Langer turns to a more explicit discussion of the thorny issue of animal communication, she is even more controversial and counterintuitive, but in my view nevertheless still arguable, than in the discussion of the preceding cases. Langer's focal thesis is: animals do not communicate in any sustainable or precise sense of that term. In place of the concept of "communication" Langer proposes to use "communion," to cover those domains of their "mutual bond apart from sexual union and fighting" (*M-II* 202). Communion has no propositional contents, being practiced and felt "without highly cerebral responses" (*M-II* 202).

> Communion is a mutual awareness, a sense of safety in nearness and, amongst gregarious animals, sometimes in numbers. It is not established and upheld by signals, gestures of submission or dominance, but primarily by physical contacts, extended by smell and, in some species, sounds and movements which pass on bodily feelings, large or small alarms, expectations, impulses. A school of fish or a swarm of locusts move as one body. Many animals are so suggestible that the first "intention movement" toward an act, made by another individual, evokes their own impulse to perform the whole act themselves. (*M-II* 202)

According to Langer, animals make no demands or proposals, do not offer to surrender, do not give marching orders, do not explicitly indicate the direction of flight, and so forth. "These are all naïve anthropomorphisms" (*M-II* 202).

A closer look at Langer's discussion, however, does not deny the permeation of animal life by signs. What she denies is the "intention" to use and manipulate signs in an explicit way. "In animal communion signs do not refer to acts or situations, but are always genuine parts of acts; and where they function as cues, they are genuine parts of situations in which the recipients of the cues initiate or change their acts. Consequently an act that arises in a situation prepared by other creatures (conspecific or not) embodies the subact or subacts which entered into its motivation, and is to that extent already a conjoint act" (*M-II* 203–204). Animals perceive whole acts, Langer says, which are to be countered or completed, as the case may be. "What looks to human eyes like cooperation to get something done is perception of an act in progress which functions as a lure to pursue its development, literally to 'get into the act' and to carry it to completion. The practical result need not be preconceived or foreseen at all; but if it entails relief from empathic stress (as in the case of freeing or aiding a fellow or a young one), it is 'reinforced,' i.e., its repetition in other situations is encouraged" (*M-II* 204). Such a thesis is a direct challenge to any naïve "continuity" hypothesis that asserts no qualitative difference between humans and the other primates. But it introduces no "substantial" break in nature.

Langer then discusses the cases of bees, ants, and chimpanzees in light of these contentions.

As to insects in general, Langer asserts that they have "simple responses, but not simplified human ones" (*M-II* 204). In the case of bees, the hive must not be thought of in human terms. The "dancing" bee, Langer says, is not giving instructions or factual information. What is happening, as Langer interprets the matter, is the *motivation* of the next cycle in the foraging act by bees who have been in physical contact with her. There is a "handing over" from one sensitive individual to another. Furthermore, the "queen" is a queen only according to our analytical apparatus and metaphorical projection. In fact, Langer thinks, "she represents every sterile worker's sex organ" (*M-II* 205). Indeed, she becomes the focal point of the hive and a locus of excitement and interest. "All kinds of cathexis may attach to her, and a constant mild tension somewhat like a sexual excitation seems to surround her wherever she is. When a swarm moves, she is usually deep inside it" (*M-II* 206). In the case of ants we can see "even more clearly the principles of holistic act perception, suggestibility, rhythmic perseveration even in overt behavior, empathy, and communion by constant touching, licking, sharing food by trophallaxis" (*M-II* 206). Ant communities have "excitement centers," and ants stir one another up to engage in conjoint action. Their excitability and empathic relations allow more than one animal to participate in "one obviously holistic act" (*M-II* 207). This is not a matter of ordering, demanding, or conveying "objective ideas," which Langer assimilates to animals that possess language in the human sense, that is, us.

As to the most famous non-human mammalian case, that of chimpanzees, Langer, based on research results at the time she was writing, is both more circumspect and highly suspicious of the claims made for their linguistic ability. She admits "the facts" about the learning of vocabulary in ASL format, facilitated by the innate ability of chimpanzees to make quick and elaborated arm and hand movements. Langer thinks that on the basis of the investigations of chimpanzees it is possible to see the line separating animal interaction—which is both emotional and pragmatic—and "genuine human communication" (*M-II* 212), which involves conversation, not just asking for objects but answering and asking questions. There was, however, Langer admits, some spontaneous naming of objects seen but not wanted, but *what does such an event really mean?* Compared to the famous case of Helen Keller, what was lacking? Did Washoe undergo any "sudden, world-opening experience" similar to Keller's? Langer answers, no. "In all her contact with people who speak with her in sign language, this ape (as far as I know) has never asked a question or made a comment, i.e., a remark about anything. Besides immediate demands and protest, all her verbal behavior is naming directly perceived things, or sometimes—rarely—missing counterparts of them. Conversation has no sources in her word-stocked brain; as Goethe said, 'Wörter machen nicht Worte'"(*M-II* 213). This would be the critical principle for interpreting all later research into the language abilities of chimpanzees. Langer's point is philosophical and semiotic—and, it appears, well-grounded.

Langer, consequently, wants to stay resolutely within the framework of a rich conception of instincts, which must supply the interpretive keys to understanding the mental functions of animals. Instinct must not be deprecated by such strategic maneuvers as ascribing to animals concepts in the strict sense, the explicit grasp of causal relations, or the making of plans of purposive action. A more solid theory of instinct, Langer thinks, allows us to see clearly "what must have happened at that critical line which the human stock has crossed, and the highest other animals have not" (*M-II* 214). It is not that human life does not have an instinctual base. It does. But it is confused and masked "by conception and the communicative power and peril of language" (*M-II* 214).

So, according to Langer, the ultimate roots of "the great shift" from animal mentality to the human mind is to be sought there. Let us now take up this complex of issues as Langer reflects on them in her project of reinterpretation and conceptual reconstruction.

8

The Symbolic Animal

From Specialization to Symbolization

Langer's culminating thesis is that the rise of the symbolic animal that is the human being is a history of coincidences, resulting in a true novelty, the phenomenon of mind, not just mentality. Mind, in the fully human sense, according to Langer, is defined by the rise of language and thought, and it is rooted in the power of symbols and symbol use. This is what is "special" about human beings. But to arrive at this special place in nature the Hominidae had to pass through a long process of specialization on multiple levels. This specialization also entailed a process of growth and elaboration of feeling, connected with the supreme brain possessed by humans. These processes had, to be sure, a genetic base, whose potentialities were expressed through long-term tendencies in a variety of ambient conditions. Langer fully acknowledged that evolution proceeds through the development and selection of inherited genetic potentialities, which are elicited by both internal and external conditions, although "organisms always contain vast numbers of inactive genes" (*M-II* 226). At the same time there are many alternative ways for organisms to live. No asset is indispensable "until it has become so by being exploited" (*M-II* 228). Specialization, as Langer understands it, is one of the cardinal principles of evolution, but it implies no teleological tendency. The different types of specialization both enable and preclude certain types of "fit" between organisms and their ambients. Moles, beavers, and oysters represent different examples of this.

Specialization, as Langer thinks of it, does not necessarily lead to "fixation in a narrow ambient or to over-growth of special features" such as horns, tusks, or scales. The oyster and the clam are not paradigms for other organisms. The development of the flexible and multi-functional cat's mouth and elephant's trunk has endowed these animals with tremendous assets. In the case of the elephant, Langer claims, "by making this organ a prehensile effector as well as a double receptor, the development of the elephant's nose into a trunk has given him an asset surpassed only by the human hand" (*M-II* 238f.). The human hand, we will see, is a pivotal instrument of humanization, allowing a distinctive range of behavioral acts, which, of course, are more variable than the acts of growth and form that gave rise to it. "Some special traits, behavioral or anatomic, found in very distantly related animals are, however, probably not convergent developments, but similar potentialities at different stages of realization" (*M-II* 240). The ultimate thrust of Langer's discussion of specialization as a general problem is that "vast possibilities are handed down from unimaginable antiquity, to be brought to light by coincidences of organic and ambient conditions" (*M-II* 241). Humans are not so radically different genetically from other organisms, even plants, Langer holds and modern genetics confirms, "but the particular turn his development has taken has shifted his mental functions into a new dimension," even if humans are "probably as full of unrealized potentialities as the lower creatures" (*M-II* 241).

Human specialization Langer takes to be exemplified in a number of distinctively human features, operative prior to symbolization. We have, it appears, no evidence of a "prehensile proto-human foot" (*M-II* 243). There is no fossil record of an "evolutionary halfway station between the simian and the human foot" (*M-II* 246). This anatomical specialization is an enabling condition of both the upright posture and the human use of the hand. The primate foot that we actually have has simply not been modified in the direction of the ape's, but has retained, indeed amplified or potentiated, the "common cursorial form" (*M-II* 247). As to the human hand and arm, they "show the typical anthropoid form, specialized for climbing and reaching, clinging and swinging, catching, holding, perhaps even brachiating" (*M-II* 247). At the same time, humans remained fundamentally terrestrial as well as omnivorous, combining harvesting and hunting. Langer admits that it is purely speculative and deeply hypothetical just how the upright posture played its role in the evolution of "large-brained, small-faced bipeds" that we are. Whatever the actual mechanisms, due to a bipedal bearing, there emerged greater and greater differences between humanoids and "the others," centered in the specialization of the brain and the evolution of the cerebral complex. The electro-chemical substrates and processes of these anatomical structures, when reaching their highest intensity, "are most ready to attain psychical levels. This leads to a great refinement and quickening of every sort of feeling, peripheral and central, i.e., receptive, somatic, emotive, or of nameless other kinds; and it is in this advance that further changes, facilitated or even motivated by the erect carriage, have fallen in with the paramount change, to support it on its evolutionary course" (*M-II* 255). Here is found the significance of the freeing of the hands, a major asset in the process of humanization.

While it is clear that the hand has a definite manipulative power, Langer points out that its greatest role is due to "its gradual specialization as a sense organ" (*M-II* 257; see Tallis 2003 for deep investigation of the philosophical dimension of the hand). The hand's sensibility is epicritical—matched perhaps only by the elephant's trunk but not by many creatures' vibrissae. It mediates a wealth of perceptual details. "But the human hand is a complex organ in which the distribution of sensory nerves and the extremely refined musculature coincide, as they do in our eyes and ears, to implement perception or form, location, size, weight, penetrability, mobility and many consequent values" (*M-II* 257). Hence, the qualities of surfaces (rough, smooth, varied, patterned) as well as their thermal characters are grasped through the hand's wide variety of movements, fingerings, and coordinations. The two hands working together, in terms of both surface sensory reactions and underlying structures, mediate a single complex impression. They are "engaged together in the tactual perception of substances: feelings of pressure and release of pressure, of warm and cold impingements, pinpointed encounters with resistance, oiliness, wetness, and mixtures like sliminess, hairiness, stickiness. The result is that we have not only a report of surface and edges, but of volume imbued with multimodal, often nameless qualities" (*M-II* 258). Langer acknowledges previous work on the sensory capacity of the hand by Katz and Révész, which focused on detection of form for practical purposes or the recognition of the purely "functional" nature of a tactual perception, which is in some ways analogous to a glance at an object. The "thing" and the hand, Langer adds, are not treated by them in their full cultural importance due to an oversight of "the aesthetic perceptiveness of the hand" (*M-II* 259). Here we have the strong phenomenon of our reception of aesthetic qualities: "purely tactual pleasure as of cool or warm waters, living grass, leaves and petals, fur or human hair, and, contrariwise, repellent impingements of crude, grimy or decayed matter, unhealthy skin, contacts which may invoke disgust and even downright horror. That seems to be a human response; apes will pick up the filthiest items" (*M-II* 259). Langer remarks, looking ahead to later discussions, as well as pointing back to earlier ones, that aesthetic tactual values are transformed and easily take on metaphorical significance. So, "hard," "soft," "liquid," "rough," and a host of other terms originating in the tactual domain get taken up into speech and from their earliest uses "designate more than tactual qualities" (*M-II* 259). They "meet and merge" with emotional elements that are not existentially current, such as sexual, maternal, or hostile feeling toward other beings. In this way they become "modes of consciousness, felt attitudes, which motivate the earliest artistic expressions, dance and vocalization" (*M-II* 259). Thus the incredible development of the human fingertips and the wide range of activities in which they engage, a theme explored, in a different musical context, by David Sudnow in his *Ways of the Hand* (2001).

Langer points out that the perceptiveness of the hand is just one, albeit extremely important, component in the human high development of sensibility, "especially in articulated, usable sensibility" (*M-II* 260). Moreover, the forward-directedness of the eyes is "another chance asset for the enhancement of sensibility, for such eyes can be focused together on an object, and for near vision binocular focus certainly yields greater precision than any other method of fixating objects" (*M-II* 261). The complex of upright posture, made possible by the distinctively human foot, the incredibly developed hand, the placement of the eyes, and the growth of a large cerebral mass, makes up a "whole complex" unlike any other in the animal world. The human brain then becomes the point of intersection and *fons et origo* of human powers, the locus for the *differentia specifica* between man and beast. Here Langer follows Arnold Gehlen in marking this difference, which is characterized by "the production and use of symbols and their paramount value in all our further mental functions, their distinction from the alleged 'signals' of animal communication and from symptoms or other indicators, and the subjective-objective dialectic pattern that builds up 'experience' of the human sort" (*M-II* 261). This pattern is further marked by the developing habit of finishing many impulses, which would otherwise overwhelm the organism, not physically as direct responses, but in the brain, in mental acts (*M-II* 262). Behavioral consummation, Langer proposes, goes over into the formation of images, clearly in the visual system or in the musculature system by means of a "momentary tensing of muscles and a fleeting fantasy of aggressive response, which stands in for the unperformed act" (*M-II* 262). This notion of "standing in for" is crucial for Langer's whole argument, being a pivot of the "semiotic turn."

Langer's thesis is that this activity of the internalization of impulse and its transformation into images is not purely defensive, a way of dealing with a surplus of impressions. The overstimulation of the cerebral organ, which introduces new activity, "encourages the agent to observe things that play no direct part in his current business, just to make images of them, probably without knowing that he is doing so. This practice widens his ambient inestimably far beyond any other creature's" (*M-II* 262). Indeed, there is created a kind of "inner ambient" in which cerebral acts are completed that could be overtly consummated, exemplified paradigmatically in dreams. Humans can produce fictitious images, which remain internal to the organism, and which "change the 'set' or 'mood' of the responding organism" rather than eliciting overt reactions. Some persons have a tendency to "produce purely fictive original percepts, either involuntarily (as in dream) or by volition, which are followed by after-images, just as externally induced object visions are" (*M-II* 264). The common optic structures of primate brains, embodied in a "neural mechanism of visual imagination," at least in humans, allows, therefore, the production of retinal images in the absence of objects. This function, the function of imagination, can be, indeed has been, extended into other sensory systems and can thereby be established as a "cortical faculty in its own right. Here it becomes the groundwork of symbolization, conception, and all other peculiarly human forms of cerebration; the evolution of mind is on its way" (*M-II* 264).

It is at this point, finally, that Langer turns explicitly and thematically to the intertwining of symbols and the evolution of mind.

Langer begins her discussion of symbols and the evolution of mind by noting that the cortical development of the Hominidae is connected with—she does not say "caused by"—constant activation, leading to "a high, steady, ever-accelerating development" (*M-II* 265). There consequently develops in such an endowed organism a massive differentiation and mutual conditionings of acts and impulses, depending on the various situations, internal and external, in which the organism stands. Langer does not engage the structure of symbols immediately and head-on. Following resolutely, with what we have seen is a phenomenologically sensitive eye, her genetic path, she starts the discussion of the evolution of symbols with an analysis of the formal structures of perception, the grasping of a fixated shape. Following up some hints from Donald Hebb and others, she foregrounds first the "phase structure" of attention and of perception. Perception, she argues, is not really an uninterrupted steady or unchanging "state," but rather "a slowly advancing act: by frequent, though irregular, recurrence of an effective stimulus in a phase sequence of related acts" (*M-II* 266). This notion we are already familiar with. Langer also specifies another way of renewing the matrix of perceptual impulses; namely, directly repeated acts have a tendency "to set up a rhythm by their own characteristic rise and fall" (*M-II* 266). Attention rhythms, Langer thinks, "depend on peripheral stimuli and vary with the sensory modalities involved," but the "rhythms of thought seem to be determined by central action" (*M-II* 267).

Langer tries to trace an arc, rooted in cerebral activity, from the phenomenon of REM, through dreams and the formation of images, and through the originary nature of physiognomical seeing to the rise of symbolization, which is exemplified first and foremost through the emergence of language. As usual, one must always keep in mind, Langer's procedure is to blend the empirical, the interpretative, and the conceptual-reconstructive. Langer's ultimate concern is the articulation of feeling, culminating in the rise of the psychical phase of acts. Langer admits that the beginning of feeling is not something that can be definitively established, although she thinks it is safe to assume a behavioral point of origin, with, in the course of evolution, broadly conceived, prior levels that may have been felt gradually sinking into a clearly non-psychical domain and others being raised to a higher level. But Langer's main claim is that the organism as a matrix of acts is an integrated system of both felt and unfelt acts. As to REM, Langer hypothesizes that their function is to maintain a normal and continuous level of cerebral activity, to perform "a general restimulating activity" (*M-II* 273).

Cerebral activity, deriving from sensory impressions, however, does not have to be consummated in the musculature, leading to action and pragmatic behavior. It can, indeed in one sense must, be consummated in the brain, and not just when the organism is awake. Sensory impressions could be so overwhelming and constant that acts of perception could not fully digest them. These impressions would then be processed only when the brain has been partially relieved of its integrating function by sleep. The consummation of cerebral activities would then be, first of all, "the dreamed image" (*M-II* 277). So, Langer argues, we have the need for stimulation, the gradual increase of stimulation, and then the transformation of unprocessed percepts into dream images. This in one sense relieves our "excessive sensibility" (*M-II* 277), which cannot accomplish all its tasks in our waking state. But humans are also embroiled in "too many emotive impulses" for them to be able to spend them freely and overtly, "especially in the social context of human life" (*M-II* 277).

> Emotional reactions are always to our own impulses in situations which do not immediately let them pass into action, that is, obstructions, long or briefly met needs, and especially conflicting motivations, which may be large or almost imperceptibly small. The small ones are the neglected ones, of which we may take no notice at all. They just belong to the fabric of the ever-moving situation in which one lives. Yet they may summate to impart a general feeling tone to the passage of life in its situational context. (*M-II* 277f.)

This notion of a "feeling tone" is, I think, the same as Whitehead's notion of an "affective tone." I have also repeatedly pointed out that Dewey's rich and nuanced analysis of "quality" supports and expands the point, too. Langer's analysis, no matter how "abstract," always remains open to the full richness of concrete experience, the logic of whose meaning-structures she dedicated her life to charting.

Dreams are unsurprisingly called "symbolic forms" by Langer. The dream image is, in spite of being "composed," "one momentary apparition" (*M-II* 278). The old sensory impressions that have been embodied in it are "a quality made visible—sometimes an innocent enough object, a bag, a fishing pole, a restaurant counter—but with a feeling of unknown significance; or a creature, human or animal, with physiognomic character above all other traits. This 'expressiveness' is what dominates the 'dream work' of composition" (*M-II* 278). Langer's detailed emphasis on "physiognomic" meaning or significance here recalls the analysis of expressive meaning by Cassirer, Dewey, and Polanyi. The image bears, indeed, "the whole cargo of emotional acts" (*M-II* 279). Even if, upon awakening, the events of the dream cannot be recalled, the actual images of the dream are colored by their affective, emotive charge. They are just as "really" bound to the image as are its form or its literal meaning (*M-II* 279). The dream image itself, it is clear, may not be appropriate to the normal, everyday experience of the dreamer. "But it is highly appropriate to primitive impulses, wishes and fantasies which cannot be allowed to enter into waking life and consequently are relegated to the covert activity of dreaming" (*M-II* 279). The materials of dreaming are subject to the distortions, contractions, and substitutions charted by Freud, with whom Langer finds herself in deep agreement, at least on these issues if not on others. These materials come from a wide variety of sources and contexts: they are derived, Langer perspicuously points out, "from unnoticed or unimportant details in previously perceived situations, events, pictures and communications" (*M-II* 280). Langer is interested in the role that "trivial, subconscious or unconscious, indirectly seen forms" play in dreams. We are all familiar with this phenomenon from our own experience.

Langer proposes an answer that is not ultimately identical with Freud's but that still does not negate Freud's answer. It rather encompasses it, as she claims, and is based on her analysis of acts. "All neglected, unrecognized though physically received impressions are unfinished business" (*M-II* 282). It is the distinctive role of imagination, in the case of dreams, to function as an "organic process of finishing frustrated perceptions as dream figments" (*M-II* 283). While in the early stages of human evolution dreaming may not have occurred exclusively or even mainly in the sleep, and may indeed have been clearly involuntary, "what finally emerged was the power of image-making" (*M-II* 283). For Langer it is important to recognize that this power is not restricted to any one sensory modality. As Langer says, "pictures, distinctive sounds and rhythmic motions are natural sources of spontaneous images, which occur especially when current stimuli are reduced—in sleep, in drowsiness, or hypnotic gazing at hearth-fire, moving water, or the like" (*M-II* 283). These last domains were subjected to deep reflective examination by Gaston Bachelard in a wide variety of works (see for example Bachelard 1964, 1969, 1971). Moreover, the ultimate fate of dream details is to elude verbalization, both of the actual imagery and of the virtual history that together make up the major elements of dream. Both the images and the virtual history share the property of being charged with intense emotive feeling. This feeling is an expressive meaning, a qualitative meaning, dependent upon recognition of a physiognomical character (*M-II* 284). These characters in the case of dreams do not have meaning purely in their own right but, as Freud argued, stand in for "entirely different" meanings and objects.

For Langer "it is in dream that the imaginative powers are born and exercised without effort or intention, unfold, and finally possess all departments of sense and activate another great class of largely uncomprehended phenomena, the products of memory" (*M-II* 288). But dreams are only the first step in the symbolic evolution of the mind in its human form. Its undirected process is superseded by the directed process of imagination, "an entertainment of images and often verbalized concepts whereby we organize our practical knowledge and, especially, orient our emotional reactions to the ever-emergent situations which form the scaffold of life" (*M-II* 288). This is a process of "deliberate envisagement" (*M-II* 288). The objects of this envisagement are "things not present and situations not actually given" (*M-II* 288). We reach a pivotal point in the great shift with this transition: "the completion of autogenic, emotive impulses, which involves the genesis of the decisive humanizing process, symbolization" (*M-II* 288f).

For Langer a "genuine symbol" is first and foremost an instrument of conception (*M-II* 289). It is grounded in "the characteristic mental function, semantic intuition—the perception of meaning" (*M-II* 289), which has emerged out of unconscious functions, where the mechanisms of symbol-making are found, but where the explicit symbolic relation of image to its corresponding concepts is not yet manifest to the image-maker. The semantic mechanisms at work here, we have seen, Langer takes over from Freud: condensation, distortion, and substitution. But, she makes clear, they still function apart from waking life and the public world. While in the animal world objects are closely bound to situations and the acts which are elicited by them, humans can operate with abstracted forms.

> [T]he pure apparition of a memory image without its setting in actions and events is arresting; and since in human memory it usually has some aura of its dream cathexis, this sudden fantasy looms up as an abstracted form, usually with a "physiognomic" appearance. Apart from action, albeit only the virtual action of dream, its notable features are visual traits of shape, color, attitude and expression. Even things and surroundings may be remembered with the peculiar intensity of dream images, while the story that involves them has left no trace of its passage. (*M-II* 290f.)

Here we have the movement to "pure form." When such a pure form has been abstracted it can be used—indeed, is used—to interpret and to mold actual perceptions. The image and the object share an identical form, according to Langer's constant refrain, recognized in our power to discern sameness or similarity through semantic intuition. In the case of perception, however, the affective charge immanent in the image, its emotional quality, can pervade the perceptual object itself, since it is in a sense viewed through the lens of the image. The deep and problematic ambiguities and feeling tones of the image, rooted in the dream work, are in this way carried over to the waking world.

Langer thinks, clearly rightly, that this transition, from form perception to the sense of significance, is a momentous step. But it is still not the stage of free symbolization. The image functions like a symbol, but the significance grasped is not so much *of* the symbol as *in* the symbol. It is exemplified in physiognomical seeing, which even the animals below humans achieve, but which is potentiated in the case of humans. Physiognomical seeing, "the immediate reception of expressive value in visual forms" (*M-II* 294), is absolutely central to Langer's (and not just hers) whole rational reconstruction of human mentality. It is further found operative in such phenomena as "the intuitive apprehension of symbolic import in sounds, movements, shapes and rhythmic changes like swinging, revolving, and flowing" and is a kind of sense of "import" without a clear and defined object (*M-II* 294). This sense of import is the perception of a significance that is "felt as a power rather than a symbolic value" and that is grasped as a physical potency rather than an intellectual potency. Langer here accepts, in effect, the anthropological thesis concerning the original form of early religious consciousness, which is an instance of "mythic thinking." But Langer thinks this primitive sense of significance is already present in the non-human world, although not functioning thematically or explicitly. It is grounded in "feelings of vague import" (*M-II* 295).

Langer's discussion is very familiar to students of the anthropology of religion, especially readers of Rudolf Otto's *The Idea of the Holy* (1923). She speaks of the originary nature of the sense of awe, of the expressiveness of certain expressive forms, an aura of vague significance, and the evoking of a primitive sense of holiness. Certain figures, objects, places become endowed with a deep, even if inarticulate, significance. Behavior before these entities led to a continuation of "the tendency to formalization" (*M-II* 295). Non-practical movements before them have a tendency to become formalized. This is the realm of expressive, emotionally engendered movements, indeed, the matrix of ritual, ceremony, symbolic acts, superstition. Communal formalized action Langer sees as the necessary but not sufficient antecedent stage to ritualization, which involves a transition to explicit consciousness. Admitting that one will never know how genuine ritual actually began, Langer proceeds, echoing her discussion from *Philosophy in a New Key,* to offer once again a most tentative "rational reconstruction" of the origin of speech and language—with specific attention to its generative ritual matrix.

For Langer it is practically axiomatic that it is in speech that we find the pivot of the "great evolutionary shift from animal existence to human estate" (*M-II* 298). "Speech is a process which has created an instrument, language" (*M-II* 298), but Langer also in *Mind* wants to reject out of hand the notion that what she calls "directive communication—i.e., warning, commanding and conveying information" is the original motivation of "the utterances that give rise to speech" (*M-II* 298). Following once again a seminal pair of articles by J. Donovan, she will propose a ritual dance origin of speech. But, as a close textual examination will show, the analysis is highly speculative, filled with multiple instances of "may have," "probably," "could hardly have been," and so forth. Ritual dance was not oriented, Langer hypothesizes, toward communication but toward communion. There is a movement in dance from "simian gregariousness" to "organized assemblage" (*M-II* 302), a movement from "bodily contact to mental contact" (*M-II* 302). What effected the movement, Langer proposes, is the use of formalized gesture, both vocal and somatic, which generates images, most "probably visual-kinesthetic envisagements," which the group shares. Dance, Langer argues, is structured and constrained by distinctive sound patterns, whether emerging from the bodies of the dancers or produced by drums, beating sticks, or something similar. These rhythmic sound patterns furnish the matrix of and elicit the acts of the participants. At the same time, Langer opines, the various sound and gestic patterns function as images, which gradually were able to convey a conceptual meaning; that is, they took on a symbolic function. The patterns could have been merely expressive or clearly mimetic. "If the action . . . was, say, swinging a club, or even felt like that expansive act, the image may be of swinging, or of whirling clubs, lifted arms or what not; but whatever it is, it symbolizes the activity, the people and objects involved in it; and especially the emotional values of the event. The image with its whole cargo of feeling is the marginal effect of the sound pattern when it is intoned apart from the dance" (*M-II* 306). In this way a vocal gesture comes to "denote" an object or action, not "signalize or demand" it (*M-II* 306). Functioning as a constructed and controlled image it becomes a "genuine conception" (*M-II* 306). The vocal fragment, part of the whole vocal-gestic structure, becomes the carrier of the symbolic function, not the private images accompanying the joint activities of the participants in the dance.

Langer, with good reason, does not think that this symbolic function of vocal structures could have arisen by contract or explicit agreement or convention. "No one chose a name at all; no one had any idea of what a name was" (*M-II* 307). The noted "transparency," "arbitrariness," and "situation-independent" character of "words" could not possibly, Langer thinks, be present at the beginning of the great shift to human linguistic consciousness. But, Langer holds, all this is, in the last analysis, extremely conjectural. "We have no real clue to give factual support to the 'festal' thesis" presented by Donovan (*M-II* 309). Indeed, most importantly, Langer does not think that language is really a totally unified phenomenon.

> There may be so many elements interacting to make up language that some of them may be ancient and common to many animals, some peculiar to the Hominoidiae, some to mankind alone. So, for instance, the two quite separate elements of reference and of direct address to one or more persons may stem from different sources and have entered into language at different times. But surely the catalyst which precipitated the new and unique power of speech was symbolic conception, the intuition of meaning. (*M-II* 310)

In this way the need for contact between fellow creatures, which is a practically universal phenomenon among "higher creatures," in the case of humans shifts from actual to symbolic levels (*M-II* 311). The symbolic function, in the phatic mode, takes over from a broken instinctive unity. All of the human being's imaginative powers get "concentrated on a symbolic act to develop and hold the nascent conception at the heart of it, and to let other equally vague figments become entrained by its formulation in the course of its awesome, prerational, gestic and vocal expression" (*M-II* 313). This is a process of "freeing a fragment of the vocal pattern" to function for a very different use and extraneous application, and this does not necessarily emerge as an effect or concomitant of the celebration of communion.

There is needed, accordingly, another step that encompasses "more elements of thought and envisagement" (*M-II* 313) than festal celebration, exemplified in group dance. Langer proposes magic-making. Langer's position on magic is actually structural rather than strictly speaking genetic. Magic is clearly centered on

objects with "some suggestive form, like the root of the mandrake, many naturally sculptured forms of stone or wood, physiognomic aspects of old trees, and
things with mysterious properties, such as flints from which sparks can be struck
and conch shells wherein the roar of the ocean sounds when they are held to
one's ear" (*M-II* 313). Magic, furthermore, involves power, where symbolism and
causal efficacy get fused and identified. But magic likewise involves enactment
and also a directive component whereby the world is "addressed." Langer will
discuss magic in more detail in a later chapter. Her analysis, once again, is based
on Cassirer's analysis of the semiotic levels of consciousness and of its originally
"mythic" matrix.

Langer looks upon ritual and myth as possible first sources of language, but
she freely admits, and rightly so, the clearly hypothetical character of her proposals. What she finds extremely improbable is that "language arose from some
kind of previous communication by improvements that had survival value"
(*M-II* 314). But Langer will simply not accept that animal contact is authentic
communication, although one must admit that the issue is perhaps more terminological than substantive. The reason for her insistence is to mark the difference
in principle between animal mentality and the human mind, in spite of her sustaining a radically naturalistic position on the unity of nature. For her, human
mentality transcends the animal pattern.

> The great individuation made by subjective activity, the symbolic finishing of exces-
> sive nervous impulses within the nervous system itself, breaks the system of instinc-
> tive responses and begets the first processes of ideation, which eventuate in wild ex-
> pressions, dance, magic, then the wishing of curses and blessings on other creatures
> and investing implements such as arrows, fishhooks or weapons with potency and
> luck by solemn rites, and hallowing the places for dancing or feasting with sacrifi-
> cial bloodshed. Speech was born, I believe, in such high reaches of proto-human ac-
> tivity, and gathered form when one individual knew by the symbolic utterance of
> another what that other was thinking about. For with such concentrated expression
> came real envisagement, the beginning of reflection, thought. (*M-II* 314)

Although it is hard to accept some of the problematic premises in the preceding
passage—for example, the existence of weapons, cursing and blessing, sacrifice
as belonging to proto-human activity—Langer's theoretical point is well taken:
concentrated expression ultimately culminated in mentioning or naming, carried by a syllabic complex. In this way the speaking beings were able to "realize
and hold" strange ideas and wild fantasies, which, nevertheless, at the early stage
still were found within a situation where the line between imagination and fact
is not stable or defined.

For Langer the movement to mind is also dependent on the change from "animal memory to human recollection of past events, which made the time dimension of the mind" (*M-II* 315) a main theme of twentieth-century philosophy. Also, in her rational reconstruction, Langer contends that the quotidian uses of language were not the chief matrix. Quotidian uses were supervenient, she thinks, in fundamental agreement with Cassirer, upon the less "realistic" frames of ritual and magic, which did not have to be thought of in those terms by the practitioners. But Langer in *Mind* clearly is following once again Wegener's great insight into language developing by emendation and division, that is, by the gradual distillation or segmentation of global utterances into "smaller semantic units" that were then related by means of all the paraphernalia of syntactic forms. This gave a kind of dynamism and flexibility to quotidian language that the more conservative and archaic forms of symbolization did not have.

Langer's general ringing conclusion is the following:

> The rise of language in the Hominidae marked the completion of the "Great Shift" from animal to man. The power of speech transformed the genus *Homo* and every aspect of its ambient; for with speech came thought and remembrance, intuition, conception and reason. With words—in dim, distant and very long ages—some strange, unimaginable ancestors of ours built up the human world. (*M-II* 316)

This human world is a world of symbols, the subject of chapter 18 of *Mind*, "Symbols and the Human World." Let us take a closer look at what Langer has to say here and what it adds to her picture of the human world.

Symbols and the Human World

Langer always, from the very beginning of her career, thinks of language as constitutive for human mentality. She speaks of the function of words as carving out and fixating objects, thus giving them a defined status and allowing them to maintain their identity across situations and perceptual occasions. Language, we have seen Langer claiming, perhaps committing the fallacy of the false alternative, is not to be identified first and foremost with communication, which she accuses both John Dewey and George Herbert Mead of doing (*M-II* 298n68), in a rather mistaken manner, since their positions are much more nuanced than she gives them credit for. For Langer it is most important above all to affirm that language "is intrinsic to thinking, imagining, even our ways of perceiving" (*M-II* 318). The originary act of the mind is identification "of any items of experience evoking expectation or interest" (*M-II* 318). Identification leads to classification, the establishing of dominant orders, but there is no one paradigmatic, language-independent classification system, although humans are liable to treat their classification systems as "natural." Language, following Langer's analysis, divides the world up into objects, acts, beings, conditions, relations, or events and then further into kinds, which group the aforementioned. It informs thinking, to be sure, but, Langer says, "the influence of language goes even further, for it extends into people's ways of perceiving what meets their senses" (*M-II* 319). Not only might the categories of our thinking be different if we indwelt a different system or mode of speech, but our deepest perceptual commitments would be different, too. Moreover, no language system is in any real sense "primitive." These are valid and substantial insights.

Langer reaffirms time and again that "language is not a code invented as a signaling device or, indeed, for any other purpose, but is a biological trait of mankind" (*M-II* 324). Langer thinks that as a system each language is adequate for what it has to do, that is, it satisfies the "mental needs and capacities of the society" in which it is found (*M-II* 324). Separate languages go their own way from a common root in a quite autonomous fashion. Language, for Langer, penetrates into the deepest part of the human estate, into the emotive and instinctive realm, and "lifts them from their animalian state to a new, peculiarly human level" (*M-II* 324). At the same time it penetrates into all sorts of higher, principally cortical mechanisms. Thus, while communication is clearly and undeniably one of the principal functions of language, it is the "cognitive" role of language, which is entirely "natural," that Langer wants to insist upon and foreground as fundamental, without, however, supplying a knockdown argument.

Langer returns in this chapter to the problem of the "beginning" of language, but from a different speculative angle. One of the noticeable biological facts is the "trait of vocalizing in the course of some well-formed, repetitious actions," which humans share with many other creatures. One is not only engulfed in the activity, with all the attendant feedback, but engulfed in a deep sensory way with the sounds. Vocal elements in this way could have developed to accompany various types of activities, even taking on a kind of autonomous development and differentiation. The well-known development of the cerebral hemispheres along with the progressive development of the sound repertoire, Langer says, "favored the potentialities of speech" (*M-II* 327). Indeed, Langer is right that the asymmetric development of the brain indicates a deep somatic base for language, as even more recent research has shown (Lieberman 1991, Deacon 1997).

A further component in the development of language as a symbolic tool, rather than a primarily communicative one, Langer connects with the peculiarity of the human hand, a topic we have already touched upon. In what, once again, does the superiority and distinctiveness of the human hand consist? Not primarily in its prehensile uses, Langer answers, but rather in its "epicritical sensibility and its expressive power" (*M-II* 329). Human handedness and human speech develop together, with a clear cortical substrate and support, both making up a hemispheric dominance that is peculiar to humans. The dominant hemisphere in humans is where symbolic thinking and purposeful manipulation of objects are intertwined and rooted. Language, consequently, is, from the biological side, rooted in cerebral specialization, though it was not "caused" by it, while on the "semiotic" side it is rooted in distinctively symbolic, not communicative, functions. The word, in Langer's almost Jamesian way of thinking, "holds a concept, while percepts change and leave nothing but a conceptual trail of successive phases of an over-all event, symbolized by the 'word'" (*M-II* 333). The problem is how to hold the various phases together. In the case of vision or visual impressions we have an ongoing way to hold the phases together in space since they are "psychically co-present" (*M-II* 333). In the case of hearing, however, which is crucial in the production and perception of speech, the "specious present" that holds the phases together is extended not in space, but in time. "Time is the new dimension which verbalizing and its mental consequence, symbolic thinking, have imposed on the human ambient, making it a world, with a homogeneous spatial frame and a history" (*M-II* 333).

The consciousness of time generates memory, which Langer subjects to a schematic, yet illuminating, analysis. At its most basic level, she points out, short-term or current memory is needed to maintain the unity of an evolving act, since one has to "remember the purpose." In the case of hearing and understanding a piece of discourse, such as a sentence or a melody, "it is essential that each subact be remembered at least to the extent of psychically retaining its contribution to the advancing conception of the whole" (*M-II* 335–336). This is a process of cumulative retention, and it manifests part of the operative logic of the great transition of humans out of the rest of the primate order. Cumulative retention generates time-consciousness as a permanent background to human existence. In fact, Langer ultimately distinguishes five different types of memory: (1) old childhood memories, (2) biographical memory, (3) factual memory, (4) inductive memory, the power of memorizing, and (5) a primitive sort of memory such as "object memory, the basis of recognition" (*M-II* 330–340). This mixture of types of memory, she claims, most likely arises from different mental functions, a topic we cannot pursue in the present context. But the possibility of "thinking again," which is the heart of memory quite generally, is deeply connected with symbolism, for "it is the symbol—whatever it may be—that can be envisaged, thought, and thought again" (*M-II* 340), no matter which memory-frame is determinative.

Memory on its most elementary level gives rise to "knowledge by acquaintance." This type of knowledge is based on our ability to automatically isolate a stimulus from rival impingements by an act of attention that "abstracts a percept from the whole sensuous array, and this percept promptly takes on the character of an image, without requiring much spontaneous imagination" (*M-II* 341). Indeed, Langer goes on to say that "the percept is a hybrid of sense impression and dreamlike image" (*M-II* 341). But the percept can be not just an object, but a scene, a dramatic pattern, rather than a set of factual impressions, involving a "constant dialectic of sensory and imaginative activity," which make up the fabric of human "experience," and which make up human memory, "a psychical background of each normal person's current consciousness and future envisagement. It is this structure that constitutes what we mean by the 'life of the mind'" (*M-II* 342). This life is an intricate web of peripheral impact and autonomous action, or objective and subjective feeling. Every objective impingement on our senses gets "emotionally tinged and subjectified" (*M-II* 342). This process of subjectification entails, Langer thinks, that "every internal feeling tends to issue in a symbol which gives it an objective status, even if only transiently" (*M-II* 342). There is a swing and sway and wide diversity between "emotional, subjective, creative impulses and analytic perception and symbolic objectification" to be found around the world (*M-II* 342). But the end result, no matter what the weighting, is the development of a "sense of pastness," which is constitutive of biographical memory. This type of memory is, Langer rightly asserts, "about the most complex mental function of ordinary human life, running like a spine through each individual history, and concatenating the human agent's mental acts into a life of the mind" (*M-II* 344). This life is marked by "the felt dialectic of sensory impact and conceptual interpretation" (*M-II* 344), operating at all levels of human experience. This is a profound and laconic formulation of vast existential import.

There is, however, no unbroken flow of memory, especially on the social and public level. Langer explains why. "History is a fabric of memories, convergent circumstantial evidence (i.e., records, chronicles) and rational construction; it is like a fine, strong, woven web in which there is hardly a single thread that could bear much of any sharp pull on itself alone without breaking" (*M-II* 344). But the formative element of biographical memory for Langer is thought to be verbal conception. This seems to be the *conditio sine qua non* of a creature's being able to have a sequential memory of its life. Here is another role for language and propositional thinking. Indeed, language is even involved in a special way in the performance of inductive memory by reason of a kind of self-induction that is involved in "committing something to memory" or "learning by heart" (*M-II* 345).

Langer aptly draws here a most insightful parallel between memorizing language and the processes "involved in memorizing music and possibly ritual movements, elaborate gestures as in dance and other essentially rhythmic actions" (*M-II* 345). Rhythm penetrates all these processes, furnishing an enabling frame, rooted in our bodily being.

Langer recurs often, with sensitivity and nuance, to the universal relevance of language. It "penetrates the entire system of cerebral activities, so that perception and fantasy and memory, intuition and even dreaming take their special human forms under its continual and increasing influence" (*M-II* 345). There is a kind of negative evidence from the pathology of language that shows the incredible diversity of tasks and categories that are joined together in a unity and that can fall apart, with differential loss of the ability to name or even recognize animate or inanimate objects, for instance. "It appears that some process of classification goes on before any conscious conceptual identification of objects. The basic perceptual distinctions and imposition of categories on experience, though apparently peculiar to humanity and therefore, in evolutionary terms, higher processes based on general primate mentation, seem to pervade and modify the elementary functions on which they have grown up" (*M-II* 346). This preconscious activity parallels similar types of processes of valuation, as we have already seen. This imposition of categories is, then, a complex, multilayered process, rooted in a universal human ability that has been "built up from a great number of mental traits, entrained in the course of a long cerebral evolution by the basic process of finishing excessive neural impulses in the brain itself as symbolic images and utterances" (*M-II* 347).

The pathology of language, which has been widely studied, shows the multiform nature of this cerebral embedding of language and the multiple roles language plays in building up the human world. Langer is, as we have repeatedly seen, of the opinion that, for example, the "rhythm and continuity of communicative speech and the conceptual use of words are distinct elements, which may be of different origin" (*M-II* 348). Donovan's thesis of the festal or dance origin of speech may bear both upon the first aspect, the communicative, in spite of Langer's downplaying of the primacy of the role of the communicative function of language, and upon the origin of the second cognitive aspect, which nevertheless may be much more mundane and practical, bound to the immediate lifeworld in its multiple contexts. Langer also recognizes, as a general observation in the philosophy of language, that normally words do not have sharply defined meanings as elements of a code, but are bound together in a relational complex such that the blocking of one word often results in the accession of another that is sufficiently related for the choice not to be arbitrary. They belong to the same conceptual "range" or "sphere" of consciousness. Karl Bühler (1934) made a similar point in his language theory, as did many other "linguistic field" theorists, such as Jost Trier, in the early part of the twentieth century. Moreover, the naming and reading of numbers seems to escape from damage when other words, "spoken or written, can no longer be produced at will" (*M-II* 349), a topic that is central to Mithen's *The Singing Neanderthals* (2006). Indeed, Langer thinks that it is possible that number concepts do not belong to our ordinary vocabulary repertoire, but developed possibly by other means than number words, whether gestic or otherwise. Though language absorbed and transformed the number sense, it is still possible that it has retained a kind of independence. "A similar distinction sometimes appears in the apprehension of musical form and the ability to read musical notation despite verbal aphasia and alexia. Such notation belongs to no alphabetical writing, i.e., renders no words of any language, and heard or read musical forms have no linguistic meanings, so (like numbers) they may escape the influence of disease affecting the capacity to use words, or written symbols for spoken words" (*M-II* 350).

The conclusion for Langer, which is well supported, is to recognize "the complexity and spread of the origins from which man's ability to talk has arisen" (*M-II* 350). The complexity, it is clear, is to be found not just on the production side but also on the reception side. Langer makes the following reservations, which clearly have their base in her prior analyses of the live body. Listening, she says, involves "more than auditory reception, namely, a play of impulses which reach the speech apparatus without coming to overt expression" (*M-II* 351). Language penetrates deep down into human perceptual and emotive systems. Its development "bears all the marks of organic process" (*M-II* 351). Metaphor becomes pervasive, giving "richness and vivid quality" to speech. Indeed, with regard to language, Langer says that "in its totality, its sound and rhythm and especially its figurative expressions, it reflects the tempo and emotional base line of the population that speaks and thinks in it; and thought which rises far above that level is apt to employ unusual words and metaphors" (*M-II* 351). Langer also makes a point that is perhaps too often ignored: archaic and foreign languages are used in religious ceremonies for various reasons—to frame the religious ritual and separate it off from the commonplace, to give a specific aesthetic force to the ceremonies, or even to reaffirm a first language of worship for those who have been displaced from their emotional foundations. Polyglotism reveals even more aspects of the penetration of language. Poetic ability, Langer asserts, is rarely found beyond bilingualism (Vladimir Nabokov is perhaps one of the great exceptions). In the case of brain lesions it is often later-acquired languages that are lost, though there are exceptions. Polyglot persons will find that they select a language depending on the task at hand, including the change of interlocutor. "A language fully possessed is a system of conception; its figures of speech are figures of thought" (*M-II* 353). Langer is well aware that language reaches far beyond thought, far beyond "cortical, rational and semi-rational processes" (*M-II* 353). It penetrates into "the emotional sphere, coloring fantasies and wishes and even perceptions; some moods dispose a polyglot individual to favor his earliest, baby-hood language, some a later-acquired one if, for instance, it seems more adult and public" (*M-II* 353). Surprisingly, and maybe not correctly in light of her previous discussion of the rise of images, Langer even thinks that all dream material "passes through the speech apparatus, where the 'dream thought' is subverbally formed; which means that those illustrated narratives, our dreams, are something thought" (*M-II* 353). At the same time, however, human dreaming is certainly thoroughly informed by language, which has permeated all psychic levels.

Langer, it is evident, thinks of the mind as being extraordinarily complex and many-faceted, without necessarily using hierarchical language. This is apparent from the tenor and vast array of topics and positions she passes in review in the chapter on symbols and the human world. According to her analysis, acts intervene upon acts in unexpected and powerful ways, overriding the pivotal distinction running through Langer's thought of peripheral impact, coming from outside, and autogenic action, originating from within. In one sense our own thoughts can interrupt our "train of thoughts." The inside has its own outside, and can feel the supervenient thought as impact. "The human brain is so elaborate, and functionally so departmentalized, that one act may impinge on a whole system of other processes; and one word may be the symbol that triggers such a mental and even physical emergency" (*M-II* 354). Such an observation recalls James's descriptions of the stream of consciousness in his *Principles of Psychology* and, as Donald Dryden has shown, also has importance for aesthetic analysis and production (Dryden 2001).

The important point for Langer is that the unique trait of humans is symbolic conception and expression, which has an enormous intraorganic influence. These powers are first of all powers for the formulation or articulation of ideas, first to oneself, in such a way that they transcend the present situation. The origin of the concept of reality is found here, Langer thinks, arising in verbal intercourse and communication, which function in a realm of values in principle different from those of the other animals. The following passage indicates, once again, that the contrast between the "cognitive" and the "communicative" functions of language is perhaps not consistently held by Langer in spite of herself.

It is in society, and more particularly in the verbal intercourse called conversation, that men have acquired what the most intelligent other animals have never developed—intellect. Animal mentation and human intellect rest on different principles. The most organized animal community is not comparable to human society, for only the latter is based on intellectual and moral values—personal responsibility, standards of justice, honor and loyalty to a social order. Society, like the spatiotemporal world itself, is a creation of man's specialized modes of feeling—perception, imagination, conceptual thought and the understanding of language. The rise of his typical way of life as a member of a continuous recognized society, built up on the ancient and gradual separation of the evolving Hominidae from all other, differentially evolving primate lines, in its advance constantly epitomizes the great shift from beast to man. (*M-II* 355)

Symbolic Forms and Cultural Order

The extraorganic, as opposed to the intraorganic, consequences of this great shift Langer will trace and discuss in the third and final volume of her trilogy, which continues her methodology of combining philosophical reflection with scientific "speculation." In this volume Langer turns to the cultural "big picture," recapitulating some of the central themes of her earlier work such as the symbolic nature of myth and ritual and the movement to the "scientific" worldview and at the same time broaching in a systematic way topics that have been latent in her reflections up to now: the discovery of death and the rise of the tragic vision of life, the symbolic import of the rise and breaking of "high civilizations." These are admittedly weighty and complicated topics, which we can only sketch here, but which Schultz (2000) has discussed in detail with an explicit comparison to Cassirer's parallel reflections. Our main task is to see how such concerns grow organically and even necessarily out of the main trajectories of Langer's previous concerns.

Langer wants to support at every stage her sober semiotic naturalism. There are no breaks in nature, coming in from the "outside." At the same time, Langer is no reductionist, as we have seen. Mind, in the human sense, is not just animal mentality writ large. It is built on a different principle, the principle of symbolization. The first human beings were "symbol-mongers" (*M-III* 4). But, rather than starting with the arbitrary "invention" of symbols, Langer foregrounds, we have seen, the phenomenon of physiognomical seeing, which isolates "visual forms by their physiognomic appearances more than by contours, textures, or colors, seeing unreal shapes, eyes, and potential movement everywhere in the bush" (*M-III* 4), the theme, I have already noted, of Stewart Guthrie's *Faces in the Clouds*

(1993). Physiognomical seeing, however, is not just a way of grasping a kind of significance that is "qualitative," but it perceives the world consonant with the act-character that is ascribed to events. This is an extremely important insight. "The natural way to imagine an event is in the form of an act" (*M-III* 5), although there is no necessity in all cases to hypothesize an agent "behind" the act. The key insight, Langer thinks, echoing Cassirer (and Vico), is to realize that it is a serious mistake to project the "scientific attitude" back into the first stages of symbolization that mark "the primitive mind." It is Langer's deepest thesis that the great amount of data bearing upon the logic of myth and of mythic consciousness is to be found in the complex of categories that include principally the act-form and motivation.

Langer is certainly right in asserting that the "primitive symbolic mind" did not operate according to the logic of scientific causality. Both practical and imaginative activity were governed by the logic of motivation. The premise was: there are no unmotivated events, which is very different from thinking of the world in terms of an interlocked system of causes and effect. The world was thought of in terms of actions and events, not causes and effects. "The world picture created by the 'scientific attitude' is, thus, radically different from the 'natural' view of events based on the feeling of organic processes, i.e., in the pattern of impulse, effort and realization" (*M-III* 8). Thinking about and acting in the world in "the mythic mode" (*M-III* 8) does not entail a transition to "the scientific mode" when a practical task has to be accomplished. The "natural" view of events, Langer points out, is "based on the feeling of organic processes, i.e., in the pattern of impulse, effort, and realization. . . . Living and non-living things are not conceptually distinguished. . . . Even as they cook, build, plant, or shape their hunting gear, they ["primitive" people] handle the material as something active, not passive" (*M-III* 8). Ritual action, with its vocal accompaniments, enters into practical action, "making the procedure comprehensible as it is carried on. . . . The motivational conception of events expresses, by its formulation of them, the act of conceiving them; the product of thinking reflects the basic pattern of the thinking process itself, much as the living body, the product of growth, expresses the dynamics of the physiological acts of growing" (*M-III* 9). The primitive symbolmonger lives in a different universe from the scientific fact-monger.

When this universe comes really to expression, with the consequent rise of imagination, "it added a whole new dimension to man's world, the supernatural dimension," and "a prodigal imagination finds scope for marvelous inventions" (*M-III* 11). These inventions make up the world of myth. Langer selects a number of myths or mythic narratives to pass in review. Their details need not concern us here, but their theoretical or symbolic points are of the utmost importance. For

Langer, based on Cassirer's insights, really wants to establish a distinctive form of consciousness or mode of apprehension as the key to myth. The *motivational* and the *causal* are not the same type of access-structures to experience, nor are they identical interpretive frameworks. But the peculiarity of prehistoric mentality is not completely explained by such a distinction, nor are the exclusive primitive traits of the logic of experience, which at any rate are still operative in our own subjective experience, topics explored by Schultz (2000). Langer points out that the prehistoric mind apparently believed its assertions, even if to us they seem fantastic. What lies behind this phenomenon?

Langer, following some hints of Daniel Essertier (1927), suggests, as a structural point, that "assertion is one of the primary acts of mind, both in phylogeny and in ontogeny" (*M-III* 20). It has a double function: "affirmation of an idea and of the mind itself" (*M-III* 21). This function, which is clearly operative in the "early mind," is never really or entirely transcended. It is not just a primitive humanizing requirement but apparently a permanent one. All humans experience the need to make assertions in order to assure themselves of their own mental power. Assertion is accompanied by a passionate feeling, what Polanyi called a persuasive passion (1958: chapter 6), attendant upon a prior heuristic passion. Religious fundamentalism clearly illustrates this point, although all creedal professions, fundamentalist or not, also do so, as does science, or politics, as a deeply passionate enterprise. There is, clearly, as we all know, a deep emotional value in conservatism and dogmatism. Langer has put her finger on it. Indeed, the original religious world, in Langer's conception, was a "spirit-world," a world of agents, who indeed clearly also affirm themselves.

The import of Langer's analysis here is universal and has, on her reckoning, vast implications. "It is in making assertions about the world as a whole that the mind affirms itself as a whole; hence the sacredness and inviolability of the cosmic myths that are incorporated in religions" (*M-III* 25). Certain types of myths, or at least mythic forms, "tend to disappear as the higher divinities are developed and exalted in religious conception," although the universal themes of origins, both of humans and of the cosmic order itself, remain and are garbed in different and new symbolic imagery (*M-III* 25). Langer speaks here to the deepest issues in the philosophy of religion, approaching it from the point of view of her symbolic project.

> Myths of creation and long-past events, of impending dangers or conquests, and of life continued in other realms after death have been as important to man's orientation in his mind-made world as his belief in the snake or stony rim that encircled the ocean to hold it in place, the heavens above his head and the hells beneath his feet, for as such fabled geography first gave the world spatial dimensions, so the

> myths of origins and superhuman adventure have given it the character of dura-
> tion, or time. (*M-III* 26)

Motivational thinking, which Langer calls "intuitive perception" (*M-III* 26),
does not think of time as a linear one-dimensional structure that is indiffer-
ently divisible into units. For such a form of thinking "time is a stream of acts"
(*M-III* 26) with forms, proportions, and interrelations that are integrated into an
ever-present now, the specious present. This gives each moment of time a different qualitative feel, depending on the mix of events in the mode of memory.
The past both has the feeling of ineluctable "givenness" and provides "motivations of present overt and, particularly, covert acts" (*M-III* 26). But it is the Future, which certainly rests on many of the same elements as the Past, that makes
up the "situation of emergent acts" (*M-III* 27). The Future is the realm of potentialities, of projects.

So, as Langer and a host of distinguished forebears have pointed out, the Past
exists in the mode of memory. It is closed, inalienable, and irreparable. The future
is open-ended, an emergent field. "Mythical beings and acts are contemplated
with a 'sense of pastness,' i.e., are conceived in the literary mode of memory,
but their occurrence was 'in the beginning,' 'very long ago,' before mankind as
it is known today existed" (*M-III* 28). But the Future is also removed from actuality, as in the case of mythic narratives of the "hereafter," which is a distinctively
imaginary Future (*M-III* 29). So, for Langer, mythic consciousness encompasses
within the structure of a present consciousness these two "ecstatic" symbolic projections of time, which are filled with mythic images, narratives, and longings.
These images and narratives have the same motivations as dreams, that is, they
arise from and are embodied in "natural symbols," which are spontaneously produced in order to express "ideas that are intellectually too advanced, too great
with implications, or emotionally too disturbing for conscious formulation and
expression in words" (*M-III* 29). Dreams, when articulated and embodied in linguistic symbols, ultimately issue in myths.

As to their intrinsic semiotic properties, Langer rightly and pertinently argues
that myths share with dreams the feature of being over-determined. They, like
dreams, are symbolic figments in a wide system of significance. Myths are in essence favored fantasies, stories that express and embody the deepest feelings of
the group and in one way perform an emotional catharsis. Myths are not bound
by a literal or discursive logic, a position we are familiar with from our discussion
of *Philosophy in a New Key*. Myths are the places where "precocious insights" come
to expression: "conceptions of life, with little distinction between human and
animal or even plant life, and all the circumambient forces of nature, winds, wa-

ters, earthquake, and fire; beginnings, growth and its metamorphoses; and the intolerable, unbelievable breakdown of every personal life in death" (*M-III* 31). Out of the vast realm of objects and events that make up the life-world of humans arise the great "natural symbols" of uncontrollable processes, natural heroes, opportunities and threats, and so forth. The "culture heroes," deities, and spooks, which reside in the primitive imagination, are themselves over-determined and carry the deepest existential significance. Langer is offering here a framework for the hermeneutics of myth that is flexible, open-ended, and remarkably free from a rigid set of systematic and theoretical premises and procedures.

The ultimate motivation of myth, if Langer is right, is deep, unconscious, and evolutionary. It involves, at its earliest stages, an effort, not necessarily self-conscious, "to conceive world and man in terms of symbolic imagery and dream-like action" (*M-III* 32). Such an effort, however, is not restricted to myth, which has a narrative form, but is clearly equally, and maybe even more, apparent in ritual, which, Langer thinks, is "almost certainly older than narrative" (*M-III* 32). Ritual takes its point of origin in emotional, self-expressive movement, which has both a tendency to become formalized and also the quality of a feedback structure: a kind of auto-suggestion or reciprocal suggestion. Ritual, it must be seen, is addressed to some agent. It has a sacred objective and functions by a kind of logic of enactment of attitude by those who participate in it. "This in turn fixes the attitude and articulates more detailed symbolic elements in the ritual, exploiting the expressive possibilities of gesture, posture, utterance, and sometimes the look and feeling of manipulated objects, in which some mysterious import is seen as an inherent quality, 'holiness,' until the addressed being takes shape for contemplation as deity, ancestral spirit, or totem" (*M-III* 33; see Handelman and Lindquist 2004).

The *spirit-world*, it is Langer's proposal, arises out of this mythic-ritual matrix, which is conceptual-performative in nature, permeated by the "various beliefs in supernatural agents, enchanted places, staggered planes of existence, and the mythic past where everything began" (*M-III* 33). Examples of all these domains come readily to mind. The weaving of ritual actions into everyday activities, which the anthropologists have often noted and interpreted in multiple ways, is meant to give these activities the "stamp of ancestral sanctions" (*M-III* 34), to enforce "patterns of sentiment" (*M-III* 34), and to express a sacred tradition (see Innis 2004 for a more extensive treatment). Anyone familiar with ritual can identify these features across many different ritual domains, including the political, as Fingarette (1972) has discussed in a Confucian context. Langer thinks that the West, with the ascendancy of causal thinking, has torn asunder this ritual sacred web, substituting for concepts of impulse and agency those of impersonal progressive events, although there is still a volatile mix of modes of thinking present in large groups of people even in "advanced" societies. While such a substitution has clearly occurred in the West, Langer notes, in an insightful but incomplete discussion, that there are, or were, "high" civilizations that have still maintained the motivational conception of the world. An exemplary case of this is ancient China, which was by no means primitive in its definitive achievements.

Ancient China was based upon ritual practice, the establishing and enacting of formal frames for feeling. The meaning of these rituals can be conceived on many levels. The range in China was, in Langer's sonorous formulation, from "the peasantry's primitive ancestor worship to the sage's contemplation of the cumulative values of life underlying the successive waves of death-bound generations" (*M-III* 37). The point was to give form to feeling, "rather than repressing it or letting it break loose in an uncontrolled flood" (*M-III* 38). The hermeneutics of such rituals must break with literal or naïve realist assumptions as necessarily implied. While on the popular level, as opposed to the level of the sages, the spirit-world was intensely personalized, this is not necessarily the case, nor must it be. Herbert Fingarette has tried, in fact, to give a rehabilitation of ritual in his *Confucius: The Secular as Sacred.* At the same time, the tendency toward literalization has been historically predominant and effective, with ritual being transformed into magic, which Langer calls "this universal human foible" (*M-III* 39). The question is, why "such a fundamental tendency to unrealism in the most intelligent animal" (*M-III* 40)? The answer cannot easily be given along Darwinian lines. So, how does one attain an answer? This Langer proposes to do in her chapter on "The Dream of Power."

Magic and the Spirit-World

What is, for Langer, the theoretical and conceptual point of an analysis of magic for a model of mind that is based on a comprehensive philosophy of symbolism?

Langer holds that magic must be understood in the context of the "spirit-world," one of her main interpretive categories. Magic is for a sophisticated person one of the most perplexing practices in precivilized life, but Langer rejects the notion that magical acts are really just substitute acts. Its persistence and ubiquitous presence in societies "point to some deeper roots" (*M-III* 43). But Langer will not propose that magic is more than incidentally "a vehicle for symbolic expression of desires" (*M-III* 44). Indeed, paradoxically, in one sense there is something impersonal or disinterested in magic, in that the magician often is not personally involved in the material outcome of the magical act. His offices can be, and often are, hired by someone who clearly has something at stake. Magic is, in fact, "always mystical and fascinating, with some touch of the supernatural, but does not seem unnatural; for in magic-practicing societies the distinction between earthly and unearthly powers is not sharp" (*M-III* 44). The spirit-world is a world of agents, though they are not anthropomorphized. But, one may ask, if magic does not involve anthropomorphization, what does it involve?

The insightful answer that Langer supplies, with keen analogical reasoning and phenomenological sense, is that it involves a specifically human ability to project bodily feeling into forms presented to the eye (*M-III* 46), something that the other primates do not have, she claims. Citing some famous experiments of Wolfgang Köhler, Langer reports that "external objects enter an animal's awareness only as elements in its own acts, and in doing so are assimilated to its behavior and treated as parts of itself" (*M-III* 47). This means, for example, in the case of Köhler's famous apes, that their "static sensations are in no way 'projected' into the visual aspects" of objects in their surroundings. The static sensations remain in the ape's "kinesthetic and equilibrant mechanisms" (*M-III* 48). With humans, however, subjective elements are "projected" into a percept "given to a distance receptor such as the eye" (*M-III* 48). This is an act of objectification.

> It lets the subjective element come back as an impingement and be perceived as an external datum, i.e., as a quality belonging to an independently existing object; and that object, which thus presents our own sensory feeling to us, is a primitive symbol, conveying the first retainable idea of an all-important sensation and, at first perhaps solely, the possibility of its loss. Body feelings may be the first thing man projected and thus, all unwittingly, imputed to everything he objectified as material bodies in his world. The very existence of "things" is modeled on his inward expectation of strains, directions, and limitations of his felt actions; the wholeness and simplicity of molar objects is that of his own soma. (*M-III* 48)

At the beginning, Langer proposes, the conceptual value of the feelings projected into outward things "is entirely embedded in the presenting form" (*M-III* 48). The feeling is grasped as a *quality* of the thing perceived. This is a kind of "conceptual seeing." The objectification of, for example, the subjective sense of balance is the "subjectification of the protosymbolic object as an image" (*M-III* 49). More extensively, any subjective feeling can be projected in such a way that its quality "comes back to its producer as an image" of whatever feeling modality lies at its point of origin. Langer thinks, with reliance on Philippe Fauré-Fremiet, that the process of experiencing, exemplified clearly in seeing, is a "dialectical interchange of objectification and subjectification, external dictate and autogenic creation" (*M-III* 49). Percepts are endowed with feeling and found significant. The projection of our muscular and gravitational sense into external things leads us to "see our other feelings reflected in their shapes, which consequently seem to present attitudes—threatening or peaceful, tense or free or somnolent. And with expressive attitudes they objectify emotional feelings, which seem to be in them, even when they do not happen to be ours at the moment" (*M-III* 50). Langer is here having recourse once again to the phenomenon of "physiognomic seeing" (*M-III* 50). Perception, in its physiognomical mode, "carves out" channels of apprehension, which get embodied and developed in myths and dream figments. All the individuated forms of nature can thereby through the power of language take on symbolic values that are associated with centers of superhuman wills and powers that surround the human race.

The primary issue in light of this objectified and subjectified symbolic fact is to find a way of dealing with these forces. Physical actions are to no avail against gods, ghosts, and demons. Langer proposes that the only recourse is symbolic action, an exercise of power, to be sure, but *mental power*. Mental power is experienced directly by the agent as a kind of invisible doing. It is this directly undergone experience that "underlies the notion of exerting a non-mechanical influence on the course of events, without physical contact, without push or pull on the external objects and persons involved" (*M-III* 51). It is not that causal relations are not known at all. Langer thinks that they are merely taken for granted and *devalued* in the context that elicits magical actions. These actions are not measured by standard "realistic" norms. They are symbolic processes, and *eo ipso* their functions are conceptual. Rooted as they are in perceptual interpretations, with the consequent articulation of gestalten, magic actions take place within a shifting world of perceptual configurations, "figurations on a precarious, tentative background that threatens at every moment to swamp the virtual array and alter the focus-created image" (*M-III* 53). Magic, then, is governed by a deep principle of perspective, a phenomenon charted in the psychology of perception. The "control" of the changing "apparition" in the perceptual field, when it engages "natural conformations" that allow a process of "seeing-in," in Wollheim's (1980: 205–226, 1987: 43–100) sense of the term, is subject to a kind of "arbitrary lability." That is, seeing shapes in clouds, jumping flames, stunted trees, and so forth is a prototypical magical act. They are active shapes and become ascribed to all sorts of living or living-like beings. "As the magician gains new potentialities, so does the spirit-world he faces" (*M-III* 57).

What is the result of this process, whose origin and development, as here given, is, Langer admits, "a purely hypothetical reconstruction" (*M-III* 57)? Trying to avoid all forms of dogmatism and grounding her assertions in a kind of semiotic phenomenology of the forms of consciousness, Langer points out that "the result of this spread of imputed magic to the whole living world—which, for primitive men, may take in not only animals and plants but stones, stars, rainbows, and man-made things like tools and traps—is that the earth is peopled with a host of uncertain characters which may be anything or anyone other than themselves, by temporary self-transformation" (*M-III* 57). Thus, on Langer's account, magic "is in essence an expression of ideas, and as such is symbolic" (*M-III* 59), though with deep psychological and affective effects. Magical rituals are not imitations. They are *forms of participation,* and a magical act "is an incentive move to start the desired action of the natural or supernatural beings that have its completion in their power" (*M-III* 61). A magical ritual is the "priming and starting of an act" that goes beyond the magician. While there is clearly a mimetic element to it, the "unconscious motive of the mimesis is intellectual: to comprehend the fears and expectations of life and thus make their impact as negotiable as possible" (*M-III* 62). This is the import of the dramatization of belief that is magical ritual. But it has multiple goals and purposes: "to influence nature, to formulate ideas, to unite people with each other and with all the spirits in their ambient in primitive communion, and to assure them of the power of their superlative asset, their humanity, their Mind" (*M-III* 62). This is a powerful and insightful characterization.

Langer, then, connects the motivational structure of magic to the act-form, as we have seen, one of the weight-bearing, and indeed controversial, concepts of her analytical framework. The act-form in the case of magic is eminently participatory. The agents addressed are expected to *fall in with* the actions performed, which themselves are filled with, in Langer's wonderful formulation, "the universal rhythm which pervades the interpenetrating spheres of divinity and humanity" (*M-III* 64). Magic involves transference of impulse from humans to the spirit-world, a transference that can be structured in excruciatingly formal detail, as in magical rites to ensure the fertility of the soil, a practice continued long after "pre-history" had passed, as the medieval historians have charted. This complex of formal detail enters into and constitutes the dramatic form of the magical ritual, which is designed to be *isomorphic with what it wishes to happen.* Langer has recourse to her old terminology of *Philosophy in a New Key* and *Feeling and Form* by speaking of mimetic ritual as presentational symbols or semblances, where there is "no clear distinction between symbol and meaning. The image is the thing itself in the drama" (*M-III* 66). While, to be sure, not all magic has the form of a pantomimic dance, it nevertheless still utilizes techniques of the theater, "symbolic representations which mean real events and are identified as such" (*M-III* 69). Mental concentration is the key psychic factor on the part of the magician and of the participants in the magical rite. Magical powers, however, are clearly not universally benign, nor does Langer say they are. They can be used for good or evil, depending on their sphere of application.

Langer, further, in continuity with her basic agreement with and translation of Cassirer's root insights, recognizes implications and roots of the great phenomenon of word magic. This is exemplified strongly and importantly in the weighty phenomenon of divine names, a central theme in Cassirer's *Language and Myth* (1925), which Langer translated. "The power of a holy name is just about the greatest power a human being can invoke, since it carries the essence of the god himself; and it is, of course, correspondingly dangerous to speak" (*M-III* 81). The name does not just mediate the reality, it *is* the reality. It is intrinsically, that is, ontologically, efficacious. "Where all happening seems like action, all nature may be expected to respond to our verbal utterances" (*M-III* 81). The ontological nature of the word, I would add, is illustrated not just in "primitive religions" but also in the agentization, if not personification, of the Word in Judaism and Christianity, albeit with quite different developmental consequences. Speech, as Langer presents the matter, is a proxy for the mental and conceptual aspects of the spirit-world. Thus, it is not just a sequence of actions that governs magic but verbal sequences, which have to be repeated without formal error in order to guarantee success. But both actions and speech emerge from a center of "purely felt powers," which are not only recognized as one's own but also ascribed to both animate and inanimate objects.

Magic is for Langer, then, "the dream of power" (*M-III* 85). Humans, as anyone possessed of the most minimal historical sense is aware, can pursue power to the very limit, vying with one another for possession of its key, even deeply into the realm of the pathological, a theme pursued by both Cassirer and Langer. Langer hypothesizes that in "savage societies" (a term she continued to use to the end) there is a state of constant fear and defense. This state is rooted in the fear of death, which is thought of as "always brought upon one by a hostile act of a human or superhuman agent. Death is not something natural" (*M-III* 85). Primitive societies are defined by, although they do not thematize it explicitly, an image of life as a stream, "which gathers up all trickles and rills that enter it and carries them along, mingled but present," even if they have "passed away" or "passed over." Death, as originally apprehended, is always motivated, and hence the powers that be must always be placated or appeased. Retaliation from the otherworld is always possible and to be avoided and is, indeed, always the cause of death. Primitive humans, Langer claims, repudiated the "idea of death as an inevitable close of their brief earthly careers" (*M-III* 87). The primary feeling is the basic feeling of life itself and its indefinite and ineluctable continuation. It took a great effort of overcoming to "recognize the closed form and the brevity of each personal life" (*M-III* 88). When this happened, death is recognized as "inherent in the form of life itself" (*M-III* 88). This insight, and its acceptance, Langer says, mark a major turning point in the history of Mind. This is a profound insight and shows how the modeling of the symbolic mind opens onto the deepest existential issues.

Death

Langer readily admits the strangeness of looking upon the recognition of death as a milestone of conceptual insight, an opening of a way "to a rational concept of human mentality" (*M-III* 89). The insight is rooted in the process of individuation and the consequent principle of entrainment, "which simplifies the tangle of separately directed impulses by massing their expressions into a few organizing acts" (*M-III* 91). Langer's construction of the philosophical implications of a generalized biology proposes that centralization and integration go hand in hand and effect a highly articulated organism. In humans the evolutionary process has led the brain to engage in more and more *symbolic play,* the results of which are inscribed on the brain itself, and by extension on the total field of impulses found within the matrix, the agent. Langer avails herself of the metaphor of inscription: every act of an organism leaves a trace, whether it is a metabolic act, a behavioral act, or an act of mentation. The brain itself "tends to individuate, and to establish a dependent yet distinct pattern of mental life within the physical life of the organism, even while it serves that organism as a vital part. It achieves a partial individuation, a functional matrix, which appears subjectively as a sort of homunculus or autonomous 'inner man,' the Mind" (*M-III* 95). In this way, Langer proposes, the human brain transcends its original cybernetic function and becomes a center of interest in itself, indeed, a mind. "It is a physiologically based, intraorganic functional entity, a relatively independent complex of vital rhythms supporting facultative mental acts" (*M-III* 97). It is the result of the process of individuation understood as an intraorganic process in which "deep linkages" (*M-III* 98) between impulses and acts are set up and stabilized in "a highly organized matrix" (*M-III* 98). When this process of individuation crosses into the human domain there are added to the somatic, muscular, and even perceptual acts of animals quite different psychic phases, composed largely of symbolic elements. "Consequently the partial individuation of the mind produces a peculiarly non-physical appearance of what seems to each person the essential agency within his own body" (*M-III* 99). This is an astounding proposal that cuts elegantly and effectively to the quick of the so-called *homunculus* problem that has vexed the philosophy of mind from time immemorial. Maybe it even dissolves it and leaves us to pursue other matters of a more phenomenological and existentially vital sort.

Langer proposes that there arises in this process, in fact, a novel sense of life, a *Lebensgefühl* that is ultimately different from the communal *Lebensgefühl* that marks primitive life. This feeling on the human level is not episodic but continuous, and it culminates in a sense of personal agency (*M-III* 102) that is grasped as a kind of integrated "inner space" or "inner realm" where inner stirrings and outer impingements are integrated into "consciousness" (*M-III* 101). The philosophical lesson here is that consciousness, as a matrix of acts, is not a static substance, but a process. It is concomitant with the "emergence of biological form into feeling" that "comes with the progressive elaboration of mental acts" (*M-III* 102). These become so close-woven "that it makes the individuated mental life seem like a single, all-embracing act" (*M-III* 102). In this way there is a transition from *Lebensgefühl* to *Ichgefühl* (*M-III* 103). With the arising of this "I-feeling" comes also the definitive recognition of the fact that death is inherent in individual life, an insight that is consciously resisted, or tacitly, but adamantly, denied. Death is ultimately understood as a passively undergone event, inevitable, and expected, due not to any agency but to nature's own way. Langer admits that we cannot date historically this insight, but reckons that it must have been resisted strongly until the resistances were overcome in the process of individuation. The act-form leads to the semblance of an independent mind that "has" the rest of the organism, rather than the other way around. A human individual feels its own agency as "his unique, autonomous Self living its unique, inviolable life" (*M-III* 107). Writing at practically the end of her own life, Langer states that "with the idea of such a personal, single act of living comes the understanding of the place of death in nature. Death is inherent in human life itself, and as life is power, so death is defeat of man's power. The defeat may come soon or late, but come it will for every individual" (*M-III* 107).

Individuation ultimately leads to the recognition that death is an inescapable fact, with all the terrors that accompany this recognition. Our life-act belongs to us, and it is our one and only life. Life, that is, our life, does not continue on. In a passage that is written from the perspective of ripe years and that applies to the very project she was working on, Langer remarks that "each person must expect to leave his unfinished works or parts undone" (*M-III* 108). Here arrives one of the great insights of human life: life has a tragic rhythm, tracing one parabolic curve from youth to death. Langer thinks of life itself, not just art, in terms of rhythm. Each life has its own inward rhythm, and it is the inward rhythm that makes individuals different and constitutes their distinctive, and non-reproducible, personalities. The rhythm of each life has the typical structure of the act-form: rising impulse, spanning tensions, cadence, "the decline to death" (*M-III* 109). The life of each individual is a "highly articulated rhythm" (*M-III* 109). This rhythm can be presented in the dramatic mode, and Langer sees Greek tragedy as the place where this first consciously occurred, with its focus on the individual and his ineluctable fate, as opposed to the different rhythm of comedy, whose ultimate focus is on the "social rhythm," which belongs to the "indefinitely self-rejuvenating life of the stock" (*M-III* 110). These are topics that Langer treated insightfully and precisely in *Feeling and Form.*

The recognition of death, Langer continues, can lead to despair, but not necessarily. The inevitability of death can be, indeed has consistently been, met by "a radical deepening of religious feeling and dawning of religious ideas" (*M-III* 110). The subjectification of death as an individual and personal event involved also making more subjective the "relation of men to their gods" (*M-III* 111). This subjectification of the gods involved a subjectification and personalization of power, a kind of infinite reservoir upon which men could draw by prayer. Out of this conceptual shift grew the great monotheistic religions with their higher moral standards and their conception of an all-powerful, but ethically constrained and invisible, deity. In spite of this conceptual superiority, however, humans' relations to such a divine power still were deeply dependent upon or utilized mythic elements in ritual form, and indeed continue to be and do so. Langer's theory here, I think, is not just a hypothetical reconstruction of origins but a description of permanent features and tendencies of consciousness. Thus, the constant insertion, or argument for their necessity and authority, of intermediaries between the individual and a remote godhead. Moreover, people find it extremely difficult to imagine their own annihilation, and the act-form develops into the notion of self-consciousness and its persistence after death. But this postmortem existence is hard to get a hand on, although one would like to find a way of ensuring it by means of ritual and sacrifice. The phenomenology of religion has shown us that these take very different, yet internally related, forms in primitive and advanced stages of religious consciousness. The great advance, connected with individuation on the one side and with the philosophical concepts of "soul" and "self" on the other, is the conception of life as a unity, "which allows it to be judged as a single act" (*M-III* 116). The transition to life as a single act entails the ascension of life to being thought of as a pattern of moral actions rather than a sequence of ritual acts. Conformation of behavior to the will of the godhead becomes the rule of life. This is a "momentous change" (*M-III* 117), the consequences of which are clearly still with us in multiple forms.

Ritual atonement, which also still plays a role in certain theological currents, is diminished or devalued—or at least in principle enabled so to be. The pattern of a whole moral life becomes the principal factor in determining the mortal fate of the individual. "The price of our individuation is a heavy one in many ways, but heaviest, perhaps, in this deepened consciousness of personal continuity and, therewith, of cumulative responsibility" (*M-III* 117). For the adult consciousness, ultimately, responsibility leaves a permanent imprint on the individual consciousness. No magic power, independent of an act of inner will and transformation, can substitute for personal power and its cumulative effects. To meet the divine demands is a lifelong task (*M-III* 118) and not something that can be accomplished in ad hoc fashion. There is no escaping either responsibility or death, and they are intrinsically connected with one another. This is a kind of "defeat," Langer argues, the recognition of our powerlessness over against something inevitable, our death as an individual event that is not connected with tribal action or a communal flow of life. We are thereby, on Langer's rational reconstruction of the "inner history of spirit," confronted with the rise of ethical consciousness, with ethos as "the fundamental quality of acts of human conception" (*M-III* 119). Out of this recognition and emergence flow a set of cultural and historical consequences that Langer attempts to sketch in the last two major chapters of the third volume of *Mind*. Much of the material is not original. But the goal of Langer's presentation is to *describe the matrices* in which mind has developed. There are clear analogies here, indeed throughout the whole discussion, to Hegel's reconstruction of an ideal or inner history of spirit in his *Phenomenology of Spirit*.

What light do these final reflections throw on our theme, "the symbolic mind"?

Restoring Balance

Individuation, as Langer conceives of it, leads to a tendency to imbalance in human life, a tendency that has to be constantly fought against or counteracted. The question we are led to pose is, then, How do humans—how *should* humans—in the process of individuation maintain their balance? The "balance" that Langer is referring to is what she calls the "ethnic balance," an "equilibrium between the drives of mental individuation and the integrity of the biological continuum, the rhythmically self-perpetuating stock" (*M-II* 125). Or, put in another way, it is a matter of maintaining, or even constructing, a balance or equilibrium between committed self-assertion and the claims of the social matrices to which each individual belongs, in fact, *has* to belong. Because "the principle of balance runs pervasively through all human life" (*M-III* 125), Langer wants to find out just what means have been employed to attempt to keep the two poles from becoming over-weighted. The means are symbolic means, and at the earliest stages of distinctively human development they encompass punishment, ritual, the construction of fetishes, sacrifice, and the development of a distinctively religious form of consciousness.

The focal point of these activities ultimately has to do with the problem of death and the attempt to find a framework that will heal this "rift" in human existence and human consciousness. Individuation, we have seen, on Langer's conception, is connected with a growing sense of *agency* and a consequent growing sense of *responsibility* for one's actions. When the mind develops interests of its own, its trajectory is toward self-assertion and the pursuit of individual interest. Self-assertion and individual interest, it is clear, must be checked so as to maintain "the biological claims of the stock upon each living generation" (*M-III* 123). Punishment, Langer thinks, is to be most fundamentally understood in this context, and it often takes on the form of ritual punishment for ritual faults. Punishment imprints a cultural rule on action, making us aware of limits and of the claims of the group. In this sense Langer thinks of custom as having a kind of sacred status or value. Punishment, then, is a "symbol of censure and recall to the social order" (*M-III* 125). "The primal and perennial work of social organization is not to fix the bounds of behavior as permanent lines, which would make all evolutionary process impossible, but to retrieve the vital balance every time some act, public or private, has upset it" (*M-III* 125). Even the birth of a child could be considered as upsetting the balance, although it is not the "fault" of the child and the resulting action is not to be thought of as "punishment." It is in such a way, Langer claims, that the phenomenon of circumcision is to be thought of, which has a "primitive symbolic function" (*M-III* 126), namely, "the branding of the organ of procreation as a possession of society" (*M-III* 128), that is, as marking one as belonging contractually to a specific group. The dialectical tension between the development of individual minds and the matrix of social life is exemplified here in a most perspicuous manner. One is thereby marked for tribal or national involvement by such a symbolic act, with very real and noticeable physical effects. "The essential process is to effect some visible symbol of the young person's socialization, the limitation of his selfhood, to be borne on his body for life" (*M-III* 128). However, the branding can also be ritually established without a bodily sign. This can happen by means of a "promise, an oath, a spoken commitment. The accompanying rite may be a sacrifice or a manipulation of sacred objects, a transient ordeal, or a presentation with or without priestly or choric dance and prayer" (*M-III* 129). Such is baptism, for instance, or ordination. Infant baptism clearly expresses "a social claim, even though it is consciously thought to bestow personal salvation" (*M-III* 129).

Langer passes in review the phenomenon of fetishes, which involves the symbolic projection "of the nameless feeling of mind-action into an arrangement of such things as potsherds and a hoe handle; the fetish represents human mental power and, characteristically, is supposed to contain and exercise the efficient 'principle' it embodies for its user" (*M-III* 132). It is clear that this phenomenon is a permanent possibility of human consciousness and not just something that belongs to its "early" stages, although it is certainly "primitive" with respect to the development of the "higher" forms of religion, whose most typical expression is to be found in sacrifice. Langer describes sacrifice as "that basic rite, perhaps the most ancient in the world" (*M-III* 132). Sacrifice's inner telos is to restore the ethnic balance in light of the experienced transgression of a stable order by the exercise of autonomous, mental power. Sacrifice is meant "to symbolize the retrieval of a balance" (*M-III* 133) in light of the committed self-assertion. The self-feeling that accompanies the mind's individuation, Langer contends, has to be balanced "*in toto* by an equally generalized ritual of maintained communion" (*M-III* 134). So, sacrifice, whose range of possible enactments is exceedingly large, was in essence "a symbolic restoration of balance between individual freedom and hereditary responsibility" (*M-III* 135).

The history of religions shows that they range from the most material act to "inner" acts of deep contrition and repentance, as one passes from more "savage" conceptions of the supernatural to modern religion with its moral and ethical vision. Religion in all its forms, Langer clearly holds, is of another order than everyday life. One must always maintain oneself in some sort of balance with this order, however it is interpreted. At the same time religion is the root and source of culture and subject to all the wild growths of the imagination, but also furnishes a stable frame to constrain such a growth. Paradoxically, therefore, the original function of religion "may have been to keep men's minds in balance with the rest of nature" (*M-III* 138) while at the same time being an essential tool in "the denial or masking of death" (*M-III* 138), which ultimately is *the* "natural" event par excellence. Religion goes over into myth here, with its projections, in various shades and with varying degrees of clarity, of a world of everlasting life, which are adhered to with labile degrees of conviction. There is a constant tension between wanting to live forever and the "desire for maximal experience" (*M-III* 138). However, "with the wish for fullness of life there comes a higher potentiality for action, a great new mental potentiality" (*M-III* 138). But, as Langer continually tries to show, the greater the mental power the greater not just the instability that can be introduced into the web of relationships but the types of means needed to redress the balance. In general there has been a gradual *interiorization* of sacrifice and ritual and the elaboration of complex symbolic forms to exemplify and induce the new balance.

Death remains the central focus of Langer's discussion of the ethnic balance, which in many ways is both a wandering and at times surprising discussion. In accord with her central concern, however, Langer asserts that to come to grips with death humans have need of "an imaginable symbol" (*M-III* 144). What she calls "the solemn image of *Moira* expresses a fairly intellectualized emotional feeling" matched in one way by the Scandinavian symbolic image of the Norns. The *Moirai* spin, determine, and end human lives. They are Fate personified, just as in one sense Allah became "a mold for the sense of inevitability" of death that was present in the seventh-century Arabian mind. But popular fatalism is not the same as the construction of an elaborate symbolic edifice for dealing with death, which religion for Langer essentially is, even to the point of finding a way of making an "infinite payment" in the form of an ultimate sacrifice or ransom. Salvation could even be thought of as being "bought," as in one Christian interpretation of the sacrifice of Christ, the infinite nature of whose sacrifice was proportionate to the infinite nature of the "original fall." Although advanced, liberal Christian theology has for the most part abandoned such a notion, it is still present in more conservative or orthodox strands of thought.

The joining of religion and the problem of death is really for Langer an exemplification of the persistent tension between symbols of power and symbols of life. It is indeed the movement to and development of *life-symbols* that mark the higher stages of religion, which themselves still are embroiled in the practices of sacrifice, both physical and symbolic. Restoration of balance is the guiding thread. In Christianity it is joining of the cross, the symbol of death, with the resurrection, the symbol of life, where one of the great symbolic complexes is to be found. This, Langer contentiously holds, is the Christian development of the Jewish blood rite, "for the concept of atonement by blood sacrifice underlay the subsequent Greco-Judaic development of the Christian myth" (*M-III* 150). Both—life and death—are "realities" to be held together in irreducible fashion, while in Brahmanic thought, for instance, with its conception of the "veil of Maya," there is only one ultimate reality, Absolute Being without qualification or duality. The polarity intrinsic to Western monotheism is superseded. This is a powerful and insightful comparison, the details of which need not concern us in the present context.

The "shift from the ideal of sheer power to that of intensified life," which Langer thinks is crucial to the progressive individuation of mind, took on massive form, she points out, in the cases of the Egyptian pyramids, the Buddhist stupas, and the prime symbolic image of the lingam. The pyramid is clearly a symbolic image of power, phallic, in fact, "obstinately defying time and transience" (*M-III* 150). It is eternal and royal power in stone. But the stupa, Langer insightfully asserts, presents a "softer" meaning.

> It figures somewhat as a life symbol from its very beginning. Like all indigenous In-
> dian architecture, it seems to emerge and grow from the ground itself rather than
> to have been placed on it; the great mound resembles a breast of the earth, a sym-
> bol of life-giving, more than an image of human power and arrogance. It belongs,
> of course, to a much later civilization [than the Egyptian], which had undoubtedly
> long passed the crucial confrontation with the fact of mortality. (*M-III* 151)

The reverse transition from breast to phallus is found in the development of the
lingam, both as a modification of the form of the stupa and as a life symbol in itself, leaving the traces of power behind. It takes on, it is obvious, a markedly or-
ganismic form.

So, there is a passage, both ideal and historical, which Langer wants to chart,
from the "ideal of infinite power to that of endless life," effected through the
"ritual centering on an image which represents that highest value" (*M-III* 152).
The symbolism of the *egg* as the germ of life becomes a prime symbol. There is
consequently, following Langer's analysis, a most interesting progression, both
real and ideal, from fetishes, magical actions, ritualization of activity, physical
and spiritual sacrifice, to the great architectural symbols of power and life. This
is, as Langer traces it, a kind of ideal semiotic or symbolic history. Power and life:
we humans, as symbolic animals, are caught in the middle. Maintaining our balance is always precarious, and we are the fulcrum between these two antago-
nistic forces. The question that Langer poses in the penultimate chapter of her
trilogy is whether we are witnessing a transition where the fulcrum of social
equilibrium is now "not between men and Supernaturals, but in society itself"
(*M-III* 154). What can Langer mean when she speaks of "a moment of pause" in
the human world's "otherworldly concerns," and the confrontation of the task
of "meeting the challenge of its own technical and economic construction of a
world-wide civilized society" (*M-III* 154)? While, to be sure, religious and moral
codes are a kind of record of the evolution of *subjective* new experience, civilization, for its part, has inscribed itself *objectively* on the face of the earth.

The Breaking and the Rise of Civilization

Why, one might still ask, does Langer deal with the rise of civilization under the
rubric of "the breaking"? The "breaking" of what? And is this a descriptive or a
normative concept?

It is clear, as I have been pointing out, that Langer is reprising in these chapters, with multiple motivations, the whole issue of life-symbols, broached in *Philosophy in a New Key,* but doing so under the rubric of the evolution of mind quite
generally.

Langer, we must keep constantly in mind, is offering a sketch of a kind of inner logic of the "life history of the mind" attendant upon the rise of civilization, which is coincident with the rise of cities and urban centers. Cities were the loci for the rise of common undertakings under the auspices of forceful personalities. This is the first type of "breaking," which is a "break in the tribal pattern of human society" (*M-III* 157). This is an acknowledged historical fact. We need not concern ourselves with the pocket history of the rise of cities that Langer presents. The "breaking" of the tribal consciousness, it is well known, led to intense concentrations not just of material wealth but of knowledge and inventions and then ferocious clashes between opposing centers: religious and economic warfare. Civilization, Langer sees and affirms, involves the constant breaking of the old orders, with mass migrations and wanderings, organized warfare, and pervasive instability becoming permanent factors in human life. Langer sees civilization as generating all sorts of possibilities of an "unbalanced mentality" (*M-III* 191), appearing in appalling form in the twin phenomena of cannibalism and human sacrifice, especially as practiced by the Amerindians, where it took on grotesque proportions. Although, as Langer points out, Topiltzin Quetzalcoatl and Akhenaton both made attempts "to introduce a humane religion based on worship of the sun as a symbol of life and a ritual of equally symbolic, largely bloodless sacrifices of tamales, snakes, butterflies, and flowers" (*M-III* 191), their efforts were premature. In the case of the Amerindians the results of the failure were pathological in the extreme: bloody ritual sacrifice in which captured warriors were slaughtered by the thousands on the altars to ward off "dangers." This "psychotic compulsion to human sacrifice was the macabre symptom of the Mesoamerican's excessive freedom from foreign influences" (*M-III* 193). The "breaking" of an essentially mythic and tribal consciousness did not occur—and perhaps, one could hesitantly admit, can never be a permanent achievement.

The symbolic lesson to be drawn here is more important than any detailed summary of Langer's own summary of the pathologies of civilization and the dangers of not recognizing its own inner logic. An evolving mind, Langer holds, "requires limitations of opportunity to achieve a unified phyletic career; it needs the pression of complex and crowding humanity to hold its form and balance in the ecological stream" (*M-III* 194). Langer's strong claim is that progressive mental life needs external hardships, *especially on the conceptual level.* This is, in a kind of Hegelian formulation, the presence of the negative, the social and conceptual negative that "gives life and thought its dialectical form" (*M-III* 194). According to Langer, the speciation of the human race takes place through a sequence of crises: speech, fantasy, ritual, and the "breaking" of tribal feeling. These crises mediate "the cultural move to civilization" (*M-III* 194), which as a process of social individuation "honors the individual as an end in itself, not as a thing of relative value, however high, but as the ultimate measure of all value" (*M-III* 195). With such a comment Langer clearly and forcefully exposes some of the normative implications of her rational reconstruction of the history of mind. It is the recognition of the primacy of the individual, at least the conceptual recognition even if the practical consequences trail far behind, that constitutes the "moral advance" of society (*M-III* 196). It is a "conceptual" revolution in the standard, if not the actual results, of behavior that results ultimately from the "breaking." "And what holds true for the moral character of Mind does so as well for its intellectual quality. A new great age is long prepared, and finally is born with the rise and expansion of a new idea which automatically transforms the outlook and reach of human mentality, in our present evolving age, even to effect the evaluation and re-evaluation of the criteria of thought itself. That is the office of philosophy" (*M-III* 196).

Civilization, Langer claims, moves by qualitative shifts. In this process there has to be maintained "a certain balance between its highest and lowest degrees of change" (*M-III* 196). This balance is effected in the midst of multiple conflicting currents that one must strive to hold in some sort of equilibrium. The goal, attained only in Europe, Langer holds, is a "many-sided mental development, religious, artistic, and, above all, intellectual" (*M-III* 197). This front moves forward by "reciprocal checks" (*M-III* 197). Little did Langer guess just what would happen when cultural currents that recognized no reciprocal checks that marked the Western world began to confront "Europe" both from within and without.

Langer ends her trilogy with a reflection on "mathematics and the reign of science" under the rubric of "the open ambient." It contains a brief and schematic summary of the relations between language and number as two different ways of comprehending the world. Many of her points have been made in other places in her work, but her schematization indicates just what she thought the ultimate upshot of her studies to be, especially as they bear upon their epistemological import.

Langer, we have seen, thinks of the mind as the functional complex of the brain, which has been subject to a distinctive and revolutionary evolution. This evolution has led to a number of great shifts, and one of the first steps in this process, we have seen, is the rise and growth of speech. Linguistic forms play an essential and generative role not just in conceptualizing experience, but in "establishing memory, and recording the fictions of dream and free fantasy, expectation and fear" (*M-III* 204). Civilization would be impossible without language and speech, although they are no guarantee of its integrity. One of the first and universal forms of conceptualization was the grasping of events under the form of acts, of agents. But the upward march of Mind led to the formulation of the cognate notions of *cause* and *fact*. Echoing one of the central theses of the last chapter of *Philosophy in a New Key*, Langer thinks of "fact" as a "highly interesting cognitive construct" (*M-III* 205). This construct became "the harbinger of a new core of knowledge, setting up an explicit logical standard and stringent methodology, great with a radical change of attitude, intellectual ambition, and its own frustrating mistakes" (*M-III* 205). The modern world is, at least theoretically, built on the foundation of "fact," if not of facts. And the notion of a fact is derived from our being language animals and not primarily "in fact" from language in its purely theoretical or abstract uses. Discursivity is not identical with the theoretical.

Langer claims that it is, indeed, a mistake to think of formalized or abstract language as the all-encompassing model of articulation. Ordinary language for Langer is marked by vagueness and inexactness, not by an "inherent tendency to pinpoint exact literal meanings" that are then applied metaphorically in other situations. Words "organize our thinking around centered conceptual symbols, however vague those central images or other carriers of meaning may be, and define a context in which that core of meaning is embedded; it is the contexts which are not at all a logician's idea" (*M-III* 208). These contexts make up a shifting ambient, and language enables us to "negotiate the turns" of what Langer calls a "mental kaleidoscope" (*M-III* 208). Linguistic forms are, therefore, intrinsically labile, flexible, open-ended, with no definite semantic boundaries. Once again Langer continues the work of such powerful thinkers as Bühler (1934), Gardiner (1933), and Barfield (1973). What we think of as "ordinary language" "shows no steady tendency to impose a coherent pattern on the world of facts which it constantly creates for us" (*M-III* 209). Ascribing a weasel quality to words, Langer sees the distinctively linguistic construction of abstract concepts as an achievement that arises either deliberately or also spontaneously as a kind of precipitate, where ultimately all the peripheral relations set up in the language field are seen to revolve around "a central concept common to all the grammatical variants of a verb or other highly inflected part of speech and make it stand more and more *in abstracto*" (*M-III* 209).

Nevertheless, science, as theory, is not based on language, but on another symbolic principle: number. Number performs two essential functions: enumerating and calculating. Langer thinks that language and speech appear to have had "a separate origin and prehistory" from numerical systems and that numbers and words have "different primitive characteristics" (*M-III* 210; see Mithen 2006).

Numbers are devoid of what seems the semantic engine of language, the tendency to metaphorical extensions of meaning, although they do have mystical associations. Langer helpfully remarks that

> counting, which seems simple to us, has really been one of the difficult problems of abstraction and presentation, for it has required a shift from essentially physical consummations to symbolic ones in the human brain. Its elements—similar conceptual units following each other in a series—are almost certainly first presented by the visual and kinesthetic perception of our own bipedal steps, under control of old cerebral mechanisms. Their expression belongs to the legs and feet, whose functions are among the least intellectual of our voluntary behavioral acts. (*M-III* 210)

Langer, in fact, hypothesizes (it cannot be more than that) that number arose from the dance, with the need of maintaining distinct, self-identical units or steps. More generally Langer relies on some research materials on the origins of numbers to show the roots of number in the human body quite generally, not just kinesthetically but also structurally. Not only does the body move in rhythmic fashion, but its bilateral symmetry, Langer observes, allows human to develop "the most complex specializations" (*M-III* 214), many of which involve a perpetual retrieval of balance.

Langer hypothesizes that the drum and the hand were crucial in the development of number, for they were essential ingredients in the development and stabilization of the "step." The hand has clearly become for humans a dominant structure.

> The walking step may have furnished the first sense of equally spaced similar units, and the dance imposed its elaborations on them, but it was very probably the drum, activated by the hands, that clinched the evolutionary shift, already prepared in several ways—the decimal systems born of finger-counting, which, despite their varying details (lifting or flexing the fingers, starting with thumb or little finger, left or right, etc.), embody the same algorithmic principle of naming ten numerals . . . and composing all higher numerosities out of these in a simple order of positions. (*M-III* 215–217)

Language and the number sense, then, at the end of Langer's intellectual journey, come together, mediated by the hand. Calculation and symbolization emerge together, giving us a semiotic tool of inestimable power and scope. But such a symbolic system, Langer realizes, which drives science in directions that ordinary language cannot go, is a revolutionary force, overthrowing previous images of world order and worldview. "We live in a precipitous, heady transitional age, the Age of Science" (*M-III* 219). The future, built on such a base, is truly an open ambient, which is subject itself to its own instabilities. Langer concludes:

It will surely take long and different ages to retrieve the moral and mental balance mankind itself has blasted in the last three or four centuries (to start only with the time of terrifying acceleration), and there is no way of guessing whether or how we shall retrieve it, because that newest of natural phenomena—Mind—still faces the mystery of all things young, the secret of vital potentiality. (*M-III* 219)

So concludes Langer's monumental attempt, spanning half a century, to chart the symbolic matrices and history of Mind. What, in conclusion, are we to ultimately make of the philosophical project as a whole?

9

Placing Langer's
Philosophical Project

Dimensions of Langer's Project

Langer's remarkable intellectual trajectory is informed by a robust mix of conceptual reconstruction and interpretation and an exemplification of a novel, reconfigured method of philosophical reflection. It is not a case of "typical" or "pure" philosophizing, nor does it engage in pyrotechnical displays of philosophical swordplay. It is by no means a singularly unique or unparalleled way of doing philosophy, but it is, I have tried to show, certainly distinctive and of the utmost importance.

As to conceptual reconstruction, Langer focuses on the pivotal notions needed to formulate in a non-reductive fashion a precise and comprehensive model of mind as a completely natural phenomenon. The dialectical play of these notions oscillates, as we have seen, between biological and the philosophico-semiotic poles, with numerous psychological and historico-cultural way stations in between. Her central thesis is that Mind, in the human sense, is a functional matrix of acts, not a substance, and is defined by diverse and stratified powers of symbolization and sign use. The process of *Minding* gives rise to the *Semiotic Self*. The task she set herself was to chart the elements, processes, and outcomes of these acts and their symbolic tools and underpinnings.

Langer's conceptual reconstruction is accompanied by a nuanced respect for the results of scientific research, but her conceptual scaffolding is oriented not toward the discovery of new facts but toward interpretations, and reinterpretations, of "proposed and established positions." As to the exploitation of novel sources, Langer weds her conceptual reconstruction to materials that are not always in the forefront of current discussions. Nor does she strive toward an exaggerated novelty of position. A rather large bulk of her resources is rarely purely philosophical in the traditional sense. Many of these resources stem from research traditions rather foreign to "normal" philosophical work, and a substantial chunk of them, especially those in French and German, are better described as systematically informed *retrievals* from the past than as the mere rescuing of "neglected figures" with no intrinsic bearing on present problems. Langer's retrievals, in fact, engage current trends in the "sciences of mind" in a substantial way. The principal foci are:

- the centrality of diverse kinds of symbolic processes ranging from the basic affective-perceptual stratum up to the highest reaches of the symbolic artifacts of high cultures
- the intertwining of the biological and the psychological
- the role of the imagination and the essentially creative, metaphorical nature of mind
- the expansion of psychological concerns to the socio-cultural realms
- the significance of art
- the interlocking multimodality of the various disciplines engaged in the research projects that go under the name of the "cognitive sciences."

Langer's efforts have a deep and clear theoretical intent. The materials upon which she relies are often unorthodox and span many different disciplines and problem areas, from cell biology and the cognitive psychology of imagination to advanced music theory and the origins of religion. We have seen at crucial places in the preceding chapters how Langer used, extended, and transformed her sources, using them both as supports and as goads. But while Langer's work has a differentiated empirical base, it does not run the risk of being "superseded" by empirical discoveries. Operating on a different level, she is engaged in systematic interpretation and generalization, not the discovery of new facts. Vincent Colapietro is correct when he writes, "For Langer herself, the semiotic turn in philosophical discourse reinforced the distinction between philosophy and science, while at the same time drove the work of philosophers closer to that of scientists" (1997: 5).

Consequently, as to the dimension of philosophical reflection, Langer's approach to her problems illustrates the nature of an attempt at the "transforma-

tion of philosophy" or at a way of doing "philosophy in a new key." From the beginning philosophy for Langer was, and remained, a matter of the analysis of
"meanings." This was the explicit and self-consciously asserted theme of her first
book, *The Practice of Philosophy,* and this focus remained permanent and determinative up to the end. But Langer's approach, while fully cognizant of the nature of logic, eschewed all forms of logicism and abstract speculation. There is an
intertwining of phenomenological description and conceptual analysis and schematization that runs throughout her work. Langer was intensely focused on the
twin themes of "the mind of meaning" and the "meaning of mind." Mind and
meanings become reciprocal heuristic keys to one another. The realms of human meanings, embodied in the field of symbolic projections, which have to be
charted and related to one another, become a set of access-structures to the human mind. The mind becomes the "locus" or "place" for the generation and interpretation of meanings(s). Minding is, at bottom, semiosis, the creation and interpretation of signs, symbols, and meanings. And this process encompasses the
total range of human "feeling."

Langer's project, consequently, operates on two intersecting levels: (1) descriptive-phenomenological and (2) conceptual-constructive.

Langer's "data field" is the whole domain of human culture, which is for her
"mind writ large." The German Idealists called this sphere "objective mind."
Treating cultural forms both as sources of insight and as exemplifications of the
power of mind gives a universal quality to Langer's reflection. Nothing human
is alien to her. Inquiring into the nooks and crannies of human cultural activity
leads her, and her readers, to engage the very structures and forms of their own
experiencing. In this sense Langer's work forces us into a kind of self-reflection
that is meant to make us familiar with the lived feelings involved in the processes
of symbolic formation and transformation. Symbolic forms are not just frames
we think about in philosophy; they are frames within which we live and become
human. Langer's reflections have a kind of admirable descriptive adequacy that
is missing from many philosophical analyses, which are often conceptually top-
heavy and descriptively thin. Langer's philosophical procedures are descriptively
"thick." And many of her examples are easily identifiable in the everyday experiences of her readers: the variety of signs and sign uses, the role of language in
informing experience, the sense of the sacred, the performance of ritual, the encounter with works of art, the sense of conceptual and civilizational imbalances,
the consciousness of death, and so forth. What Langer has attempted to do is construct a coherent frame within which meaning-configurations can be situated
and placed over against one another.

This turn to thick description allows Langer, or rather forces her, to attempt to construct a conceptual framework that gives *analytical adequacy* to the descriptive adequacy, though not completeness, that marks her work. This framework is defined by a set of central categories of remarkable power:

- *symbolic transformation* as the defining feature of the human mind
- *abstraction* and *grasp of form* as pivotal acts of minding
- *discursive* and *presentational* forms as the two great symbolic tracks on which minding runs
- *life-symbols* that are rooted in symbolically pregnant images
- *forms of feeling* that are embodied in artworks and that reveal the *logic of sentience* or the *morphology of feeling*
- *primary illusions* as constituting the *artistic import* of different art genres
- *Mind* as an achievement of higher-order processes of *feeling*

and a host of others that we have passed in review in the course of our discussion. These notions have what I have been calling great "heuristic fertility." They allow us to focus upon a wide range of cultural phenomena and to uncover their deep logic and forms of relationship. They show the human world, which was Langer's primary concern, to be a web of meaning that we both spin out of ourselves and spin ourselves into. In Langer the analytical, the hermeneutic and interpretive, and the self-reflective all intersect with one another as essential aspects of one universal philosophical task: they grasp the human world as a world of generated meanings embodied in symbolic forms.

The fusion of the descriptive-phenomenological and the conceptual-constructive dimensions situates and qualifies Langer's "rejection" of the traditional way of doing philosophy. This is certainly a judgment, perhaps more rhetorical than strictly substantive, on Langer's part of philosophy's exhaustion, on the level of both types of questions and types of answers. Strangely enough, it is not that Langer thought of previous philosophies as being "wrong-headed" or simply "mistaken" in their types of questions and methods of inquiry. In spite of her essentially systematic interests, Langer thought of philosophy as fundamentally situated in history. This applied also to her own philosophical endeavors, which were inspired by the "symbolic turn" in a vast array of disciplines and sciences, ranging from biology through psychology, sociology, the history of religions, literary theory, psychoanalysis, formal logic, and so forth. Such advances had critical consequences, in her opinion, for the tasks of philosophy. Philosophy itself, no superscience with a God's-eye view and with empirical intent, was to turn away from facts to meanings. This was the core thesis of Langer's very first book—a thesis she defended to the end of her life. But, strangely enough, such a notion paradoxically makes philosophy more empirical rather than less, *since meanings, embodied in symbol systems, are themselves objective structures in the world.* Philosophy, in one of its tasks, then, engages this symbol world in its breadth and depth, specifying its generating conditions, its constitutive structures, and its formed content. Philosophy is "empirical" in the non-scientific sense that it is a "reflective experiencing and analysis" of embodied meanings. It is experiential and analytical at the same time. *Reflective analytical experiencing:* such a notion brings philosophy into close contact with all the humanistic disciplines. What distinguishes philosophy is to a great degree attributed to the rather different weightings given to its formal and critical dimensions, which do not contravene its hermeneutical dimension.

Positive Results of Langer's Philosophical Project

The positive results of Langer's philosophical project, as well as some issues left open by it, can be encapsulated in the following theses, which have been explored in the preceding chapters.

First of all, Langer has indeed showed us *a* "new way" to do philosophy, but not, I think, *the* new way. I have tried to show that her procedures do not attempt to supplant other approaches, but instead to extend, reformulate, and exploit them. She has supplied rather a differently configured frame within which various issues can be situated and explored, and she has shown how her own version of the "semiotic" turn, that is, a philosophy focused on "the symbolic mind," can supplement as well as engage concerns and results from other philosophical traditions, especially the American pragmatist tradition. Of special interest, I have indicated, is the transformation and reformulation of the notion of "experience." Langer has shown how to combine in a nuanced way the "experiential" and the "semiotic," pushing meaning "up" and pushing it "down" in clearly defined ways. Her philosophy, like much of the American philosophical tradition, is both a *philosophy of experience* and a *philosophy of meaning.* Her "new key" shows how these two central philosophical foci can be related to one another and integrated, just as Peirce's theory of signs and Dewey's pragmatist analysis of experiencing did. Philosophy, on Langer's terms, is not bare conceptual analysis nor the rearrangement of facts, but a broadly conceived analysis of essentially *embodied* meanings, in the broadest sense of that term. Philosophy for Langer, as for Cassirer, is, or was intended to be, the comprehensive and comparative study of symbolic forms, each of which has its own "logic" or irreducible way of making meaning. Language, myth, ritual, sacrament, religion, art are all both the *instruments* and the *results* of symbolic transformation, the essential act of mind—or the act essential to mind. This "semiotic" turn, for which Langer retained Cassirer, not Peirce, as its prime exemplar or inspiration, is accomplished effectively and deeply in her work. She did it in a sober, non-histrionic way, avoiding all trendiness and empty literary fireworks as well as superfluous technical flourishes, while going beyond Cassirer's sources and duplicating many of Peirce's theses, which from the substantive point of view she is in full agreement with, especially with respect to the critique of immediacy, the universality of interpretation, the irreducibility of different types of sign and meaning-systems, and so forth. But Langer was never tempted by Peirce's leanings toward objective idealism.

The philosophical and semiotic analysis of meanings, Langer clearly shows, has a pervasive phenomenological dimension or descriptive thickness. It is not merely abstract and schematic, without content or substantive import. The analytical and the descriptive, we have seen, are intertwined in Langer's reflections. She wants to indicate the *point* of her analysis while giving enough paradigmatic examples to show that her conclusions are not really top-down impositions of premises, but generalizations, as well as abductions, from more limited domains. This is in accord with her conception of philosophy as proceeding through progressive generalizations and creative schematization of concepts. This makes up what I call Langer's "double-bladed" approach to philosophy: an upper blade of categories and concepts and a lower blade of empirical materials. The job of the philosopher, she has showed us, is to bring these two blades together with all the "friction-filled cutting" that is involved. It is utilization of this double philosophical method, of top down and bottom up, that makes Langer's way of doing philosophy so fruitful and exciting and that in the later parts of *Mind* engages us with matters of the deepest civilizational and existential import.

Second, Langer's philosophical procedures show how the conceptual, the hypothetical, and the empirical can be brought into dialectical unity. Langer has a clear conceptual framework with its key pivotal distinctions, as I have already noted, and does not shy away from the hypothetical, or abductive, side of philosophical reflection. This hypothetical side is mainly connected with what I have called Langer's "rational reconstruction" of "origins" of the various symbolic matrices, which she herself admits are purely speculative. But her controversial approach to the origin of language, for example, is also to some extent empirical, that is, since she is concerned to observe how language actually works, not how it should work. That is, her approach is not stipulative, but stays close to "living language." While ostensibly, at the beginning of her work, she took her clues from the types of considerations that Wittgenstein and Russell engaged in, it is clear that Langer never really took the "picture theory of meaning" or the notion of a "logical picture" in more than an extended metaphorical sense, although she was thoroughly grounded in the technical side of logic. But she did want to show that these notions could be flexibly generalized in a non-trivial way and integrated into a wider framework, while accepting certain restrictions on free-floating and irresponsible theoretical inventions. To the very end of her intellectual career Langer never repudiated her concern for the "logical dimension." While in one sense Wittgenstein and Russell were concerned with the "meanings of logic," Langer, following Cassirer, was in a more broad sense concerned with the semiotic "logic of meanings," which went far beyond the traditional concerns of logic in the restricted sense.

Third, Langer's philosophical "sobriety" marks a significant difference between her work and certain, but not all, strands of the semiotic traditions developed in the twentieth century. In particular, Langer rejected, perhaps without even confronting in any fashion, the universalization of the linguistic model that followed the development of structuralist linguistics by the philosophical and literary followers of Saussure. Nevertheless, as we have seen, there is no downplaying of language in Langer's work, nor was she innocent of work in linguistics proper. Language, for Langer, is a distinctive and unique human achievement of symbolization. It *penetrates* to the very depths of human mentality, which it also *supports*. For her, language is not the autonomous system that much structuralist thought affirmed, with its "displacement" of the signifying subject and its forced and unavoidable dwelling in the "prison-house of language." Language for Langer is certainly no prison-house, but neither is it always clearly a "happy home" for the understanding, since it is also the source of our greatest illusions and of the fallibility of belief systems. It is something in between, both potentiating our mental powers and exposing them to mortal perils and grotesque distortions.

Fourth, out of Langer's primary notion of symbolic transformation, which supplies the comprehensive matrix of her work, comes her most important, indeed essential, distinction: between discursive and presentational forms. Both of these forms, Langer has shown, are *intrinsically rational* and *give us knowledge*. They are forms or modes of symbolization. By recognizing and validating the cognitive value of these forms Langer is able to broaden the scope of knowing and to overcome all tendencies to logocentrism while still acknowledging the centrality of language in making us human. It is, in fact, the language animal that systematically produces presentational forms, no matter what the sense modality. These forms are rooted in the human organism's image-making needs and capacities. Word and symbolic image, saying and showing, discursivity and presentationality, these are equipotential and intertwined powers of human rationality. Both are essential forms of *authentic symbolization*. This classification schema, which is marked by an essential contrast and duality, encompasses but does not necessarily supplant in analytical range and nuance the triadic schema of Peirce, whereby signs are sorted into iconic, indexical, and symbolic types in accordance with his theory of categories, to which Langer does not advert. But Langer clearly recognizes the bases of Peirce's classification: indexes are based on some sort of "existential" connection with their objects, icons on some sort of "resemblance" between themselves and their objects, and symbols on a "convention" or "agreement." The differences in classification are, in my opinion, mainly terminological, although Peirce's analytical framework leads in the long run to more fine-grained differentiation of the formal inner spaces of signs and to the ability to develop the notion of an "interpretant," that is, the proper significate effect of a sign, in more detail than Langer does. For both Langer and Peirce, though, the move to symbolization and to the conscious control or awareness of signs is essential. Once we reach the human realm, where signs are recognized *as* signs, Langer and Peirce have established, we are everywhere in the realm of what Peirce called thirdness, the realm of conscious mediation. For both of them, in the words of Peirce, "thinking is a kind of conduct, and is itself controllable, as everybody knows. Now the intellectual control of thinking takes place by thinking about thought. All thinking is by signs; and the brutes use signs. To do so is manifestly a second step in the use of language" (*CP-V* 534). Peirce admits that "the brutes are certainly capable of more than one grade of control; but it seems to me that our superiority to them is more due to our greater number of grades of self-control than it is to our versatility" (*CP-V* 533). Both Langer and Peirce throw powerful and complementary light on this complex of issues surrounding a properly formulated "semiotic pragmatism."

Fifth, Langer's validation of the notion of a presentational form as a true symbol allows her to grapple in a systematic fashion with some of the most pressing and seemingly irresolvable issues of aesthetics. Her notions of a "form of feeling" or "morphology of feeling" are defined by their essential presentationality, by their irreducibility to the discursive domain. Langer's nuanced approach to art theory is well grounded and coherent, primarily oriented to the objective art symbol or artwork, but it is not complete, nor is it mutually exclusive of other approaches with which it is not in any necessary conflict, such as the pragmatist and phenomenological traditions, which foreground more explicitly the experiential dimensions of the aesthetic encounter. Nevertheless, Langer by no means ignores the experiential dimension, but it makes its appearance in a rather different way in her art theory. For what is experienced first and foremost for her is the "primary illusion" made manifest by the art symbol.

Langer's notion of a primary illusion of each art form has both descriptive and critical value. It is descriptive in the sense of attempting to give us a "feel" for what is distinctive about each art genre, given Langer's premises. It is critical in the sense of deriving the primary illusions from a recognition of what the art genre must be, given that it is the result of a specific type of "abstraction." Langer's critical point is that ignoring the form of abstraction carried out by a specific art genre will make it impossible to grasp the genre's primary illusion. Langer has clearly shown that art genres are not defined by the subject matter, motif, or theme, although they do play a substantial role in their functioning. Langer's aesthetic semiotic "formalism," however, is not a traditional formalism. It is not empty but exceedingly "full" in the experiential sense and thus open to alternative expansions and supplementations. Langer has constructed a formal frame, not a formalistic frame. If there is any serious weakness in her approach it is to underemphasize to a certain, but not debilitating, degree the content side of art, its orientation toward and interpretation of a "world." While I think that Langer's notion of a "form of feeling" is extremely enlightening, "feeling" is, as I have been emphasizing, bipolar, and it is the feeling of a *world* that also is presented, a world that also has its "objective" structures and relations and contents, albeit drenched with "affective tones." The "cognitive" and the "affective" are indissolubly joined in Langer's aesthetics, just as they were in Dewey's.

Sixth, Langer's substantive conclusions are both conceptual and empirically based. It could be asked sympathetically, as Arthur Danto did, to what degree the conceptual discoveries and proposals are so intertwined with their empirical bases that they could be superseded by the addition of new empirical discoveries, especially in the anthropological and cultural sciences. Langer's concerns with "origins," it must be admitted, are semiotically, not historically, motivated. She admits frequently and openly the hypothetical nature of many of her theses: about the origin of language, the origin of religion, the origin of the idea of death, and so forth. What she is really interested in are the originating *matrices* of meaning, the permanent frames in which humans carry out their symbolic lives. This focal interest not so much in the origins of meaning as in the matrices of meaning is played out on the psychological, the cultural, the historical, and the conceptual levels. In this sense Langer's concerns are structural and constitutive and indeed even, in certain ways, quite independent of actual questions of historical origin, though clearly not entirely. This is an exemplification, once again, of her idea that philosophy is concerned with interpretations—and with the interpretation of interpretations.

Langer, in fact, does not try in any way to reduce the analysis of meanings and their matrices to a discovery of their points of origin. She is interested in "origins" in the sense of a kind of retroductive genetic analysis, but also in the sense of a kind of rational reconstruction based upon admittedly tentative historical data. The concepts and phenomena themselves, structures of meaning, that she is concerned with have a permanent stable value; indeed, they are semiotic emergences, conceptual (and historical) achievements. Thus, for example, while there are, as we have seen, cerebral conditions for the rise of symbolization, once symbolization has emerged as a structure in its own right with its own logic, this logic can be examined by itself, descriptively and normatively, without referring constantly to its cerebral conditions. I think we are confronted with the same sort of relationship in the much-mooted work in "cognitive neuroscience" and the attempts to find the neural correlates of experienced conscious states. Whether such a task can ever be achieved and whether it can ever really escape its medical importance, which is immense, I think that, philosophically if not therapeutically, Langer has shown that the enterprise of identifying and describing conscious states or forms of sentience can proceed quite independently of the neurological dimension, which is, in fact, parasitic upon the descriptive inventory of these states and forms, a point I have made elsewhere (Innis 2002a) in a discussion with Mark Johnson. The so-called mind-body problem is a conceptual, not an empirical, problem. But it could even be argued, on Langerian grounds, that the whole problem has been posed in the wrong way. The "mind" is a self-organizing matrix of acts, of events, that arises when neural and bodily conditions have reached a certain stage. It is not a thing or a substance. It is a way of acting of an organism, and the human organism is a symbolic organism. We are, as Terrence Deacon put it, a "symbolic species." Langer wants to show us just what this entails and what the philosophical consequences are. We are both symbolic, organic, and materially physical at the same time. This is Langer's parallel schematization to Merleau-Ponty's differentiation, in *The Structure of Behavior,* of the ideal, the vital, and the physical orders.

Langer's conceptual scheme, consequently, functions as a heuristic aid to more concrete, empirical investigations. It tells us what kinds of things to look for, what kinds of things we should be concerned with. It does not tell us exactly what we will find, so it is subject to a kind of revision. Langer's work, then, is not purely empirical and verifiable in the empirical sense. It must be validated, expanded, and confirmed rather than "put to the empirical test." In this sense Langer's work is hermeneutical and interpretive—and it must be contested on that level first and foremost. The main issue is that of conceptual and descriptive adequacy.

Philosophy, however, is clearly conceived by Langer as a synthetic discipline, working closely with the empirical sciences. As a descriptive and structural analysis of meaning, philosophy is clearly not unrelated to the results and concerns of the empirical sciences of meaning such as anthropology, cognitive psychology, and the history of religion, and to the various practices of the arts as well as their practitioners' reflections upon them. The synthetic, generalizing characteristic of philosophical reflection flows directly from the project of the analysis of meanings. Philosophy, Langer definitively shows, does and should interact both with the cultural sciences, which chart the social matrices and forms of meaning, and with the empirical sciences of mind, which deal with the organic conditions of possibility of symbolization.

Finally, Langer's mature philosophical position places both *symbolization* and *feeling* at the very center of her account of the mind. Her concept of *symbolization*, already in place in her earliest work, is both broad and precisely nuanced, but it is used in a context-dependent kind of way. There is shown to be, as Langer's work progressed, an intricate and indispensable network of connections between *symbolization and imagination*, understood as the power of creating images, both internal and external. Symbolization takes many forms: linguistic, artistic, mythic, religious, philosophical, mathematical, and so forth. *Feeling* is the cover term for the passage to the psychic level, the passage to "felt mentality." It encompasses, Langer has established, every movement of subjectivity and consciousness. These movements and forms of consciousness strive toward "expression" in external symbols, which become the access structures to the life of feeling. We come to know what our mental powers are by reading their features off the play of symbols, in Langer's sense of that term. Langer's whole philosophical project exemplifies the Goethean adage, which also echoes the deepest trajectories of Spinoza's thought, that what is inner is outer and what is outer is inner. Langer's "semiotic turn" in philosophy, which focuses on what Peirce called "the entire phenomenal manifestation of mind" (Peirce 1868: 53), exemplifies the cognate insight expressed by Umberto Eco, when, speaking of "signification"—that is, what Langer called symbolic transformation—he claimed that "it encompasses the whole of cultural life, even at the lower threshold of semiotics" (Eco 1976: 46). This is the essential lesson that Langer wanted to teach us in her monumental attempt to "push meaning up and down."

References

Abram, David. 1996. *The Spell of the Sensuous: Perception and Language in a More-than-Human World*. New York: Random House.

Addiss, Laird. 1999. *Of Mind and Music*. Ithaca, N.Y.: Cornell University Press.

Åhlberg, Lars-Olof. 1994. "Susanne Langer on Representation and Emotion in Music." *British Journal of Aesthetics* 34, no. 1: 69–80.

Alexander, Christopher. 2002a. *The Phenomenon of Life*. Book One of *The Nature of Order: An Essay on the Art of Building and the Nature of the Universe*. Berkeley: Center for Environmental Structure.

———. 2002b. *The Process of Creating Life*. Book Two of *The Nature of Order*.

———. 2004. *The Luminous Ground*. Book Four of *The Nature of Order*.

———. 2005. *A Vision of a Living World*. Book Three of *The Nature of Order*.

Arnheim, Rudolf. 1966. *Toward a Psychology of Art*. Berkeley and Los Angeles: University of California Press.

———. 1969. *Visual Thinking*. Berkeley and Los Angeles: University of California Press.

———. 1974. *Art and Visual Perception*. Berkeley and Los Angeles: University of California Press.

———. 1986. *New Essays on the Psychology of Art*. Berkeley and Los Angeles: University of California Press.

Auxier, Randall. 1997. "Susanne Langer on Symbols and Analogy: A Case of Misplaced Concreteness?" *Process Studies* 26, no. 1–2: 86–106.

Bachelard, Gaston. 1964. *The Psychoanalysis of Fire*. Trans. Alan C. M. Ross. Preface by Northrop Frye. Boston: Beacon Press.

———. 1969. *The Poetics of Reverie: Childhood, Language, and the Cosmos*. Trans. Daniel Russell. Boston: Beacon Press.

———. 1971. *On Poetic Imagination and Reverie*. Trans. with introd. Colette Gaudin. Indianapolis: Library of Liberal Arts.

Barfield, Owen. 1973. *Poetic Diction: A Study in Meaning*. Middletown, Conn.: Wesleyan University Press. Originally published in 1928.

Buchler, Justus. 1990. *Metaphysics of Natural Complexes*. Albany, N.Y.: SUNY Press.

Budd, Malcolm. 1985. *Music and the Emotions*. London: Routledge.

Bühler, Karl. 1934 [1990]. *Theory of Language*. Trans. Donald A. Goodwin. Amsterdam: John Benjamins.

Burnshaw, Stanley. 1970. *The Seamless Web*. New York: George Braziller.

Campbell, James. 1997. "Langer's Understanding of Philosophy." *Transactions of the Charles S. Peirce Society* 33, no. 1 (Winter): 133–147.

Cassirer, Ernst. 1925 [1946]. *Language and Myth*. Trans. Susanne K. Langer. New York: Harper and Bros.

———. 1929 [1957]. *The Philosophy of Symbolic Forms*. Vol. 3. New Haven, Conn.: Yale University Press.

———. 1946. *The Myth of the State*. Foreword by Charles W. Hendel. New Haven, Conn.: Yale University Press.

Clarke, D. S. 2003. *Panpsychism and the Religious Attitude*. Albany: State University of New York Press.

Colapietro, Vincent M. 1989. *Peirce's Approach to the Self: A Semiotic Perspective on Human Subjectivity*. Albany, N.Y.: SUNY Press.

——— 1997. "Susanne Langer on Artistic Creativity and Creations." In *Semiotics 1997*, ed. C. W. Spinks and John Deely. New York: Peter Lang.

———. 1998. "Symbols and the Evolution of Mind: Susanne Langer's Final Bequest to Semiotics." In *Semiotics 1998*, ed. C. W. Spinks and John Deely. New York: Peter Lang.

———. 2007. "Steps toward an Ecological Consciousness: Loyalty to the Inherited Matrix of Experimental Intelligence." In *Education for a Democratic Society*, ed. John Ryder and Gert-Rüdiger Wegmarshaus. Amsterdam: Rodopi.

Conrad, Klaus. 1954. "New Problems of Aphasia." *Brain* 77: 491–509.

Crosby, Donald A. 2005. *Novelty*. Lanham, Md.: Lexington Books.

Dalton, Wayne A. 1974. "The Status of Artistic Illusion in Concrescence." *Process Studies* 4, no. 3 (Fall): 207–211.

Damasio, Antonio. 1994. *Descartes' Error: Emotion, Reason, and the Human Brain*. New York: G. P. Putnam's Sons.

———. 1999. *The Feeling of What Happens*. New York: Harcourt.

———. 2003. *Looking for Spinoza: Joy, Sorrow, and the Feeling Brain*. New York: Harcourt.

Davies, Stephen. 1994. *Musical Meaning and Expression*. Ithaca, N.Y.: Cornell University Press.

Deacon, Terrence. 1997. *The Symbolic Species: The Co-Evolution of Language and the Brain*. New York: Norton.

Dewey, John. 1896. "The Unit of Behavior." In Dewey 1931c.

——— 1908. "The Practical Character of Reality." In *Essays, Philosophical and Psycho-*

logical in Honor of William James. New York: Minton, Balch. Reprinted in Dewey 1931c.

———. 1931a. "Affective Thought." In Dewey 1931c.

———. 1931b. "Qualitative Thought." In Dewey 1931c.

———. 1931c. *Philosophy and Civilization.* New York: Putnam's.

———. 1934 [1987]. *Art as Experience.* Carbondale: Southern Illinois University Press.

Donovan, J. 1891/1892. "The Festal Origin of Human Speech." *Mind* (O.S.) 16: 498–506; 17: 325–339

Dryden, Donald. 1997a. "Susanne K. Langer and American Philosophic Naturalism in the Twentieth Century." *Transactions of the Charles S. Peirce Society* 33: 161–182.

———. 1997b. "Whitehead's Influence on Susanne Langer's Conception of Living Form." *Process Studies* 26: 62–85.

———. 2001. "Susanne Langer and William James: Art and the Dynamics of the Stream of Consciousness." *Journal of Speculative Philosophy* 15: 272–285.

———. 2003. "Susanne K. Langer." *Dictionary of Literary Biography.* Vol. 270: *American Philosophers before 1950,* ed. Philip B. Dematteis and Leemon B. McHenry, 189–199. Farmington Hills, Mich.: Gale.

———. 2004. "Memory, Imagination, and the Cognitive Value of the Arts." *Consciousness and Cognition* 13: 254–267.

——— 2007. "The Philosopher as Prophet and Visionary." *Journal of Speculative Philosophy* 21, no. 1: xxx.

D'Udine, Jean. 1910. *L'Art et le geste.* Paris: Alcan.

Eco, Umberto. 1976. *A Theory of Semiotics.* Bloomington: Indiana University Press.

Edelman, Gerald M. 2004. *Wider Than the Sky: The Phenomenal Gift of Consciousness.* New Haven, Conn.: Yale University Press.

Essertier, Daniel. 1927. *Les formes inférieures de l'explication.* Paris: Alcan.

Fauré-Fremiet, Philippe. 1934. *Pensée et re-création.* Paris: Alcan.

———. 1940. *La Recréation du réel et l'équivoque.* Paris: Alcan.

Fingarette, Herbert. 1972. *Confucius: The Secular as Sacred.* New York: HarperCollins.

Gardiner, Alan. 1933. *The Theory of Speech and Language.* Oxford: Clarendon; 2nd ed. 1951.

Gadamer, Hans-Georg. 1986. *The Relevance of the Beautiful and Other Essays.* Trans. Nicholas Walker. Ed. and intro. Robert Bernasconi. Cambridge: Cambridge University Press.

Gilmour, John. 1986. *Picturing the World.* Albany, N.Y.: SUNY Press.

Gombrich, Ernst. 1979. *The Sense of Order: A Study in the Psychology of Decorative Art.* Ithaca, N.Y.: Cornell University Press.

Goodman, Nelson. 1976. *Languages of Art.* Indianapolis: Hackett.

———. 1978. *Ways of Worldmaking.* Indianapolis: Hackett.

Guthrie, Stewart. 1993. *Faces in the Clouds: A New Theory of Religion.* New York: Oxford University Press.

Handelman, Don, and Galina Lindquist. 2004. *Ritual in Its Own Right.* New York: Berghahn.

Hansen, Forest. 1993. "Philosophy of Music Education in a Slightly New Key." *Philosophy of Music Education Review* 1, no. 1 (Spring): 61–74.

Harrison, Jane. 1908. *Prolegomena to the Study of Greek Religion.* 2nd ed. Cambridge: Cambridge University Press.

Hausman, Carl R. 1993. *Charles S. Peirce's Evolutionary Philosophy.* Cambridge: Cambridge University Press.

Heelan, Patrick. 1983. *Space—Perception and the Philosophy of Science.* Berkeley and Los Angeles: University of California Press.

Heidegger, Martin. 1960. *Der Ursprung des Kunstwerkes.* Mit einer Einführung von Hans-Georg Gadamer. Stuttgart: Reclam.

Hildebrand, Adolf. 1932. *The Problem of Form in Painting and Sculpture.* New York: G. E. Stechert.

Innis, Robert. 1977. "Art, Symbol, Consciousness." *International Philosophical Quarterly* 17, no. 4: 455–476.

———. 1981. *Karl Bühler: Semiotic Foundations of Language Theory.* New York: Plenum.

———. 1994. *Consciousness and the Play of Signs.* Bloomington: Indiana University Press.

———. 1999. "John Dewey et sa glose approfondie de la théorie peircienne de la qualité." *Protée* 26, no. 3: 89–98.

———. 2001. "Perception, Interpretation, and the Signs of Art." *Journal of Speculative Philosophy* 15: 20–33.

———. 2002a. *Pragmatism and the Forms of Sense: Language, Perception, Technics.* University Park: Penn State University Press.

———. 2002b. "Homing in on the Range: Comments on Mark Johnson's 'Cowboy Bill Rides Herd on the Range of Consciousness.'" *Journal of Speculative Philosophy* 16, no. 4: 264–272.

———. 2004. "The Tacit Logic of Ritual Embodiments." In *Ritual in Its Own Right: Exploring the Dynamics of Transformation,* ed. Don Handelman and Galina Lindquist. New York: Berghahn.

———. 2007. "Dimensions of an Aesthetic Encounter." In *Semiotic Rotations: Modes of Meanings in Cultural Worlds,* ed. SunHee Kim Gertz, Jaan Valsiner, and Jean-Paul Breaux. Charlotte, N.C.: Information Age Publishing.

Jakobson, Roman. 1960. "Linguistics and Poetics." In *Language in Literature,* ed. K. Pomorska and S. Rudy. Cambridge, Mass.: Harvard University Press.

Johnson, James R. "The Unknown Langer: Philosophy from the New Key to the Trilogy of Mind." *Journal of Aesthetic Education* 27, no. 1 (Spring): 63–73.

Johnson, Mark. 1987. *The Body in the Mind: The Bodily Basis of Meaning, Imagination, and Reason.* Chicago: University of Chicago Press.

———. 2007. *The Meaning of the Body: Aesthetics of Human Understanding.* Chicago: University of Chicago Press.

Jonas, Hans. 1966. *The Phenomenon of Life: Toward a Philosophical Biology.* New York: Harper and Row.

Jones, Judith. 1998. *Intensity: An Essay in Whiteheadian Ontology.* Nashville, Tenn.: Vanderbilt University Press.

Kanizsa, Gaetano. 1980. *Grammatica del vedere*. Bologna: Il Mulino.

Keller, Helen. 1936. *The Story of My Life*. Garden City, N.Y.: Doubleday, Doran. 1st ed. 1902.

Kivy, Peter. 2002. *Introduction to a Philosophy of Music*. Oxford: Clarendon Press.

Köhler, Wolgang. 1947. *Gestalt Psychology*. New York: H. Liveright.

Kruse, Felicia. 2005. "Emotion in Musical Meaning: A Peircean Solution to Langer's Dualism." *Transactions of the Charles S. Peirce Society* 41, no. 4 (Fall): 762–779.

Lachmann, Rolf. 1993a. "Der philosophische Weg Susanne K. Langers (1895–1985)." *Studia Culturologica* 2: 65–90.

———. 1993b. "Susanne K. Langer: Primär- und Sekundärbibliographie." *Studia Culturologica* 2: 91–114.

——— 1997. "From Metaphysics to Art and Back: The Relevance of Susanne K. Langer's Philosophy for Process Metaphysics." *Process Studies* 26: 107–125.

———. 2000. *Susanne K. Langer: Die lebendige Form menschlichen Fühlens und Verstehens*. Munich: Fink.

Lakoff, George, and Mark Johnson. 1999. *Philosophy in the Flesh: The Embodied Mind and Its Challenge to Western Thought*. New York: Perseus.

———. 2003. *Metaphors We Live By*. Chicago: University of Chicago Press.

Lang, Bernhard. 1997. *Sacred Games*. New Haven, Conn.: Yale University Press.

Lieberman, Philip. 1991. *Uniquely Human: The Evolution of Speech, Thought, and Selfless Behavior*. Cambridge, Mass.: Harvard University Press.

Liszka, James. 1996. *A General Introduction to the Semeiotic of Charles Sanders Peirce*. Bloomington: Indiana University Press.

Martin, F. David. 1972. *Art and the Religious Experience: The "Language" of the Sacred*. Lewisburg, Pa.: Bucknell University Press.

Martin, James Alfred, Jr. 1990. *Beauty and Holiness: The Dialogue between Aesthetics and Religion*. Princeton, N.J.: Princeton University Press.

Martland, Thomas. 1981. *Religion as Art: An Interpretation*. Albany: State University of New York Press.

McDermott, John. 1976. *The Culture of Experience: Philosophical Essays in the American Grain*. New York: New York University Press.

———. 1986. *Streams of Experience: Reflections on the History of Philosophy and American Culture*. Amherst: University of Massachusetts Press.

McGandy, Michael. 1993. "Communication and Its Limits: Expression and Communication in Langer's Aesthetics." *Conference: A Journal of Philosophy and Theory* 4, no. 1: 21–35.

Mithen, Steven. 2006. *The Singing Neanderthals: The Origins of Music, Language, Mind, and Body*. Cambridge, Mass.: Harvard University Press.

Murray, Gilbert. 1925. *Five Stages of Greek Religion*. Oxford: Clarendon Press.

Nelson, Beatrice K. 1994. "Susanne K. Langer's Conception of 'Symbol'—Making Connections through Ambiguity." *Journal of Speculative Philosophy* 8, no. 4: 277–296.

Oppenheim, Frank M. 1987. *Royce's Mature Philosophy of Religion*. Notre Dame, Ind.: University of Notre Dame Press.

———. 2005. *Reverence for the Relations of Life: Re-imagining Pragmatism via Josiah Royce's Interactions with Peirce, James, and Dewey.* Notre Dame, Ind.: University of Notre Dame Press.

Otto, Rudolf. 1923. *The Idea of the Holy: An Inquiry into the Non-Rational Factor in the Idea of the Divine and its Relation to the Rational.* Trans. John W. Harvey. London: Oxford University Press.

Pater, Walter. 1908. *The Renaissance: Studies in Art and Poetry.* New York: Dover.

Peirce, Charles S. 1868. "Some Consequences of Four Incapacities." In *The Essential Peirce: Selected Philosophical Writings.* Vol. 1 (1867–1893). Ed. Nathan Houser and Christian Kloesel. Bloomington: Indiana University Press, 1992.

———. 1958. *Collected Papers.* Cambridge, Mass.: Belknap Press of Harvard University Press. (Cited as *CP* followed by volume number and paragraph).

Percy, Walker. 1977. "Symbol as Need." In Walker Percy, *The Message in the Bottle.* New York: Picador.

Philippe, Jean. 1903. *L'image mentale (évolution et dissolution).* Paris: Alcan.

Pirsig, Robert. 1974. *Zen and the Art of Motorcycle Maintenance: An Inquiry into Values.* New York: HarperCollins.

Polanyi, Michael. 1958. *Personal Knowledge: Towards a Post-Critical Philosophy.* London: Routledge.

———. 1966. *The Tacit Dimension.* Garden City, N.Y.: Doubleday.

Potter, Vincent. 1996. *Peirce's Philosophical Perspectives.* Ed. V. M. Colapietro. New York: Fordham University Press.

Powers, John. 2006. "Susanne Langer's Philosophy of Mind: Some Implications for Media Ecology." In *Perspectives on Culture, Technology and Communication: The Media Ecology Tradition,* ed. Casey M. K. Lum. Cresskill, N.J.: Hampton Press.

Prall, David. 1936. *Aesthetic Analysis.* New York: Thomas Y. Crowell.

Pratt, Carroll. 1931. *The Meaning of Music.* Whitefish, Mont.: Kessinger.

Raffman, Diana. 1993. *Language, Music, and Mind.* Cambridge, Mass.: MIT Press.

Rappaport, Roy. 1999. *Ritual and Religion in the Making of Humanity.* Cambridge: Cambridge University Press.

Reichling, Mary. 1993. "Susanne Langer's Theory of Symbolism: An Analysis and Extension." *Philosophy of Music Education Review* 1, no. 1: 3–17.

———. 1995. "Susanne Langer's Concept of Secondary Illusion in Music and Art." *Journal of Aesthetic Education* 29, no. 4 (Winter): 39–51.

———. 2004. "Intersections: Form, Feeling, and Isomorphism." *Philosophy of Music Education Review* 12, no. 1 (January).

Reid, Louis Arnaud. 1929. "Beauty and Significance." *Proceedings of the Aristotelian Society* (N.S.) 29: 123–154.

Reimer, Bennett. 1970. *A Philosophy of Music Education.* Englewood Cliffs, N.J.: Prentice Hall.

Ribot, Th. 1926. *Essai sur l'imagination créatrice.* Paris: Alcan.

Richmond, John W. 1999. "Reconsidering Aesthetic and Religious Experience: A Companion View." *Journal of Aesthetic Education* 33, no. 4 (Winter): 29–49.

Royce, Josiah. 1913 [2001]. *The Problem of Christianity.* Introductions by Frank M. Oppenheim and John E. Smith. Washington: Catholic University of America Press.

Rue, Loyal D. 1994. *By the Grace of Guile: The Role of Deception in Natural History and Human Affairs.* New York: Oxford University Press.

——. 2000. *Everybody's Story: Wising Up to the Epic of Evolution.* Albany, N.Y.: SUNY Press.

Sandelands, Lloyd. 1998. *Feeling and Form in Social Life.* Lanham, Md.: Roman and Littlefield.

Sapir, Edward. 1921. "Language." In *Selected Writings of Edward Sapir on Language, Culture, and Personality,* ed. David G. Mandelbaum. Berkeley and Los Angeles: University of California Press.

Schapiro, Meyer. 1994. *Theory and Philosophy of Art: Style, Artist, and Society.* New York: George Braziller.

Schultz, William. 2000. *Cassirer and Langer on Myth: An Introduction.* New York: Garland Publishing.

Scully, Vincent. 1979. *The Earth, the Temple, and the Gods: Greek Sacred Architecture.* New Haven, Conn.: Yale University Press.

Sebeok, Thomas. 2001. *Signs: An Introduction to Semiotics.* Toronto: University of Toronto Press.

Shelley, Cameron. 1998. "Consciousness, Symbols, and Aesthetics: A Just-So Story and Its Implications in Susanne's Langer's *Mind: An Essay on Human Feeling."* *Philosophical Psychology* 11, no. 1: 45–66.

Soltes, Ari. 2005. *Our Sacred Signs.* New York: Westview Press.

Sonner, Rudolf. 1930. *Musik und Tanz: von Kulttanz zum Jazz.* Leipzig: Quelle und Meyer.

Sudnow, David. 2001. *Ways of the Hand: A Rewritten Account.* Cambridge, Mass.: MIT Press.

Tallis, Raymond. 2003. *The Hand: A Philosophical Inquiry into Human Being.* Edinburgh: Edinburgh University Press.

Thompson, D'Arcy. 1942. *On Growth and Form,* 2nd ed. 2 vols. 1st ed., 1917. Cambridge: University Press.

Thompson, Evan. 2007. *Mind in Life: Biology, Phenomenology, and the Sciences of Mind.* Cambridge, Mass.: Belknap Press of Harvard University Press.

Tuan, Yi-Fu. 1977. *Space and Place: The Perspective of Experience.* Minneapolis: University of Minnesota Press.

——. 1995. *Passing Strange and Wonderful: Aesthetics, Nature, and Culture.* New York: Kodansha International.

Uexküll, Jakob von. 1940. *Theory of Meaning.* Trans. Barry Stone and Herbert Weiner. Special issue of *Semiotica* 42, no. 1 (1982): 25–82.

Van der Leeuw, Gerardus. 1963. *Sacred and Profane Beauty: The Holy in Art.* New York: Holt, Rinehart, and Winston.

Van Roo, William, S.J. 1981. *Man the Symbolizer.* Rome: Gregorian University Press.

Voegelin, Eric. 1952. *The New Science of Politics.* Chicago: University of Chicago Press.

Volkelt, Hans. 1912. *Über die Vorstellungen der Tiere*. Leipzig: Engelmann.

Vološinov, V. 1930. *Marxism and the Philosophy of Language*. Trans. Ladislav Matejka and I. R. Titunik. New York: Seminar Press.

Watling, Christine. 1998. "The Arts, Emotion, and Current Research in Neuroscience." *Mosaic* 31, no. 1 (March): 107–125.

Weber, Andreas. 2002. "Feeling the Signs: The Origins of Meaning in the Biological Philosophy of Susanne K. Langer and Hans Jonas." *Sign Systems Studies* 30, no. 1: 183–200.

Wegener, Philipp. 1885 [1991]. *Untersuchungen über die Grundfragen des Sprachlebens*. Ed. E. F. K. Koerner. Amsterdam Studies in the Theory and History of Linguistic Science, ser. II. Classics in Psycholinguistics, vol. 5. Amsterdam: J. Benjamins.

Wehr, Wesley. n.d. "Susanne K. Langer: The Evolution of a Friendship." Unpublished manuscript.

Wentworth, Nigel. 2004. *The Phenomenology of Painting*. Cambridge: Cambridge University Press.

Wheelwright, Philip. 1968. *The Burning Fountain: A Study in the Language of Symbolism*. Bloomington: Indiana University Press.

Wigman, Mary. 1935: "The New German Dance." In *Modern Dance,* ed. Merle Armitage, compiled by Virginia Stewart. New York: E. Weyhe.

Wollheim, Richard. 1980. *Art and Its Objects*. Cambridge: Cambridge University Press.

———. 1987. *Painting as an Art*. Princeton, N.J.: Princeton University Press.

Zevi, Bruno. 1957. *Architecture as Space*. New York: Horizon Press.

Index

Robert E. Innis is Professor of Philosophy at the University of Massachusetts, Lowell. He is author of *Semiotics: An Introductory Anthology* (Indiana University Press, 1985) and *Consciousness and the Play of Signs* (Indiana University Press, 1994). His most recent book is *Pragmatism and the Forms of Sense: Language, Perception, Technics.*